THE JOB SAFETY AND HEALTH ACT OF 1970

Text

Analysis

Legislative History

Prepared by the Editorial Staff of
The Bureau of National Affairs, Inc.

OPERATIONS MANUAL

PUBLISHED BY THE BUREAU OF NATIONAL AFFAIRS, INC.
WASHINGTON, D.C.

Standard Book Number: 87179-129-3

Library of Congress Catalog Card Number: 78-156236

"This publication is designed to provide accurate and authoritative information in regard to the subject matter covered. It is sold with the understanding that the publisher is not engaged in rendering legal, accounting or other professional service. If legal advice or other expert assistance is required, the services of a competent professional person should be sought." (From a Declaration of Principles jointly adopted by a Committee of the American Bar Association, and a Committee of Publishers and Associations.)

PRINTED IN THE UNITED STATES OF AMERICA

31

TABLE OF CONTENTS

INTRODUCTION

The Occupational Safety and Health Act of 1970 requires safe and healthful working conditions for virtually every employee in the United States.

Effective April 28, 1971, the law directs the Secretary of Labor to set and enforce safety and health standards for businesses affecting interstate commerce—an estimated 4.1 million establishments with 57 million employees. The only employers exempted are the United States and state and local governments. But there are special provisions requiring standards for them.

Employers are required to furnish a place of employment free from "recognized hazards" and to comply with occupational safety and health standards. Beyond this, however, employers must make investigations of their establishments and meet extensive record-keeping requirements.

The law provides specific procedures for setting standards. There are three varieties—interim, permanent, and emergency. Temporary variances are permitted, and adversely affected parties may seek judicial review of standards.

Enforcement is a dual process. The Labor Department makes inspections and issues citations. An independent Occupational Safety and Health Review Commission performs the adjudicatory functions. If dangers are caused by new processes, equipment, materials, or emergency situations, the Secretary of Labor must ask for court injunctions to close the affected area until standards are met.

States are encouraged to set and enforce their own occupational safety and health standards, but the federal standards will be the yardstick for approval of state plans. Grants are provided to assist the states in developing and administering their plans.

Research in the occupational safety and health field, including the psychological factors is to be conducted by the Department of Health, Education, and Welfare, with a new National Institute for Occupational Safety and Health in charge of the program.

In addition, the law authorizes direct loans to small businesses to help them comply with the new standards, requires federal agencies to conduct occupational safety and health programs, and creates a National Commission on State Workmen's Compensation Laws to undertake a study of state laws.

This operations manual is devoted to an analysis of the major provisions of the statute. It explains its background, meaning, and effect. The analysis and appendices of pertinent reports and congressional debates are designed to give employers, employees, governmental agencies, unions, and associations a broad-range view of the new job safety and health law.

CHAPTER 1

THE LAW IN BRIEF

In adopting the Occupational Safety and Health Act of 1970, Congress did not embark on completely uncharted waters. For guidance, it had the experience under the special safety and health laws for the maritime, coal mining, and construction industries; the safety and health regulations for government construction, service, and manufacturing and supply contracts; and the standards established under numerous state laws.

But the magnitude of the new undertaking is staggering. Coverage extends to the farthest reaches of the congressional power to regulate commerce. An estimated 57 million employees in 4.1 million establishments are within its protection. The thrust of its provisions is broad and diffuse.

• For the Department of Labor, there are far-reaching new responsibilities—regulatory, administrative, and enforcement. The number of employees ultimately involved could reach as high as 2,000.

• For the Department of Health, Education, and Welfare, there are new tasks in safety and health research, training, and employee education.

• For the federal courts, there is a new grant of jurisdiction in enforcement proceedings brought under the Act.

• And for employers throughout the country, there will be problems of determining what the Act requires and how to remain in compliance.

New Agencies Created

The Act also creates some new agencies to perform specific functions. First, there is the Occupational Safety and Health Review Commission, which will serve as a review tribunal in enforcement actions by the Labor Department. In the Department of Health, Education, and Welfare, there will be the National Institute for Occupational Safety and Health. It will carry out research, training, and education functions. Finally, there will be a National Advisory Committee on Occupational Safety and Health and a National Commission on State Workmen's Compensation Laws.

WHAT THE LAW SEEKS TO DO

The Act is a labor-standards law—more akin to the Fair Labor Standards Act than to the Taft-Hartley Act. Its heart is the promulgation and enforcement of safety and health standards. But there also is an administrative adjudicatory function vested in the Occupational Safety and Health Review Commission. The Commission is given jurisdiction to review citations of violation and proposed assessments of penalty by the Secretary of Labor. Orders of the Commission are, in turn, reviewable by the federal courts of appeals.

Issuance of Standards

The Act specifies three procedures for the issuance of standards—one for "interim" standards, one for "permanent" standards, and one for "emergency temporary standards." In brief, here are the rules:

• *Interim Standards*—The rule-making requirements of the Administrative Procedure Act do not apply to the promulgation of early standards. They are to be issued by the Secretary of Labor "as soon as practicable" during the period beginning with the effective date of the Act, April 28, 1971, and ending two years after. An interim standard may be a "national consensus standard" or an "established federal standard." If there is a conflict among any of these standards, the Secretary is directed to adopt the one that assures the greatest protection of the safety or health of the employees.

A "national consensus standard" is defined as one that meets these requirements: It has been issued by a nationally recognized standards-producing organization under procedures whereby it can be determined that interested and affected persons have reached substantial agreement on its adoption; it was formulated in a manner that afforded an opportunity for diverse views to be considered; *and* it has been designated as such a standard by the Secretary after consultation with other appropriate federal agencies.

An "established federal standard" is defined as "any operative occupational safety and health standard established by any agency of the United States and presently in effect, or contained in any Act of Congress in force on the date of enactment of this Act."

• *Permanent Standards*—The procedure for establishing permanent standards is much more detailed and follows the rule-making provisions of the Administrative Procedure Act. It applies to the promulgation, modification, or revocation of a standard. In some respects, it resembles the industry-committee procedure used in setting minimum wage rates under the Fair Labor Standards Act.

The process begins when the Secretary of Labor determines on the basis of available information that a standard should be issued, modified, or revoked. He then may request the recommendations of an advisory committee consisting of not more than 15 members, including representatives of employers and employees involved, one or more designees of the Secretary of Health, Education, and Welfare, and one or more representatives of state safety and health agencies.

The Secretary then publishes a proposed rule, either on his own or on the basis of the recommendations of the advisory committee if one was requested. Following the publication of the proposed rule, interested persons may file written comments or objections and request a public hearing on the proposal.

The new standard is not promulgated until all the procedures are completed. Even then, the Secretary may delay its effective date for as long as 90 days to permit all concerned to become familiar with its requirements.

• *Emergency Temporary Standards*—Such standards may be made effective immediately upon publication in the *Federal Register,* subject to two conditions. The Secretary must determine (1) that employees are exposed to grave danger from exposure to substances or agents determined to be toxic or physically harmful or from new hazards, *and* (2) that such emergency standard is necessary to protect employees from such danger.

Upon publication of such an emergency temporary standard, the Secretary is required to commence a rule-making proceeding in which the emergency standard will serve as a proposed rule. A permanent standard must be issued to replace the emergency standard within six months.

Enforcement of Standards

The primary responsibility for enforcing the Act will rest in the Department of Labor, which will have a new Assistant Secretary for Occupational Safety and Health. In addition, the Secretary of Labor is authorized to place an additional 25 positions in the grades GS-16, 17, and 18 to carry out the Department's responsibilities under the Act.

Inspections of establishments to determine whether violations exist may be made by the Labor Department either on its own initiative or at the request of an employee or a representative of employees. Such a request must be in writing and must set forth with "reasonable particularity" the grounds for believing that a violation threatening physical harm or imminent danger exists.

Representatives of the Department have the right to enter any establishment subject to the Act "without delay and at reasonable times." But the Act does specify that inspections be made during regular working hours and other reasonable times and within reasonable limits and in a reasonable manner.

If an inspection leads the Department to believe that a violation has been committed, it must issue a citation to the employer with "reasonable promptness." No citation may be issued more than six months after the occurrence of the alleged violation. Once a citation has been issued, the enforcement procedure is as follows:

• The Department notifies the employer of the penalty, if any, it proposes to assess. The employer then has 15 days to notify the Department whether he wishes to contest the proposed penalty. If the employer decides not to contest the citation and proposed penalty and no employee or employee representative contests the reasonableness of the period for abatement of the violation, the citation and assessment of penalty become a final order of the Review Commission—not subject to review by any court or agency.

• If the Department has reason to believe an employer has not corrected a violation within the period specified for abatement in the citation, it notifies the employer of the failure and the proposed penalty. Here again, the employer has 15 days in which to notify the Department that he will contest the penalty. If there is no contest, the notice and proposed penalty become a final, unreviewable order of the Commission.

• If there is a contest, the Review Commission affords the parties an opportunity for a hearing and then issues an order, based on findings of fact, affirming, modifying, or vacating the Secretary's citation or proposed penalty. The Commission also may grant other appropriate relief, and it may use hearing examiners in its proceedings.

• Any person adversely affected or aggrieved by an order of the Commission may obtain review by filing a petition in a federal court of appeals within 60 days after issuance of the order. The petition may be filed in the circuit in which the alleged violation occurred, in that in which the employer has his principal office, or in the U.S. Court of Appeals for the District of Columbia. In the same way, the Secretary may obtain review or enforcement of any final order of the Commission.

Imminent-Danger Procedures

The bill originally adopted by the Senate provided for administrative closing of a work site in cases in which an inspector determined that an "imminent danger" existed. The Conference Committee, however, adopted the provisions of the House bill, which established an injunctive procedure for such closings.

As adopted, the Act gives federal district courts jurisdiction, upon petition by the Secretary of Labor, to restrain "any conditions or practices in any place of employment which are such that a danger exists which could reasonably be expected to cause death or serious physical harm immediately or before the imminence of such danger can be eliminated through the enforcement procedures otherwise provided by this Act." The proceedings will be governed by Rule 65 of the Federal Rules of Civil Procedure, except that no temporary restraining order issued without notice may be effective for longer than five days.

The Act places responsibility on an inspector to inform the affected employees and employer in such imminent-danger cases. Moreover, if the Secretary of Labor "arbitrarily or capriciously" fails to seek relief in such as case, he may be sued by any employee who is injured as a result.

WHAT THE PENALTIES ARE FOR VIOLATIONS

The penalty provisions in the Senate bill were harsh. They specified mandatory penalties for all violations that were not of a *de minimis* nature. But the House bill provided for both mandatory and discretionary penalties. The conferees accepted the House version.

Here is a rundown of the penalties:

• For wilfully or repeatedly violating standards under the Act, an employer *may* be assessed a civil penalty of not more than $10,000 for each violation.

• For a citation for a "serious violation," an employer *shall* be assessed a civil penalty of up to $1,000 for each such violation.

• For a citation for a violation specifically determined not to be of a serious nature, an employer *may* be assessed a civil penalty of up to $1,000 for each such violation.

• For failing to correct a violation for which a citation has been issued within the period permitted for its correction, an employer *may* be assessed a civil penalty of not more than $1,000 for each day during which such failure or violation continues.

• For wilfully violating any standard, rule, order, or regulation under the Act that caused death to an employee, an employer *shall*, upon conviction, be punished by a fine of not more than $10,000 or by imprisonment for not more than six months, or by both. If, however, the conviction is for a violation committed after a first conviction, the punishment *shall* be a fine of not more than $20,000 or imprisonment for not more than one year, or both.

• For giving advance notice of any inspection to be conducted under the Act, without authority from the Secretary or his designees, a person *shall*, upon conviction, be punished by a fine of not more than $1,000 or by imprisonment for not more than six months, or by both.

• For knowingly making any false statement, representation, or certification in any application, record, report, plan, or other document filed or required to be maintained under the Act, a person *shall*, upon conviction, be punished by a fine of not more than $10,000 or by imprisonment for not more than six months, or by both.

• For killing a person while he is engaged in investigative, inspection, or enforcement functions under the Act, a person *shall* be punished by imprisonment for any term of years or for life.

• For violating any of the posting requirements under the Act, an employer *shall* be assessed a civil penalty of up to $1,000 for each violation.

Commission's Authority

As made clear by the use of the words "may" and "shall," there are both discretionary and mandatory penalties. There also are both civil and criminal penalties.

Authority to assess all civil penalties under the Act is vested in the Review Commission. It is required to give due consideration to the appropriateness of the penalty, weighing such factors as the size of the employer's business, the gravity of the violation, the good faith of the employer, and the record of prior violations. Civil fines collected are to be paid to the Secretary of Labor for deposit in the U.S. Treasury.

The amount of the penalty imposed upon an employer depends in some circumstances on whether the violation is a "serious" one. Section 17(k) states that "a serious violation shall be deemed to exist in a place of employment if there is a substantial probability that death or serious physical harm could result from a condition which exists, or from one or more practices, means, methods, operations, or processes which have been adopted or are in use, in such place of employment unless the employer did not, and could not with the exercise of reasonable diligence, know of the presence of the violation." It is not a precise definition, and it will require interpretation.

HOW THE ACT AFFECTS OTHER LAWS

At the time the Occupational Safety and Health Act was adopted, there were in effect several federal laws dealing with specific types of employment. There also were a number of state laws dealing with safety and health.

How the new Act affects existing laws—state and federal—is set out in Section 4. The relationships are complicated. In some instances, standards established under the new Act supersede the earlier standards. In others, the earlier standards continue to be effective. Here are the rules:

• The Act does not apply to employees for whom safety or health standards have been established by other federal agencies, or by federal or state agencies acting under the authority of Section 274 of the Atomic Energy Act of 1954, as amended.

• Safety and health standards issued under the Walsh-Healey Act, the Service Contract Act, and the National Foundation on Arts and Humanities Act are to be superseded on the effective date of corresponding standards issued under the new Act and determined by the Secretary of Labor to be more effective. Meanwhile, standards issued under the earlier laws will be considered standards under the new Act until superseded.

• Nothing in the Act is to be construed to supersede or in any other manner to affect the common-law or statutory rights, duties, or liabilities under any workmen's compensation law with respect to injuries, diseases, or death of employees arising out of employment.

To deal with the problem of duplication of standards, the Secretary of Labor is required to report to Congress within three years after the effective date of the Act. The report must contain recommendations for legislation to avoid unnecessary duplication and to achieve coordination between the Act and other federal laws.

WHAT THE LAW MEANS TO EMPLOYERS

The impact of the new legislation will fall directly on those included within the definition of "employer." The definition is brief. The term "employer," it states in Section 3(5), means "a person engaged in a business affecting commerce who has employees, but does not include the United States or any State or political subdivision of a State."

The phrase "affecting commerce" is the test of coverage under the National Labor Relations Act, and it has been given a broad construction in a series of decisions under that Act. It does not require that products be shipped across state lines. It is sufficient that raw materials, power, or communications used cross state lines.

Duties of Employer

The Act imposes two basic duties upon an "employer." He is required:

• To "furnish to each of his employees employment and a place of employment which are free from recognized hazards that are causing or are likely to cause death or serious physical harm to his employees."

• To "comply with occupational safety and health standards promulgated under the Act."

But these are not the only duties imposed on employers by the Act. They must permit Labor Department investigators to enter their establishments "without delay and at reasonable times." Then there are record-keeping requirements.

An employer is required to make, keep, and preserve such records regarding his activities relating to the Act as the Secretary of Labor, in cooperation with the Secretary of Health, Education, and Welfare, may prescribe by regulation as necessary or appropriate for the enforcement of the Act or for development of information regarding the causes and prevention of occupational accidents and illnesses.

The investigative and record-keeping provisions do not end with this general provision. Other obligations that may be imposed on employers include:

• The conduct of periodic inspections and the posting of notices to keep employees informed of their rights and obligations under the Act.

• The maintenance of accurate records of and the preparation of periodic reports on work-related deaths, injuries, and illnesses other than minor injuries requiring only first-aid treatment and that do not involve medical treatment, loss of consciousness, restriction of work or motion, or transfer to another job.

• The maintenance of accurate records of employee exposures to potentially toxic materials or harmful physical agents that are required to be monitored under the temporary standards provisions of Section 6 of the Act.

In a gesture toward employers, the Act does specify that any information obtained by the Secretary of Labor, the Secretary of Health, Education, and Welfare, or a state agency under the Act shall be obtained with "a minimum burden upon employers, especially those operating small businesses." If an investigation is made, the employer may have a representative accompany the Government inspector.

WHAT THE LAW MEANS TO EMPLOYEES

The basic objective of the law is to protect employees against safety and health hazards. But it also imposes a duty on employees. Section 5(b) states:

"Each employee shall comply with occupational safety and health standards and all rules, regulations, and orders issued pursuant to this Act which are applicable to his own actions and conduct."

Apart from Section 5(b), the Act's provisions relating to employees are concerned primarily with rights. As a counterpart to the duty imposed on an employer, an employee has a right to a place of employment that is free from recognized hazards that are causing or are likely to cause death or serious physical harm. To implement this right, the Act gives an employee or his representative the right to request an inspection of an establishment if he believes that a violation of a safety or health standard exists or that an imminent danger exists.

If an inspection is made, an employee or a representative of employees must be given the opportunity to accompany the Labor Department investigator for the purpose of aiding the inspection. Moreover, if the Labor Department determines that there are no reasonable grounds to believe that a violation or danger exists, it is required to notify the employee or his representative in writing.

A provision similar to Section 8(a)(4) of the National Labor Relations Act and Section 15(a)(3) of the Fair Labor Standards Act protects an employee against discrimination for filing a complaint, instituting a proceeding, or testifying in a proceeding under the Act. Federal district courts have jurisdiction over suits involving alleged violations of this provision and may award appropriate relief to the employee, including reinstatement in his job with back pay.

WHAT THE LAW MEANS TO LABOR UNIONS

Labor unions are affected by the Act in two ways. First, they will have the same rights and obligations of other employers in their role as employers. Second, they will have certain rights as representatives of employees. These rights include the following:

• The right to file written objections and to request a public hearing on a proposed safety or health standard promulgated by the Secretary of Labor.

• The right to request that the Labor Department make an inspection of an establishment in which it is believed that a violation of a safety or health standard exists or in which imminent peril is believed to exist.

• The right to accompany the Labor Department inspector in an investigation to determine whether violations of the safety and health standards established under the Act exist.

• The right to bring an action in a federal district court against the Secretary of Labor on behalf of an employee injured as a result of the failure of the Secretary "arbitrarily or capriciously" to seek relief under the "imminent peril" provisions of the Act.

WHAT THE LAW MEANS TO THE STATES

There is no general federal preemption under the Act. Instead, there is a sharing of responsibility for the issuance and enforcement of safety and health standards. There also are provisions for grants to states to assist them in carrying out responsibilities they assume under the Act.

First, there is a blanket statement that nothing in the Act shall prevent any state agency or court from asserting jurisdiction under state law over any safety or health issue regarding which there is no standard in effect under Section 6 of the Federal Act.

But this is not all. There also are provisions under which a state may assume responsibility for developing and enforcing safety and health standards in areas in which the Federal Government has acted.

Rules for State Plans

To assume such responsibility, a state must submit a plan to the Secretary of Labor for his approval. The Secretary must approve such a plan if, in his judgment, it meets the following requirements:

• The plan designates a state agency or agencies as the agency or agencies responsible for administering the plan throughout the state.

• The plan provides for the development and enforcement of standards that are or will be at least as effective in providing safe and healthful employment as standards issued under the Federal Act and which, when applicable to products used in interstate commerce, are required by compelling local conditions and do not unduly burden interstate commerce.

• The plan provides a right to enter and inspect work places that is at least as effective as that provided by Section 8 of the Federal Act. Moreover, it must include a prohibition on advance notice of inspections.

• The plan must provide satisfactory assurance that the agency will have the legal authority and the qualified personnel necessary for the enforcement of the standards.

• The plan must give satisfactory assurance that the state will devote adequate funds to the administration and enforcement of the standards.

• The plan must contain satisfactory assurance that the state will establish and maintain an effective and comprehensive safety and health program for all employees of public agencies of the state and its political subdivisions.

• The plan must require employers in the state to make reports to the Secretary of Labor in the same manner and to the same extent as if the plan were not in effect.

• The plan must require the state agency to make reports to the Secretary of Labor in such form and containing such information as the Secretary may require.

Review Procedure

The Secretary of Labor may not reject a plan submitted by a state without first giving the state due notice and the opportunity for a hearing. Moreover, a state may obtain review of a decision of the Secretary rejecting or withdrawing approval of a plan in the federal court of appeals for the circuit in which the state is located. Unless the court finds that the Secretary's decision is not supported by "substantial evidence," it must affirm it.

This does not end the proceedings, however. The state or the Secretary may ask the U.S. Supreme Court to review the decision of the Court of Appeals either on certiorari or certification, as provided in Section 1254 of Title 28 of the U.S. Code.

There are other provisions that make the procedure for state participation even more complicated. After the Secretary of Labor has approved a state plan as meeting the requirements set out above, he *may*, but is not required to, exercise his authority to enforce standards established under the Federal Act until he determines that the criteria for state plans are being applied. But this determination *shall* not be made for at least three years after the approval of the state plan. Thereafter, the federal standards will give way to those under the state plan.

The Secretary of Labor, however, still retains jurisdiction to make a continuing evaluation of the manner in which the state plan is being operated. If he determines after due notice and opportunity for a hearing that the state plan is not meeting the standards, he may withdraw approval. As noted above, however, the state may obtain review of the Secretary's action in a federal court of appeals.

Grants to States

To assist the states in developing occupational safety and health plans, Section 23 of the Act authorizes the Secretary of Labor to make grants to the states in the fiscal year ending June 30, 1971, and the two succeeding fiscal years to assist them in doing the following:

• Identifying their needs and responsibilities in the area of occupational safety and health.

• Developing state plans that meet the requirements of Section 18 of the Federal Act.

• Developing plans for (1) establishing systems for the collection of information concerning the nature and frequency of occupational injuries and diseases; (2) increasing the expertise and enforcement capabilities of personnel engaged in the program; and (3) otherwise improving the administration and enforcement of state occupational safety and health laws.

Applications for grants will be approved or rejected by the Secretary of Labor after consultation with the Secretary of Health, Education, and Welfare. Those made for the purposes mentioned above may not exceed 90 percent of the total cost of the application.

In addition, the Secretary of Labor is authorized to make grants to states to assist them in administering and enforcing occupational safety and health plans approved by the Secretary under Section 18. The federal share under such a grant may not exceed 50 percent of the total cost to the state of the program.

WHAT THE LAW MEANS TO FEDERAL AGENCIES

Agencies of the Federal Government, like agencies of state and local governments, are excluded from the definition of an "employer" under the Act. But this does not mean that the agencies have no obligations under the Act.

To obtain approval of a plan under Section 18, a state must provide satisfactory assurance that it will establish and maintain an effective and comprehensive occupational safety and health program for all employees and public employees of the state and its political subdivisions.

Section 19 declares it to be the responsibility of the head of each federal agency to establish and maintain an effective and comprehensive occupational safety and health program. The program must be consistent with the standards established for private industry under Section 6.

Specifically, the head of each agency, after consultation with representatives of the employees, must do the following:

• Provide safe and healthful places and conditions of employment, consistent with the standards for private industry.

• Acquire, maintain, and require the use of safety equipment, personal protective equipment, and devices reasonably necessary to protect employees.

• Keep adequate records of all occupational accidents and illnesses for proper evaluation and necessary corrective action.

• Consult with the Secretary of Labor with respect to the adequacy in form and content of the records kept.

• Make an annual report to the Secretary of Labor regarding occupational accidents and injuries and the agency's safety and health program.

The Secretary of Labor, for his part, is required to provide the President with a summary or digest of the reports submitted to him by the agencies. In carrying out his functions in this area, the Secretary is to have access to records and reports kept and filed by federal agencies under the Act unless an executive order specifically requires that they be kept secret in the interest of national defense or foreign policy. In such an event, the Secretary is to have access to such information as will not jeopardize national defense or foreign policy.

CHAPTER 2

BACKGROUND AND LEGISLATIVE HISTORY

The first nationwide job safety and health legislation was signed by President Richard M. Nixon December 29, 1970, as the Occupational Safety and Health Act of 1970, Public Law 91-596.

The law was preceded by what Senator Jacob K. Javits (R-NY), a key figure in the final compromise, called "the most bitter labor-management political fight in years."

The need for the legislation had been well documented. The Democrat-controlled 91st Congress put a high priority on passage of a job safety bill. President Nixon added Republican support in a Message to Congress August 6, 1969, followed by specific Administration recommendations.

The legislation was jeopardized at virtually every stage of congressional consideration, however, with major disagreement over key provisions. Support for the Administration's position ran high in the House, and resulted in rejection of the House Education and Labor Committee's bill in favor of a modified Administration version.

Compromise came easier in the Senate, with that bill reflecting Senate Labor and Public Welfare Committee recommendations and Republican modifications.

Additional compromises in conference between the Senate and House produced a bill acceptable to both Houses and the Administration.

NEED FOR LEGISLATION

Statistics on industrial accidents and health hazards made a strong case for federal intervention. Each year 14,000 workers died and 2.2 million were disabled by accidents in the workplace, former Labor Secretary George P. Shultz testified during Senate hearings.

Work-related deaths and accidents meant estimated annual losses of $1.5 billion in wages and $8 billion in the gross national product.

Even these figures undercounted disabling injuries by from 8 to 10 percent, according to an unpublished study prepared for the Department of Labor by health and safety expert Jerome B. Gordon. If industrial accident statistics compiled by the Department also included nondisabling serious accidents accounting for less than a day's work, the yearly total would be 25 million rather than 2.2 million injuries, Mr. Gordon said.

In a 1967 study, the Surgeon General estimated that 65 percent of the workers in 1,700 industrial plants potentially were exposed to harmful physical agents, yet only 25 percent of these workers were protected adequately. On the basis of this study, it was estimated that 390,000 new cases of occupational disease occurred each year.

Known hazards went unchecked. Lead and mercury poisoning

affected substantial numbers of workers. Asbestosis, clinically defined over 40 years ago, remained a threat. Allied diseases increased in number. The danger of byssinosis for workers in cotton mills, recognized in the United States in the fifties, grew unabated.

New dangers posed equally complex problems. The Public Health Service estimated that a new, potentially toxic chemical was introduced into industry every 20 minutes. New energy sources and processes— atomic energy, laser beams, ultra-sonics, and microwaves—complicated industrial health problems.

Farmworkers suffered the effects of newly developed and increasingly dangerous pesticides, herbicides, and fungicides.

Regulation Efforts

Some states had acted to establish and enforce safety and health standards, but only a few had modern laws and adequate resources for administration and enforcement. At least eight states had no identifiable programs in occupational health at all. Four states had no inspection personnel and only three states had over 100 inspectors. Total state safety inspectors numbered only 1,600, which, combined with fewer than 100 federal inspectors, totaled less than half the number of fish and game wardens in the country.

Health and safety programs merited up to $2.70 per worker per year in some states, while others spent less than one cent.

Employers had taken the initiative in some areas, with programs and campaigns to educate and protect their employees. Industrial members of the National Safety Council and trade associations boasted injury rates well below those of nonmembers in the same line. Companies that invested in health and safety of employees, however, claimed an economic disadvantage compared to those who did not.

Union membership provided some protection. Sixty-five percent of collective bargaining agreements contained some type of health and safety clause. But millions of non-union workers were left uncovered.

Federal programs were spotty, concentrated on selected industries such as longshoring, railroading, federally contracted construction and service suppliers, atomic energy, and mining. Federal financial and technical support had risen and fallen over the years, but it never had been enough to have any real significance.

BACKGROUND OF THE LAW

The Federal Government entered the safety and health area in 1890, when the first federal legislation governing safety standards and inspection practices for coal mines was passed. Three years later safe equipment specifications were mandated for railroad cars and engines, and in the ensuing years a series of control laws for railroads was enacted.

Occupational health programs consisted mainly of research and studies, beginning with the creation of the Public Health Service in 1902. The Bureau of Mines, concerned with health and safety research for underground operations, was established in the Department of the

Interior in 1910. In 1914, the predecessor of the Occupational Health Division in the Department of Health, Education, and Welfare was formed.

At the same time, private groups sprang up, composed of professionals in the gradually expanding field of occupational health and safety, as well as industrialists and public-spirited citizens.

None of these programs had any real impact on a national scale. While virtually every state had some kind of industrial health and safety law by 1920 and most regulated mining, follow through was haphazard.

The growth of the labor movement in the early 1930s revived federal involvement slightly, and the Davis-Bacon Act of 1931 had a fringe effect on workers subject to its provisions. In 1936 the Walsh-Healey Public Contracts Act prescribed health and safety standards for workers engaged in Government contract work, but enforcement was lacking. In the mid-thirties, the creation of the Bureau of Labor Standards within the Labor Department stimulated the development of voluntary safety codes, and involved the Government in consultative and training efforts for state and private safety organizations.

Both the depression and World War II interfered with overall activity in the health and safety field. Labor was concerned with wages and establishment of union rights; management was in no position to expend time or money on non-profit making endeavors during the lean years. Winning the war took precedence over other considerations in the early forties.

By the mid-forties federal activities were at a low ebb, but the high increase in work-related injuries during the war caused a brief flurry of interest, and the first Presidential Conference on Industrial Safety was called in 1948 by President Harry S. Truman. These conferences continued through the Eisenhower Administration.

Congressional Interest

In 1951 Senator Hubert H. Humphrey (D-Minn) introduced a bill calling for uniform national health and safety codes and uniform enforcement standards. Like the several bills offered by others in the next 10 or 12 years, it got nowhere.

A trend to federal concern for specific industries with abnormally high accident rates did develop, and several laws were passed in the 1950s which regulated maritime safety (longshoring), and tightened up mine regulations.

By the sixties a new factor entered the picture—environmental control. As the country became conscious of air and water pollution, a parallel concern about the polluted working environment developed. This coincided with several other elements—sharp increase in industrial accidents starting in 1958, research into the danger of new chemicals and other physical agents, and general prosperity which enabled unions to work for non-wage demands and management to pay for needed controls. The groundwork for comprehensive legislation was laid.

Nonetheless, the Federal Government was reluctant to enter the total job safety field. In 1958, Congresswoman Leonor K. Sullivan (D-Mo), in response to an industrial disaster in St. Louis, requested then Secretary of Labor James Mitchell to draft legislation setting mandatory standards for the safe use of hazardous materials in industry. He declined on the ground that the problem did not warrant federal intervention.

In 1965, H.R. 1179, the first bill dealing with general industrial hazardous materials, outside of the Atomic Energy Act, was introduced. It died, but that same year the McNamara-O'Hara Public Service Contract Act was passed, extending to Government service suppliers the same protection as in the Walsh-Healey Act. The National Foundation for the Arts and Humanities Act, which also had health and safety provisions, became law the same year.

The 90th Congress

On January 23, 1968, President Lyndon B. Johnson proposed "the Nation's first comprehensive Occupational Health and Safety Program to protect the worker on the job."

In broad outline, President Johnson requested legislation to strengthen the authority and resources of the Secretary of Health, Education, and Welfare for an extensive program of research, as a basis for setting comprehensive health and safety standards.

Under the plan, the Secretary of Labor would set and enforce standards and could impose strong sanctions, including civil and criminal penalties. Federal assistance for states to develop and strengthen their own occupational health and safety programs, was part of the package.

The Johnson bill was introduced in the House by Congressman James G. O'Hara (D-Mich). Following hearings by the House Education and Labor Select Subcommittee on Labor, which ended in March 1968, Congressman William D. Hathaway (D-Maine) offered a revised version which was reported out of the full committee July 16. The Rules Committee refused to clear the bill, however, and it died.

The Senate Labor and Public Welfare Subcommittee on Labor held a series of meetings on the Administration measure, introduced in the Senate by Ralph Yarborough (D-Texas) as S. 2864. With the demise of the House bill, the Senate Subcommittee took no further action.

HOW THE LAW EVOLVED

The 91st Congress was more receptive to occupational safety and health legislation, and early in the session passed coal mine, construction, and railroad safety acts.

A primitive version (H.R. 3809) of the bill eventually reported by the House committee was introduced by Congressman James O'Hara January 6, 1969, with 17 cosponsors.

On May 16, Senator Harrison Williams (D-NJ), with Senators Edward Kennedy (D-Mass), Walter Mondale (D-Minn), and Ralph Yarborough (D-Texas) dropped a job safety bill (S. 2193) in the Senate hopper.

Although President Nixon called for "proposals to help guarantee the health and safety of workers" in his Domestic Programs and Policies Message to Congress on April 14, 1969, it was not until August 6 that the Administration proposals were spelled out. Following the President's August 6 message, Administration bills (H.R. 13373 and S. 2788) were introduced.

The early bills, although considerably less detailed than subsequent versions, contained many of the seeds of conflicts to come.

Principal Disputes

President Nixon recommended that a new National Occupational Safety and Health Board set and enforce standards. Democrats wanted the same authority vested in the Secretary of Labor. This division posed formidable problems during congressional debate.

Almost all of the conflicts which plagued the legislators divided along labor-management lines, with management favoring the Administration approach and labor endorsing the Democratic version.

The important and troublesome issues included provisions relating to the general duty requirement for employers, "walk-around" rights of employers and employees during federal inspection tours, plant closings in cases of "imminent danger," and citation and posting requirements.

Fears that employers' rights under due process might be abrogated on the one hand, or that employees might be denied their right to protection or access to relevant information on the other, also hampered agreement.

The Hearings

Intensive hearings were conducted by both the House and Senate Labor Subcommittees.

In contrast to testimony at the 1968 hearings, management abandoned its opposition to federal involvement in favor of the Nixon Administration's approach to separation of standard-setting, investigatory, and enforcement powers. Organized labor went straight down the line for vesting full responsibility in the Labor Department and lent its full weight to Mr. O'Hara's bill.

The House Subcommittee held 13 days of hearings in Washington, D.C., in September, October, and November 1969, with an additional two days in November in San Francisco.

Senate hearings ran intermittently between September 1969 and May 1970 for a total of 12 days. Field hearings were conducted in New Jersey, Pennsylvania, and South Carolina in April 1970.

Events in the House

Early in 1970 the long process of compromise began. With the fall 1969 hearings completed and H.R. 3809 as a basis, Congressman Dominick V. Daniels (D-NJ), House Labor Subcommittee chairman, began preparation of a new bill.

Mr. Daniels' proposal went through seven versions before final presentation to the House Subcommittee.

The bill was approved by the Democrats, and the Subcommittee me
March 19. Republican amendments were rejected and the Subcommittee
concluded its business on March 25. In retaliation for alleged Democra
unwillingness to compromise, Republican Committee members boycotted
the final session.

H.R. 16785, the clean bill reported out of the Subcommittee in the
face of the Republican hold-out, was taken up by the full Committee on
April 14. Republican hopes for compromise appeared dim, but a revised
Administration bill, worked out by Congressman William A. Steiger
(R-Wis), was presented to the full Committee at its first working
session.

Mr. Steiger's compromise was defeated by a straight party vote
and Committee sessions were suspended as the two sides sought to work
out their differences.

The Democrats scheduled an open meeting for June 3, but the Republicans failed to attend. Subsequent quorum calls by the Committee
also fell short.

In a last-ditch effort to bring the adversaries together, the Republicans devised another draft, in cooperation with Labor Department representatives, and Congressmen William A. Hathaway (D-Maine) and
Phillip Burton (D-Calif). This version, which failed, would have set up
an Occupational Safety and Health Court, similar to the United States
Tax Court, to adjudicate violations.

On June 13, H.R. 16785 was approved by the House Labor Committee, along straight party lines, save for one Republican defector, Congressman Alphonzo Bell of California, who said he voted just to get the
bill out.

In an appendage to the Committee report, 12 of the 15 Republican
members declared the bill unacceptable. Six also castigated separately
the Committee bill as a "tragedy without equal." Another three, presumably acquiescing in the report, signed neither statement. Congressman Phillip Burton (D-Calif) offered a concurrent view, with the
reservation that the Committee bill might prove too weak. (The text of
the report appears in Appendix C.)

Congressman William H. Ayres (R-Ohio) later hoped to induce the
Rules Committee to consider a substitute to be introduced by Mr. Steiger
in place of the Committee bill. This tactic failed, however.

The Rules Committee refused the Committee bill a hearing prior to
the House summer recess, running from August 14 to September 10. It
was not until September 22 that H.R. 16785 was granted a rule, a week
after H.R. 19200, a modification of the Administration bill, was introduced by Mr. Steiger, with Congressman Robert Sikes (D-Fla) as cosponsor. Mr. Steiger made clear his intention to bring up his bill on the
floor and have it replace the Committee measure.

On November 23, almost a week after the Senate version of the bill had been passed, H.R. 16785 reached the House floor.

Mr. Daniels presented a series of amendments designed to accommodate most Republican objections—except for divesting the Secretary of Labor of his standard-setting authority.

Resentment to the tardy compromise ran high. Furthermore, as Mr. Sikes pointed out, the proposed amendments left many controversial issues untouched.

The fundamental dispute of who was to set standards was one. Criteria for standards to be developed was another. In addition, walkaround provisions, i.e., the right of employees and employers to accompany the federal inspector, had not been resolved.

Mr. Steiger read a letter of support for H.R. 19200 from the Secretary of Labor, after which further action was postponed until the following day, when the Steiger-Sikes substitute was accepted first by a teller vote of 185-114, and then by a 220-172 roll call vote, as an amendment to the Committee bill.

Events in the Senate

The Senate hearings were under way during March and April, while the House Subcommittee was struggling to come to agreement. The Senate Labor Subcommittee had no intention of waiting for the House to complete action on the measure, but no executive meetings to consider the bill were expected until July 1970.

Like his counterpart in the House, Senate Labor Subcommittee Chairman Harrison J. Williams (D-NJ) had quorum troubles, and for a while it appeared he would have to bypass the Subcommittee if he hoped to report out a bill at all. At the end of August he managed to attract a quorum and by September 9, some problems had been hammered out at two executive sessions. The bill was sent to the full Committee, where consideration began September 16.

Through diligence and hard work, and perhaps with the unfortunate example of the House proceedings before them, the Senate Committee members effected substantial changes in the bill, many significant ones with Republican sponsorship.

Important as these amendments were, however, they still left pending the questions of basic administrative arrangements and aspects of imminent danger closings.

The Committee did encounter some difficulties. On several occasions, a rarely used parliamentary device prevented executive sessions from being held while the Senate was in session. The tactic only delayed the inevitable; there was sufficient agreement within the Committee to report the bill on September 25, by a 17 to 2 vote.

On September 29, Senator Peter H. Dominick (R-Colo) introduced S. 4404, the Senate equivalent of H.R. 19200, with the intention of offering it on the floor as a substitute for the Committee bill.

Originally scheduled for floor debate during the week of October 5, action on S. 2193 was postponed for a week on request of the minority. On October 13, Senator Mike Mansfield (D-Mont) requested unanimous consent to set aside other pending business, stating that additional requests for delay by the Republicans violated a tacit understanding on procedures made at the time of their initial request.

A Republican filibuster against the unanimous consent motion followed.

On October 14, the Senate agreed to make the bill the pending business of the Senate following the election recess.

On November 16, Mr. Williams moved almost immediately to table the Dominick substitute, and his motion carried 41 to 39. It was then agreed to vote on amendments to the Committee bill.

The spirit of compromise was in the air, although the first amendment, offered by Senators William B. Saxbe (R-Ohio) and Richard S. Schweiker (R-Pa), to require a court order for closing a plant due to imminent danger was rejected 42 to 40.

Mr. Javits introduced his proposition for a three-man appeals commission, joined by Mr. Dominick as cosponsor. Mr. Javits accepted the descriptive title of "Commission" from the Dominick bill to replace his proposed terminology of a "Panel." The amendment passed, 43 to 38.

The Senate difficulty with the imminent danger provision finally was resolved by a Javits amendment. This, coupled with an earlier amendment, enabled the Williams bill to come to a final vote and win Senate approval.

THE FINAL AGREEMENT

The conference to iron out differences between the Senate and House bills began December 8. It took five sessions, some of which lasted for more than seven hours to conclude what Congressman Carl D. Perkins (D-Ky) termed a "difficult conference."

At a long meeting on December 11, tentative agreement on the general duty clause was reached, with the compromise eventually accepted. The conferees also came together on provisions for inspection, investigations, and record-keeping.

About midway through the conference, the Senate conceded to the House on the imminent danger clause.

Mr. Steiger had proposed retention of the House provision on standards setting, but with the Secretary of Labor as chairman, and the Secretary of HEW as a member. When that tactic failed, he suggested that the Secretary of Labor set the standards, with review by a separate appeals board.

The Democrats appeared adamant on giving standards setting to the Secretary of Labor, and the House conferees caved in. Later accusations by Mr. Sikes that a longer holdout by the House could have saved the House provision partially were confirmed by admission of some Senators that a potential Senate counterproposal never had a chance to be heard.

A second issue which hamstrung the conferees during the final meeting on December 14 concerned formal *vs* informal rulemaking procedures. The Senate view of informal procedures prevailed over the objections and attempts at compromise by Mr. Steiger.

At the end of the day on December 14 there was some question whether the Republican House conferees would sign the conference report. A key figure was Mr. Steiger. Although still dismayed by some aspects of the report, Mr. Steiger announced his support of the conference report on December 15. He denied, however, that a letter from Secretary of Labor James Hodgson endorsing the compromise or pressure from the White House had influenced his decision.

The compromise went first to the Senate, which accepted it after only 10 minutes of discussion.

It was not quite so easy in the House, where debate lasted an hour. Congressmen Sikes and William J. Scherle (R-Ind) argued for voting against the measure, amidst a series of laudatory speeches. At the end of debate, the conference report was adopted, 308 to 60 in the early afternoon of December 17.

The Occupational Safety and Health Act of 1970 was ready for President Nixon's signature.

In a signing ceremony held at the Labor Department, Mr. Nixon noted the compromise that had been made at each step. "This bill," he said, "represents in its culmination the American system at its best."

CHAPTER 3

SAFETY AND HEALTH STANDARDS

Traditionally, the landmark pieces of labor legislation—the Fair Labor Standards Act, the Taft-Hartley Act, the Landrum-Griffin Act, and the Civil Rights Act of 1964—spelled out a list of specific "do's and don'ts" for employers or unions to follow. The Occupational Safety and Health Act of 1970 departed from this tradition in that it did not set forth the ground rules and the prohibitions, but instead only established the machinery for grinding them out.

Congress recognized that "industrial safety and health problems are as complex and changing as American industry itself" and that "they cannot be solved by a lengthy list of prohibitions spelled out in a statute." (116 Cong. Rec. S 17470, Oct. 8, 1970) Instead, the law empowers an administrative agency to issue detailed safety and health regulations, called standards, that will have the force and effect of law.

Three basic types of standards are called for under the new law: (1) interim standards that could be promulgated immediately, since they are based on already existing federal and "consensus" standards that were developed after obtaining the views of interested parties; (2) permanent standards that would replace or supplement the interim standards after allowing an opportunity, through advisory committees and hearings, for affected employers and employees to have a voice in the standard-setting process; and (3) temporary emergency standards that could be issued immediately when new health and safety findings indicate that employees are exposed to grave dangers.

THE INTERIM STANDARDS

The intent of the interim standards provision is to give the Secretary of Labor a speedy mechanism to promulgate standards with which industry already is familiar. It was recognized in Congress that these interim standards might not be as effective or as current as the permanent standards that subsequently will be promulgated, but it was felt that the interim standards would be useful immediately to provide a nationwide floor of minimum health and safety standards.

Every covered employer is required to comply with the interim standards promulgated by the Secretary of Labor. The interim standards may come from only two sources—national consensus standards or established federal standards. These two types of standards are discussed in detail below.

Procedure—The law contemplates that the Secretary of Labor immediately will issue interim standards, without going through the time-consuming process of formal procedures. The use of an informal, shortened rule-making procedure is permitted. The House bill specified that a

23

public hearing must be afforded to interested parties before standards are promulgated. This provision was not included in the final version. Instead, the Secretary is authorized to promulgate interim standards without a hearing. (116 Cong. Rec. H 11899, Dec. 17, 1970)

The Secretary is directed to promulgate interim standards "unless he determines that the promulgation of such standard will not result in improved safety or health for specifically designated employees." (Sec. 6 (a))

Effective date—The interim standards are to be issued "as soon as practicable" after the April 28, 1971, effective date of the law. They are to remain in effect for a two-year period ending April 28, 1973, or until superseded by a permanent standard issued under the Secretary's general authority to promulgate, modify, or revoke any standard under the Act. (Sec. 6(a))

The interim standards are effective immediately upon publication in the *Federal Register*. The House bill contained a provision specifying that 90 days after promulgating interim standards, the Secretary must begin procedures for setting permanent ones. This was dropped from the final version.

Conflict—In the event of conflict among the consensus or established federal standards, the Secretary is directed to promulgate the one that assures the greatest protection of affected employees. (Sec. 6(a))

The Federal Standards

Existing federal standards for safety and health may be promulgated by the Secretary of Labor as standards under the new law immediately after the effective date of the Act.

In authorizing the promulgation of interim standards without a hearing, the legislators reasoned that these standards already had been subjected to the procedural scrutiny mandated by the law under which they were issued. Such standards, moreover, incorporate, by reference, many voluntary industrial standards.

The existing federal standards have been issued under numerous federal safety laws, such as the Walsh-Healey Act, Service Contract Act, Construction Safety Act, Arts and Humanities Act, and Longshoremen's and Harbor Workers' Compensation Act. These pre-existing federal standards applied to at least 25 million workers prior to the enactment of the Occupational Safety and Health Act.

Walsh-Healey Act

In the ceremony at the Labor Department when President Nixon signed the new law, Labor Secretary James D. Hodgson indicated that a first step after the effective date of the law would be to extend to all employers covered by the law the safety and health standards previously required only of U.S. Government contractors under the Walsh-Healey Act. This Act specifies that no work under a Government contract covered by the law (contracts for manufacturing or supplying goods in an amount in excess of $10,000) may be performed in establishments or under conditions that are unsanitary, hazardous, or dangerous to the health and safety of the employee.

Regulations have been issued by the Secretary of Labor setting forth minimum standards of safe and healthful conditions of work to assure compliance with the law. These regulations deal with such subjects as injury frequency rates, exposure to radiation, noise, gases, vapors, fumes, dusts, and mists, hazardous chemicals, and other hazards. (For the text of these regulations, see Appendix J.)

The regulations also require covered contractors to comply with standards issued by the two consensus standards organizations—the American National Standards Institute and the National Fire Protection Association—plus standards issued by the American Society of Mechanical Engineers and the American Society for Testing and Materials. The part of the regulations that deals with "gases, vapors, fumes, dusts, and mists" also specifies that contractors must act in accordance with standards adopted by the American Conference of Governmental Industrial Hygienists, the Compressed Gas Association, the National Committee on Uniform Traffic Laws and Ordinances, and the American Welding Society.

A listing of addresses where the standards, specifications, and codes of these organizations may be obtained appears in Appendix J.

Construction Safety Act

Considerable effort was made in the debate preceding adoption of the overall Occupational Safety and Health Act to clarify the overlap between that Act and the Construction Safety Act. The House and Senate conferees on the bill agreed, it was stated, that the Secretary of Labor is supposed to develop health and safety standards for federal building contractors under the Construction Safety Act and then use the same "mechanisms and resources" to develop health and safety standards for all of the other construction workers (those on privately financed work) newly covered by the overall Act, including those engaged in alterations, repairs, painting, and/or decorating. (116 Cong. Rec. H 11811, Dec. 16, 1970)

One of the conferees, Congressman William A. Steiger (R-Wis), explained that it was the intent of the conferees that (1) there should be no duplication under the two laws, (2) there should be no more burden imposed on the construction industry under the new law than on any other industry, and (3) the Secretary of Labor in working with the advisory committees under the new law should work "toward an effective coordination between the two acts." (116 Cong. Rec. H 11897, Dec. 17, 1970)

Congressman Carl D. Perkins (D-Ky), chairman of the House Education and Labor Committee, agreed with this interpretation and added that if "the Secretary proceeded under one Act and failed—or succeeded—he then could not resort to the penalty proceedings in the other Act" with respect to a contractor covered by both laws. (116 Cong. Rec. H 11897-11898, Dec. 17, 1970)

Other Safety Laws

In addition to Walsh-Healey and Construction Safety, the new law mentions these pre-existing federal laws with safety provisions:

Service Contract Act—This Act parallels the Walsh-Healey Public Contracts Act and covers private firms performing service contracts with the U.S. Government for amounts in excess of $2,500. Service contracts covered by the Act include contracts for laundry and dry cleaning, custodial and janitorial work, packing and crating, guard duty, food and cafeteria service, and miscellaneous housekeeping functions. The Act specifies that covered contracts must contain a provision that none of the work under the contract will be performed under working conditions that are "unsanitary or dangerous to the health or safety of service employees."

Regulations issued under the Act require employers to comply with standards issued by nationally recognized professional organizations. Specifically mentioned in this regard are the two consensus standards organizations—the American National Standards Institute and National Fire Protection Association—plus the American Society of Mechanical Engineers, the American Society for Testing and Materials, and the American Conference of Governmental Industrial Hygienists.

On January 22, 1970, all safety and health rules adopted under the Walsh-Healey Act and the Longshoremen's and Harbor Workers' Compensation Act were made applicable, where relevant, to contractors under the Service Contract Act.

National Foundation on Arts & Humanities Act—This Act covers professionals retained under programs receiving federal assistance from the National Foundation of the Arts and Humanities, or from any of its subdivisions or agents under the Act, as well as laborers and mechanics employed by contractors or subcontractors on construction projects assisted under the Act. The Labor Secretary is authorized to issue regulations governing wages and working conditions (safety and health) to ensure that covered workers receive at least the wages and working conditions prevailing in the locality.

Regulations issued under the Act specify that until such time as the Labor Department is able to study in depth the safety and health hazards peculiar to the production of the arts and related projects, the Secretary will accept as prima facie evidence of compliance with the Act, compliance with existing federal standards or other nationally recognized standards. The regulations list as acceptable "nationally recognized standards" those developed by the National Bureau of Standards; American National Standards Institute, Inc.; National Fire Protection Association; American Society of Mechanical Engineers; and the American Society for Testing and Materials.

Longshore Safety—The Labor Department was given authority to regulate safety and health in longshoring by 1958 amendments (P.L. 85-742) to Section 41 of the Longshoremen's and Harbor Workers' Compensation Act. The Labor Department issued its first set of regulations under this Act in 1960.

The federal authority under the Act applies only to navigable waters and hence ends at the gangway. Dockside operations come under the jurisdiction of the bordering state.

A consensus safety code covering dockside operations has been developed by the American National Standards Institute, Inc. This standard was published in 1969 and will become a standard under the new law if and when the Labor Secretary adopts the ANSI consensus standards as interim standards during the first two years of the new safety law's operation.

Enforcement Choices

The new law provides that safety standards under the other laws administered by the Secretary of Labor, such as Walsh-Healey and Construction Safety, will be superseded when more effective standards are promulgated under the new law, but until then they are deemed standards under the new law. (Sec. 4(a)(2)) This means that the enforcement procedures of the new law are added to the enforcement procedures of the other laws. (116 Cong. Rec. H 11811, Dec. 16, 1970)

When the standards under the old laws are superseded by standards promulgated under the new safety law, the newly promulgated standards will become standards under both the new law and the old laws, "thereby preserving remedies available under existing laws," according to Mr. Steiger. (116 Cong. Rec. H 11899, Dec. 17, 1970)

The remedies provided by the other laws are unchanged, including provisions authorizing cancellation of the offending employer's Government contract and blacklisting him from receiving other Government contracts.

In any enforcement proceeding against a Government contractor covered by both the new law and one of the old laws, the principle of collateral estoppel will apply, which means that the same facts can't be litigated twice, once under one law and the second time under the other. Mr. Perkins explained the intent of the conferees as follows:

"The Secretary was intended to have alternatives available to him. That is, he may elect to pursue the procedure for enforcement laid out in either Act and may seek to have imposed the penalty authorized by either Act. He may not, however, pursue enforcement under one Act and then—whether having failed or succeeded—attempt to pursue the procedure provided in the other Act. The provisions for contract termination and blacklisting may be applied, of course, in appropriate cases and their imposition will not preclude the possibility of a civil penalty, in addition." (116 Cong. Rec. H 11894, Dec. 17, 1970)

Mr. Steiger also noted that it was the express intent of the conferees that the Secretary of Labor proceed initially under the new law, and that the Review Commission's findings of fact under this law would be binding upon the Secretary and the employer in determining whether an additional remedy should be imposed under one of the other laws. Under the doctrine of collateral estoppel, it was observed, if the Secretary lost an issue in a proceeding under any of the overlapping laws, he would be barred from raising that issue again. (116 Cong. Rec. H 11898, Dec. 17, 1970)

Guide to Interim Federal Standards

Prior to the passage of the Occupational Safety and Health Act, the Bureau of Labor Standards issued a handbook of guides to the safety and health standards for federal contracts under the Walsh-Healey Act and the Service Contract Act. Since these standards will become interim standards under the new law, this handbook offers employers a guide to where they stand under the law during the period of up to two years in which the interim standards are in effect.

"Anyone who complies with this [handbook] will be in compliance with the new law," Robert D. Gidel, deputy director of the Bureau, said.

The handbook—"Inspection Survey Guide, a handbook of guides and references to Safety and Health Standards for Federal Contract Programs"—is about three fourths of an inch thick, but is only a small fraction of the size of the material it condenses. "We took a seven-foot shelf of standards and translated it," Mr. Gidel said.

For each "hazard category" that is digested briefly in the guide, there is a reference to where it appears in the Code of Federal Regulations, the consensus standards of ANSI, or elsewhere.

Part A of the book, "Pre-Operational Requirements," has chapters on Walking-Working Surfaces; Illumination; Stairs-Stairways; Ladders and Scaffolds; Ventilation-General Comfort; Life Safety (Building Exits); Fire Suppression Equipment; Electrical Wiring; Apparatus, and Equipment; Boilers, Heaters and Cooling Equipment, Pressure Vessels and Piping; Elevators, Bowered Platforms, Manlifts, Hoisting Machinery, Equipment and Devices; Industrial Sanitation, and Medical Services and First Aid Facilities.

Part B on "Operational Requirements" covers Material Handling; Hand and Portable Powered Tools and Other Hand-held Equipment; Machine Guarding and Mechanical Safety; Material Hazards; Materials Storage; Surface Preparation, Finishing, and Preservation; Personal Protective Equipment; Industrial Environment; Welding, Cutting, Heating, and Brazing; Mining, and Program Factors.

There are appendices on Material Handling Gear and Appurtenances; Machine Guarding, Safe Openings and Guarding Materials; Table for Storage of Hazardous Materials; Safety Data Sheet; Safety and Health Standards for Federal Service Contracts; Safety and Health Standards for Federal Supply Contracts, and Glossary.

Copies of "Inspection Survey Guide," BLS Bulletin 236, may be obtained from the Superintendant of Documents, U.S. Government Printing Office, Washington, D.C. 20402, for $2.25 a copy.

The Consensus Standards

In addition to the standards under existing federal safety laws, the only other source mentioned in the new law for interim standards is the consensus standards. The Secretary is required, during the law's first two years, to promulgate as interim standards under the law all national consensus standards unless he determines that a standard would not result in improved safety or health for all or some of the affected employees. (Sec. 6(a))

The Act's definition of a "consensus standard" is one which has been adopted under procedures which have given diverse views an opportunity to be considered and which indicate that interested and affected persons have reached substantial agreement on its adoption. (Sec. 3(a)) Use of these procedures, it was felt, made it appropriate for the Labor Secretary to adopt these standards without a public hearing or other formal proceedings.

Two private organizations are the major sources of consensus standards—the American National Standards Institute, Inc., and the National Fire Protection Association. The standards they produce are the only ones available in many areas. These two groups together produce only about 13 percent of all safety standards. As the House Labor Committee Report noted, they have done very little in the way of developing occupational health standards.

The consensus standards have been criticized primarily on two grounds: (1) they are produced by private organizations, which are susceptible to the pressures of commercial trade association interests, and (2) the consensus standard organizations have been slow in developing and updating safety standards.

American National Standards Institute, Inc.

ANSI is a voluntary, non-profit organization with representation from scientific, technical, trade, professional, consumer, and labor organizations. These groups numbered about 160 in 1970 and, according to ANSI, represent roughly 95 percent of the standards developing capability in private industry.

Depending upon their primary interest, organizations select membership in either ANSI's Member Body Council, which is responsible for standards development and administration, or the Consumer Council, which advises on consumer matters and reviews standards of interest to consumers.

In addition to this organizational representation, ANSI has some 900 individual companies as company members. These companies are not directly involved in standards development or approval and have direct votes only on matters of policy. They provide financial support for ANSI, but there is a ceiling on how much any one company may contribute. This ceiling is intended to keep major companies or combinations thereof from dominating standards approval.

The financial support from industry and organizations accounts for less than 50 percent of ANSI's operating budget. The remainder is received from sales of standards and from special projects.

The ANSI standards are promulgated for voluntary use, but hundreds of them have found their way into local, state, and national law and regulation. These standards were adopted in the regulations issued under the Walsh-Healey Act, for example. (See Appendix J for text of these regulations.)

At the working level in developing standards, ANSI utilizes technical advisory boards (18 in total in 1970) and standards committees (227 in 1970). ANSI membership is not required for participation in the technical work of these boards and committees. The volunteer members are recruited for their background and experience and normally are nominated by trade associations, labor unions, consumer groups, and affected agencies of federal, state, and local governments.

Standards proposed by a standards committee are submitted to ANSI's Board of Standards Review, whose members represent a cross section of standards interest. Proposed standards also will be released for public review and comment to the trade and general press, ANSI members, and interested government agencies. This review procedure is new and was adopted in response to criticisms that ANSI committees in the past have been "closed shops" and have failed to consult fully with affected groups.

Once approved by the Board of Standards Review, the proposed standard becomes an "American National Standard" of ANSI.

ANSI has some 3,000 standards ranging from specifications for nuts and bolts and electrical wiring to safety requirements for power mowers and household appliances.

National Fire Protection Association

NFPA develops its standards in much the same manner as ANSI. It has produced National Fire Codes that are available in 10 volumes with individual codes, standards, and practices also available in pamphlet form.

The titles of the codes are flammable liquids; gases; combustible solids, dusts, and explosives; building construction and facilities; electrical; sprinklers, fire pumps, and water tanks; alarm and special extinguishing systems; portable and manual fire control equipment; occupancy standards and process hazards, and transportation.

A complete listing of pamphlet editions is available from the Association and will be supplied free upon request. (See Appendix J)

Advantages and Drawbacks of Consensus Standards

In "Status of Safety Standards," a review of safety and health standards in effect in 1968, the Bureau of Labor Standards cited several advantages to adopting consensus standards. It noted that such standards:
• Represent a national consensus of all interested parties.
• Permit a pooling of resources, competent skills, talent, experience, and technology—a "combo" impossible for a single agency, public or private, to duplicate.
• Represent a feasible compromise between protection and production and therefore are more readily accepted by those regulated.
• Present greater opportunity for federal and state governments to join forces with industry and labor to develop or update standards.
• Help reduce the proliferation of individual standards and guides, both in government and in private industry, which have reached unmanageable proportions.
• Remove the need for the Federal Government to duplicate the work done to date in the areas where sound safety and health standards exist.

But this same report noted that over 60 percent of the ANSI safety standards were out of date and needed serious revision. At the time of the 1968 study, nearly 60 percent of the consensus standards were five or more years old—the largest percentage 10 years-plus. Based on past performances, only about one fifth of these standards would be revised or affirmed in any one year. The study also found at least 50 areas where national standards either did not exist or were inadequate.

Partly in response to this criticism, ANSI revised its procedures to speed up the production of standards. As a result, the yearly production, which had been 413 standards in 1967, rose to about 1,000 in 1969. ANSI estimated that it could take about 1,000 approval actions each year.

Voluntary standards set by the consensus method were criticized in the House Labor Committee report as "representing the lowest common denominator of change in the status quo that is necessary to achieve acceptance."

The Proprietary Standards

The bill that passed the Senate and the bill that was reported out by the House Labor Committee would have permitted the Secretary to use proprietary standards for interim regulation. The proprietary standards are those that have been promulgated by national organizations, but by nonconsensus method, i.e., a method that does not involve the interchange of views of experts and interested parties that is part of the consensus method.

Many of the proprietary standards are produced by various industries, professional societies, and associations. Included are such groups as the American Conference of Governmental Industrial Hygienists, the Manufacturing Chemists Association, and the Associated General Contractors. Policy in these organizations is determined by a straight membership vote, not by consensus.

The law as passed dropped the provision in the Senate bill that would have permitted the use of proprietary standards. However, the primary intent of the Senate bill was to enable the Secretary of Labor to use the proprietary standards of the American Conference of Governmental Industrial Hygienists, which set threshold limit values (TLVs) for airborne contaminants. The Senate conferees receded on this point because the ACGIH standards have been incorporated by reference into the Walsh-Healey Act, which makes them part of the federal standards that will be adopted as interim standards under the new law. (As noted under the discussion of the Walsh-Healey Act, the proprietary standards of several organizations have been incorporated into the Walsh-Healey Act, and hence will come under the new law as federal standards.)

During the Senate hearings, an Administration spokesman indicated that the ACGIH standards might almost be considered consensus standards. He remarked:

"It should be noted that the vast majority (over 400) of those health standards promulgated by the Department of Labor under the Walsh-Healey Public Contracts Act . . . were developed and recommended by the Threshold Limit Committee of the American Conference of Governmental Industrial Hygienists (ACGIH). Although there was no input from labor and very little input from industry in the development of these professional standards, they can be considered *de facto* consensus standards because of their wide acceptance and usage by industry, labor, state, and local occupational health agencies, and the governments of Canada and Great Britain." (Hearings before the Senate Subcommittee on Labor, p. 152)

THE PERMANENT STANDARDS

The consensus and federal standards that are issued as interim standards under the new law should provide a sound foundation for a national safety and health program. However, Congress recognized that it is essential that these standards be improved constantly and replaced as new knowledge and techniques are developed. Moreover, many occupational hazards—particularly those affecting health—are not covered by any of the existing standards. For these reasons, the Act sets forth procedures by which new standards may be promulgated and the interim standards may be revised and revoked.

Briefly, here is now the procedure works:

• A new or revised standard may be suggested by "an interested person," a union, a nationally recognized standard-setting organization, the Secretary of HEW, the National Institute for Occupational Safety and Health, a state or political subdivision, or the Labor Secretary himself.

• The Secretary may initiate proceedings either by (1) appointing an advisory committee whose recommendations the Secretary would use for proposing standards to be published in the *Federal Register,* or (2) dispensing with the advisory committee and simply publishing proposed standards in the *Federal Register.*

• In either case, interested parties would have 30 days within which to submit their views and to request a public hearing.

• If a hearing is requested, it is to be of the informal type authorized for rule-making by the Administrative Procedure Act in which no formal record is made.

• Within 60 days after the hearing is completed, the Secretary would issue the new or revised standard. If he deemed it necessary, the Secretary could delay the effective date of the new standard. (Sec. 6(b))

This procedure is discussed in more detail below.

Advisory Committees

The Secretary of Labor has the authority under the new law to set the machinery in motion for new or revised safety and health standards by simply publishing proposed standards in the *Federal Register.* It is expected, however, that where the subject matter is controversial, the Secretary first will appoint advisory committees to help him devise the proposed standards.

If an advisory committee is appointed, it is required to make its recommendations within 90 days, although the Secretary may extend this to 270 days. (Sec. 6(b)(1)) If the Secretary determines that regulations should be proposed, he must do so within 60 days of receipt of the advisory committee recommendations. If an advisory committee fails to report back within the period designated by the Secretary, he may publish his own proposed standards within 60 days of the date he had set for the committee's recommendations. (Sec. 6(a) (2))

An advisory committee appointed to assist the Secretary in developing standards may not consist of more than 15 members. It *must* include at least one member designated by the Secretary of Health, Education, and Welfare, and at least one representative of state health and safety agencies. It *must* include an equal number of persons qualified by experience and affiliation to present the views of employers and of employees.

The advisory committee *may* include representatives of nationally recognized standards-producing organizations and representatives of professional organizations of technicians or professionals specializing in occupational safety and health. The number of nongovernmental members may not exceed the number of members representing federal and state agencies. (Sec. 7(b))

The advisory committee meetings must be open to the public and an accurate record is to be kept and made available to the public. This provision, which was in the House bill but not the Senate bill, is designed to assure a full exchange between members of the advisory committee, to preserve a record of what they do, and to avoid undue secrecy on vital matters. No member of the committee (except for the representatives of employers and employees) is to have an economic interest in any proposed rule so that members would be free from economic or psychological coercion in their decision-making. (Sec. 7(b))

The House Labor Committee, which drafted the language that ended up in the law's provision on advisory committee membership and meetings, commented:

"Standards ought to be judged objectively as to whether they do, in fact, give maximum and reasonable protection to the health and safety of workers. Industry wants to be assured that it will be heard and its technical input properly evaluated. Other interested persons also wish to make effective presentations. Public hearings before technical advisory committees will better accomplish this since the openness of meetings imposes an extra duty of preparation and rebuttal."

Hearings on Proposed Standards

Whether the Secretary uses an advisory committee or not, any proposal for new or revised standards must be published in the *Federal Register*. Interested persons have a period of 30 days after publication to submit data or comments and to request a public hearing. (Sec. 6(b)(2))

If written objection is made and a hearing requested, the Secretary will publish a notice specifying the objections made and setting a time and place for hearing. (Sec. 6(b)(3). The hearing would be of the informal type authorized for rule-making by the Administrative Procedure Act.

The type of hearing to be held before a permanent standard is promulgated stimulated debate in Congress between advocates of formal hearings and those of informal hearings. Those favoring use of formal procedures argued that this was necessary to assure the fullest involvement and participation in the development of safety and health standards and to assure that a standard is based on substantial evidence on the record.

Under the informal proceeding provided for in the law, no formal record is made and, critics asserted, the standards could not be tested to see if they were based on substantial evidence of record. Advocates countered that this informal procedure is used in almost all comparable statutes, is fully consistent with administrative due process, and permits a speedy promulgation of standards with a fair opportunity for those affected to be heard.

The formal procedures were rejected as too complicated and time-consuming for setting standards. As it is, the machinery for establishing permanent standards could take well over a year—90 to 270 days for an advisory committee to come up with recommendations, up to 60 days for publication of the proposed standards in the *Federal Register*, 30 days for interested parties to file comments and request a hearing, and an indeterminate period of time for holding a hearing and promulgating a final version of the permanent standard.

The possibilities for delay inherent in this procedure for setting permanent standards prompted the legislators to authorize use of interim standards in the first two years of the new law.

Criteria for Permanent Standards

In setting standards dealing with toxic materials or harmful physical agents, the Secretary is directed by the law to observe certain criteria. In general, the Secretary is told to set the standard that most adequately assures, *to the extent feasible on the basis of the best available evidence,* that no employee will suffer material impairment of health or functional capacity even if he is exposed to a hazard for all his working life. (Sec. 6(b) (5))

This language was picked up from the Senate bill, and during the debate on that bill, Senator Harrison J. Williams (D-NJ) offered the following explanation of the provision:

"It will provide a continued direction to the Secretary that he shall be required to set the standard which most adequately and to the greatest extent feasible assures, on the basis of the best available evidence, that no employee will suffer any material impairment of health or functional capacity even if he has continual exposure to the hazard for the period of his working life.

"Certainly that is the objective, and included within this concept of unimpaired health and functional capacity is protection against diminished life expectancy." (116 Cong. Rec. S 18355, Nov. 17, 1970)

To clarify the meaning, Senator Peter H. Dominick (R-Colo) sought and obtained Mr. Williams' assurance that the interpretation of this provision meant that "the Secretary has got to use his best efforts to promulgate the best available standards, and in so doing, that he should take into account that anyone working in toxic agents or physical agents which might be harmful may be subjected to such conditions for the rest of his working life." The objective, Mr. Dominick continued, is to set a standard "so that we can get at something which might not be toxic now, if he works in it a short time, but if he works in it the rest of his life, it might be very dangerous." (116 Cong. Rec. S 18355, Nov. 17, 1970)

During the debate it was stated that the intent was not to require the Secretary to come up with a standard that would protect every worker, for the rest of his life, against any foreseeable hazard from toxic or harmful physical agents.

The law also specifies that:

• Standards shall be based on research, demonstrations, experiments, and such other information as may be appropriate.

• In addition to seeking the highest degree of protection for the employee, the Secretary also should take into consideration the latest scientific data in the field, the feasibility of these standards, and experience gained under this and other health and safety laws.

• Whenever practicable, the standard promulgated shall be expressed in terms of objective criteria and of the performance desired. (Sec. 6(b)(5))

Differences from Consensus Standards

If the Labor Secretary adopts a permanent standard that differs "substantially" from an existing national consensus standard, he must state reasons why the standard he adopted will better effectuate the purposes of the Act. (Sec. 6(b)(8))

During the Senate debate on this provision, several reasons were advanced for its need:

• The people should have an explanation of why the Secretary is departing from an existing consensus standard.

• Consensus organizations, such as ANSI, should be assured that the Act is not intended to preempt or limit their activity or importance.

• The consensus organizations also should be assured that the new National Institute for Occupational Safety and Health created by the Act "will take full advantage of the extensive expertise represented by members of technical societies and private standards-development organizations which serve an important purpose and which should continue to function in the private sector of occupational health and safety." (116 Cong. Rec. S 18356, Nov. 17, 1970)

Label Requirements

Standards are to prescribe the use of labels or other forms of warning to alert employees to the hazards to which they are exposed, relevant symptoms and appropriate emergency treatment, as well as proper conditions and precautions of safe use or exposure. The standards also are to prescribe suitable protective equipment and technological procedures to be used in connection with these hazards. In the case of toxic substances or harmful physical agents, monitoring and measuring may be required.

The label requirements were included in response to repeated testimony on the many problems caused by the continued presence and use of carcinogenic and toxic substances and processes in the workplace. The Senate Committee report said:

"Basically, the worker needs to have adequate advance knowledge of hazards in order to protect himself from damaging exposures. He needs proper protective equipment and the information necessary to treat emergencies if they arise. He should not be economically coerced into a hazardous job. Since inadvertent exposure to unknown products or processes often causes severe and immediate reactions, the exposed worker must know what type of exposure he has suffered in order to use proper treatment. The worker especially needs this information in cases of toxic substances which have delayed or latent ill effects."

Monitoring and measuring of employee exposure "at such locations and intervals, and in such manner as may be necessary for the protection of employees" is *required.*

In addition, the standard is to prescribe, where appropriate, the type and frequency of medical examinations of or other tests to employees when necessary to determine whether exposure has been or *may be* harmful. The employer is to bear the cost, unless such medical examinations are in the nature of research—then the Secretary of HEW will pick up the tab.

An informal rule-making process is permitted for modification by the Secretary of Labor, in consultation with the Secretary of HEW, of the labeling, monitoring, and medical examination requirements.

Delay in Effective Date

The Secretary is permitted to delay the effective date of a new standard to permit affected employers to familiarize themselves and their employees with its requirements. Such a delay may not exceed 90 days. (Sec. 6(b)(4))

This 90-day time limit is not intended, however, to preclude the possibility that a particular standard may provide for graduated requirements to take effect progressively on specific dates even though the intervals between the effective dates of such graduated requirements may exceed 90 days.

For example, a standard applicable to a particular industry could provide that, 90 days after issuance, the sound level in the workplace may not exceed X decibels; that six months after issuance, the sound level may not exceed X-5 decibels; and that one year after issuance, the sound level may not exceed X-10 decibels. (116 Cong. Rec. H 11899, Dec. 17, 1970)

Temporary Variances

Any employer affected by a particular standard may apply to the Secretary for a temporary order granting a variance provided that he (1) notify his employees so they are afforded the opportunity to participate in hearings on the variance, and (2) submit evidence in the record that he will provide to his employees employment that is as safe and healthful as would prevail if he complied immediately with the standard. (Sec. 6(b)(6)(A))

Reasons for Variance

Such an order is to be granted only if the employer shows he is unable to comply with a standard for specific and limited reasons—the unavailability of professional or technical personnel, or of necessary materials or equipment, or because necessary construction or alteration of facilities cannot be completed in the time required. In deciding whether to allow a variance, the one factor that may *not* be considered is the economic implications of a standard for the employer.

Duration of Variance

An order permitting a variance may be issued in any given case for a maximum of one year and may not be renewed more than twice.

Interim Orders

A temporary order permitting a variance usually is granted only after notice to employees and opportunity for a hearing. However, the Secretary may issue one interim order pending the holding of a hearing.

Application Requirements

An application for a variance must contain:

• A statement of the standard or portion thereof from which a variance is sought.

• A representation, supported by qualified persons with first-hand knowledge of the facts, that the employer is unable to comply with the standard, with a detailed statement of the reasons.

• A statement of the steps the employer has taken and will take (with specific dates) to protect employees against the hazard covered by the standard.

• A statement of when the employer expects to be able to comply with the standard and the steps he has taken and will take (with specific dates) to come into compliance.

• A certification that he has informed his employees of the application and of their right to petition for a hearing, with a description of how they were informed. (Sec. 6(b)(B))

Research Variances

Special variances may be granted if the Secretary of Labor or Secretary of HEW determines that a variance is needed to permit an employer to participate in an approved experiment designed to demonstrate or validate new and improved health-safety techniques. (Sec. 6(b)(6)(C))

Note: The provision detailed above appears in the subsection of the law dealing with temporary variances from permanent standards. A separate provision in the law provides a procedure for seeking permanent (but revocable) variances from any standards—interim, permanent, or temporary—promulgated under the law. This provision is discussed on the following page.

TEMPORARY EMERGENCY STANDARDS

Because of the obvious need for quick response to new safety and health findings, the Act authorizes the Secretary to issue emergency temporary standards without regard to the normal rule-making requirements and to take effect immediately. (Sec. 6(c))

The legislative history makes it clear that it was intended that this procedure not be utilized to circumvent the regular standard-setting procedures. Its intended use is for those limited situations where such emergency standards are necessary because employees are exposed to grave danger from substances or agents determined to be toxic, or from physically dangerous agents, or from new hazards. The Secretary must determine that a temporary emergency standard is necessary to protect the employees from such a danger.

In describing the restrictions on the use of emergency standards, Mr. Perkins said:

"Thus, where the state of the act is incomplete or in some way lacking so that a determination cannot be made as to whether such a standard will protect employees, in such instances the Secretary would utilize the regular standard-setting procedures . . . and not the emergency standard-setting authority." (116 Cong. Rec. H 11899, Dec. 17, 1970)

Time Limits

Upon publication of an emergency temporary standard, the Secretary must begin a regular standard-setting procedure for such hazard, with the emergency standard serving as a proposed standard under this procedure. The proceedings must be completed within six months. (Sec. 6(c)(3))

PRIORITY FOR STANDARDS

A provision was inserted during the Senate debate to make it clear that the Secretary needn't wait to promulgate interim or permanent standards "across the board" but rather could take up the more urgently needed standards first. In determining this priority for establishing standards, the Secretary is directed to give due regard to the following:

• The urgency of the need for mandatory safety and health standards for particular industries, trades, crafts, occupations, businesses, workplaces, or work environments.

• The recommendations of the Secretary of Health, Education, and Welfare regarding the need for mandatory standards in determining the priority for establishing such standards.

VARIANCES

Two separate provisions of the law authorize variances from standards promulgated by the Secretary of Labor. The two provisions deal with:

Temporary Variances

A detailed procedure is specified for seeking a temporary variance from a permanent standard. The intent of this provision is to give an employer a period of time in which to come into compliance with a new permanent standard. Since this procedure applies solely to permanent standards, it is discussed above under the section dealing with permanent standards.

Permanent Variances

A separate provision of the law authorizes the granting of permanent variances under which the employer is fully excepted from the standards. These requirements must be met before such a variance can be granted:

• The affected employees must be given notice and a chance to participate in a hearing on the proposed variance.

• The employer must show by a preponderance of the evidence that the conditions, practices, methods, etc., that he uses or proposes to use will provide employment and places of employment that are as safe and healthful as those that would prevail if he complied with the standard.

• If a variance is issued, it must prescribe the conditions the employer must maintain and the practices he must follow to the extent that they differ from the standard in question.

Revocation

An order or rule granting a variance may be modified or revoked any time after six months from its issuance upon application by the employer or his employees, or by the Secretary on his own motion, if it is shown that the conditions for its issuance are not being met. (Sec. 6(d))

JUDICIAL REVIEW

An employer or other person "adversely affected" may challenge a standard in the courts in either of two ways: (1) he may seek judicial review within 60 days of the promulgation of the standard by filing a challenge in the U.S. court of appeals in the circuit in which he resides or has his principal place of business. (Sec. 6(b)); or (2) he can obtain judicial review during the enforcement proceeding by appealing an adverse ruling of the enforcement commission in the appropriate U.S. court of appeals. (The latter method of obtaining judicial review is discussed in Chapter 4 on Enforcement.)

One of the reasons for providing this dual right of judicial review was to assure that small employers would receive their day in court. If the exclusive method for judicial review were to file a challenge within 60 days of a standard's promulgation, the practical effect, it was feared, would be that "trade associations and the giant corporations, having an abundance of legal manpower, would monopolize the right of review and thereby deny small employers and companies their day in court." (116 Cong. Rec. S 18264, Nov. 16, 1970)

The filing of a petition in an appeals court challenging a newly promulgated standard does not operate as a stay of the standard, unless the court so orders.

In reviewing a standard, the courts are to regard the Secretary's determinations as conclusive "if supported by substantial evidence in the record considered as a whole."

EMPLOYER'S GENERAL DUTY

On the theory that precise standards to cover every conceivable situation will not always exist, the law includes a "general duty" clause under which employers are required to maintain workplaces free from "recognized hazards" that are causing or are likely to cause death or serious bodily harm.

During the hearings and debate on this provision, it was brought out that 35 or more states have provisions of this type and that similar provisions are found in other federal safety laws, such as the Walsh-Healey Act, the Service Contract Act, and the Longshoremen's and Harbor Workers' Compensation Act. The need for such a "general obligation" clause was urged before both the Senate and House Labor Subcommittees by Governor Howard Pyle, president of the National Safety Council, who said:

"The absence of such a general obligation provision would mean the absence of authority to cope with a hazardous condition which is obvious and admitted by all concerned for which no standards have been promulgated."

Limited Scope

Objection was voiced to the general duty clause as first written on the ground that it is unfair to employers to require compliance with a vague, open-ended mandate, under which the employer in effect is told to "do good and avoid evil." The clause was redrafted, however, and proponents of the revised clause were careful to explain its limited scope. Here are some of the points made:

• There is no penalty for violation of the clause. It is only if the employer refuses to correct the unsafe condition after it has been called to his attention and a citation is issued that a penalty may be imposed. And before that may be done, the employer would be entitled to a full administrative hearing followed by judicial review, if he disagrees that the situation is unsafe. (116 Cong. Rec. S 18250, Nov. 16, 1970)

• The general-duty clause applies only to "recognized" hazards, which are the type of hazards that can be detected readily on the basis of the "basic human senses." Hazards that require technical or testing devices to detect them are not intended to be within the scope of the clause. (116 Cong. Rec. H 11899, Nov. 17, 1970)

• The "recognized" hazard is one that is generally known to be hazardous, not one that a particular inspector happens to think is hazardous. A "recognized" hazard relates to "the standard of knowledge in the industry." (116 Cong. Rec. H 10625, Nov. 23, 1970)

• The general-duty clause should not be used to set ad hoc standards. The law already provides procedures for setting temporary emergency standards. It is expected that the general duty requirement will be relied upon infrequently and that primary reliance will be placed on the specific standards that will be promulgated under the Act. (116 Cong. Rec. H 11899, Nov. 17, 1970)

CHAPTER 4

ENFORCEMENT

Enforcement of the Occupational Safety and Health Act, which was a point of major controversy during congressional debate, will be under close scrutiny for many years to come.

"There must be close scrutiny, constant policing, and prompt and adequate enforcement to make sure the goal of this legislation is realized," AFL-CIO President George Meany said on final congressional action. "We intend to make sure this is done, and if the enforcement machinery in this bill fails, we will immediately petition the Congress to strengthen and improve it," he added.

The law will not produce miracles, I. W. Abel, president of the Steelworkers and the AFL-CIO Industrial Union Department warned. "We must insist that Congress appropriate sufficient funds to make it effective and meaningful. We must insist that the Nixon Administration, and particularly the U.S. Department of Labor, staff the program with concerned and dedicated personnel in numbers adequate to do the job."

Congress will be on the alert, too. One of the new law's authors, Senator Harrison A. Williams, Jr. (D-NJ), chairman of the Senate Labor Subcommittee, said before the bill was signed, "Hopefully, this legislation will be vigorously enforced and our national neglect will be a thing of the past. I know that I will personally do everything I can to make sure that this law is enforced fairly and yet most stringently."

The Labor Department will be in the spotlight, as Secretary James D. Hodgson indicated at the ceremony marking the signing of the bill. "For the Department of Labor this act opens a whole new vista," he said. "We plan to launch its administration with all the vigor and momentum we can generate. From this day forward, the health and safety of the American workers has become a top priority activity for this department."

These, then, are the pressures and promises surrounding enforcement of the new law.

GENERAL DUTY PROVISION

The law puts an affirmative duty on each employer (1) to "furnish to each of his employees employment and a place of employment which are free from recognized hazards that are causing or are likely to cause death or serious physical harm to his employees," and (2) to "comply with occupational health and safety standards promulgated under this Act."

Section 5, the general duty provision just quoted, also requires that each employee "shall comply with occupational safety and health standards and all rules, regulations, and orders issued pursuant to this Act which are applicable to his own actions and conduct."

The general duty provision was put in the bill partly in recognition of the fact that "specific standards could not be fashioned to cover every conceivable situation and that lives should not be put in jeopardy merely because some specific standard has not been promulgated to cover a situation which from all appearances is dangerous." (116 Cong. Rec., S 17571, Oct. 8, 1970)

The House Labor Committee report on its bill said, "The general obligation clause is necessary in order to encourage compliance with the congressional intent set forth in Section 2(b), 'To assure as far as possible every man and woman in the nation safe and healthful working conditions'."

INSPECTIONS

With 4,100,000 establishments covered by the law, by Labor Department estimate, it is apparent that many work places will not be scheduled for a regular Government inspection for years, if ever, in the normal order of things.

For the places that are inspected, the Labor Department intends to use a "worst first" approach, concentrating its resources first on the industries with the greatest safety or health hazards.

The Senate Labor Committee report on the bill recommended this approach, saying, "In recognition of the possibility of limited inspection manpower in the earliest phases of the program, the Committee expects that the Secretary will initially place emphasis on inspections in those industries or occupations where the need to assure safe and healthful conditions is determined to be the most compelling."

The "worst first" approach will not mean immunity from inspections for employers in less hazardous industries, however.

Regular Inspections

The Government inspector is authorized to inspect the place of employment "and all pertinent conditions, structures, machines, apparatus, devices, equipment, and materials therein."

On presenting his credentials, the inspector is entitled to be admitted to any covered employer's premises promptly and at reasonable times to make an inspection. The inspector must conduct his inspection and investigation during regular working hours "and at other reasonable times and within reasonable limits and in a reasonable manner."

As part of his investigation, he may question the employer, owner, operator, agent, or employees privately. (Sec. 8(a))

The employer or his representative may go along with the inspector, and so may a representative authorized by the employees, during the physical inspection of the work place "for the purpose of aiding such inspection." If there is no authorized employee representative (which the Secretary will define in his regulations), the inspector is required to consult with "a reasonable number of employees concerning matters of health and safety in the workplace." (Sec. 8(e))

The Senate Labor Committee report said, "It is expected that such consultation shall be undertaken with a view both to apprising the inspector of all possible hazards to be found in the workplace, as well as to insure that employees generally will be informed of the inspector's presence and the purpose and manner of his inspection."

In the Administration bill p a s s e d by the House, the employee representative was allowed to go along on the inspection only if the employer representative did also. The conferees took the Senate provision. The Senate Labor Committee report gave this explanation of the provision:

"During the field hearings held by the [Senate Labor] Subcommittee, the complaint was repeatedly voiced that under existing safety and health legislation, employees are generally not advised of the content and results of a federal or state inspection. Indeed, they are often not even aware of the inspector's presence and are thereby deprived of an opportunity to inform him of alleged hazards. Much potential benefit of an inspection is never realized, and workers tend to be cynical regarding the thoroughness and efficacy of such inspections. Consequently, in order to aid in the inspection and provide an appropriate degree of involvement of employees themselves in the physical inspection of their own places of employment, the Committee has concluded that an authorized representative of employees should be given an opportunity to accompany the person who is making the physical inspection of a place of employment. . . . Correspondingly, an employer should be entitled to accompany an inspector on his physical inspection, although the inspector should have an opportunity to question employees in private so that they will not be hesitant to point out hazardous conditions which they might otherwise be reluctant to discuss."

No Advance Notice

During hearings on this law and the Federal Coal Mine Health and Safety Act of 1969, there were many complaints that employers are tipped off in advance of visits by Government safety inspectors and clean up violations before the inspectors appear on the scene.

The Senate bill and the House Labor Committee bill both contained penalties for giving advance notice without official authorization.

Those supporting the Administration bill strongly were opposed to making it a criminal violation to give unauthorized advance notice of an inspection. Comparing the Senate Labor Committee bill and the Administration bill, Senator William B. Saxbe (R-Ohio) said, "This provision of the reported bill is probably the clearest example of the police oriented approach that permeates that [Senate Labor Committee] bill. The reported bill obviously does not consider the occupational safety and health proposal as remedial social legislation. Rather than guiding employers by showing them how best to improve working conditions, the reported bill assumes that many employers are furtive wrongdoers who must be caught in the act. A criminal provision of this type has no place in legislation which primarily seeks to enlist the necessary goodwill and cooperation of employers." (116 Cong. Rec. S 17471, Oct. 8, 1970)

Nevertheless, the Senate and House conferees decided to keep a ban on unauthorized advance notice of an inspection and to provide a criminal penalty for violations. The penalty on conviction is a fine of up to $1,000 or six months imprisonment, or both. (Sec. 17(f))

Congressman William A. Steiger (R-Wis), a cosponsor of the Administration bill in the House, commented on this section in his statement on the conference report:

"It is clear from the language that giving advance notice of inspections is not prohibited where the Secretary believes such notice will further the interests of the Act. However, there will be some cases where it will be important that no prior notice be given and therefore the penalty is provided for giving unauthorized notice." (116 Cong. Rec. H 11900, Dec. 17, 1970)

Special Inspections

The law provides that any employee or representative of employees (which is to be defined by the Secretary in regulations) who believes that there is a violation of a health or safety regulation serious enough to threaten physical harm, or that an imminent danger exists, may notify the Secretary and request an inspection.

The notice has to be in writing eventually but may start with a phone call. It must describe the grounds for asking the inspection and be signed by the employees making the request. Only the copy going to the Secretary or his representative has to carry these signatures. A duplicate copy, which must be given to the employer by the time of the inspection, will not show who requested the inspection and the information cannot be made public at any time, if the employees prefer it that way.

The Senate Labor Committee report on the bill said, "While the bill provides that a request for a special inspection shall be reduced to writing, the Committee intends that notification may first be made by telephone, and that where an imminent harm is threatened, such as in an imminent danger situation, the Secretary should not await receipt through the mail of the written notification before beginning his inspection."

An inspection will not automatically follow an employee request. The Secretary must decide that there are reasonable grounds to believe that the violation or danger exists. In other words, he must satisfy himself that the allegations made in the complaint may be true.

The Secretary must make a special inspection "as soon as practicable" if he believes there is a violation or a threat of imminent danger. If, however, he finds that there is no reasonable ground for believing there is a serious violation or imminent danger, he must report this in writing to the employees or employee representative who made the request. (Sec. 8(f)(1)) The employees have a right of appeal from this denial.

Mr. Steiger said in his comments on the final bill that the employee belief on which the request for an inspection is based must be "in good faith and on a reasonable basis." It must be a belief that a violation of a standard exists that "threatens significant physical harm, or that an imminent danger exists."

"It is expected that the Secretary will use his good judgment in determining whether there are reasonable grounds to believe that a violation exists and will not permit this procedure to be used as an harassment device," Mr. Steiger said.

The language "as soon as practicable" requires the Secretary to "act expeditiously" if he finds an inspection should be made, Mr. Steiger said. The language "also is intended to prevent serious disruptions in the systematic conduct of the Secretary's inspection program," he said. "There may be other priorities which involve violations of a serious nature that are known and must be processed ahead of a given employee-requested inspection." (116 Cong. Rec. H 11899, Dec. 17, 1970)

The Senate Labor Committee indicated in its report on the bill that it expected the Secretary to put an employee complaint in perspective. The report said, "By requiring that the special inspection be made 'as soon as practicable,' the Committee contemplates that the Secretary, in scheduling the special inspection, will take into account such factors as the degree of harmful potential involved in the condition described in the request and the urgency of competing demands for inspectors arising from other requests or regularly scheduled inspections."

The House Labor Committee report took note of the fears expressed by employers, particularly in the petroleum industry, that the provision permitting employees to ask for Government inspections would be misused in labor disputes by getting struck plants closed on grounds that they are unsafe to operate with skeleton crews. The Committee report said, "Protecting the safety and health of workers certainly will be the Secretary's primary responsibility under this bill, but the Committee wishes to emphasize a strong caveat to the Secretary that illusory safety or health issues should never be used as an excuse to intervene in a labor-management dispute."

Other Employee Charges

A section which appears to be somewhat redundant (Sec. 8(f)(2)) provides that employees or their representative may report any violation they suspect to an inspector in writing prior to or during an inspection. Considering the ban on advance notice of an inspection, employees would have no way of telling an inspector during a regular inspection the things they know about safety and health conditions except through the one employee accompanying the inspector, if one does. Even this employee would have no advance notice of a regular inspection to help him prepare for it.

Section 8(f)(2) is an additional way of providing for the employees who know the work place to pass along information during a regular inspection, if they think there is a safety or health violation.

Another function that Section 8(f)(2) may serve is to allow employees or their representative to report continuing safety violations that are not serious enough to require a special inspection. Such a report might say, "When you come for an inspection, here are some things to look for."

Employee safety committees might make a practice of sending their safety complaints to the Government inspection office. The language of the law also would give this action official sanction.

The requirement that the complaint made during a regular inspection must be in writing is understood to be subject to the same proviso that was stated by the Senate Labor Committee in respect to requests for special inspections, quoted above. That would mean that the employee may make an oral complaint to an inspector on the scene, but if he plans to appeal rejection of the complaint, he must put it in writing.

Employee Appeals

The second sentence of Section 8(f)(2) is worded broadly enough to cover both the employee request for a special inspection under Section 8(f)(1) and the employee complaint of a suspected violation during a regular inspection under Section 8(a). It says that the Secretary shall set up a procedure to review "any refusal" by his representative (the inspector) "to issue a citation with respect to any such violation." After this review, the Secretary is required to give the employees requesting the review, or their representative, an explanation of why no violation was found or why the Secretary disposed of the case as he did. This is comparable to the appeal to the General Counsel from a National Labor Relations Board regional director's refusal to issue an unfair labor practice complaint under the Taft-Hartley Act.

Discrimination Prohibited

The law forbids anyone to discharge "or in any manner discriminate against" an employee because he has filed a complaint, or filed "any proceeding under or related to this Act," or caused someone else to file such proceeding, or testified, or is about to testify, or because the employee exercised any right given him by the law. (Sec. 11(c))

An employee believing that he has been fired or discriminated against in violation of this prohibition has 30 days in which to file a charge with the Secretary of Labor. The Secretary has 90 days to investigate and, if he finds that there has been a violation, he is required to bring an action in the U.S. district court on the employee's behalf. The court may order the employee reinstated with back pay as part of the "all appropriate relief" it is authorized to give.

If the Secretary does not file a court complaint in a discrimination case, he must notify the employee of his decision within the 90 days.

This section is similar in its protection to Section 8(a)(4) of the Labor Management Relations Act, 1947 (Taft-Hartley Act) and to Section 15(a)(3) of the Fair Labor Standards Act, neither of which has had to be used very much.

OTHER ENFORCEMENT METHODS

Hearings

If it should be necessary, the Secretary is authorized to hold a hearing and subpoena witnesses to attend and bring books and records, so that they may be questioned under oath. Such a procedure might well follow a serious accident, to determine the cause and whether safety or health regulations had been violated. If the Secretary's subpoena were ignored, a federal district court could issue an order to comply with it and punish for contempt of court anyone who continued to ignore it or responded incompletely. (Sec. 8(b))

Voluntary Compliance Reporting

It may be many years before some places of employment subject to the new law see a Government health or safety inspector. Certainly this may be true of "white collar" work places and those in industries with low health or safety hazards.

The Senate and House Labor Committees did not place all reliance on Government inspectors' visits to get compliance with the law, however. They gave the Secretary authority to require employers to conduct their own periodic inspections and report their findings. The conferees struck out any requirement that an employer must report his own violations.

What remains in the law, in Section (c)(1), is a provision that each employer shall make "such records regarding his activities relating to this Act" as the Secretary of Labor, in cooperation with the Secretary of Health, Education, and Welfare, "may prescribe by regulation as necessary or appropriate for the enforcement of this Act . . ." and "such regulations may include provisions requiring employers to conduct periodic inspections."

The Labor Department is considering asking employers to make voluntary reports on their compliance with the law, on forms that the Government would prescribe. This is similar to the voluntary reports that many firms file with the National Safety Council.

Failure to cooperate with any voluntary reporting program promulgated by the Labor Department may mark an employer as a possible violator and a conspicuous target for early inspection.

The Senate Labor Committee saw self-inspection as a valuable supplement to the Government's inspections and not just a substitute in the early days when there will be millions of places eligible for inspection. The Committee report said, "Such a procedure could well provide a valuable, and probably indispensable supplement to the Secretary's own inspections, since it would cause an employer regularly to review conditions in the workplace which might otherwise be ignored between official inspections."

Record-keeping

Record-keeping will be an important part of enforcement. The records required will be of four kinds: (1) Those "necessary or appropriate" for enforcement of the law, (2) those "necessary or appropriate" for research, (3) those reporting deaths and injuries related to the job, and (4) those showing employee exposure to possible harm. (Sec. 8(c)(1), (2), and (3))

Some of the records may be combined. The Secretary of Health, Education, and Welfare, who will be in charge of all research under the law, and the Secretary of Labor will cooperate in drawing up the regulations on record-keeping.

Information required by the Government "shall be obtained with a minimum burden upon employers, especially those operating small businesses. Unnecessary duplication of efforts in obtaining information shall be reduced to the maximum extent feasible." (Sec. 8(d))

This was amplified in the Senate Labor Committee report, which said the Committee "recognizes the need to assure employers that they will not be subject to unnecessary or duplicative record-keeping requests . . . To that end the Committee intends that, wherever possible, reporting requirements should be satisfied by having an employer report relevant data only to one governmental agency and that other governmental agencies, if any, should then acquire their information from the original agency."

The reports on employee deaths and injuries required by the new law are much more extensive than those now required by the Bureau of Labor Statistics or any state. The only injury an employer formerly had to report was one that caused the employee to lose a day's work or more. In virtually every set of job safety hearings, whether on coal mines, metal mines, factories or whatever, there have been complaints of underreporting and of employers keeping injured employees on light work or just sitting around idle to keep injury rates down.

It no longer will be possible to conceal job injuries in this way. Employers will be required to report work-related "injuries and illnesses other than minor injuries requiring only first aid treatment and which do not involve medical treatment, loss of consciousness, restriction of work or motion, or transfer to another job." (Sec. 8(c)(2))

Under the new requirements the number of injuries that have to be reported will rise tenfold, from 2,500,000 to 25,000,000 a year, according to an estimate by Jerome B. Gordon, a consultant who studied the subject under a Labor Department contract.

It is not unusual under state occupational safety laws to require that deaths must be reported within a short time. This probably will be required under the new federal law, and perhaps reports of very serious injuries will be required on a timely basis also, as part of the recordkeeping and reporting "necessary or appropriate" to enforcement. More frequent regular reports than annual ones may be required also, at least early in the history of the law.

Monitoring

It is part of the enforcement scheme of the Act (Sec. 8(c)(3)) that employees or their representative must be given an opportunity to observe the monitoring or measuring of potentially toxic materials or harmful physical agents to determine whether the standard is being met. The individual employee, and former employee must have access to these monitoring reports so that he can see what his exposure was to the harm, real or potential. This recognizes that every employee in a plant will not have the same exposure to a harmful or potentially harmful substance or agent. It also shows concern for the employees who have left a workplace having a potential harm that may not become real for some years.

The law does not place its reliance on employee initiative in witnessing the monitoring or measuring of the harm or potential harm or in looking at the monitoring reports. It requires that each employer "shall promptly notify any employee who has been or is being exposed to toxic materials or harmful physical agents in concentrations or at levels which exceed those prescribed by an applicable occupational safety and health standard promulgated under Section 6, and shall inform any employee who is being thus exposed of the corrective action being taken." (Sec. 8(c)(3))

The use of labels as required in the standards-setting provision of the law also is a type of enforcement measure. (Sec. 6(b)(7))

Notice Posting

Employers will be required to post notices, or use other appropriate means where notices are not possible, to keep employees informed of their "protections and obligations" under the law, including the provisions of applicable standards.

Because of the reference to "applicable standards," the posting required under the Occupational Safety and Health Act of 1970 may amount to much more than putting up a single sheet of paper or poster such as is required under minimum wage laws or the Civil Rights Act of 1964. (Sec. 10(c)(1))

The rules on notice posting will be established in regulations to be issued by the Secretary of Labor.

At earlier stages of the legislation, the inspector was required to give employees or their representative a copy of his inspection report. This did not remain in the final law.

If a citation is issued, it must be posted "at or near each place a violation referred to in the citation occurred." (Sec. 9(b)) If no citation is issued and there was no employee complaint or appeal, which would require a report back from the Secretary, there is no specific provision in the law requiring that employees be informed that the employer was given a clean bill of health.

This might be done, however, under a very broad grant of authority given to the Secretary to "compile, analyze, and publish, either in summary or detailed form, all reports or information obtained under this section." (Sec. 8(g)(1)) This section also provides for using the injury and health reports for all kinds of statistical studies and research.

CITATIONS

If an inspector finds a violation of the law—a regulation, standard, rule, or order—he is required to issue a written citation describing "with particularity" the nature of the violation and the section of the law, rule, or regulation violated. (Sec. 9(a)) He must issue a citation with "reasonable promptness," which Congressman Steiger and Congressman Carl Perkins (D-Ky), chairman of the Senate-House Conference Committee on the bills, both said meant within 72 hours, except in unusual circumstances. (116 Cong. Rec. H 11893, Dec. 17, 1970)

Under earlier versions of the bill, the Administration feared that inspectors would have to issue their citations on the spot immediately after completing the inspection.

If an employer does not notify the Secretary within 15 working days that he intends to appeal the citation or penalty, it will become final at the end of that time. (Sec. 10(a))

In no event can a citation be issued more than six months after the violation occurred. If it were a continuing violation, the six months would start running from the last day the violation occurred, under the usual principal of law.

As part of the citation, the Secretary would include a time period within which the violation had to be corrected. The only requirement is that this be a "reasonable" time.

The Senate Labor Committee said in its report that the language of Section 9 "does not limit the issuance of citations to those violations which the inspector has himself witnessed. It is the Committee's intent that if an investigation should disclose that violations have occurred, even though since corrected, a citation may be issued in appropriate cases."

If an inspector finds "de minimis" (slight or minor) violations which "have no direct or immediate relationship to safety or health," he may issue a notice instead of a citation, under regulations which the Secretary will issue. The Senate Labor Committee said that the notice to be given "should detail the conditions and circumstances of the violation and prescribe the means for correcting it. However, no penalties would attach to a violation covered by such a notice."

Post-Citation Procedure

If a citation is sent after an inspector's visit, it may state the penalty, if any, for each violation listed. In any event, notice of the penalty must be given "within a reasonable time" after the inspection or investigation and must be sent by certified mail.

The notice also will tell the employer that he has 15 work days in which to appeal the citation or penalty or both. If the employer does not notify the Secretary that he plans to appeal, and if no employee or employee representative files a notice within 15 days complaining that the abatement period is unreasonable, the citation and the penalty will become final at the end of the 15 work days and cannot be appealed after that time. (Sec. 10(a))

If the Secretary has reason to believe that the employer is ignoring a citation and not correcting the violation after the period allowed for correction is over, he must give a second notice by certified mail and state the penalty being levied this time. The same procedure would have to be repeated before the Secretary could levy a new penalty if the violation continued. Each time the employer would have 15 work days in which to notify the Secretary that he intended to appeal either the latest citation or the penalty. If he did not give such notice, the Secretary's notice and penalty would become final and could not be appealed after the 15 work days had elapsed. (Sec. 10(b))

If the employer makes a good-faith appeal to the Occupational Safety and Health Review Commission, "not solely for delay or avoidance of penalties," the penalty is stayed during the review. If he loses before the Commission, the abatement time given by the Secretary runs from the time the Commission's order becomes final.

PENALTIES

The Secretary may assess a monetary penalty for a violation for which a citation was issued. He does not have to do this if the violation was not serious (and not wilful or repeated), but even for a non-serious violation he may levy a penalty of up to $1,000. (Sec. 17(c))

Penalties are mandatory, not discretionary, for a wide range of other offenses above the non-serious category.

The Senate Labor Committee advice in its report pointed away from automatic penalties being set by the Labor Department under the new law. The report said:

"The Committee recognizes that given the complexities of modern industry, violations involving the broad range of technical standards do not lend themselves to any simple determination as to the amount of civil penalties to be assessed. Therefore, the Committee believes that within the framework of the Act's penalty provisions, the Secretary should have as much flexibility as possible to enable him to assess the amount of civil penalty which he determines is appropriate to the violation in question. We would expect the Secretary, therefore, to develop an internal manual or guide which would include a set of principles to follow in determining the proper amount of civil penalties to be applied or settle such penalties through informal procedures without the need of a hearing."

Civil Penalties

The Act provides for the following penalties for violations of the law, regulations, a standard, rule, or order:

Non-Serious Violations: Up to $1,000 or no penalty, at the discretion of the Secretary. (Sec. 17(c))

Serious Violations: Up to $1,000 for each violation. (Sec. 17(b)) A serious violation "shall be deemed to exist in a place of employment if there is a substantial probability that death or serious physical harm could result from a condition which exists, or from one or more practices, means, methods, operations, or processes which have been adopted or are in use, in such place of employment unless the employer did not, and could not with the exercise of reasonable diligence, know of the presence of the violation." (Sec. 17(k))

Continuing Violations: $1,000 for each day the violation continues. (Sec. 17(d)) A continuing violation is one not corrected within the time set in the Labor Department citation or in case of a good-faith appeal to the Review Commission in the same length of time following the Review Commission's final decision.

Failure to Post Notices: Up to $1,000 for each violation. (Sec. 17(i))

Wilful or Repeated Violations: Up to $10,000 for each violation. (Sec. 17(a))

Criminal Penalties

Criminal penalties are provided as follows:

Wilful violation resulting in death: Fine of up to $10,000 or six-month imprisonment or both, on a first conviction in court. Fine of up to $20,000 or one-year imprisonment or both on a second conviction in court. (Sec. 17(e))

Violation of Advance Notice Ban: Up to $1,000 or six-month imprisonment or both on conviction in court. (Sec. 17(f))

Filing of False Document: Fine of up to $10,000 or imprisonment up to six months or both on conviction in court. (Sec. 17(g))

Assaulting or hampering the work of a Labor Department safety or health investigator or inspector: Fine of up to $5,000 or up to three-year imprisonment or both. (Sec. 17(h)(1))

Assaulting an investigator or inspector with a deadly weapon: Fine of up to $10,000 or imprisonment up to 10 years, or both. (Sec. 17(h)(1))

Murder of Labor Department safety or health investigator or inspector: Fine up to $10,000 and imprisonment "for any term of years or for life." (Sec. 17(h)(2))

The Senate Labor Committee report said, "The Secretary may compromise, mitigate, or settle any claim for such penalties." The law specifies that the Review Commission, in levying civil penalties, may take into consideration "the appropriateness of the penalty with respect to the size of the business of the employer being charged, the gravity of the violation, the good faith of the employer, and the history of previous violations."

Collection of Penalties

If the Secretary or Commission is unable to collect a penalty, the Government may bring suit to force payment in the federal district court in the district where the violation is alleged to have occurred or the employer has its principal office. (Sec. 17(1))

The district court may not try the merits of the case. Congressman Steiger emphasized in his statement on the final bill, "It should also be made clear that the provision for judicial review and enforcement of the Commission's orders contained in Section 11 are exclusive. Section 17(1) authorizing actions in the name of the United States for the collection of penalties should be construed narrowly and is intended to be limited to any collection process which may be necessary in order to actually collect the penalty." (116 Cong. Rec. H 11900, Dec. 17, 1970)

APPEAL TO REVIEW COMMISSION

If the employer wishes to appeal from the Secretary's citation or penalty, he must, within 15 working days, notify the Secretary, who in turn notifies the Occupational Safety and Health Review Commission, an independent body.

The Commission is required to hold a hearing and issue findings of fact and an order affirming, modifying, or vacating the Secretary's citation or proposed penalty, "or directing other appropriate relief." Its order becomes final 30 days after issuance, unless it is appealed to the U.S. Court of Appeals. Then a stay is not automatic. The court must take the affirmative action of granting a stay.

Employees also may get a review if they file a complaint with the Secretary, within 15 days after a citation, that the time allowed for correcting the violation is unreasonable. The Secretary advises the Commission, which then will hold a hearing and make a finding.

If the employer shows that he made a good-faith effort to comply with the abatement requirements but could not because of factors "beyond his reasonable control," the Commission is required to hold a hearing on the abatement issue. Then a new order is to be issued affirming or modifying the abatement requirements in the citation. The Senate Labor Committee said on this point:

"It is anticipated that in many cases an employer will choose not to file a timely challenge to a citation when it is issued, on the assumption that he can comply with the period allowed in the citation for abatement of the violation. In some such cases the employer may subsequently find that despite his good-faith efforts to comply, abatement cannot be completed within the time permitted because of factors beyond his reasonable control—for example, where the delivery of necessary equipment is unavoidably delayed. In order to prevent unfair hardship, the bill provided that in such instances the employer may obtain review and modification by the Secretary of the abatement requirements specified in the citation, "even though the citation has otherwise become final."

In all its hearings, the Commission is required to permit affected employees, or their representative, to participate as parties, under rules of procedure that it will lay down.

OCCUPATIONAL SAFETY AND HEALTH REVIEW COMMISSION

The Commission was set up to create an independent body outside the Labor Department to which employers could appeal a citation and notice of penalty and employees could appeal the length of time allowed for abatement of a violation.

It was one of the most contested sections of the new law, with opponents arguing that it is contrary to the way in which many laws are administered, with the same agency having authority to find violations and adjudicate the appeals from those findings. Senator Jacob K. Javits (R-NY) argued that "apparently the business community feels an infinitely greater assurance with this kind of commission than with enforcement by the Secretary of Labor." (116 Cong. Rec. S 18340, Nov. 17, 1970) The provision was in the Administration bill adopted by the House, so there was no conflict for the conferees to iron out.

The three Commission members will be appointed by the President and must be confirmed by the Senate. In the future, they will serve six-year terms, but to make the terms expire two years apart, the first three members will have a two-year, a four-year, and a six-year term. The President will designate the chairman from among the three.

The qualifications for the Commissioners set in the law are that they must have the training, education, or experience to carry out the Commission's functions. An argument was made in the Senate debate that "there are no congressional guides for the selection of members of the Commission." Mr. Javits replied, "It will be done in accordance with the way it is done in other commissions of the same character. The protection there is confirmation by the Senate."

He described the Commission as having "the same type of authority that the Federal Trade Commission exercises: The power to issue a cease and desist order which, if challenged within a given period of time, can be reviewed by the Circuit Court of Appeals. Its operation is stayed if the Circuit Court of Appeals so orders. If the Secretary desires to enforce the order through the contempt power, similarly, he can go into court in order to get the Circuit Court of Appeals to enter an order for the specific purpose, and then that order can be enforced through the contempt powers of the Circuit Court of Appeals. It is the traditional Federal Trade Commission type of procedure."

The Commission will operate through hearing examiners. That is, a hearing examiner will hear a case and then make a report and decision. The Commission may review the hearing examiner's decision if one member thinks it should. Otherwise the examiner's decision will go into effect as the final order of the Commission 30 days after the decision is issued. Mr. Javits pointed to this as a potential time saver and "a very quick way of dealing with relatively minor situations."

A record will be made of the proceedings before a hearing examiner, and if the Commission decides to review a case, it may do so by studying the record and the briefs submitted by the parties. It is not required to hear oral arguments, although it may do so. Two members of the Commission will constitute a quorum for doing business.

The Commission will have the same investigatory powers as the National Labor Relations Board does under Section 11 of the Labor Management Relations Act, 1947 (Taft-Hartley Act). This section covers issuance of subpoenaes, service of notices, and such matters connected with hearings.

The Commission's headquarters will be in Washington, D.C., but the hearings may be held in the field if the Commission decides "the convenience of the public or of the parties may be promoted, or delay cr expense may be minimized."

The Act does not say how long an employer will have to bring his case before the Commission, or the employees to bring their complaint over an abatement period, except that notice of either appeal must be given to the Secretary within 15 working days after his action. The Commission, no doubt, will issue regulations governing the time for bringing the case to it, and other procedural matters.

Commission Hearings

Commission hearings on appeals must be held in accordance with the Administrative Procedure Act (Section 554 of Title 5, United States Code). The pertinent parts of this section follow:

"(b) Persons entitled to notice of an agency hearing shall be timely informed of—

(1) the time, place, and nature of the hearing;

(2) the legal authority and jurisdiction under which the hearing is to be held; and

(3) the matters of fact and law asserted.

When private persons are the moving parties, other parties to the proceeding shall give prompt notice of issues controverted in fact or law; and in other instances agencies may by rule require responsive pleading. In fixing the time and place for hearings, due regard shall be had for the convenience and necessity of the parties or their representatives.

"(c) The agency shall give all interested parties opportunity for—

(1) the submission and consideration of facts, arguments, offers of settlement, or proposals of adjustment when time, the nature of the proceeding, and the public interest permit; and

(2) to the extent that the parties are unable so to determine a controversy by consent, hearing and decision on notice and in accordance with sections 556 and 557 of this title.

"(d) The employee who presides at the reception of evidence pursuant to section 556 of this title shall make the recommended decision or initial decision required by section 557 of this title, unless he becomes unavailable to the agency. Except to the extent required for the disposition of ex parte matters as authorized by law, such an employee may not—

(1) consult a person or party on a fact in issue, unless on notice and opportunity for all parties to participate; or

(2) be responsible to or subject to the supervision or direction of an employee or agent engaged in the performance of investigative or prosecuting functions for an agency.

An employee or agent engaged in the performance of investigative or prosecuting functions for an agency in a case may not, in that or a factually related case, participate or advise in the decision, recommended decision, or agency review pursuant to section 557 of this title, except as witness or counsel in public proceedings. This subsection does not apply—

(A) in determining applications for initial licenses;

(B) to proceedings involving the validity or application of rates, facilities, or practices of public utilities or carriers; or

(C) to the agency or a member or members of the body comprising the agency.

"(e) The agency, with like effect as in the case of other orders, and in its sound discretion, may issue a declaratory order to terminate a controversy or remove uncertainty."

The Commission may impose all the civil penalties provided in the law. These are the same monetary penalties as may be proposed by the Secretary of Labor and do not require conviction in a court of law.

The Commission is given greater latitude than is explicitly stated for the Secretary, however. It is authorized to give "due consideration to the appropriateness of the penalty with respect to the size of the business of the employer being charged, the gravity of the violation, the good faith of the employer, and the history of previous violations."

JUDICIAL REVIEW

"Any person adversely affected or aggrieved" (the employer or the employees who may have been made a party to the case before the Commission) may appeal the Commission's decision to the U. S. Court of Appeals. The court chosen must be the one where the violation occurred or the employer has his principal office, or it may be in the District of Columbia. The appeal must be filed within 60 days after the Commission issues its order, and the court must hear the case "expeditiously."

The court does not re-try the case, but must accept the Commission's findings of fact if they are supported by "substantial evidence on the record considered as a whole." No objection to the Secretary's citation or penalty that was not made to the Commission can be made to the court, except in extraordinary circumstances. If a party thinks more evidence should be heard and can convince the court that it is material evidence and there were reasonable grounds for not presenting it before, the court may remand the case to the Commission to take the new evidence. The Commission then will hold a hearing and may modify or set aside its previous order. The case then would go back to the Court of Appeals for new review. (Sec. 11(a))

The Secretary of Labor also may appeal a Commission decision to the U.S. court of appeals, but he is limited to the circuit where the violation occurred or the employer has his principal office. He may not file in Washington, D.C. The reason for this was to keep an employer from being forced to come to Washington to defend a case, since the Government has lawyers all over the country. The Secretary also may file a petition asking the court (in the same two choices of circuits) to enforce a Commission order that an employer refuses to obey. If an enforcement petition is filed more than 60 days after a Commission order was issued and no petition for review has been filed by the employer, the employer cannot attack the Commission's findings of fact or its order and the order will be conclusive.

If the Court of Appeals has to cite an employer for contempt for refusing to obey its order, it may assess the penalties provided in the penalties section "in addition to invoking any other available remedies."

Appeals may be taken from a U.S. court of appeals to the Supreme Court in accordance with Section 1254 of Title 28, United States Code. The Supreme Court also is supposed to consider the case for review "expeditiously."

IMMINENT DANGER

The imminent danger section of the law, Section 13, deals with safety and health conditions that are so serious that they must be dealt with immediately rather than wait for the slower method of issuing a citation.

No section of the new law aroused more controversy. The dispute was over whether a Labor Department inspector should be able to close a work place if he found an imminent danger so threatening that there would be no time to have a federal district court order the shutdown. In the earlier drafts, an inspector's closing order could have stayed in effect for 72 hours before being tested in court. The provision underwent several changes and in the end it was decided to require that a court order be issued before a work place could be closed down.

The section will come into use if an inspector finds "conditions or practices . . . such that a danger exists which could reasonably be expected to cause death or serious physical harm immediately or before the imminence of such danger can be eliminated through the enforcement procedures otherwise provided by this Act." (Sec. 13(a))

The inspector must tell the employer and employees of the danger and that he is recommending that a court injunction be sought. (Sec. 13(c))

The Secretary of Labor then would file a petition with a U.S. district court to issue an injunction ordering the work place closed to employees until the danger was over and describing the corrective steps to be taken to end it. An exception to the barring of employees would be made for those whose presence is necessary to correct the danger, or to keep a continuous process operation in shape to resume normal operations, or to permit a shutdown of operations in a safe and orderly manner. (Sec. 13(a))

The court's first action, a temporary restraining order, would be effective for no longer than five days. At the end of that time, the Secretary would have to go back to court to justify any extension of the order. (Sec. 13(b))

If the Secretary "arbitrarily or capriciously" failed to apply for a court order, any employee who "may be" injured by reason of that failure, or an employee representative, could bring court action for a writ of mandamus to compel the Secretary to apply for a closing order "and for such other relief as may be appropriate."

The district court in which the employee court action could be brought would be the one in which the imminent danger was claimed to exist, or the company had its principal office, or in the District of Columbia.

During the hearings and debate, it was made clear that the inspector's finding of an "imminent danger" need not apply to a whole plant. A section of a plant or even a single machine might be found too dangerous for employees to use.

Very rarely is the Secretary expected to have to go into court for an order to close an unsafe work place. As Senator Richard Schweiker (R-Pa) pointed out in the Senate debate, "Employers do not want their plants to blow up any more than the employees do. In the average case where the Labor Department finds a real danger in a plant, I would expect the employer to agree with the Department and close the plant or the portion of the plant voluntarily himself."

Both he and Mr. Saxbe indicated their belief that a closing order, rather than a voluntarily closing, would be necessary only when the employer and the inspector differed in their opinions of whether there was an "imminent danger." In that case, they said, the "objective disinterested view of a court is absolutely necessary" and "the Department should have to sustain a burden of proof in persuading a federal district judge that the closure of the plant is necessary."

The proponents of the clause giving the inspector, with higher Labor Department approval, a right to close a plant for 72 hours without going to court where that is impossible argued that such a provision is in 29 state laws. Mr. Saxbe replied, "It is seldom used because the inspector is reluctant to use it even when his superior agrees. Then when he does want to use it, as I am informed in some situations in New York, he, not being a policeman, cannot do it. He has to go to the court and go out and get a policeman to enforce the order."

Although the provision for closing without a court order was not dropped from the Senate bill but was later in conference, Mr. Saxbe's further comments may be helpful in showing the situations in which an "imminent danger" may arise. "When this subject was discussed," he said, speaking of the Senate Labor Committee, "we went into great length on an individual machine, an oil slick on the floor, noxious fumes being emitted, or a leaky pipe—things that would create an imminent danger. When they red tag this, they close down this machine or this area of the plant, and not the plant." (116 Cong. Rec. S 18336, Nov. 17, 1970)

Mr. Williams also put "imminent danger" closings, whether by an inspector or a court, in context when he said, "in connection with imminent danger, under the Committee bill, the continuous operations can go on. There will be no complete shutdown . . . Even in an area where the work stops, there is no cooling off of all the fires of operation." (116 Cong. Rec. S 18270, Nov. 16, 1970)

CHAPTER 5

RECORD-KEEPING AND REPORTS

Congress encountered an appalling lack of accurate statistical information in the occupational health and safety field during its deliberations on the new legislation. Numerous provisions have been written into the Act to overcome this deficiency and, while the requirements may appear to be nothing more than closing the barn door after the horse is gone, employers and state and federal agencies will be faced with stiff statutory obligations for some time to come.

The law mandates improved record-keeping on work-related deaths and injuries. In addition, records are to be maintained on illnesses and exposure to potentially toxic substances.

Congress failed, however, to spell out the record-keeping requirements in any detail. It put both the Secretary of Labor and the Secretary of Health, Education, and Welfare in the picture, with broad authority to establish the necessary regulations. There is a requirement though that the Secretaries work together to minimize the record-keeping requirements.

BACKGROUND

Prior to the enactment of the occupational safety and health law, a private consultant conducted a study of the Bureau of Labor Statistics' industrial accident data. Results of the study indicated that an estimated 8 to 10 percent—or 200,000 cases—of disabling injuries were unreported each year. It further was estimated that if serious work injuries were reported, rather than just disabling injuries (those that cause a loss of at least a day's work), the number would be 1,000 times what had been reported, or 25 million injuries a year, compared to the 2.5 million reported.

Jerome B. Gordon, author of the study, blamed what he called BLS' "dismal and unfortunate" failure in its job accident statistics on industry dominance of the reporting programs relied on. BLS statistics have been based on reports from 16 states using the American National Standards Institute method of recording and measuring work injury experience. (ANSI has proposed a new system, described below, for recording injuries.)

As a consequence of this report and other complaints that job accidents were under-reported, a broad requirement was written into the law that the Secretary of Labor, in cooperation with the Secretary of Health, Education, and Welfare, would compile accurate statistics on all disabling, serious, or significant injuries and illnesses to develop full information on the incidence, the nature, or causes of such injuries and illnesses. This broad requirement for statistics required an equally broad reporting requirement for employers.

RECORD-KEEPING

Extensive record-keeping requirements are authorized by Section 8 of the law. Regulations are to be drafted by the Secretary of Labor, in cooperation with the Secretary of Health, Education, and Welfare.

Employers are directed to "make, keep and preserve" and make available to the Secretaries four types of records:

- Records "necessary or appropriate" for enforcement of the Act.
- Records "necessary or appropriate" for research.
- Records reporting deaths and injuries related to the job, and
- Records showing employee exposure to possible harm.

The record-keeping regulations may include provisions requiring employers to conduct periodic inspections. In addition, the regulations will require that employers, through posting of notices or other appropriate means, keep their employees informed of their protections and obligations under the law, including the provisions of applicable standards.

Reports required on employee deaths and injuries will be much more extensive than those previously required by the Bureau of Labor Statistics. Employers will be required to report work-related "injuries and illnesses" other than minor injuries requiring only first aid treatment and which do not involve medical treatment, loss of consciousness, restriction of work or motion, or transfer to another job. (Sec. 8(c))

Full and accurate information is a "fundamental precondition for meaningful administration" of the new law, the Senate Labor Committee report said. It maintained, however, that existing information was inadequate. The new reporting requirements are essential, the report said. It added:

"The committee recognizes the fact that some work-related injuries or ailments may involve only a minimal loss of work time or perhaps none at all, and may not be of sufficient significance to the Government to require their being recorded or reported. However, the committee was also unwilling to adopt statutory language which in practice might result in under-reporting. The committee believes that records and reports prescribed by the Secretary should include such occurrences as work-related injuries and illnesses requiring medical treatment or restriction or reassignment of work activity, as well as work-related loss of consciousness."

The Government is to obtain information "with a minimum burden upon employers, especially those operating small businesses. Unnecessary duplication of efforts in obtaining information shall be reduced to the maximum extent feasible." (Sec. 8(d)) On this the Senate Labor Committee Report said:

"The committee recognizes the need to assure employers that they will not be subject to unnecessary or duplicative record-keeping requests and has specifically stated this intent in section 8(d). To that end the committee intends that, wherever possible, reporting requirements should be satisfied by having an employer report relevant data only to one Governmental agency and that other governmental agencies, if any, should then acquire their information from the original agency."

Both the Labor Secretary and the Secretary of HEW are authorized to compile, analyze, and publish, either in summary or detailed form, all reports or information obtained under Section 8 of the law.

Toxic Materials and Harmful Agents

Accurate records also will be required on employee exposure to potentially toxic materials or harmful physical agents. (Sec. 8(c) (3))

Toxic materials include gases, solids, dust, fumes, vapors, and chemicals. Harmful physical agents include noise, vibrations, and radiation.

The employer is required to monitor these materials and agents under Section 6 of the law to make sure that they comply with the standards set by the Secretary.

Employees or their representatives are to be given an opportunity to observe monitoring or measuring, and to have access to the records thereof. (See Chapter 4.)

STATISTICS

Under Section 24, Statistics, the Secretary of Labor, in consultation with the Secretary of Health, Education, and Welfare, is directed to undertake a program of collection, compilation, and analysis of occupational safety and health statistics. Employments covered by this provision and the types of injuries and illnesses on which statistics must be collected are specified.

In carrying out this program, the Secretary of Labor is authorized specifically to do the following:

• Promote, encourage, or directly engage in programs of studies, information, and communication concerning occupational safety and health statistics.

• Work with the states (or other political subdivisions) by making grants to assist them in developing programs on such statistics, up to 50 percent of the state's total cost; and to make use of the services, facilities, or employees of state agencies, with or without reimbursement.

• Arrange by grants or contracts to conduct research and investigations that "give promise of furthering the objectives of this section."

• Prescribe by regulation the necessary reports to be filed by employers based on the records called for under Section 8(c).

The final provision of Section 24 states explicitly that existing agreements between the Labor Department and the states for the collection of statistics remain in effect until superseded by grants or contracts under the new law. This provision came from the House bill. (116 Cong. Rec. H 11814, Dec. 16, 1970)

Both House and Senate versions of the bill provided for statistics programs, although in the Senate version this was included in the section relating to grants to the states. As originally passed, both versions gave the Secretary of Labor complete authority in this area; the requirement that he consult with the Secretary of HEW in carrying out the statistics program came from an amendment offered by the Senate managers in joint conference. (116 Cong. Rec. H 11814, Dec. 16, 1970) Presumably, the intent is to make sure programs undertaken by the Secretary of Labor under this section will be coordinated with the research of the National Institute for Occupational Health and Safety in HEW.

The language specifying the types of work injuries and illnesses on which statistics must be collected did not appear in the bills of either the House or Senate, but was added in the conference by Senate amendment. Generally, the wording here is the same as that of Sec. 8(c) (2) on record-keeping and reporting requirements, except that Section 24 calls for statistics on all disabling, serious, or significant injuries or illnesses, *whether or not involving loss of time from work*. This could involve much more extensive reporting by employers.

In effect, the provisions for statistical programs are more comprehensive both in coverage of employment and of types of information to be reported than are other sections of the law.

PROPOSED REPORTING SYSTEM

The American National Standards Institute has proposed a national system for recording occupational injuries and illnesses which parallels the one called for under the occupational safety and health law. The proposal, prepared by a top-level study committee appointed at the request of the Secretary of Labor, is designed to provide an annual profile on the number of occupational injuries and illnesses occurring in the American workplace.

Included in the proposed system are a simple method for recording these injuries and illnesses, a suggested work sheet or log to be used in recording and reporting, and an annual summary sheet. It would require that all reportable occupational injuries and illnesses, including two-visit physician treatment cases, be counted. Exceptions and exemptions in existing reporting systems are eliminated. The category of occupational illnesses in current usage has been expanded; the arbitrary charges for number of days for deaths and permanent impairments are not included, but a count of workdays lost is required. The measure of injury and illness rates has been simplified and expressed in terms more readily understood by management, the Institute asserts. The measure in the proposed system is "injuries per 100 full-time employees per year," rather than the traditional per-million man-hours. (Copies of the Proposed National System for Uniform Recording and Reporting of Occupational Injuries and Illnesses are available for $3 each from the American National Standards Institute, Inc., 1430 Broadway, New York, N.Y.)

CHAPTER 6

FEDERAL AND STATE RELATIONS

Federal involvement in job safety and health is mandated by the Occupational Safety and Health Act. It was not the congressional intent, however, to ban the states from the worksite.

The Act encourages the states to retain or gain control of occupational safety and health programs. It even offers financial incentives for doing so. But the dominant federal role is made clear—federal standards and enforcement are to be the yardstick.

The law was predicated on an experience of poor state programs and enforcement. The more aggressive states in occupational safety and health—California and New York for instance—can be expected to take a serious look at the possibilities of state programs. For others, the choice will be easy—no state program means no commitment of state funds. Federal incentives, after all, require some expenditure on the part of the states. Federal enforcement does not.

STATE INVOLVEMENT

Among the many controversies surrounding proposed occupational safety and health legislation, the subject of federal-state relations was absent. All bills introduced from the Johnson Administration proposal on suggested safeguarding state standards which were more stringent than those promulgated at the national level.

Various legislative proposals suggested that states be allowed to administer health and safety plans which satisfied minimum standards to the satisfaction of the Secretary of Labor. Several additions, refinements, and clarifications went into the final language, however, among them special provisions for product safety standards, interim provisions for state programs, and modifications for coverage of employees of state and local governments.

The First Two Years

With the approval of the Secretary of Labor, a state is permitted to continue to enforce its standards during the first two years of operation under the Act, or until the Secretary of Labor has taken action on a plan submitted by the state for an occupational health and safety program. (Sec. 18 (h))

The provision for state enforcement during the first two years is intended to cover the anticipated hiatus between the effective date of the federal law and the time when the Government program has standards which it is geared to enforce. The provision resulted from an amendment, which was adopted, by Congressman William D. Hathaway (R-Maine). A Senate version of the amendment would have required the state standard not to be in conflict with the adopted federal standard or to be stronger. Mr. Hathaway explained why he felt that this was too restrictive as follows:

"If, for example, you had a federal standard that said workbenches should be three feet apart and if there were a state standard that said they should be 2½ feet apart, then under the Senate amendment that was approved and agreed to, the state standard could not be effective, because it would be in conflict. The Secretary may say 'We had better have a 2½-foot standard at least until the three-foot standard is ready to be enforced'." (116 Cong. Rec. H 10684, Nov. 24, 1970)

State Plans

The law places no restrictions whatever on states in areas where no federal standards exist. Under the law, any state agency or state court may assert jurisdiction under state law over any occupational health and safety issue not covered by a federal standard. (Sec. 18 (a))

In areas where the Secretary of Labor has issued standards, he has the initial discretion, subject to court review, on whether to allow a state to exercise jurisdiction over that area. He is, of course, offered guidance by the Act on when he should allow state standards and enforcement to apply.

If the Secretary disapproves a state plan, he must grant the state "due notice" and opportunity for a hearing prior to taking adverse action. (Sec. 18 (d))

Overlapping Jurisdictions

Once approval of a state plan is given, a period of overlapping jurisdictions begins which is ended only when the Secretary of Labor determines that the state actually is doing what it said it was going to do and is satisfying the law's requirements for a state program. This period will be at least three years, during which the Secretary may continue enforcement activities in the state.

Following the period of overlapping, the state is given its "second papers," and federal involvement subsides. The Secretary may continue enforcement actions brought under Sections 9 and 10, however. (Sec. 18 (e))

Nothing in the Act bars the Secretary from enforcing federal standards for which there are no comparable state standards, but with a comprehensive state health and safety program in operation, federal inspection efforts may be small.

Revocation

A state plan can lose its franchise if the Secretary finds substantial failure to comply with any of the provisions of the plan or any assurance the provisions may contain. (Sec. 18 (f))

The Secretary has a statutory obligation to review operation of a state plan continuously by monitoring reports concerning operations under the program and by continuing with federal inspections in the state. Should he suspect the state plan and operation to be deficient, he is to notify the state and provide an opportunity for a hearing.

If a state is deficient, the Secretary is directed by the law to withdraw approval of the state plan. The state retains jurisdiction only over enforcement cases already instituted. (Sec. 18 (f))

Judicial Review

Review of the Secretary's decision to revoke a state plan or to deny a state plan initial approval may be had in the U.S. court of appeals for the circuit in which the state affected by the decision is located. The state may file a petition to modify or set aside the Secretary's decision or a portion of his decision within 30 days of receipt of the Secretary's notice of such a decision. (Sec. 18 (g))

The Secretary is to be furnished a copy of the state's petition. He, in turn, is to furnish the court the record upon which his judgment was based.

The court is directed to affirm the decision of the Secretary, provided it is "supported by substantial evidence," a standard of review selected over a finding that the Secretary's decision was "arbitrary and capricious." (116 Cong. Rec. S 18354, Nov. 17, 1970) The right of final judicial review rests with the Supreme Court.

ESSENTIAL INGREDIENTS OF STATE PLANS

The Secretary of Labor has some discretion in deciding whether to grant approval to a state plan, but he is given a shopping list to use in examining state proposals. If an item on the list is not in the plan the Secretary is not permitted, by statute, to grant approval. The list contains eight key items. (Sec. 18 (c))

Briefly, the Act requires a state plan to:

• Designate a state agency or agencies to administer the plan. (Sec. 18(c)(1))

• Provide for development and enforcement of standards which will be as effective as the standards adopted under Section 6. (Sec. 18(c)(2))

• Provide for a right of entry and inspection which is as effective as that contained in the Act and which contains a prohibition on advance notice of inspections. (Sec. 18(c)(3))

• Assure that the agency charged with administration will have legal authority and qualified personnel to enforce the standards developed. (Sec. 18(c)(4))

• Give assurances that the state will devote adequate funds for administration and enforcement. (Sec. 18(c)(5))

• Provide for coverage of state and local employees to the extent possible. (Sec. 18(c)(6))

• Require employers to make reports to the Secretary of Labor to the same extent as if the plan weren't in effect. (Sec. 18(c)(7))

• Provide that the state agency will make reports to the Secretary of Labor as required. (Sec. 18(c)(8))

Standards

While all the items are important, perhaps the most weighted is the second, that which requires a plan to provide for development of standards and enforcement which will be as effective as federal standards and enforcement. The requirement brings up the question of how standards may be weighed against one another.

Specific standards are not required before a state plan is approved. Section 18(c)(2) asks that a plan provide for "the development and enforcement of safety and health standards relating to one or more safety or health issues, which standards (and the enforcement of which standards) are or will be at least as effective in providing safe and healthful employment and places of employment as the standards promulgated under Section 6 which relate to the same issues, and which standards, when applicable to products which are distributed or used in interstate commerce, are required by compelling local conditions and do not unduly burden interstate commerce." A state agency might begin by adopting federal standards and then proceed with its own revisions of them. California's standards were developed in this manner, first by adopting a set of nationally-recognized standards and then beginning a process of revision and emendation which led to the standards which it now has.

The degree of latitude possible for state standards will vary with the subject. Climatic conditions could be the reason for a particular deviation or stiffening in the standards. Other geographical features could affect standards necessary to protect workers as well—whether a state borders on the ocean or is inland, whether it is dry or wet, urban or rural, and the like.

States will be required to show "compelling local conditions" when state standards are at variance with federal standards applicable to products which are distributed or used in interstate commerce. (Sec. 18(c)(2)) This particular provision, introduced by Senator William Saxbe (R-Ohio) in the Senate and Congressman Tom Railsback (R-Ill) in the House, was offered to avoid the confusion which could exist if a significant number of the states all had standards which called for manufacturing variations in the same basic product, a product manufactured for a national market.

A feature of the Act allowing the Secretary of Labor to grant companies variances from federal standards (Sec. 6(d)), may find its way into state programs, allowing a specified state official or agency to make a determination that alternate means will provide employment as safe and healthful at a particular worksite as if the state standards were in effect. The same safeguards which the Act places on this prerogative would seem also to be required in a state plan—a hearing and, where appropriate, an inspection, plus an opportunity to revoke the modified rule or order six months after its issuance.

Enforcement

A staff of "qualified personnel" with legal authority necessary for the enforcement of the state's standards is specifically required by Section 18(c)(4). This staff is to be under a state agency or agencies designated to administer the state's program (Sec. 18(c)(1))

A right to entry and inspection of all workplaces within the state plan's jurisdiction is required. This right must be as effective as that provided by the Act in Section 8 and contain a prohibition against advance notice of inspections. It is Section 8 of the Act which contains authorizations for record-keeping, imminent danger provisions, and the like (See Chapter 4). Further, the plan must give satisfactory assurances that the state will devote "adequate" funds to administer and enforce its standards. This requirement (Sec. 18(c)(5)) will depend on such factors as the coverage contemplated by the state plan and the standards the state decides to administer. Should it seek to administer a fully comprehensive program, a per-worker outlay equivalent to what the Federal Government has provided might be deemed required. This amount would be reduced by whatever federal grants the state could secure, however.

A state plan will not be able to exempt employers from making reports to the Secretary of Labor to the same extent as if the plan were not in effect. Section 18(c)(7) requires the state plan to make such reports mandatory under its provisions.

The state agency is required, in fact, to supply whatever reports the Secretary of Labor requests. Approved plans will provide that such reports will be made according to Section 18(c)(8).

FEDERAL AND STATE EMPLOYEES

Special provisions are made for coverage of federal and state and local employees. Section 19 sets up responsibilities for federal agencies. The Act itself doesn't cover state employees, but it makes their coverage mandatory in federally approved state plans.

Federal Program

Federal agencies must follow the new national standards as they "establish and maintain an effective and comprehensive occupational safety and health program" designed to "provide safe and healthful places and conditions of employment." Enforcement provisions of the Act are suspended, but each agency is charged with developing an effective program of inspections and safeguards to preserve the health of the Government worker. In accordance with the request of the Government Employees Council of the AFL-CIO, consultation rights for employee representatives are written into the Act. (Sec. 19(a))

Federal agency heads are required to do the following:
- Set up programs in line with standards set by the Labor Secretary,
- Acquire materials and devices necessary to protect employees,
- Keep records of occupational accidents and illnesses in compliance with direction offered by the Secretary of Labor.
- Make an annual report to the Secretary.

The Secretary of Labor is directed to digest the agency reports and report to the President, who in turn will give Congress an accounting of federal activities in this sphere.

The Secretary of Labor has access to federal agency records required by the Act except those records and reports whose disclosure would jeopardize national defense or foreign policy. (Sec. 19(d))

State Programs

Section 18 (c) (6) sets out a requirement a state plan must meet prior to approval by the Secretary of Labor. A plan must contain "satisfactory assurances that such state will, to the extent permitted by its law, establish and maintain an effective and comprehensive occupational safety and health program applicable to all employees of public agencies of the state and its political subdivisions, which program is as effective as the standards contained in the approved plan." The difference between this version and that rejected in the House when the Steiger-Sikes substitute was approved lies in the added words "to the extent permitted by law."

The problem arises not with employees of the state but with employees of local jurisdictions. A state's control over local jurisdictions is frequently very slight, since the rights of counties and muncipalities often are established by charter or constitution. The Secretary of Labor is asked only to see that the state plan pushes its jurisdiction to its fullest extent.

FEDERAL GRANTS TO STATES

The primary vehicle for involving states in the enforcement of occupational health and safety is federal grants to the states. These can be of four kinds:
- Development grants where the federal share may be as high as 90 percent.
- Operating grants where the federal share may be as high as 50 percent.
- Grants to assist states in developing and administering programs dealing with occupational health and safety statistics.
- General research contracts to assist the Secretary of Health, Education, and Welfare in carrying out his duty to develop the science of job safety and health.

Grants for development of state programs are limited to the first years under the Act. The Secretary of Labor's authority to disburse development grants to a state agency upon application expires on June 30,

1973, but a review of the entire grant program is required by that time, together with recommendations for its future, suggesting the possibility of an extension of the development program.

Uses which a state may make of a development grant are outlined in Section 23(a) and include:

- Identification of needs and responsibilities.
- Developing plans under Section 18.
- Developing plans for collection of information, increasing expertise and enforcement capabilities of personnel engaged in job safety and health, and improving the administration and enforcement of laws and standards in this area.

The Secretary of Labor is required to consult with the Secretary of Health, Education, and Welfare in the person of the director of the National Institute for Occupational Safety and Health on approving development grants.

For operating grants the Labor Secretary has sole discretion on the amount to be given, except that he is limited to 50 percent, the money must be for a state plan approved under Section 18, and differences in shares to the states must be based on objective criteria.

Apart from operating and development money, the states and subdivisions of the state have other sources of money open to them through the Act. These include:

- Grants from the Secretary of Labor to assist states in developing and administering programs dealing with occupational safety and health statistics up to the amount of 50 percent.
- Contracts from the Secretary of Health, Education, and Welfare under Section Section 20(c) for the purpose of exploring general health and safety questions which would further HEW's research function— and which possibly could have an especial impact on occupational safety and health within the state.
- Grants or contracts for training and employee education. (Sec. 21(a))

The primary avenue for federal assistance, however, will remain the grants for development and for operating state plans. Recipients of grants are required to keep records as prescribed by the Secretary of Labor and the Secretary of Health, Education, and Welfare which make account of disbursements as well as the complete financial records of the project for which the grant is used. The financial records will be open to audit, according to Section 25, by the agents of the Secretaries or of the Comptroller General of the United States.

FUTURE ROLE

The number of states which presently could qualify their programs in occupational health and safety is open to conjecture. Former Labor Secretary George P. Shultz noted during the hearings that three states have been "most outstanding" with their programs—New York, Pennsylvania, and California—but that a listing without closer examination of the programs would be foolhardy.

The number of states which will attempt to qualify state plans for enforcement of state-developed standards also is open to question. Will states view the monetary grants as affording an opportunity for becoming involved in occupational health and safety to a greater extent than possible before, or will they forgo any expenditure at all with the belief that federal involvement in the jobplace has relieved the states of the burden they have been carrying?

The reasons why a state would want to administer a program which without its administration would be carried on by the Federal Government can be guessed. First, there are the closer ties a state has with the citizens within its jurisdiction; it is one layer of government closer to their problems. In the eyes of these citizens the state government may be more responsive to their needs. Business in the state might feel that its interests could be safeguarded to a greater extent if the state to which it contributes revenue has the powers an occupational health and safety plan contemplates. Broader legislation could be adopted, some perhaps putting a greater degree of responsibility on the worker to follow safe practices. The labor interests in a state might feel that a state plan could afford broader coverage to the workers in the state, and that problems could be handled more swiftly and with greater sensitivity to the interests of particular labor groups if the enforcement power is closer to home.

A state with a program already in operation has a considerable investment in experience with the particular state problems, a staff of employees, and administrative structures which would be invaluable to the employees in the state. Should such a program be nipped, the experience and structures would be broken up, perhaps not to be assimilated in a federal effort. Should it continue, operating and development grants could give it the opportunity to grow and improve.

Weighed against these reasons for state enforcement of state regulations are problems of cost. Many state and local jurisdictions have felt a financial pinch in recent years. Pleas for revenue sharing are more and more frequent. Federal responsibility for job health and safety could be viewed by a state with growing governmental costs as a chance to prune away one function. There is also a political problem of satisfying the interests of diverse groups in a piece of legislation, and it is possible that the political leaders of a state may see more advantage in leaving well enough alone.

CHAPTER 7

RESEARCH AND TRAINING

Among the least controversial provisions of the new law are those aimed at providing the "research, information, education, and training in the field of occupational safety and health" mentioned in the preamble to the Act. The lack of research knowledge, of trained personnel, and of statistical information—all vital to effective administration of the law—was mentioned repeatedly in the hearings by members of both political parties and spokesmen for employer, union, government, and private organizations.

The importance attached to research and training is indicated in Section 2 on congressional findings and purpose. The Senate version of this section stated merely that the Act would provide "for research relating to occupational safety and health." The House bill, which became the basis for the final language of this section, listed the following:

• Research in the field of occupational safety and health, including the psychological factors involved, and development of innovative methods, techniques, and approaches for dealing with occupational safety and health problems. (Sec. 2(b)(5))

• Exploration of ways to discover latent diseases and to establish causal connections between diseases and the work environment, and other research relating to health problems, in recognition of the fact that occupational health standards present problems often different from those involved in occupational safety. (Sec. 2(b)(6))

• Establishment of medical criteria which will insure insofar as practicable that no employee will suffer diminished health, functional capacity, or life expectancy as a result of his work experience. (Sec. 2(b)(7))

• Training programs to increase the number and competence of personnel engaged in the field of occupational safety and health. (Sec. 2(b)(8))

Provisions of the law implementing these purposes authorize the undertaking of a massive research effort by the Federal Government. In general, these provisions are from the final Senate bill, which was the more comprehensive of the two approaches and the only one establishing a new National Institute for Occupational Safety and Health within the Department of Health, Education, and Welfare. Over-all, HEW is given major responsibility for research activities under the new law.

GENERAL RESEARCH RESPONSIBILITIES

Section 20 of the Act directs the Secretary of HEW, after consultation with the Secretary of Labor and other appropriate federal officials, to conduct "research, experiments, and demonstrations relating to occupational safety and health, including studies of psychological factors involved, and relating to innovative methods, techniques, and approaches for dealing with occupational safety and health problems." Specific areas of research activity (described in more detail below) include development of criteria for the Secretary of Labor to use in promulgating health and safety standards, publication of lists of known toxic substances, programs for working with employers in collecting on-the-job data, and other studies.

The Secretary of Labor also is given authority to arrange for studies, to be undertaken by public agencies or private organizations, relating to his responsibilities under the Act. The Senate bill specified that such studies were to be related "to the establishing and applying of occupational safety and health standards under Section 6 of this Act," but this restriction was omitted from the final bill.

During the Senate hearings, HEW anticipated that studies by the Labor Department would be "in areas in which we are not working, such as studies relating to the operation of particular types of industrial machines." (Hearings before the Senate Subcommittee on Labor, p. 163). In any event, this provision as enacted calls for the Secretary of Labor to cooperate with the Secretary of HEW to avoid any duplication of research efforts.

Other subsections of Section 20 specify:

• The Secretary of HEW has authority to make inspections and question employers and employees (as also provided under Section 8) in carrying out the research activities.

• Information obtained from research conducted by HEW and the Department of Labor is to be disseminated to employers, employees, and organizations by the Secretary of Labor.

• All functions of the Secretary of HEW, to the extent feasible, are delegated to the director of the National Institute for Occupational Safety and Health established by Section 22.

DEVELOPMENT OF CRITERIA FOR STANDARDS

Development of scientific criteria for the Secretary of Labor to use in setting or revising standards under Section 6 is the responsibility of the Secretary of HEW, and he is required to consult with the Secretary of Labor in developing specific plans for the research necessary to produce the criteria, including criteria identifying toxic substances. Criteria developed on the basis of this research or other available information are to be published annually by HEW. (This requirement was not included in the Senate version of the bill but was in the House bill.) Under the Senate bill, criteria dealing with toxic materials and harmful physical agents and substances were to be developed to demonstrate exposure levels at which a worker would experience no impairment of health or functional capacities or diminished life expectancy; the House bill had no such provision. The compromise provision as passed calls for the development of such criteria to describe exposure levels that are safe for various periods of employment, *including but not limited to* the exposure levels at which no employee will suffer impaired health or functional capacity or diminished life expectancy as a result of his work experience. (116 Cong. Rec., H 11814, Dec. 16, 1970)

Definitions

The term *criteria* as used in the Act was defined in the House Education and Labor Committee report as "scientifically determined conclusions based on the best available medical evidence; they are commonly presented in the form of recommendations describing medically acceptable tolerance levels of exposure to harmful substances or conditions over a period of time. They may also include medical judgments on methods and devices used to control exposure or its effects."

Standards as developed by the Secretary of Labor "will reflect the criteria described above," the report noted, but "they may be modified by practical considerations such as feasibility, means of implementation, and the like. They will specify the conditions that will be required to be present in the working place."

Shortcomings of Existing Criteria

The need for extensive research for the development of criteria was emphasized by many witnesses during the hearings, including Dr. Roger Egeberg, Assistant Secretary of HEW for Health and Scientific Affairs. He said, "We need a continuing flow of knowledge as the basis for standard-changing, for we cannot assume that any health or safety standard can ever be good for all time." (Senate hearings, p. 99)

The report of the Senate Labor and Public Welfare Committee noted that a large proportion of the safety standards presently in use are seriously out of date and that there are many occupational hazards—particularly those affecting health—not covered by any standards at all. A statement submitted to the Senate Subcommittee by the director of the Bureau of Occupational Safety and Health listed the following "substances and/or conditions for which no adequate standards exist and for which standards should be promulgated: cotton dust; coal tar pitch volatiles; petroleum coke; proteolytic enzymes; heat stress; diesel exhaust gases; grain dust; and rubber dust." (Senate hearings, p. 161)

Another problem discussed in the hearings was that it sometimes had taken years to issue certain standards, often because of lack of criteria data; the House Committee report stressed "the need to have these criteria developed as rapidly as possible."

LISTS OF TOXIC SUBSTANCES

Another major research responsibility of the Secretary of HEW is the annual publication of a list "of all known toxic substances by generic family or other useful groupings, and the concentrations at which such toxicity is known to occur." (Sec. 20(a)(6)) The first such list is to be published before October 28, 1971. The Senate bill provided that the list would include substances "used or found in the workplace," but this limitation was omitted from the final bill.

Upon written request by an employer or authorized representative of employees, the Secretary of HEW is to determine whether a substance found at a workplace has potentially toxic effects. This provision was included in both House and Senate bills. The Senate version also included the following additional requirements, which were retained in the final measure:

• The request must specify "with reasonable particularity" the grounds on which it is being made.

• The determination is to be submitted to both employers and employees affected as soon as possible.

• If the determination is that the substance *is* potentially toxic at the concentrations used or found in the work place, and no applicable standard is in effect, the Secretary of Labor is to be so advised and given all pertinent criteria so that he may take action. (116 Cong. Rec. H 11814, Dec. 16, 1970)

The final provisions of the law relating to toxic substances are far less comprehensive than those suggested by various witnesses during the hearings. The Oil, Chemical & Atomic Workers union, for example, said the bill should include immediate provision, to every worker, of a complete list of the chemicals with which he works, including the latest toxicological information on each, and a central clearing house for information on chemicals, which workers anywhere in the United States could telephone at any time, day or night, in order to obtain data on substances. (Senate hearings, p. 1032)

The original House bill did include much more comprehensive provisions with respect to toxic substances. The report of the House Labor Committee stated, "Basically, the worker needs to have adequate advance knowledge of hazards in order to protect himself from damaging exposures."

The original bill required that, when there was a determination that a substance was toxic, employers must provide employees with information as to the hazards, symptoms, treatment, and precautions involved, and with necessary protective equipment. It also permitted an employee to absent himself from that specific danger for its duration without loss of pay. This so-called "strike with pay" provision was deleted from the proposed bill by the House Subcommittee before the bill came to a vote. (116 Cong. Rec. H 10617, Nov. 23, 1970)

EMPLOYER INVOLVEMENT

Employers can be required by the Secretary of HEW to measure, monitor, and make reports on the exposure of employees to potentially toxic substances or harmful physical agents. (Sec. 20(a) (5)) The purpose of the requirement is to furnish data necessary for developing criteria for standards and provide information on toxic substances.

Financial Assistance

Upon the request of any employer required to participate in research activities, HEW is to "furnish full financial or other assistance" to defray the added cost to that employer. There was no provision for financial assistance in either bill originally; it was added to the Senate version by an amendment proposed by Senator Saxbe (R-Ohio), in Committee. The House conferees agreed to the provision with the understanding that regulations issued under the subsection "will be limited to those instances in which there is a reasonable probability of developing information on toxic substances or harmful physical agents." (116 Cong. Rec. H 11814, Dec. 16, 1970)

Section 20 also authorizes the Secretary of HEW to establish programs of medical examinations and tests for employees. An exception is made for those who object to medical exams or treatment on religious grounds unless they are necessary to protect the health and safety of others. Payment to employers for expenses in connection with medical exams is not provided explicitly in this subsection, although Section 6(b)(7) states, "In the event such medical examinations are in the nature of research, as determined by the Secretary of Health, Education, and Welfare, such examinations may be furnished at the expense of the Secretary of Health, Education, and Welfare."

A provision in the House bill called for congressional appropriations to enable the Secretary of Labor to provide monitoring equipment for all employers required by any standard, rule, or regulation to measure the exposure of employees to unhealthy environments. This was not included in the final Act, and financial assistance is to be provided for purchase of monitoring equipment only if it is required by HEW as part of a research effort, as is the case with expenses for medical exams. (116 Cong. Rec. H 11814, Dec. 16, 1970)

Inspections

The Secretary of HEW is given the authority to make inspections and question employers and employees to carry out his functions under the Act. (Sec. 20(7)(b))

An HEW spokesman testified during Senate hearings that the purpose of this subsection was to "mandate entry for health purposes, so that we can gather the kind of information and statistics that are needed to develop criteria and standards to carry out the preventive action." In discussing research in the textile industry, he said, "It isn't always easy to gain access to a mill to find out what is wrong with it and what is making their workers ill, which is one of the problems that we think the legislation that is before you will help to clear up." (Senate hearings, p. 157)

The HEW Secretary's right of inspection also is spelled out in Section 8, which provides that he shall prescribe such rules and regulations as he may deem necessary, including rules and regulations dealing with the inspection of an employer's establishment. (Sec. 8(g)(2))

OTHER RESEARCH STUDIES

Other studies called for specifically under Section 20 include industry-wide studies of the effect of chronic or low-level exposure to industrial materials, processes, and stresses on the potential for illness, disease, or loss of functional capacity in aging adults. (Sec. 20(a)(7)) A report on these studies is required within two years and annually thereafter. This provision came from the Senate bill; there was no comparable subsection in the House bill.

Another provision, which came from the House bill, calls for special research projects related to new problems, including those created by new technology in the field of occupational safety and health, and for research into the motivational and behavioral factors relating to the field. (Sec. 20 (a) (4))

In addition to all the types of studies spelled out in Section 20, a wide range of other projects could be undertaken under the broad research authority given the Secretary of HEW. The Senate Labor Committee report listed the following which the Committee believed important:

• Studies of the toxic effects of exposure to particular combinations of chemical and physical agents.

• Development of appropriate instruments for monitoring the extent of environmental hazards in the workplace, including personal monitoring devices to be used by individual workers.

• Studies of mental and personality disorders attributable to occupational stresses.

• Development of reliable tests for identifying and predicting the degree of individual tolerance to workplace hazards, and medical surveillance programs to provide early detection of incipient health deterioration.

• Studies of the potential genetic effects of complex chemicals and other material in the work environment.

NATIONAL INSTITUTE FOR OCCUPATIONAL
SAFETY AND HEALTH

A new National Institute for Occupational Safety and Health (NIOSH) within HEW is provided for by Section 22 of the Act. The new Institute is to (1) develop and establish recommended occupational safety and health standards, and (2) perform all functions specified to be performed by the Secretary of HEW under the research and training provisions (Sections 20 and 21) of the law.

The Institute is to be headed by a director to be appointed for a six-year term by the Secretary of HEW. On his own initiative, or upon request of the Secretary of Labor or the Secretary of HEW, the director of NIOSH is authorized:

• To conduct research and experiments needed to develop criteria for new and improved occupational safety and health standards.

• To make recommendations for new and improved standards on the basis of such research and experiments. Any standards so recommended must be sent immediately to the Secretaries of Labor and HEW.

To carry out these responsibilities, the director is given the following authority:

• Prescribe necessary regulations.

• Receive and dispose of money and other property (restricted or unrestricted in its use).

• Appoint necessary personnel and determine their compensation in accordance with civil service rules.

• Use the services of experts or consultants and of voluntary and noncompensated personnel.

• Enter into contracts, grants, or other arrangements.

• Make necessary expenditures.

The director must make an annual report to the Secretary of HEW, the President, and Congress of the operations of the Institute, including a detailed statement of all private and public funds received and spent, and any recommendation he deems appropriate.

Neither House nor Senate bill originally provided for the delegation of HEW functions to a separate Institute. It was added to the Senate bill by an amendment proposed by Senator Javits (R-NY) in Committee and retained in the final meaure. The reasons for establishing such an Institute were set forth in the Senate Labor Committee Report as follows:

"The establishment of this institute will elevate the status of occupational health and safety research to place it on an equal footing with the research conducted by the HEW into other matters of vital social concern, particularly in the health area. Such an institute will be able to attract the qualified personnel necessary to engage in occupational health and safety research if we are to make any real progress in reducing job-related injury and disease under the Act, and will much more easily attract the substantial increase in funding which will be necessary to achieve the purposes of this Act.

"Equally important, the research and recommendations of the institute will be of critical importance in continually improving occupational health and safety standards promulgated under this Act. The primary source of these standards at this time is the various consensus and proprietary organizations such as the American National Standards Institute and the American Conference of Governmental Industrial Hygienists. Without in any way denigrating the substantial contributions to occupational health and safety which such organizations have already made, and which they will undoubtedly continue to make, it is apparent that the Government must develop a capacity for developing these standards which will operate independently of self-interest groups."

Relationship to Private Groups

The effect of the new Institute on the several private organizations and associations already doing much of the research relating to health and safety standards was a matter of some concern. While it is assumed that the Institute will begin with the present Bureau of Occupational Safety and Health as a nucleus, there is no clear indication of what other Government agencies or private institutions might eventually come under its umbrella.

During the hearings, Mr. Javits said ". . . it may very well be that an institute like this would give a creative role for the trade unions, as well as the employer organizations, and other sources of support," the implication being that he anticipated that organizations outside the Government would contribute to the research efforts of whatever institute was established. The status of these organizations vis-a-vis the Institute was not brought up until the final Senate debate. At that time Mr. Javits assured these organizations that he did not view the establishment of NIOSH as jeopardizing their existence, saying:

"The other aspect of the matter is that the bill provides for a National Institute of Occupational Health and Safety, and it is important to assure these outside organizations, which are very important in this field, that the Institute is not designed in any way to preempt or limit the activity or importance of national consensus organizations such as the American National Standards Institute. These organizations have made valuable contributions in this field in the past, and I hope they will continue to do so in the future. This is so that they may be reassured that the Institute represents no threat to them.

"The other point I should like to make with respect to reassuring these organizations is to confirm the fact that it is expected that the director of the new institute will take full advantage of the extensive expertise represented by members of technical societies and private standards-development organizations which serve an important purpose and which should continue to function in the private sector of occupational health and safety." (116 Cong. Rec. S 18355, Nov. 17, 1970)

TRAINING AND EMPLOYEE EDUCATION

Activities related to training and employee education specifically authorized by Section 21 of the Act include the following:

• The Secretary of HEW, after consultation with the Secretary of Labor and with other appropriate federal agencies, is directed to conduct programs, either directly or by grants or contracts, (1) of education to provide the personnel needed to implement the new law, and (2) to provide information on the importance of and proper use of safety and health equipment.

• The Secretary of Labor also may conduct, directly or by grants or contracts, short-term training programs of personnel carrying out the provisions of the Act.

• The Secretary of Labor, in consultation with the Secretary of HEW, is directed to provide (1) programs for training employers and employees in accident prevention, and (2) consultation to employers, employees, and employee organizations, as to means of preventing occupational injuries and illnesses.

Both Senate and House Committee reports emphasized that no matter how good the final bill was, its purposes could not be achieved without qualified, trained personnel.

Provisions of the House and Senate bills relating to training and education were virtually identical, and no amendment was made in the final version of the Act. The three separate areas of training and education provided for are discussed below.

Training of Professional Manpower

The Secretary of Health, Education, and Welfare is to develop programs for the education of safety and health personnel to provide a substantial increase in the competent professional manpower necessary to carry out the research effort called for by the new law.

A shortage of professional occupational health and safety personnel was cited many times during the hearings. In the safety area, it was noted that there are fewer than 100 federal safety inspectors and only 1,600 state inspectors.

In occupational health, the situation appeared to be even worse. According to the Senate Committee report, "The hearings revealed a dearth of occupational health specialists in the country—probably no more than 700 are available to meet the demands of a national program to provide healthful working conditions."

According to the American Medical Association, 5,000 new full-time and part-time physicians and 10,000 nurses are needed to fill the in-plant health services of industry. Figures presented by HEW indicated a serious shortage of personnel in all areas of occupational health.

Types of professional training programs that may be undertaken under this provision of the law are indicated by suggestions from various witnesses in the hearings. For example:

• In-service training programs to give recent college graduates an intensive course in occupational safety and health. The Bureau of Occupational Safety and Health already has developed such a program. (Senate hearings, p. 138)

• Training of paraprofessionals to take over many of the details that use up much of the time and energy of the professionals, such as training of technicians to take samples, monitoring the effects of operation engineering controls, and conducting routine laboratory analyses. *(Ibid.)*

• Grants to colleges that have specific prescribed curricula leading to degrees in industrial safety and/or health. At present, there are comparatively few such institutions. A 1969 study by the American Society of Safety Engineers indicated that four-year under-graduate degrees in safety engineering are offered by only five institutions and graduate degrees by 14 institutions. (House hearings, p. 526)

• Contracts with universities for the development of additional college-level programs similar to the one being undertaken for the Bureau of Mines to train safety inspectors. Once the curriculum and materials are developed, contracts can be extended to other universities to do the training. (House hearings, p. 1312)

• Grants-in-aid to enable engineers, chemists, and other scientists to do post-graduate work in industrial health. (Senate hearings, p. 408)

Short-term Personnel Training Programs

The Labor Department has the job of providing short-term training to inspectors and other enforcement officers in both federal and state agencies. Not included specifically in the Act, but included in both House and Senate reports on the legislation, was a statement that the Secretary of Labor, working with the Civil Service Commission, should "continue to establish qualifications for federal occupational safety personnel which have a meaningful relationship to standards promulgated under this Act. It is absolutely essential that all who are carrying out duties under this Act will be fully qualified to do so."

This provision, and the accompanying statement, reflect the concern expressed during the hearings about the personnel who would be responsible for enforcement of the new law. Congresswoman Edith Green (D-Ore), for example, in questioning the then Secretary of Labor George P. Schultz, said, "In other legislation I have been concerned with the enforcement procedures and with the people who go out in the field who are either eager beavers or who don't know what they are doing." (House hearings, p. 364)

Spokesmen for employer groups also expressed some anxiety on this point. The Associated General Contractors asked for assurance that only competent persons become inspectors, saying, "We believe that this is extremely necessary because such people should be well-trained and requirements should be established for personnel authorized to investigate work sites." (Senate hearings, p. 763)

Another aspect of this problem was brought out by a spokesman for the steel industry, who pointed out that without certified field personnel "the necessary technical communications between industry representatives and inspectors cannot be achieved and would only create a bottleneck in obtaining our goal of a safe and healthy environment for the workers." (*Ibid.*, p. 409)

Employer-Employee Training Programs

The third type of training effort authorized by the new law is aimed at promoting greater awareness of safety in the workplace. In the House debate, Congressman John P. Dent (D-Pa) described the purpose of this section as follows:

"Unsafe acts or unsafe work practices are frequently the result of failure to train workers in safe work practices. Unsafe work practices may be of many forms: using the wrong tool, using a tool incorrectly, failure to use guards or protective equipment, taking unnecessary chances, and assuming an awkward position, to name but a few. Such unsafe practices indicate lack of effective safety training and safety training should be a part of the routine job training. In order to promote this greater awareness of safety in the workplace the bill provides for employee and employer training with special emphasis on technical assistance to both labor and management for the adoption of sound safety and health practices." (116 Cong. Rec. H 10635, Nov. 23, 1970)

The Secretary of Labor is given the major responsibility for the employer-employee training programs, but in consultation with the Secretary of HEW. In the hearings, it was pointed out that the need for these programs is greatest in smaller companies that can't afford their own safety specialists or industrial hygienists. In many instances the only information, training, or advice for the small companies comes from their insurance company or the state, in those few states that have large-scale safety and health programs. New York, for example, provides a consulting service that includes speakers for safety seminars sponsored by various industry groups and programs for labor unions. This is the type of program that would be provided by the Federal Government, where it is not available on the state level, under this provision.

CHAPTER 8

OTHER PROVISIONS

Congress pushed federal involvement to new heights in the Occupational Safety and Health Act, but it also served notice on the states that more is yet to come. A national study of workmen's compensation plans —an area controlled by the states—was launched.

The study, to be performed by a new National Commission on State Workmen's Compensation Laws, is one of the final provisions of the Act. Other provisions that helped round out the law include sections on economic assistance to small business, confidentiality of trade secrets, a national advisory committee, and the law's effect on existing legislation.

STATE WORKMEN'S COMPENSATION LAWS

A National Commission on State Workmen's Compensation Laws is established by Section 27 of the Act. The Commission is to undertake a comprehensive evaluation of state laws and report its findings and recommendations to the President and Congress by July 31, 1972.

Despite a general awareness of inadequacies in state workmen's compensation plans, Congress has refrained from infringing on this area of state jurisdiction. The original proposals for national job safety standards avoided the subject entirely.

The provision in the law comes from an amendment sponsored by Senator Javits (R-NY), which was accepted by the Senate Labor and Public Welfare Committee before the bill reached the Senate floor.

The study of workmen's compensation laws "could be one of the most significant parts of the bill," Mr. Javits warned during Senate debate. "I know how nearly everyone feels about a federal workmen's compensation system, which is all the more reason why there should be a much greater degree of adequacy among the states." (116 Cong. Rec. S 18363, Nov. 17, 1970)

Proper care was taken in the Senate Labor Committee report not to recommend federalization of existing workmen's compensation plans, but the door was left open for the study Commission to make this recommendation. The report said:

"The Committee wishes to emphasize that by authorizing this study it is not impliedly recommending federalization of the existing workmen's compensation system or its merger with the O.A.S.D.I. program. Nor is it willing to accept the notion that workmen's compensation would, under any and all circumstances, remain a matter completely within the prerogatives of the states. Just as the Federal Government has a responsibility to assure that American workers are protected from job-related injury and disease, it also has an interest in insuring that those American workers who do suffer job-related injury or disease are adequately compensated and treated.

"Whether, and to what extent, the Federal Government should become directly or indirectly involved in assuring the adequacy of workmen's compensation will be one of the matters considered by the Commission in framing its recommendations. Indeed, one of the primary purposes of authorizing this study and report is to provide a basis for an informed decision by Congress of this question in the future."

Scope of the Study

Congress gave the new Commission a full agenda. The list of subjects to be studied is not all inclusive, however. The Commission has authority to search into other areas not mentioned in the Act.

The compensation study and evaluation of state laws *must* include the following:

• Amount and duration of permanent and temporary disability benefits and the criteria for determining the maximum limitations thereof.

• Amount and duration of medical benefits and provisions insuring adequate medical care and free choice of physician.

• Extent of coverage of workers, including exemptions based on numbers or type of employment.

• Standards for determining which injuries or diseases should be deemed compensable.

• Rehabilitation.

• Coverage under second or subsequent injury funds.

• Time limits on filing claims.

• Waiting periods.

• Compulsory or elective coverage.

• Administration.

• Legal expenses.

• Feasibility and desirability of a uniform system of reporting information concerning job-related injuries and diseases and the operation of workmen's compensation laws.

• Resolution of conflict of laws, extraterritoriality and similar problems arising from claims with multistage aspects.

• Extent to which private insurance carriers are excluded from supplying workmen's compensation coverage and the desirability of such exclusionary practices, to the extent they are found to exist.

• Relationship between workmen's compensation on the one hand, and old-age, disability, and survivors insurance and other types of insurance, public or private, on the other hand.

• Methods of implementing the recommendations of the Commission.

The listed subjects include most of the standards for workmen's compensation laws recommended by the Department of Labor and the International Association of Industrial Accident Boards and Commissions. It also includes matters which the Senate Labor Committee said it believes deserve particular attention.

The Commission Structure

The National Commission on State Workmen's Compensation Laws will be composed of 15 members, appointed by the President. The membership is to come from state boards, representatives of insurance carriers, business, labor, members of the medical profession having experience in industrial medicine or in workmen's compensation cases, educators having special expertise in the field of workmen's compensation, and representatives of the general public. The Secretaries of Labor and Health, Education, and Welfare are to be *ex officio* members of the Commission.

The President is to designate one of the members to serve as chairman and one to serve as vice chairman. Eight members of the Commission will constitute a quorum.

The Commission or any subcommittee or members thereof may hold hearings, take testimony, and sit and act at such times and places as the Commission deems advisable for accomplishing the required study.

All the federal departments and independent agencies are directed to furnish the Commission information it deems necessary to carry out its functions.

The law gives the chairman of the Commission the power to appoint an executive director and "such additional staff personnel as he deems necessary."

Contracts also are authorized between the Commission and federal or state agencies, private firms, institutions, and individuals for the conduct of research or surveys, the preparation of reports, and other activities necessary to the discharge of the Commission's duties.

Ninety days after the Commission submits its report, it will cease to exist.

Early Evidence

The Senate Labor Committee indicated that it didn't intentionally investigate state workmen's compensation laws, but the evidence that "inevitably" turned up during hearings and research conducted by the Committee raised "serious questions about the present inadequacy of many state workmen's compensation laws."

The Committee's report noted that workmen's compensation benefits do not appear to have kept pace with increasing wages and the rising cost of living faced by American workers, "with the result that benefits usually replace only a small fraction of the income lost due to disabling injury or disease." It noted that between 1940 and 1969 the ratio of maximum benefits to average weekly wages decreased in 44 states.

The Committee also noted that many state programs do not recognize certain types of occupational disease as compensable. Two examples cited were black lung, suffered by coal miners, now covered in the Coal Mine Health and Safety Act, and byssinosis, a respiratory disease caused by the inhalation of cotton dust produced during the processing of textiles.

The Committee report also indicated that because of exemptions based on type of employment, or number of employees, approximately 20 percent of all American workers fail to enjoy the protection of workmen's compensation. Among the workers usually excluded are agricultural employees.

The over-all ratio of compliance with recommended standards for state compensation laws is less than 50 percent, the Committee said. Similarly, a model workmen's compensation law developed under the auspices of the Council of State Governments appears to have been largely ignored.

SMALL BUSINESS ASSISTANCE

The small business provision authorizes loans to small businesses whenever the standards set by the Federal Government are so severe that they will cause a real and substantial economic injury. The loans can be made through the Small Business Administration to help businesses purchase needed new equipment or modify conditions in the shop.

In explaining this provision, Senator Dominick (R-Colo) said he thought it was needed to minimize economic injury that could occur. Citing the Minerals and Nonmetallic Mines Act as an example, he said the bill as originally passed had a provision for sanitary conditions, showers, running water, and others, that would run a "father and son" mine out of business if imposed.

The small business provision in the Occupational Safety and Health Act would eliminate this possibility, he explained.

The legislation provides that loans can be made either directly or in cooperation with banks or lending institutions through agreements to participate on an immediate or deferred basis.

NATIONAL ADVISORY COMMITTEE

A National Advisory Committee on Occupational Safety and Health is authorized by Section 7 of the Act. The Advisory Committee is in addition to the ad hoc advisory committees available to the Secretary of Labor.

The national committee is to consist of 12 members, appointed by the Secretary of Labor, four of whom are to be designated by the Secretary of Health, Education, and Welfare.

The members are to be selected on the basis of their experience and competence in the field of occupational safety and health. The Secretary of Labor is to designate one of the members as chairman, and furnish the Committee with an executive secretary and secretarial and clerical assistance.

The Committee is to advise, consult with, and make recommendations to the Labor Secretary and the Secretary of HEW. It is to hold at least two meetings each year, and all meetings are to be open to the public.

The role of the Committee was commented on by the Senate Labor

Committee in its report. The Committee said, "The Advisory Committee has an important role to perform in bringing continuing public attention and interest to bear on the Act and on its programs. Its membership should be chosen with great care and should be widely representative."

CONFIDENTIALITY OF TRADE SECRETS

Both House and Senate versions of the occupational safety and health legislation made provisions for confidentiality of trade secrets. The House proposal provided that the information should be made off the public record and kept separately. The Senate version provided that the courts or the Secretary of Labor should issue confidentiality orders. The House receded and the Senate version was adopted.

During hearings on the legislation, witnesses saw one of the major problems in carrying out the Act as being that employers might use the confidentiality of trade secrets provision unjustifiably to conceal information.

They contended that the degree of risk involved in a given work environment cannot realistically be evaluated unless the inspectors and environmental investigators have enough information to assess the adequacy of control measures.

EFFECT ON OTHER LAWS

The Act makes it clear that it will not supersede or affect any existing workmen's compensation law or enlarge, diminish, or affect common law or statutory rights, duties, or liabilities under any law related to occupational injuries, diseases, or death of employees resulting from employment.

The major difference in the Senate and House bills in the treatment of the proposed effect on other health and safety statutes was that the Senate version, which prevailed, said the Act should not apply to working conditions where other federal agencies exercise statutory authority. The House amendment excluded employees whose working conditions were regulated by other federal agencies.

The Act also provides that safety standards under any law administered by the Labor Secretary—Walsh-Healey, Service Contract, Construction Safety, Arts and Humanities, Longshoremen's and Harbor Workers' Compensation Acts—will be superseded when more effective standards are established under the new Act. (See Chapter 3)

Standards under existing laws were not repealed by enactment of the Occupational Safety and Health Act.

To deal with the problem of duplication of standards, the Secretary of Labor is required to report to Congress within three years after the effective date of the Act. The report must contain recommendations for legislation to avoid unnecessary duplication and to achieve coordination between the Act and other federal laws.

TEXT OF THE ACT

𝔄𝔫 𝔄𝔠𝔱

84 STAT. 1590

To assure safe and healthful working conditions for working men and women; by authorizing enforcement of the standards developed under the Act; by assisting and encouraging the States in their efforts to assure safe and healthful working conditions; by providing for research, information, education, and training in the field of occupational safety and health; and for other purposes.

Be it enacted by the Senate and House of Representatives of the United States of America in Congress assembled, That this Act may be cited as the "Occupational Safety and Health Act of 1970".

Occupational Safety and Health Act of 1970.

CONGRESSIONAL FINDINGS AND PURPOSE

SEC. (2) The Congress finds that personal injuries and illnesses arising out of work situations impose a substantial burden upon, and are a hindrance to, interstate commerce in terms of lost production, wage loss, medical expenses, and disability compensation payments.

(b) The Congress declares it to be its purpose and policy, through the exercise of its powers to regulate commerce among the several States and with foreign nations and to provide for the general welfare, to assure so far as possible every working man and woman in the Nation safe and healthful working conditions and to preserve our human resources—

(1) by encouraging employers and employees in their efforts to reduce the number of occupational safety and health hazards at their places of employment, and to stimulate employers and employees to institute new and to perfect existing programs for providing safe and healthful working conditions;

(2) by providing that employers and employees have separate but dependent responsibilities and rights with respect to achieving safe and healthful working conditions;

(3) by authorizing the Secretary of Labor to set mandatory occupational safety and health standards applicable to businesses affecting interstate commerce, and by creating an Occupational Safety and Health Review Commission for carrying out adjudicatory functions under the Act;

(4) by building upon advances already made through employer and employee initiative for providing safe and healthful working conditions;

(5) by providing for research in the field of occupational safety and health, including the psychological factors involved, and by developing innovative methods, techniques, and approaches for dealing with occupational safety and health problems;

(6) by exploring ways to discover latent diseases, establishing causal connections between diseases and work in environmental conditions, and conducting other research relating to health problems, in recognition of the fact that occupational health standards present problems often different from those involved in occupational safety;

(7) by providing medical criteria which will assure insofar as practicable that no employee will suffer diminished health, functional capacity, or life expectancy as a result of his work experience;

(8) by providing for training programs to increase the number and competence of personnel engaged in the field of occupational safety and health;

(9) by providing for the development and promulgation of occupational safety and health standards;

(10) by providing an effective enforcement program which shall include a prohibition against giving advance notice of any inspection and sanctions for any individual violating this prohibition;

(11) by encouraging the States to assume the fullest responsibility for the administration and enforcement of their occupational safety and health laws by providing grants to the States to assist in identifying their needs and responsibilities in the area of occupational safety and health, to develop plans in accordance with the provisions of this Act, to improve the administration and enforcement of State occupational safety and health laws, and to conduct experimental and demonstration projects in connection therewith;

(12) by providing for appropriate reporting procedures with respect to occupational safety and health which procedures will help achieve the objectives of this Act and accurately describe the nature of the occupational safety and health problem;

(13) by encouraging joint labor-management efforts to reduce injuries and disease arising out of employment.

DEFINITIONS

SEC. 3. For the purposes of this Act—

(1) The term "Secretary" mean the Secretary of Labor.

(2) The term "Commission" means the Occupational Safety and Health Review Commission established under this Act.

(3) The term "commerce" means trade, traffic, commerce, transportation, or communication among the several States, or between a State and any place outside thereof, or within the District of Columbia, or a possession of the United States (other than the Trust Territory of the Pacific Islands), or between points in the same State but through a point outside thereof.

(4) The term "person" means one or more individuals, partnerships, associations, corporations, business trusts, legal representatives, or any organized group of persons.

(5) The term "employer" means a person engaged in a business affecting commerce who has employees, but does not include the United States or any State or political subdivision of a State.

(6) The term "employee" means an employee of an employer who is employed in a business of his employer which affects commerce.

(7) The term "State" includes a State of the United States, the District of Columbia, Puerto Rico, the Virgin Islands, American Samoa, Guam, and the Trust Territory of the Pacific Islands.

(8) The term "occupational safety and health standard" means a standard which requires conditions, or the adoption or use of one or more practices, means, methods, operations, or processes, reasonably necessary or appropriate to provide safe or healthful employment and places of employment.

(9) The term "national consensus standard" means any occupational safety and health standard or modification thereof which (1), has been adopted and promulgated by a nationally recog-

nized standards-producing organization under procedures whereby it can be determined by the Secretary that persons interested
and affected by the scope or provisions of the standard have
reached substantial agreement on its adoption, (2) was formulated in a manner which afforded an opportunity for diverse
views to be considered and (3) has been designated as such a
standard by the Secretary, after consultation with other appropriate Federal agencies.

(10) The term "established Federal standard" means any operative occupational safety and health standard established by any
agency of the United States and presently in effect, or contained
in any Act of Congress in force on the date of enactment of this
Act.

(11) The term "Committee" means the National Advisory
Committee on Occupational Safety and Health established under
this Act.

(12) The term "Director" means the Director of the National
Institute for Occupational Safety and Health.

(13) The term "Institute" means the National Institute for
Occupational Safety and Health established under this Act.

(14) The term "Workmen's Compensation Commission" means
the National Commission on State Workmen's Compensation
Laws established under this Act.

APPLICABILITY OF THIS ACT

SEC. 4. (a) This Act shall apply with respect to employment per-
formed in a workplace in a State, the District of Columbia, the Com-
monwealth of Puerto Rico, the Virgin Islands, American Samoa,
Guam, the Trust Territory of the Pacific Islands, Wake Island, Outer
Continental Shelf lands defined in the Outer Continental Shelf Lands
Act, Johnston Island, and the Canal Zone. The Secretary of the Inte-   67 Stat. 462.
rior shall, by regulation, provide for judicial enforcement of this   43 USC 1331
Act by the courts established for areas in which there are no United   note.
States district courts having jurisdiction.

(b)(1) Nothing in this Act shall apply to working conditions of
employees with respect to which other Federal agencies, and State
agencies acting under section 274 of the Atomic Energy Act of 1954,
as amended (42 U.S.C. 2021), exercise statutory authority to pre-   73 Stat. 688.
scribe or enforce standards or regulations affecting occupational safety
or health.

(2) The safety and health standards promulgated under the Act
of June 30, 1936, commonly known as the Walsh-Healey Act (41
U.S.C. 35 et seq.), the Service Contract Act of 1965 (41 U.S.C. 351   49 Stat. 2036.
et seq.), Public Law 91–54, Act of August 9, 1969 (40 U.S.C. 333),   79 Stat. 1034.
Public Law 85–742, Act of August 23, 1958 (33 U.S.C. 941), and the   83 Stat. 96.
National Foundation on Arts and Humanities Act (20 U.S.C. 951 et   72 Stat. 835.
seq.) are superseded on the effective date of corresponding standards,   79 Stat. 845;
promulgated under this Act, which are determined by the Secretary   Ante, p. 443.
to be more effective. Standards issued under the laws listed in this
paragraph and in effect on or after the effective date of this Act shall
be deemed to be occupational safety and health standards issued under
this Act, as well as under such other Acts.

(3) The Secretary shall, within three years after the effective date   Report to
of this Act, report to the Congress his recommendations for legisla-   Congress.
tion to avoid unnecessary duplication and to achieve coordination
between this Act and other Federal laws.

84 STAT. 1593

(4) Nothing in this Act shall be construed to supersede or in any manner affect any workmen's compensation law or to enlarge or diminish or affect in any other manner the common law or statutory rights, duties, or liabilities of employers and employees under any law with respect to injuries, diseases, or death of employees arising out of, or in the course of, employment.

DUTIES

SEC. 5. (a) Each employer—

(1) shall furnish to each of his employees employment and a place of employment which are free from recognized hazards that are causing or are likely to cause death or serious physical harm to his employees;

(2) shall comply with occupational safety and health standards promulgated under this Act.

(b) Each employee shall comply with occupational safety and health standards and all rules, regulations, and orders issued pursuant to this Act which are applicable to his own actions and conduct.

OCCUPATIONAL SAFETY AND HEALTH STANDARDS

SEC. 6. (a) Without regard to chapter 5 of title 5, United States Code, or to the other subsections of this section, the Secretary shall, as soon as practicable during the period beginning with the effective date of this Act and ending two years after such date, by rule promulgate as an occupational safety or health standard any national consensus standard, and any established Federal standard, unless he determines that the promulgation of such a standard would not result in improved safety or health for specifically designated employees. In the event of conflict among any such standards, the Secretary shall promulgate the standard which assures the greatest protection of the safety or health of the affected employees.

80 Stat. 381;
81 Stat. 195.
5 USC 500.

(b) The Secretary may by rule promulgate, modify, or revoke any occupational safety or health standard in the following manner:

(1) Whenever the Secretary, upon the basis of information submitted to him in writing by an interested person, a representative of any organization of employers or employees, a nationally recognized standards-producing organization, the Secretary of Health, Education, and Welfare, the National Institute for Occupational Safety and Health, or a State or political subdivision, or on the basis of information developed by the Secretary or otherwise available to him, determines that a rule should be promulgated in order to serve the objectives of this Act, the Secretary may request the recommendations of an advisory committee appointed under section 7 of this Act. The Secretary shall provide such an advisory committee with any proposals of his own or of the Secretary of Health, Education, and Welfare, together with all pertinent factual information developed by the Secretary or the Secretary of Health, Education, and Welfare, or otherwise available, including the results of research, demonstrations, and experiments. An advisory committee shall submit to the Secretary its recommendations regarding the rule to be promulgated within ninety days from the date of its appointment or within such longer or shorter period as may be prescribed by the Secretary, but in no event for a period which is longer than two hundred and seventy days.

Advisory
committee,
recommendations.

(2) The Secretary shall publish a proposed rule promulgating, modifying, or revoking an occupational safety or health standard in the Federal Register and shall afford interested persons a period of thirty days after publication to submit written data or comments. Where an advisory committee is appointed and the Secretary determines that a rule should be issued, he shall publish the proposed rule within sixty days after the submission of the advisory committee's recommendations or the expiration of the period prescribed by the Secretary for such submission.

Publication in Federal Register.

(3) On or before the last day of the period provided for the submission of written data or comments under paragraph (2), any interested person may file with the Secretary written objections to the proposed rule, stating the grounds therefor and requesting a public hearing on such objections. Within thirty days after the last day for filing such objections, the Secretary shall publish in the Federal Register a notice specifying the occupational safety or health standard to which objections have been filed and a hearing requested, and specifying a time and place for such hearing.

Hearing, notice.

Publication in Federal Register.

(4) Within sixty days after the expiration of the period provided for the submission of written data or comments under paragraph (2), or within sixty days after the completion of any hearing held under paragraph (3), the Secretary shall issue a rule promulgating, modifying, or revoking an occupational safety or health standard or make a determination that a rule should not be issued. Such a rule may contain a provision delaying its effective date for such period (not in excess of ninety days) as the Secretary determines may be necessary to insure that affected employers and employees will be informed of the existence of the standard and of its terms and that employers affected are given an opportunity to familiarize themselves and their employees with the existence of the requirements of the standard.

(5) The Secretary, in promulgating standards dealing with toxic materials or harmful physical agents under this subsection, shall set the standard which most adequately assures, to the extent feasible, on the basis of the best available evidence, that no employee will suffer material impairment of health or functional capacity even if such employee has regular exposure to the hazard dealt with by such standard for the period of his working life. Development of standards under this subsection shall be based upon research, demonstrations, experiments, and such other information as may be appropriate. In addition to the attainment of the highest degree of health and safety protection for the employee, other considerations shall be the latest available scientific data in the field, the feasibility of the standards, and experience gained under this and other health and safety laws. Whenever practicable, the standard promulgated shall be expressed in terms of objective criteria and of the performance desired.

Toxic materials.

(6)(A) Any employer may apply to the Secretary for a temporary order granting a variance from a standard or any provision thereof promulgated under this section. Such temporary order shall be granted only if the employer files an application which meets the requirements of clause (B) and establishes that (i) he is unable to comply with a standard by its effective date because of unavailability of professional or technical personnel or of materials and equipment needed to come into compliance with the standard or because necessary construction or alteration of facilities cannot be completed by the effective date, (ii) he is taking all available steps to safeguard his employees against the hazards covered by the standard, and (iii) he has an effective program for coming into compliance with the standard as quickly as

Temporary variance order.

84 STAT. 1595

practicable. Any temporary order issued under this paragraph shall prescribe the practices, means, methods, operations, and processes which the employer must adopt and use while the order is in effect and state in detail his program for coming into compliance with the standard. Such a temporary order may be granted only after notice to employees and an opportunity for a hearing: *Provided*, That the Secretary may issue one interim order to be effective until a decision is made on the basis of the hearing. No temporary order may be in effect for longer than the period needed by the employer to achieve compliance with the standard or one year, whichever is shorter, except that such an order may be renewed not more than twice (I) so long as the requirements of this paragraph are met and (II) if an application for renewal is filed at least 90 days prior to the expiration date of the order. No interim renewal of an order may remain in effect for longer than 180 days.

> Notice, hearing.
>
> Renewal.
>
> Time limitation.

(B) An application for a temporary order under this paragraph (6) shall contain:

(i) a specification of the standard or portion thereof from which the employer seeks a variance,

(ii) a representation by the employer, supported by representations from qualified persons having firsthand knowledge of the facts represented, that he is unable to comply with the standard or portion thereof and a detailed statement of the reasons therefor,

(iii) a statement of the steps he has taken and will take (with specific dates) to protect employees against the hazard covered by the standard,

(iv) a statement of when he expects to be able to comply with the standard and what steps he has taken and what steps he will take (with dates specified) to come into compliance with the standard, and

(v) a certification that he has informed his employees of the application by giving a copy thereof to their authorized representative, posting a statement giving a summary of the application and specifying where a copy may be examined at the place or places where notices to employees are normally posted, and by other appropriate means.

A description of how employees have been informed shall be contained in the certification. The information to employees shall also inform them of their right to petition the Secretary for a hearing.

(C) The Secretary is authorized to grant a variance from any standard or portion thereof whenever he determines, or the Secretary of Health, Education, and Welfare certifies, that such variance is necessary to permit an employer to participate in an experiment approved by him or the Secretary of Health, Education, and Welfare designed to demonstrate or validate new and improved techniques to safeguard the health or safety of workers.

(7) Any standard promulgated under this subsection shall prescribe the use of labels or other appropriate forms of warning as are necessary to insure that employees are apprised of all hazards to which they are exposed, relevant symptoms and appropriate emergency treatment, and proper conditions and precautions of safe use or exposure. Where appropriate, such standard shall also prescribe suitable protective equipment and control or technological procedures to be used in connection with such hazards and shall provide for monitoring or measuring employee exposure at such locations and intervals, and in such manner as may be necessary for the protection of employees. In

> Labels, etc.
>
> Protective equipment, etc.

addition, where appropriate, any such standard shall prescribe the type and frequency of medical examinations or other tests which shall be made available, by the employer or at his cost, to employees exposed to such hazards in order to most effectively determine whether the health of such employees is adversely affected by such exposure. In the event such medical examinations are in the nature of research, as determined by the Secretary of Health, Education, and Welfare, such examinations may be furnished at the expense of the Secretary of Health, Education, and Welfare. The results of such examinations or tests shall be furnished only to the Secretary or the Secretary of Health, Education, and Welfare, and, at the request of the employee, to his physician. The Secretary, in consultation with the Secretary of Health, Education, and Welfare, may by rule promulgated pursuant to section 553 of title 5, United States Code, make appropriate modifications in the foregoing requirements relating to the use of labels or other forms of warning, monitoring or measuring, and medical examinations, as may be warranted by experience, information, or medical or technological developments acquired subsequent to the promulgation of the relevant standard.

Medical examinations.

80 Stat. 383.

(8) Whenever a rule promulgated by the Secretary differs substantially from an existing national consensus standard, the Secretary shall, at the same time, publish in the Federal Register a statement of the reasons why the rule as adopted will better effectuate the purposes of this Act than the national consensus standard.

Publication in Federal Register.

(c)(1) The Secretary shall provide, without regard to the requirements of chapter 5, title 5, United States Code, for an emergency temporary standard to take immediate effect upon publication in the Federal Register if he determines (A) that employees are exposed to grave danger from exposure to substances or agents determined to be toxic or physically harmful or from new hazards, and (B) that such emergency standard is necessary to protect employees from such danger.

Temporary standard. Publication in Federal Register. 80 Stat. 381; 81 Stat. 195. 5 USC 500.

(2) Such standard shall be effective until superseded by a standard promulgated in accordance with the procedures prescribed in paragraph (3) of this subsection.

Time limitation.

(3) Upon publication of such standard in the Federal Register the Secretary shall commence a proceeding in accordance with section 6(b) of this Act, and the standard as published shall also serve as a proposed rule for the proceeding. The Secretary shall promulgate a standard under this paragraph no later than six months after publication of the emergency standard as provided in paragraph (2) of this subsection.

(d) Any affected employer may apply to the Secretary for a rule or order for a variance from a standard promulgated under this section. Affected employees shall be given notice of each such application and an opportunity to participate in a hearing. The Secretary shall issue such rule or order if he determines on the record, after opportunity for an inspection where appropriate and a hearing, that the proponent of the variance has demonstrated by a preponderance of the evidence that the conditions, practices, means, methods, operations, or processes used or proposed to be used by an employer will provide employment and places of employment to his employees which are as safe and healthful as those which would prevail if he complied with the standard. The rule or order so issued shall prescribe the conditions the employer must maintain, and the practices, means, methods, operations, and processes which he must adopt and utilize to the extent they

Variance rule.

differ from the standard in question. Such a rule or order may be modified or revoked upon application by an employer, employees, or by the Secretary on his own motion, in the manner prescribed for its issuance under this subsection at any time after six months from its issuance.

Publication
in Federal
Register.

(e) Whenever the Secretary promulgates any standard, makes any rule, order, or decision, grants any exemption or extension of time, or compromises, mitigates, or settles any penalty assessed under this Act, he shall include a statement of the reasons for such action, which shall be published in the Federal Register.

Petition for
judicial
review.

(f) Any person who may be adversely affected by a standard issued under this section may at any time prior to the sixtieth day after such standard is promulgated file a petition challenging the validity of such standard with the United States court of appeals for the circuit wherein such person resides or has his principal place of business, for a judicial review of such standard. A copy of the petition shall be forthwith transmitted by the clerk of the court to the Secretary. The filing of such petition shall not, unless otherwise ordered by the court, operate as a stay of the standard. The determinations of the Secretary shall be conclusive if supported by substantial evidence in the record considered as a whole.

(g) In determining the priority for establishing standards under this section, the Secretary shall give due regard to the urgency of the need for mandatory safety and health standards for particular industries, trades, crafts, occupations, businesses, workplaces or work environments. The Secretary shall also give due regard to the recommendations of the Secretary of Health, Education, and Welfare regarding the need for mandatory standards in determining the priority for establishing such standards.

ADVISORY COMMITTEES; ADMINISTRATION

Establishment;
membership.

SEC. 7. (a) (1) There is hereby established a National Advisory Committee on Occupational Safety and Health consisting of twelve members appointed by the Secretary, four of whom are to be designated by the Secretary of Health, Education, and Welfare, without regard to the provisions of title 5, United States Code, governing appointments in the competitive service, and composed of representatives of management, labor, occupational safety and occupational health professions, and of the public. The Secretary shall designate one of the public members as Chairman. The members shall be selected upon the basis of their experience and competence in the field of occupational safety and health.

80 Stat. 378.
5 USC 101.

(2) The Committee shall advise, consult with, and make recommendations to the Secretary and the Secretary of Health, Education, and Welfare on matters relating to the administration of the Act. The Committee shall hold no fewer than two meetings during each calendar year. All meetings of the Committee shall be open to the public and a transcript shall be kept and made available for public inspection.

Public tran-
script.

(3) The members of the Committee shall be compensated in accordance with the provisions of section 3109 of title 5, United States Code.

80 Stat. 416.

(4) The Secretary shall furnish to the Committee an executive secretary and such secretarial, clerical, and other services as are deemed necessary to the conduct of its business.

(b) An advisory committee may be appointed by the Secretary to assist him in his standard-setting functions under section 6 of this Act. Each such committee shall consist of not more than fifteen members and shall include as a member one or more designees of the Secretary of Health, Education, and Welfare, and shall include among its members an equal number of persons qualified by experience and affiliation to present the viewpoint of the employers involved, and of persons similarly qualified to present the viewpoint of the workers involved, as well as one or more representatives of health and safety agencies of the States. An advisory committee may also include such other persons as the Secretary may appoint who are qualified by knowledge and experience to make a useful contribution to the work of such committee, including one or more representatives of professional organizations of technicians or professionals specializing in occupational safety or health, and one or more representatives of nationally recognized standards-producing organizations, but the number of persons so appointed to any such advisory committee shall not exceed the number appointed to such committee as representatives of Federal and State agencies. Persons appointed to advisory committees from private life shall be compensated in the same manner as consultants or experts under section 3109 of title 5, United States Code. The Secretary shall pay to any State which is the employer of a member of such a committee who is a representative of the health or safety agency of that State, reimbursement sufficient to cover the actual cost to the State resulting from such representative's membership on such committee. Any meeting of such committee shall be open to the public and an accurate record shall be kept and made available to the public. No member of such committee (other than representatives of employers and employees) shall have an economic interest in any proposed rule.

80 Stat. 416.

Recordkeeping.

(c) In carrying out his responsibilities under this Act, the Secretary is authorized to—

(1) use, with the consent of any Federal agency, the services, facilities, and personnel of such agency, with or without reimbursement, and with the consent of any State or political subdivision thereof, accept and use the services, facilities, and personnel of any agency of such State or subdivision with reimbursement; and

(2) employ experts and consultants or organizations thereof as authorized by section 3109 of title 5, United States Code, except that contracts for such employment may be renewed annually; compensate individuals so employed at rates not in excess of the rate specified at the time of service for grade GS–18 under section 5332 of title 5, United States Code, including traveltime, and allow them while away from their homes or regular places of business, travel expenses (including per diem in lieu of subsistence) as authorized by section 5703 of title 5, United States Code, for persons in the Government service employed intermittently, while so employed.

Ante, p. 198-1.

80 Stat. 499;
83 Stat. 190.

INSPECTIONS. INVESTIGATIONS. AND RECORDKEEPING

SEC. 8. (a) In order to carry out the purposes of this Act, the Secretary, upon presenting appropriate credentials to the owner, operator, or agent in charge, is authorized—

(1) to enter without delay and at reasonable times any factory, plant, establishment, construction site, or other area, workplace or environment where work is performed by an employee of an employer; and

(2) to inspect and investigate during regular working hours and at other reasonable times, and within reasonable limits and in a reasonable manner, any such place of employment and all pertinent conditions, structures, machines, apparatus, devices, equipment, and materials therein, and to question privately any such employer, owner, operator, agent or employee.

Subpoena power.

(b) In making his inspections and investigations under this Act the Secretary may require the attendance and testimony of witnesses and the production of evidence under oath. Witnesses shall be paid the same fees and mileage that are paid witnesses in the courts of the United States. In case of a contumacy, failure, or refusal of any person to obey such an order, any district court of the United States or the United States courts of any territory or possession, within the jurisdiction of which such person is found, or resides or transacts business, upon the application by the Secretary, shall have jurisdiction to issue to such person an order requiring such person to appear to produce evidence if, as, and when so ordered, and to give testimony relating to the matter under investigation or in question, and any failure to obey such order of the court may be punished by said court as a contempt thereof.

Recordkeeping.

(c)(1) Each employer shall make, keep and preserve, and make available to the Secretary or the Secretary of Health, Education, and Welfare, such records regarding his activities relating to this Act as the Secretary, in cooperation with the Secretary of Health, Education, and Welfare, may prescribe by regulation as necessary or appropriate for the enforcement of this Act or for developing information regarding the causes and prevention of occupational accidents and illnesses. In order to carry out the provisions of this paragraph such regulations may include provisions requiring employers to conduct periodic inspections. The Secretary shall also issue regulations requiring that employers, through posting of notices or other appropriate means, keep their employees informed of their protections and obligations under this Act, including the provisions of applicable standards.

Work-related deaths, etc.; reports.

(2) The Secretary, in cooperation with the Secretary of Health, Education, and Welfare, shall prescribe regulations requiring employers to maintain accurate records of, and to make periodic reports on, work-related deaths, injuries and illnesses other than minor injuries requiring only first aid treatment and which do not involve medical treatment, loss of consciousness, restriction of work or motion, or transfer to another job.

(3) The Secretary, in cooperation with the Secretary of Health, Education, and Welfare, shall issue regulations requiring employers to maintain accurate records of employee exposures to potentially toxic materials or harmful physical agents which are required to be monitored or measured under section 6. Such regulations shall provide employees or their representatives with an opportunity to observe such monitoring or measuring, and to have access to the records thereof. Such regulations shall also make appropriate provision for each employee or former employee to have access to such records as will indicate his own exposure to toxic materials or harmful physical agents. Each employer shall promptly notify any employee who has been or is being exposed to toxic materials or harmful physical agents in concentrations or at levels which exceed those prescribed by an applicable occupational safety and health standard promulgated under section 6, and shall inform any employee who is being thus exposed of the corrective action being taken.

(d) Any information obtained by the Secretary, the Secretary of Health, Education, and Welfare, or a State agency under this Act shall be obtained with a minimum burden upon employers, especially those operating small businesses. Unnecessary duplication of efforts in obtaining information shall be reduced to the maximum extent feasible.

(e) Subject to regulations issued by the Secretary, a representative of the employer and a representative authorized by his employees shall be given an opportunity to accompany the Secretary or his authorized representative during the ~~physic~~al inspection of any workplace under subsection (a) for the purpose of aiding such inspection. Where there is no authorized employee representative, the Secretary or his authorized representative shall consult with a reasonable number of employees concerning matters of health and safety in the workplace.

(f)(1) Any employees or representative of employees who believe that a violation of a safety or health standard exists that threatens physical harm, or that an imminent danger exists, may request an inspection by giving notice to the Secretary or his authorized representative of such violation or danger. Any such notice shall be reduced to writing, shall set forth with reasonable particularity the grounds for the notice, and shall be signed by the employees or representative of employees, and a copy shall be provided the employer or his agent no later than at the time of inspection, except that, upon the request of the person giving such notice, his name and the names of individual employees referred to therein shall not appear in such copy or on any record published, released, or made available pursuant to subsection (g) of this section. If upon receipt of such notification the Secretary determines there are reasonable grounds to believe that such violation or danger exists, he shall make a special inspection in accordance with the provisions of this section as soon as practicable, to determine if such violation or danger exists. If the Secretary determines there are no reasonable grounds to believe that a violation or danger exists he shall notify the employees or representative of the employees in writing of such determination.

(2) Prior to or during any inspection of a workplace, any employees or representative of employees employed in such workplace may notify the Secretary or any representative of the Secretary responsible for conducting the inspection, in writing, of any violation of this Act which they have reason to believe exists in such workplace. The Secretary shall, by regulation, establish procedures for informal review of any refusal by a representative of the Secretary to issue a citation with respect to any such alleged violation and shall furnish the employees or representative of employees requesting such review a written statement of the reasons for the Secretary's final disposition of the case.

(g)(1) The Secretary and Secretary of Health, Education, and Welfare are authorized to compile, analyze, and publish, either in summary or detailed form, all reports or information obtained under this section. *Reports, publication.*

(2) The Secretary and the Secretary of Health, Education, and Welfare shall each prescribe such rules and regulations as he may deem necessary to carry out their responsibilities under this Act, including rules and regulations dealing with the inspection of an employer's establishment. *Rules and regulations.*

CITATIONS

SEC. 9. (a) If, upon inspection or investigation, the Secretary or his authorized representative believes that an employer has violated a requirement of section 5 of this Act, of any standard, rule or order promulgated pursuant to section 6 of this Act. or of any regulations prescribed pursuant to this Act, he shall with reasonable promptness issue a citation to the employer. Each citation shall be in writing and shall describe with particularity the nature of the violation, including a reference to the provision of the Act, standard, rule, regulation, or order alleged to have been violated. In addition, the citation shall fix a reasonable time for the abatement of the violation. The Secretary may prescribe procedures for the issuance of a notice in lieu of a citation with respect to de minimis violations which have no direct or immediate relationship to safety or health.

(b) Each citation issued under this section, or a copy or copies thereof, shall be prominently posted, as prescribed in regulations issued by the Secretary, at or near each place a violation referred to in the citation occurred.

(c) No citation may be issued under this section after the expiration of six months following the occurrence of any violation.

PROCEDURE FOR ENFORCEMENT

SEC. 10. (a) If, after an inspection or investigation, the Secretary issues a citation under section 9(a), he shall, within a reasonable time after the termination of such inspection or investigation, notify the employer by certified mail of the penalty, if any, proposed to be assessed under section 17 and that the employer has fifteen working days within which to notify the Secretary that he wishes to contest the citation or proposed assessment of penalty. If, within fifteen working days from the receipt of the notice issued by the Secretary the employer fails to notify the Secretary that he intends to contest the citation or proposed assessment of penalty, and no notice is filed by any employee or representative of employees under subsection (c) within such time, the citation and the assessment, as proposed, shall be deemed a final order of the Commission and not subject to review by any court or agency.

(b) If the Secretary has reason to believe that an employer has failed to correct a violation for which a citation has been issued within the period permitted for its correction (which period shall not begin to run until the entry of a final order by the Commission in the case of any review proceedings under this section initiated by the employer in good faith and not solely for delay or avoidance of penalties), the Secretary shall notify the employer by certified mail of such failure and of the penalty proposed to be assessed under section 17 by reason of such failure, and that the employer has fifteen working days within which to notify the Secretary that he wishes to contest the Secretary's notification or the proposed assessment of penalty. If, within fifteen working days from the receipt of notification issued by the Secretary, the employer fails to notify the Secretary that he intends to contest the notification or proposed assessment of penalty, the notification and assessment, as proposed, shall be deemed a final order of the Commission and not subject to review by any court or agency.

(c) If an employer notifies the Secretary that he intends to contest a citation issued under section 9(a) or notification issued under subsection (a) or (b) of this section, or if, within fifteen working days of the issuance of a citation under section 9(a), any employee or representative of employees files a notice with the Secretary alleging that the period of time fixed in the citation for the abatement of the violation is unreasonable, the Secretary shall immediately advise the Commission of such notification, and the Commission shall afford an opportunity for a hearing (in accordance with section 554 of title 5, United States Code, but without regard to subsection (a)(3) of such section). The Commission shall thereafter issue an order, based on findings of fact, affirming, modifying, or vacating the Secretary's citation or proposed penalty, or directing other appropriate relief, and such order shall become final thirty days after its issuance. Upon a showing by an employer of a good faith effort to comply with the abatement requirements of a citation, and that abatement has not been completed because of factors beyond his reasonable control, the Secretary, after an opportunity for a hearing as provided in this subsection, shall issue an order affirming or modifying the abatement requirements in such citation. The rules of procedure prescribed by the Commission shall provide affected employees or representatives of affected employees an opportunity to participate as parties to hearings under this subsection.

80 Stat. 384.

JUDICIAL REVIEW

Sec. 11. (a) Any person adversely affected or aggrieved by an order of the Commission issued under subsection (c) of section 10 may obtain a review of such order in any United States court of appeals for the circuit in which the violation is alleged to have occurred or where the employer has its principal office, or in the Court of Appeals for the District of Columbia Circuit, by filing in such court within sixty days following the issuance of such order a written petition praying that the order be modified or set aside. A copy of such petition shall be forthwith transmitted by the clerk of the court to the Commission and to the other parties, and thereupon the Commission shall file in the court the record in the proceeding as provided in section 2112 of title 28, United States Code. Upon such filing, the court shall have jurisdiction of the proceeding and of the question determined therein, and shall have power to grant such temporary relief or restraining order as it deems just and proper, and to make and enter upon the pleadings, testimony, and proceedings set forth in such record a decree affirming, modifying, or setting aside in whole or in part, the order of the Commission and enforcing the same to the extent that such order is affirmed or modified. The commencement of proceedings under this subsection shall not, unless ordered by the court, operate as a stay of the order of the Commission. No objection that has not been urged before the Commission shall be considered by the court, unless the failure or neglect to urge such objection shall be excused because of extraordinary circumstances. The findings of the Commission with respect to questions of fact, if supported by substantial evidence on the record considered as a whole, shall be conclusive. If any party shall apply to the court for leave to adduce additional evidence and shall show to the satisfaction of the court that such additional evidence is material and that there were reasonable grounds for the failure to adduce such evidence in the hearing before the Commission, the court may order such additional evidence to be taken before the Commission and to be made a part of the record. The Commission may modify its findings as to the facts, or make new findings, by reason of additional evidence so taken and filed, and it shall file such modified or new findings, which findings with respect to questions of fact, if supported by substantial evi-

72 Stat. 941;
80 Stat. 1323.

62 Stat. 928.

dence on the record considered as a whole, shall be conclusive, and its recommendations, if any, for the modification or setting aside of its original order. Upon the filing of the record with it, the jurisdiction of the court shall be exclusive and its judgment and decree shall be final, except that the same shall be subject to review by the Supreme Court of the United States, as provided in section 1254 of title 28, United States Code. Petitions filed under this subsection shall be heard expeditiously.

(b) The Secretary may also obtain review or enforcement of any final order of the Commission by filing a petition for such relief in the United States court of appeals for the circuit in which the alleged violation occurred or in which the employer has its principal office, and the provisions of subsection (a) shall govern such proceedings to the extent applicable. If no petition for review, as provided in subsection (a), is filed within sixty days after service of the Commission's order, the Commission's findings of fact and order shall be conclusive in connection with any petition for enforcement which is filed by the Secretary after the expiration of such sixty-day period. In any such case, as well as in the case of a noncontested citation or notification by the Secretary which has become a final order of the Commission under subsection (a) or (b) of section 10, the clerk of the court, unless otherwise ordered by the court, shall forthwith enter a decree enforcing the order and shall transmit a copy of such decree to the Secretary and the employer named in the petition. In any contempt proceeding brought to enforce a decree of a court of appeals entered pursuant to this subsection or subsection (a), the court of appeals may assess the penalties provided in section 17, in addition to invoking any other available remedies.

(c) (1) No person shall discharge or in any manner discriminate against any employee because such employee has filed any complaint or instituted or caused to be instituted any proceeding under or related to this Act or has testified or is about to testify in any such proceeding or because of the exercise by such employee on behalf of himself or others of any right afforded by this Act.

(2) Any employee who believes that he has been discharged or otherwise discriminated against by any person in violation of this subsection may, within thirty days after such violation occurs, file a complaint with the Secretary alleging such discrimination. Upon receipt of such complaint, the Secretary shall cause such investigation to be made as he deems appropriate. If upon such investigation, the Secretary determines that the provisions of this subsection have been violated, he shall bring an action in any appropriate United States district court against such person. In any such action the United States district courts shall have jurisdiction, for cause shown to restrain violations of paragraph (1) of this subsection and order all appropriate relief including rehiring or reinstatement of the employee to his former position with back pay.

(3) Within 90 days of the receipt of a complaint filed under this subsection the Secretary shall notify the complainant of his determination under paragraph 2 of this subsection.

THE OCCUPATIONAL SAFETY AND HEALTH REVIEW COMMISSION

Establishment; membership.

SEC. 12. (a) The Occupational Safety and Health Review Commission is hereby established. The Commission shall be composed of three members who shall be appointed by the President, by and with the advice and consent of the Senate, from among persons who by reason of training, education, or experience are qualified to carry out the functions of the Commission under this Act. The President shall designate one of the members of the Commission to serve as Chairman.

(b) The terms of members of the Commission shall be six years **Terms.** except that (1) the members of the Commission first taking office shall serve, as designated by the President at the time of appointment, one for a term of two years, one for a term of four years, and one for a term of six years, and (2) a vacancy caused by the death, resignation, or removal of a member prior to the expiration of the term for which he was appointed shall be filled only for the remainder of such unexpired term. A member of the Commission may be removed by the President for inefficiency, neglect of duty, or malfeasance in office.

(c)(1) Section 5314 of title 5, United States Code, is amended by **80 Stat. 460.** adding at the end thereof the following new paragraph:

"(57) Chairman, Occupational Safety and Health Review Commission."

(2) Section 5315 of title 5, United States Code, is amended by add- **Ante, p. 776.** ing at the end thereof the following new paragraph:

"(94) Members, Occupational Safety and Health Review Commission."

(d) The principal office of the Commission shall be in the District **Location.** of Columbia. Whenever the Commission deems that the convenience of the public or of the parties may be promoted, or delay or expense may be minimized, it may hold hearings or conduct other proceedings at any other place.

(e) The Chairman shall be responsible on behalf of the Commission for the administrative operations of the Commission and shall appoint such hearing examiners and other employees as he deems necessary to assist in the performance of the Commission's functions and to fix their compensation in accordance with the provisions of chapter 51 and subchapter III of chapter 53 of title 5, United States Code, **5 USC 5101,** relating to classification and General Schedule pay rates: *Provided*, **5331.** That assignment, removal and compensation of hearing examiners **Ante, p. 198-1.** shall be in accordance with sections 3105, 3344, 5362, and 7521 of title 5, United States Code.

(f) For the purpose of carrying out its functions under this Act, two **Quorum.** members of the Commission shall constitute a quorum and official action can be taken only on the affirmative vote of at least two members.

(g) Every official act of the Commission shall be entered of record, **Public records.** and its hearings and records shall be open to the public. The Commission is authorized to make such rules as are necessary for the orderly transaction of its proceedings. Unless the Commission has adopted a different rule, its proceedings shall be in accordance with the Federal Rules of Civil Procedure. **28 USC app.**

(h) The Commission may order testimony to be taken by deposition in any proceedings pending before it at any state of such proceeding. Any person may be compelled to appear and depose, and to produce books, papers, or documents, in the same manner as witnesses may be compelled to appear and testify and produce like documentary evidence before the Commission. Witnesses whose depositions are taken under this subsection, and the persons taking such depositions, shall be entitled to the same fees as are paid for like services in the courts of the United States.

(i) For the purpose of any proceeding before the Commission, the provisions of section 11 of the National Labor Relations Act (29 U.S.C. 161) are hereby made applicable to the jurisdiction and powers **61 Stat. 150;** of the Commission. **Ante, p. 930.**

84 STAT. 1605

Report.

(j) A hearing examiner appointed by the Commission shall hear, and make a determination upon, any proceeding instituted before the Commission and any motion in connection therewith, assigned to such hearing examiner by the Chairman of the Commission, and shall make a report of any such determination which constitutes his final disposition of the proceedings. The report of the hearing examiner shall become the final order of the Commission within thirty days after such report by the hearing examiner, unless within such period any Commission member has directed that such report shall be reviewed by the Commission.

(k) Except as otherwise provided in this Act, the hearing examiners shall be subject to the laws governing employees in the classified civil service, except that appointments shall be made without regard to section 5108 of title 5, United States Code. Each hearing examiner shall receive compensation at a rate not less than that prescribed for GS–16 under section 5332 of title 5, United States Code.

80 Stat. 453.

Ante, p. 198-1.

PROCEDURES TO COUNTERACT IMMINENT DANGERS

Sec. 13. (a) The United States district courts shall have jurisdiction, upon petition of the Secretary, to restrain any conditions or practices in any place of employment which are such that a danger exists which could reasonably be expected to cause death or serious physical harm immediately or before the imminence of such danger can be eliminated through the enforcement procedures otherwise provided by this Act. Any order issued under this section may require such steps to be taken as may be necessary to avoid, correct, or remove such imminent danger and prohibit the employment or presence of any individual in locations or under conditions where such imminent danger exists, except individuals whose presence is necessary to avoid, correct, or remove such imminent danger or to maintain the capacity of a continuous process operation to resume normal operations without a complete cessation of operations, or where a cessation of operations is necessary, to permit such to be accomplished in a safe and orderly manner.

(b) Upon the filing of any such petition the district court shall have jurisdiction to grant such injunctive relief or temporary restraining order pending the outcome of an enforcement proceeding pursuant to this Act. The proceeding shall be as provided by Rule 65 of the Federal Rules, Civil Procedure, except that no temporary restraining order issued without notice shall be effective for a period longer than five days.

28 USC app.

(c) Whenever and as soon as an inspector concludes that conditions or practices described in subsection (a) exist in any place of employment, he shall inform the affected employees and employers of the danger and that he is recommending to the Secretary that relief be sought.

(d) If the Secretary arbitrarily or capriciously fails to seek relief under this section, any employee who may be injured by reason of such failure, or the representative of such employees, might bring an action against the Secretary in the United States district court for the district in which the imminent danger is alleged to exist or the employer has its principal office, or for the District of Columbia, for a writ of mandamus to compel the Secretary to seek such an order and for such further relief as may be appropriate.

REPRESENTATION IN CIVIL LITIGATION

SEC. 14. Except as provided in section 518(a) of title 28, United States Code, relating to litigation before the Supreme Court, the Solicitor of Labor may appear for and represent the Secretary in any civil litigation brought under this Act but all such litigation shall be subject to the direction and control of the Attorney General.

80 Stat. 613.

CONFIDENTIALITY OF TRADE SECRETS

SEC. 15. All information reported to or otherwise obtained by the Secretary or his representative in connection with any inspection or proceeding under this Act which contains or which might reveal a trade secret referred to in section 1905 of title 18 of the United States Code shall be considered confidential for the purpose of that section, except that such information may be disclosed to other officers or employees concerned with carrying out this Act or when relevant in any proceeding under this Act. In any such proceeding the Secretary, the Commission, or the court shall issue such orders as may be appropriate to protect the confidentiality of trade secrets.

62 Stat. 791.

VARIATIONS, TOLERANCES, AND EXEMPTIONS

SEC. 16. The Secretary, on the record, after notice and opportunity for a hearing may provide such reasonable limitations and may make such rules and regulations allowing reasonable variations, tolerances, and exemptions to and from any or all provisions of this Act as he may find necessary and proper to avoid serious impairment of the national defense. Such action shall not be in effect for more than six months without notification to affected employees and an opportunity being afforded for a hearing.

PENALTIES

SEC. 17. (a) Any employer who willfully or repeatedly violates the requirements of section 5 of this Act, any standard, rule, or order promulgated pursuant to section 6 of this Act, or regulations prescribed pursuant to this Act, may be assessed a civil penalty of not more than $10,000 for each violation.

(b) Any employer who has received a citation for a serious violation of the requirements of section 5 of this Act, of any standard, rule, or order promulgated pursuant to section 6 of this Act, or of any regulations prescribed pursuant to this Act, shall be assessed a civil penalty of up to $1,000 for each such violation.

(c) Any employer who has received a citation for a violation of the requirements of section 5 of this Act, of any standard, rule, or order promulgated pursuant to section 6 of this Act, or of regulations prescribed pursuant to this Act, and such violation is specifically determined not to be of a serious nature, may be assessed a civil penalty of up to $1,000 for each such violation.

(d) Any employer who fails to correct a violation for which a citation has been issued under section 9(a) within the period permitted for its correction (which period shall not begin to run until the date of the final order of the Commission in the case of any review proceeding under section 10 initiated by the employer in good faith and not solely for delay or avoidance of penalties), may be assessed a civil penalty of not more than $1,000 for each day during which such failure or violation continues.

(e) Any employer who willfully violates any standard, rule, or order promulgated pursuant to section 6 of this Act, or of any regulations prescribed pursuant to this Act, and that violation caused death to any employee, shall, upon conviction, be punished by a fine of not more than $10,000 or by imprisonment for not more than six months, or by both; except that if the conviction is for a violation committed after a first conviction of such person, punishment shall be by a fine of not more than $20,000 or by imprisonment for not more than one year, or by both.

(f) Any person who gives advance notice of any inspection to be conducted under this Act, without authority from the Secretary or his designees, shall, upon conviction, be punished by a fine of not more than $1,000 or by imprisonment for not more than six months, or by both.

(g) Whoever knowingly makes any false statement, representation, or certification in any application, record, report, plan, or other document filed or required to be maintained pursuant to this Act shall, upon conviction, be punished by a fine of not more than $10,000, or by imprisonment for not more than six months, or by both.

65 Stat. 721;
79 Stat. 234.

(h)(1) Section 1114 of title 18, United States Code, is hereby amended by striking out "designated by the Secretary of Health, Education, and Welfare to conduct investigations, or inspections under the Federal Food, Drug, and Cosmetic Act" and inserting in lieu thereof "or of the Department of Labor assigned to perform investigative, inspection, or law enforcement functions".

62 Stat. 756.

(2) Notwithstanding the provisions of sections 1111 and 1114 of title 18, United States Code, whoever, in violation of the provisions of section 1114 of such title, kills a person while engaged in or on account of the performance of investigative, inspection, or law enforcement functions added to such section 1114 by paragraph (1) of this subsection, and who would otherwise be subject to the penalty provisions of such section 1111, shall be punished by imprisonment for any term of years or for life.

(i) Any employer who violates any of the posting requirements, as prescribed under the provisions of this Act, shall be assessed a civil penalty of up to $1,000 for each violation.

(j) The Commission shall have authority to assess all civil penalties provided in this section, giving due consideration to the appropriateness of the penalty with respect to the size of the business of the employer being charged, the gravity of the violation, the good faith of the employer, and the history of previous violations.

(k) For purposes of this section, a serious violation shall be deemed to exist in a place of employment if there is a substantial probability that death or serious physical harm could result from a condition which exists, or from one or more practices, means, methods, operations, or processes which have been adopted or are in use, in such place of employment unless the employer did not, and could not with the exercise of reasonable diligence, know of the presence of the violation.

(l) Civil penalties owed under this Act shall be paid to the Secretary for deposit into the Treasury of the United States and shall accrue to the United States and may be recovered in a civil action in the name of the United States brought in the United States district court for the district where the violation is alleged to have occurred or where the employer has its principal office.

STATE JURISDICTION AND STATE PLANS

Sec. 18. (a) Nothing in this Act shall prevent any State agency or court from asserting jurisdiction under State law over any occupational safety or health issue with respect to which no standard is in effect under section 6.

(b) Any State which, at any time, desires to assume responsibility for development and enforcement therein of occupational safety and health standards relating to any occupational safety or health issue with respect to which a Federal standard has been promulgated under section 6 shall submit a State plan for the development of such standards and their enforcement.

(c) The Secretary shall approve the plan submitted by a State under subsection (b), or any modification thereof, if such plan in his judgment—

(1) designates a State agency or agencies as the agency or agencies responsible for administering the plan throughout the State,

(2) provides for the development and enforcement of safety and health standards relating to one or more safety or health issues, which standards (and the enforcement of which standards) are or will be at least as effective in providing safe and healthful employment and places of employment as the standards promulgated under section 6 which relate to the same issues, and which standards, when applicable to products which are distributed or used in interstate commerce, are required by compelling local conditions and do not unduly burden interstate commerce,

(3) provides for a right of entry and inspection of all workplaces subject to the Act which is at least as effective as that provided in section 8, and includes a prohibition on advance notice of inspections,

(4) contains satisfactory assurances that such agency or agencies have or will have the legal authority and qualified personnel necessary for the enforcement of such standards,

(5) gives satisfactory assurances that such State will devote adequate funds to the administration and enforcement of such standards,

(6) contains satisfactory assurances that such State will, to the extent permitted by its law, establish and maintain an effective and comprehensive occupational safety and health program applicable to all employees of public agencies of the State and its political subdivisions, which program is as effective as the standards contained in an approved plan,

(7) requires employers in the State to make reports to the Secretary in the same manner and to the same extent as if the plan were not in effect, and

(8) provides that the State agency will make such reports to the Secretary in such form and containing such information, as the Secretary shall from time to time require.

(d) If the Secretary rejects a plan submitted under subsection (b), he shall afford the State submitting the plan due notice and opportunity for a hearing before so doing. **Notice of hearing.**

(e) After the Secretary approves a State plan submitted under subsection (b), he may, but shall not be required to, exercise his authority under sections 8, 9, 10, 13, and 17 with respect to comparable standards promulgated under section 6, for the period specified in the next sentence. The Secretary may exercise the authority referred to above until he determines, on the basis of actual operations under the

State plan, that the criteria set forth in subsection (c) are being
applied, but he shall not make such determination for at least three
years after the plan's approval under subsection (c). Upon making the
determination referred to in the preceding sentence, the provisions of
sections 5(a)(2), 8 (except for the purpose of carrying out subsection
(f) of this section), 9, 10, 13, and 17, and standards promulgated under
section 6 of this Act, shall not apply with respect to any occupational
safety or health issues covered under the plan, but the Secretary may
retain jurisdiction under the above provisions in any proceeding commenced under section 9 or 10 before the date of determination.

Continuing evaluation.

(f) The Secretary shall, on the basis of reports submitted by the
State agency and his own inspections make a continuing evaluation of
the manner in which each State having a plan approved under this
section is carrying out such plan. Whenever the Secretary finds, after
affording due notice and opportunity for a hearing, that in the administration of the State plan there is a failure to comply substantially
with any provision of the State plan (or any assurance contained
therein), he shall notify the State agency of his withdrawal of
approval of such plan and upon receipt of such notice such plan shall
cease to be in effect, but the State may retain jurisdiction in any case
commenced before the withdrawal of the plan in order to enforce
standards under the plan whenever the issues involved do not relate
to the reasons for the withdrawal of the plan.

Plan rejection, review.

(g) The State may obtain a review of a decision of the Secretary
withdrawing approval of or rejecting its plan by the United States
court of appeals for the circuit in which the State is located by filing
in such court within thirty days following receipt of notice of such
decision a petition to modify or set aside in whole or in part the action
of the Secretary. A copy of such petition shall forthwith be served
upon the Secretary, and thereupon the Secretary shall certify and file
in the court the record upon which the decision complained of was

72 Stat. 941; 80 Stat. 1323.

issued as provided in section 2112 of title 28, United States Code.
Unless the court finds that the Secretary's decision in rejecting a proposed State plan or withdrawing his approval of such a plan is not supported by substantial evidence the court shall affirm the Secretary's
decision. The judgment of the court shall be subject to review by the
Supreme Court of the United States upon certiorari or certification

62 Stat. 928.

as provided in section 1254 of title 28, United States Code.

(h) The Secretary may enter into an agreement with a State under
which the State will be permitted to continue to enforce one or more
occupational health and safety standards in effect in such State until
final action is taken by the Secretary with respect to a plan submitted
by a State under subsection (b) of this section, or two years from the
date of enactment of this Act, whichever is earlier.

FEDERAL AGENCY SAFETY PROGRAMS AND RESPONSIBILITIES

SEC. 19. (a) It shall be the responsibility of the head of each Federal agency to establish and maintain an effective and comprehensive
occupational safety and health program which is consistent with the
standards promulgated under section 6. The head of each agency shall
(after consultation with representatives of the employees thereof)—

(1) provide safe and healthful places and conditions of employment, consistent with the standards set under section 6;

(2) acquire, maintain, and require the use of safety equipment,
personal protective equipment, and devices reasonably necessary
to protect employees;

(3) keep adequate records of all occupational accidents and ill-   Recordkeeping.
nesses for proper evaluation and necessary corrective action;

(4) consult with the Secretary with regard to the adequacy as
to form and content of records kept pursuant to subsection (a)(3)
of this section; and

(5) make an annual report to the Secretary with respect to   Annual report.
occupational accidents and injuries and the agency's program
under this section. Such report shall include any report submitted
under section 7902(e)(2) of title 5, United States Code.   80 Stat. 530.

(b) The Secretary shall report to the President a summary or digest   Report to President.
of reports submitted to him under subsection (a)(5) of this section,
together with his evaluations of and recommendations derived from
such reports. The President shall transmit annually to the Senate and   Report to Congress.
the House of Representatives a report of the activities of Federal
agencies under this section.

(c) Section 7902(c)(1) of title 5, United States Code, is amended
by inserting after "agencies" the following: "and of labor organizations representing employees".

(d) The Secretary shall have access to records and reports kept   Records, etc.; availability.
and filed by Federal agencies pursuant to subsections (a)(3) and (5)
of this section unless those records and reports are specifically required
by Executive order to be kept secret in the interest of the national
defense or foreign policy, in which case the Secretary shall have access
to such information as will not jeopardize national defense or foreign
policy.

RESEARCH AND RELATED ACTIVITIES

SEC. 20. (a)(1) The Secretary of Health, Education, and Welfare,
after consultation with the Secretary and with other appropriate
Federal departments or agencies, shall conduct (directly or by grants
or contracts) research, experiments, and demonstrations relating to
occupational safety and health, including studies of psychological
factors involved, and relating to innovative methods, techniques, and
approaches for dealing with occupational safety and health problems.

(2) The Secretary of Health, Education, and Welfare shall from
time to time consult with the Secretary in order to develop specific
plans for such research, demonstrations, and experiments as are necessary to produce criteria, including criteria identifying toxic substances, enabling the Secretary to meet his responsibility for the
formulation of safety and health standards under this Act; and the
Secretary of Health, Education, and Welfare, on the basis of such
research, demonstrations, and experiments and any other information
available to him, shall develop and publish at least annually such
criteria as will effectuate the purposes of this Act.

(3) The Secretary of Health, Education, and Welfare, on the basis
of such research, demonstrations, and experiments, and any other
information available to him, shall develop criteria dealing with toxic
materials and harmful physical agents and substances which will
describe exposure levels that are safe for various periods of employment, including but not limited to the exposure levels at which no
employee will suffer impaired health or functional capacities or
diminished life expectancy as a result of his work experience.

(4) The Secretary of Health, Education, and Welfare shall also
conduct special research, experiments, and demonstrations relating
to occupational safety and health as are necessary to explore new
problems, including those created by new technology in occupational
safety and health, which may require ameliorative action beyond that

which is otherwise provided for in the operating provisions of this Act. The Secretary of Health, Education, and Welfare shall also conduct research into the motivational and behavioral factors relating to the field of occupational safety and health.

Toxic substances, records.

(5) The Secretary of Health, Education, and Welfare, in order to comply with his responsibilities under paragraph (2), and in order to develop needed information regarding potentially toxic substances or harmful physical agents, may prescribe regulations requiring employers to measure, record, and make reports on the exposure of employees to substances or physical agents which the Secretary of Health, Education, and Welfare reasonably believes may endanger the health or safety of employees. The Secretary of Health, Education, and Welfare also is authorized to establish such programs of medical examinations and tests as may be necessary for determining the incidence of occupational illnesses and the susceptibility of employees to such illnesses. Nothing in this or any other provision of this Act shall be deemed to authorize or require medical examination, immunization, or treatment for those who object thereto on religious grounds, except where such is necessary for the protection of the health or safety of others. Upon the request of any employer who is required to measure and record exposure of employees to substances or physical agents as provided under this subsection, the Secretary of Health, Education, and Welfare shall furnish full financial or other assistance to such employer for the purpose of defraying any additional expense incurred by him in carrying out the measuring and recording as provided in this subsection.

Medical examinations.

Toxic substances, publication.

(6) The Secretary of Health, Education, and Welfare shall publish within six months of enactment of this Act and thereafter as needed but at least annually a list of all known toxic substances by generic family or other useful grouping, and the concentrations at which such toxicity is known to occur. He shall determine following a written request by any employer or authorized representative of employees, specifying with reasonable particularity the grounds on which the request is made, whether any substance normally found in the place of employment has potentially toxic effects in such concentrations as used or found; and shall submit such determination both to employers and affected employees as soon as possible. If the Secretary of Health, Education, and Welfare determines that any substance is potentially toxic at the concentrations in which it is used or found in a place of employment, and such substance is not covered by an occupational safety or health standard promulgated under section 6, the Secretary of Health, Education, and Welfare shall immediately submit such determination to the Secretary, together with all pertinent criteria.

Annual studies.

(7) Within two years of enactment of this Act, and annually thereafter the Secretary of Health, Education, and Welfare shall conduct and publish industrywide studies of the effect of chronic or low-level exposure to industrial materials, processes, and stresses on the potential for illness, disease, or loss of functional capacity in aging adults.

Inspections.

(b) The Secretary of Health, Education, and Welfare is authorized to make inspections and question employers and employees as provided in section 8 of this Act in order to carry out his functions and responsibilities under this section.

Contract authority.

(c) The Secretary is authorized to enter into contracts, agreements, or other arrangements with appropriate public agencies or private organizations for the purpose of conducting studies relating to his responsibilities under this Act. In carrying out his responsibilities under this subsection, the Secretary shall cooperate with the Secretary of Health, Education, and Welfare in order to avoid any duplication of efforts under this section.

(d) Information obtained by the Secretary and the Secretary of Health, Education, and Welfare under this section shall be disseminated by the Secretary to employers and employees and organizations thereof.

(e) The functions of the Secretary of Health, Education, and Welfare under this Act shall, to the extent feasible, be delegated to the Director of the National Institute for Occupational Safety and Health established by section 22 of this Act.

Delegation of functions.

TRAINING AND EMPLOYEE EDUCATION

SEC. 21. (a) The Secretary of Health, Education, and Welfare, after consultation with the Secretary and with other appropriate Federal departments and agencies, shall conduct, directly or by grants or contracts (1) education programs to provide an adequate supply of qualified personnel to carry out the purposes of this Act, and (2) informational programs on the importance of and proper use of adequate safety and health equipment.

(b) The Secretary is also authorized to conduct, directly or by grants or contracts, short-term training of personnel engaged in work related to his responsibilities under this Act.

(c) The Secretary, in consultation with the Secretary of Health, Education, and Welfare, shall (1) provide for the establishment and supervision of programs for the education and training of employers and employees in the recognition, avoidance, and prevention of unsafe or unhealthful working conditions in employments covered by this Act, and (2) consult with and advise employers and employees, and organizations representing employers and employees as to effective means of preventing occupational injuries and illnesses.

NATIONAL INSTITUTE FOR OCCUPATIONAL SAFETY AND HEALTH

SEC. 22. (a) It is the purpose of this section to establish a National Institute for Occupational Safety and Health in the Department of Health, Education, and Welfare in order to carry out the policy set forth in section 2 of this Act and to perform the functions of the Secretary of Health, Education, and Welfare under sections 20 and 21 of this Act.

Establishment.

(b) There is hereby established in the Department of Health, Education, and Welfare a National Institute for Occupational Safety and Health. The Institute shall be headed by a Director who shall be appointed by the Secretary of Health, Education, and Welfare, and who shall serve for a term of six years unless previously removed by the Secretary of Health, Education, and Welfare.

Director, appointment, term.

(c) The Institute is authorized to—

(1) develop and establish recommended occupational safety and health standards; and

(2) perform all functions of the Secretary of Health, Education, and Welfare under sections 20 and 21 of this Act.

(d) Upon his own initiative, or upon the request of the Secretary or the Secretary of Health, Education, and Welfare, the Director is authorized (1) to conduct such research and experimental programs as he determines are necessary for the development of criteria for new and improved occupational safety and health standards, and (2) after consideration of the results of such research and experimental programs make recommendations concerning new or improved occupational safety and health standards. Any occupational safety and health standard recommended pursuant to this section shall immediately be forwarded to the Secretary of Labor, and to the Secretary of Health, Education, and Welfare.

(e) In addition to any authority vested in the Institute by other provisions of this section, the Director, in carrying out the functions of the Institute, is authorized to—

(1) prescribe such regulations as he deems necessary governing the manner in which its functions shall be carried out;

(2) receive money and other property donated, bequeathed, or devised, without condition or restriction other than that it be used for the purposes of the Institute and to use, sell, or otherwise dispose of such property for the purpose of carrying out its functions;

(3) receive (and use, sell, or otherwise dispose of, in accordance with paragraph (2)), money and other property donated, bequeathed, or devised to the Institute with a condition or restriction, including a condition that the Institute use other funds of the Institute for the purposes of the gift;

(4) in accordance with the civil service laws, appoint and fix the compensation of such personnel as may be necessary to carry out the provisions of this section;

80 Stat. 416.

(5) obtain the services of experts and consultants in accordance with the provisions of section 3109 of title 5, United States Code;

(6) accept and utilize the services of voluntary and noncompensated personnel and reimburse them for travel expenses, including per diem, as authorized by section 5703 of title 5, United States Code;

83 Stat. 190.

(7) enter into contracts, grants or other arrangements, or modifications thereof to carry out the provisions of this section, and such contracts or modifications thereof may be entered into without performance or other bonds, and without regard to section 3709 of the Revised Statutes, as amended (41 U.S.C. 5), or any other provision of law relating to competitive bidding;

(8) make advance, progress, and other payments which the Director deems necessary under this title without regard to the provisions of section 3648 of the Revised Statutes, as amended (31 U.S.C. 529); and

(9) make other necessary expenditures.

Annual report to HEW, President, and Congress.

(f) The Director shall submit to the Secretary of Health, Education, and Welfare, to the President, and to the Congress an annual report of the operations of the Institute under this Act, which shall include a detailed statement of all private and public funds received and expended by it, and such recommendations as he deems appropriate.

GRANTS TO THE STATES

SEC. 23. (a) The Secretary is authorized, during the fiscal year ending June 30, 1971, and the two succeeding fiscal years, to make grants to the States which have designated a State agency under section 18 to assist them—

(1) in identifying their needs and responsibilities in the area of occupational safety and health,

(2) in developing State plans under section 18, or

(3) in developing plans for—

(A) establishing systems for the collection of information concerning the nature and frequency of occupational injuries and diseases;

(B) increasing the expertise and enforcement capabilities of their personnel engaged in occupational safety and health programs; or

(C) otherwise improving the administration and enforcement of State occupational safety and health laws, including standards thereunder, consistent with the objectives of this Act.

(b) The Secretary is authorized, during the fiscal year ending June 30, 1971, and the two succeeding fiscal years, to make grants to the States for experimental and demonstration projects consistent with the objectives set forth in subsection (a) of this section.

(c) The Governor of the State shall designate the appropriate State agency for receipt of any grant made by the Secretary under this section.

(d) Any State agency designated by the Governor of the State desiring a grant under this section shall submit an application therefor to the Secretary.

(e) The Secretary shall review the application, and shall, after consultation with the Secretary of Health, Education, and Welfare, approve or reject such application.

(f) The Federal share for each State grant under subsection (a) or (b) of this section may not exceed 90 per centum of the total cost of the application. In the event the Federal share for all States under either such subsection is not the same, the differences among the States shall be established on the basis of objective criteria.

(g) The Secretary is authorized to make grants to the States to assist them in administering and enforcing programs for occupational safety and health contained in State plans approved by the Secretary pursuant to section 18 of this Act. The Federal share for each State grant under this subsection may not exceed 50 per centum of the total cost to the State of such a program. The last sentence of subsection (f) shall be applicable in determining the Federal share under this subsection.

(h) Prior to June 30, 1973, the Secretary shall, after consultation with the Secretary of Health, Education, and Welfare, transmit a report to the President and to the Congress, describing the experience under the grant programs authorized by this section and making any recommendations he may deem appropriate.

Report to President and Congress.

STATISTICS

SEC. 24. (a) In order to further the purposes of this Act, the Secretary, in consultation with the Secretary of Health, Education, and Welfare, shall develop and maintain an effective program of collection, compilation, and analysis of occupational safety and health statistics. Such program may cover all employments whether or not subject to any other provisions of this Act but shall not cover employments excluded by section 4 of the Act. The Secretary shall compile accurate statistics on work injuries and illnesses which shall include all disabling, serious, or significant injuries and illnesses, whether or not involving loss of time from work, other than minor injuries requiring only first aid treatment and which do not involve medical treatment, loss of consciousness, restriction of work or motion, or transfer to another job.

(b) To carry out his duties under subsection (a) of this section, the Secretary may—

(1) promote, encourage, or directly engage in programs of studies, information and communication concerning occupational safety and health statistics;

(2) make grants to States or political subdivisions thereof in order to assist them in developing and administering programs dealing with occupational safety and health statistics; and

(3) arrange, through grants or contracts, for the conduct of such research and investigations as give promise of furthering the objectives of this section.

(c) The Federal share for each grant under subsection (b) of this section may be up to 50 per centum of the State's total cost.

(d) The Secretary may, with the consent of any State or political subdivision thereof, accept and use the services, facilities, and employees of the agencies of such State or political subdivision, with or without reimbursement, in order to assist him in carrying out his functions under this section.

Reports.

(e) On the basis of the records made and kept pursuant to section 8(c) of this Act, employers shall file such reports with the Secretary as he shall prescribe by regulation, as necessary to carry out his functions under this Act.

(f) Agreements between the Department of Labor and States pertaining to the collection of occupational safety and health statistics already in effect on the effective date of this Act shall remain in effect until superseded by grants or contracts made under this Act.

AUDITS

SEC. 25. (a) Each recipient of a grant under this Act shall keep such records as the Secretary or the Secretary of Health, Education, and Welfare shall prescribe, including records which fully disclose the amount and disposition by such recipient of the proceeds of such grant, the total cost of the project or undertaking in connection with which such grant is made or used, and the amount of that portion of the cost of the project or undertaking supplied by other sources, and such other records as will facilitate an effective audit.

(b) The Secretary or the Secretary of Health, Education, and Welfare, and the Comptroller General of the United States, or any of their duly authorized representatives, shall have access for the purpose of audit and examination to any books, documents, papers, and records of the recipients of any grant under this Act that are pertinent to any such grant.

ANNUAL REPORT

SEC. 26. Within one hundred and twenty days following the convening of each regular session of each Congress, the Secretary and the Secretary of Health, Education, and Welfare shall each prepare and submit to the President for transmittal to the Congress a report upon the subject matter of this Act, the progress toward achievement of the purpose of this Act, the needs and requirements in the field of occupational safety and health, and any other relevant information. Such reports shall include information regarding occupational safety and health standards, and criteria for such standards, developed during the preceding year; evaluation of standards and criteria previously developed under this Act, defining areas of emphasis for new criteria and standards; an evaluation of the degree of observance of applicable occupational safety and health standards, and a summary

of inspection and enforcement activity undertaken; analysis and evaluation of research activities for which results have been obtained under
governmental and nongovernmental sponsorship; an analysis of major
occupational diseases; evaluation of available control and measurement
technology for hazards for which standards or criteria have been
developed during the preceding year; description of cooperative efforts
undertaken between Government agencies and other interested parties
in the implementation of this Act during the preceding year; a
progress report on the development of an adequate supply of trained
manpower in the field of occupational safety and health, including
estimates of future needs and the efforts being made by Government
and others to meet those needs; listing of all toxic substances in industrial usage for which labeling requirements, criteria, or standards
have not yet been established; and such recommendations for additional legislation as are deemed necessary to protect the safety and
health of the worker and improve the administration of this Act.

NATIONAL COMMISSION ON STATE WORKMEN'S COMPENSATION LAWS

SEC. 27. (a) (1) The Congress hereby finds and declares that—
    (A) the vast majority of American workers, and their families,
are dependent on workmen's compensation for their basic economic security in the event such workers suffer disabling injury
or death in the course of their employment; and that the full protection of American workers from job-related injury or death
requires an adequate, prompt, and equitable system of workmen's
compensation as well as an effective program of occupational
health and safety regulation; and
    (B) in recent years serious questions have been raised concern-
ing the fairness and adequacy of present workmen's compensation
laws in the light of the growth of the economy, the changing
nature of the labor force, increases in medical knowledge, changes
in the hazards associated with various types of employment, new
technology creating new risks to health and safety, and increases
in the general level of wages and the cost of living.
(2) The purpose of this section is to authorize an effective study and
objective evaluation of State workmen's compensation laws in order to
determine if such laws provide an adequate, prompt, and equitable
system of compensation for injury or death arising out of or in the
course of employment.

(b) There is hereby established a National Commission on State   Establishment.
Workmen's Compensation Laws.

(c) (1) The Workmen's Compensation Commission shall be com-   Membership.
posed of fifteen members to be appointed by the President from among
members of State workmen's compensation boards, representatives of
insurance carriers, business, labor, members of the medical profession
having experience in industrial medicine or in workmen's compensation cases, educators having special expertise in the field of workmen's
compensation, and representatives of the general public. The Secretary, the Secretary of Commerce, and the Secretary of Health, Education, and Welfare shall be ex officio members of the Workmen's
Compensation Commission:

(2) Any vacancy in the Workmen's Compensation Commission
shall not affect its powers.

(3) The President shall designate one of the members to serve as
Chairman and one to serve as Vice Chairman of the Workmen's Compensation Commission.

Quorum.

(4) Eight members of the Workmen's Compensation Commission shall constitute a quorum.

Study.

(d) (1) The Workmen's Compensation Commission shall undertake a comprehensive study and evaluation of State workmen's compensation laws in order to determine if such laws provide an adequate, prompt, and equitable system of compensation. Such study and evaluation shall include, without being limited to, the following subjects: (A) the amount and duration of permanent and temporary disability benefits and the criteria for determining the maximum limitations thereon, (B) the amount and duration of medical benefits and provisions insuring adequate medical care and free choice of physician, (C) the extent of coverage of workers, including exemptions based on numbers or type of employment, (D) standards for determining which injuries or diseases should be deemed compensable, (E) rehabilitation, (F) coverage under second or subsequent injury funds, (G) time limits on filing claims, (H) waiting periods, (I) compulsory or elective coverage, (J) administration, (K) legal expenses, (L) the feasibility and desirability of a uniform system of reporting information concerning job-related injuries and diseases and the operation of workmen's compensation laws, (M) the resolution of conflict of laws, extraterritoriality and similar problems arising from claims with multistate aspects, (N) the extent to which private insurance carriers are excluded from supplying workmen's compensation coverage and the desirability of such exclusionary practices, to the extent they are found to exist, (O) the relationship between workmen's compensation on the one hand, and old-age, disability, and survivors insurance and other types of insurance, public or private, on the other hand, (P) methods of implementing the recommendations of the Commission.

Report to President and Congress.

(2) The Workmen's Compensation Commission shall transmit to the President and to the Congress not later than July 31, 1972, a final report containing a detailed statement of the findings and conclusions of the Commission, together with such recommendations as it deems advisable.

Hearings.

(e) (1) The Workmen's Compensation Commission or, on the authorization of the Workmen's Compensation Commission, any subcommittee or members thereof, may, for the purpose of carrying out the provisions of this title, hold such hearings, take such testimony, and sit and act at such times and places as the Workmen's Compensation Commission deems advisable. Any member authorized by the Workmen's Compensation Commission may administer oaths or affirmations to witnesses appearing before the Workmen's Compensation Commission or any subcommittee or members thereof.

(2) Each department, agency, and instrumentality of the executive branch of the Government, including independent agencies, is authorized and directed to furnish to the Workmen's Compensation Commission, upon request made by the Chairman or Vice Chairman, such information as the Workmen's Compensation Commission deems necessary to carry out its functions under this section.

(f) Subject to such rules and regulations as may be adopted by the Workmen's Compensation Commission, the Chairman shall have the power to—

(1) appoint and fix the compensation of an executive director, and such additional staff personnel as he deems necessary, without regard to the provisions of title 5, United States Code, governing appointments in the competitive service, and without regard to the provisions of chapter 51 and subchapter III of chapter 53 of such title relating to classification and General Schedule

80 Stat. 378.
5 USC 101.

5 USC 5101, 5331.

84 STAT. 1618

pay rates, but at rates not in excess of the maximum rate for GS–18 of the General Schedule under section 5332 of such title, and   *Ante*, p. 198-1.

(2) procure temporary and intermittent services to the same extent as is authorized by section 3109 of title 5, United States Code.   80 Stat. 416.

(g) The Workmen's Compensation Commission is authorized to ·nter into contracts with Federal or State agencies, private firms, ιstitutions, and individuals for the conduct of research or surveys, the ·reparation of reports, and other activities necessary to the discharge ·f its duties.   Contract authorization.

(h) Members of the Workmen's Compensation Commission shall ·eceive compensation for each day they are engaged in the perform-ιce of their duties as members of the Workmen's Compensation ·ommission at the daily rate prescribed for GS–18 under section 5332 ·f title 5, United States Code, and shall be entitled to reimbursement ·r travel, subsistence, and other necessary expenses incurred by them ι the performance of their duties as members of the Workmen's ·ompensation Commission.   Compensation; travel ex-penses.

(i) There are hereby authorized to be appropriated such sums as ιay be necessary to carry out the provisions of this section.   Appropriation.

(j) On the ninetieth day after the date of submission of its final ·port to the President, the Workmen's Compensation Commission ιall cease to exist.   Termination.

ECONOMIC ASSISTANCE TO SMALL BUSINESSES

SEC. 28. (a) Section 7(b) of the Small Business Act, as amended, is ιended—   72 Stat. 387; 83 Stat. 802. 15 USC 636.

(1) by striking out the period at the end of "paragraph (5)" and inserting in lieu thereof "; and"; and

(2) by adding after paragraph (5) a new paragraph as follows:

"(6) to make such loans (either directly or in cooperation with ιnks or other lending institutions through agreements to participate ι an immediate or deferred basis) as the Administration may ·termine to be necessary or appropriate to assist any small business ·ncern in effecting additions to or alterations in the equipment, facil-ies, or methods of operation of such business in order to comply with ιe applicable standards promulgated pursuant to section 6 of the ·ccupational Safety and Health Act of 1970 or standards adopted by a ·ate pursuant to a plan approved under section 18 of the Occupa-·onal Safety and Health Act of 1970, if the Administration deter-·ines that such concern is likely to suffer substantial economic injury ithout assistance under this paragraph."

(b) The third sentence of section 7(b) of he Small Business Act, as ιended, is amended by striking out "or (5)" after "paragraph (3)" ιd inserting a comma followed by "(5) or (6)".

(c) Section 4(c)(1) of the Small Business Act, as amended, is ιended by inserting "7(b)(6)," after "7(b)(5),".   80 Stat. 132. 15 USC 633.

(d) Loans may also be made or guaranteed for the purposes set ·rth in section 7(b)(6) of the Small Business Act, as amended, pur-ιant to the provisions of section 202 of the Public Works and Eco-·mic Development Act of 1965, as amended.   79 Stat. 556. 42 USC 3142.

ADDITIONAL ASSISTANT SECRETARY OF LABOR

SEC. 29. (a) Section 2 of the Act of April 17, 1946 (60 Stat. 91) as ιended (29 U.S.C. 553) is amended by—   75 Stat. 338.

(1) striking out "four" in the first sentence of such section an inserting in lieu thereof "five"; and

(2) adding at the end thereof the following new sentence, "O of such Assistant Secretaries shall be an Assistant Secretary Labor for Occupational Safety and Health.".

80 Stat. 462.

(b) Paragraph (20) of section 5315 of title 5, United States Code, amended by striking out "(4)" and inserting in lieu thereof "(5)

ADDITIONAL POSITIONS

SEC. 30. Section 5108(c) of title 5, United States Code, is amend by—

(1) striking out the word "and" at the end of paragraph (8

(2) striking out the period at the end of paragraph (9) an inserting in lieu thereof a semicolon and the word "and"; an

(3) by adding immediately after paragraph (9) the followin new paragraph:

"(10) (A) the Secretary of Labor, subject to the standar and procedures prescribed by this chapter, may place an add tional twenty-five positions in the Department of Labor GS–16, 17, and 18 for the purposes of carrying out his respoi sibilities under the Occupational Safety and Health A of 1970;

"(B) the Occupational Safety and Health Review Cor mission, subject to the standards and procedures prescrib by this chapter, may place ten positions in GS–16, 17, and in carrying out its functions under the Occupational Safe and Health Act of 1970."

EMERGENCY LOCATOR BEACONS

72 Stat. 775.
49 USC 1421.

SEC. 31. Section 601 of the Federal Aviation Act of 1958 is amend by inserting at the end thereof a new subsection as follows:

"EMERGENCY LOCATOR BEACONS

"(d) (1) Except with respect to aircraft described in paragraph (. of this subsection, minimum standards pursuant to this section sh; include a requirement that emergency locator beacons shall installed—

"(A) on any fixed-wing, powered aircraft for use in air cor merce the manufacture of which is completed, or which imported into the United States, after one year following t date of enactment of this subsection; and

"(B) on any fixed-wing, powered aircraft used in air commer after three years following such date.

"(2) The provisions of this subsection shall not apply to je powered aircraft; aircraft used in air transportation (other than a taxis and charter aircraft); military aircraft; aircraft used solely f training purposes not involving flights more than twenty miles fro its base; and aircraft used for the aerial application of chemicals."

SEPARABILITY

SEC. 32. If any provision of this Act, or the application of such pr vision to any person or circumstance, shall be held invalid, the remai der of this Act, or the application of such provision to persons circumstances other than those as to which it is held invalid, shall n be affected thereby.

APPROPRIATIONS

SEC. 33. There are authorized to be appropriated to carry out this Act for each fiscal year such sums as the Congress shall deem necessary.

EFFECTIVE DATE

SEC. 34. This Act shall take effect one hundred and twenty days after the date of its enactment.

Approved December 29, 1970.

◯

Public Law 91-596, 91st Congress, S. 2193
December 29, 1970

LEGISLATIVE HISTORY:

HOUSE REPORTS: No. 91-1291 accompanying H.R. 16785 (Comm. on
                Education and Labor) and No. 91-1765 (Comm. of
                Conference).
SENATE REPORT No. 91-1282 (Comm. on Labor and Public Welfare).
CONGRESSIONAL RECORD, Vol. 116 (1970):
     Oct. 13, Nov. 16, 17, considered and passed Senate.
     Nov. 23, 24, considered and passed House, amended, in lieu
                of H.R. 16785.
     Dec. 16, Senate agreed to conference report.
     Dec. 17, House agreed to conference report.

STATEMENT OF THE MANAGERS ON THE PART OF THE HOUSE

The managers on the part of the House at the conference on the disagreeing votes of the two Houses on the amendments of the House to the bill (S. 2193) to authorize the Secretary of Labor to set standards to assure safe and healthful working conditions for working men and women, to assist and encourage States to participate in efforts to assure such working conditions, to provide for research, information, education, and training in the field of occupational safety and health, and for other purposes, submit the following statement in explanation of the effect of the action agreed upon by the conferees and recommended in the accompanying conference report:

The House amendment struck out all of the Senate bill after the enacting clause and inserted a new text. The conference report recommends a substitute text for both the Senate bill and the House amendment. Except for minor, technical, and clarifying differences, this statement describes the actions of the conferees insofar as they recommend changes in the House amendment.

CONGRESSIONAL FINDINGS AND PURPOSE

The findings and purposes of the Senate bill and the House amendment were consistent but the House provisions were more detailed. The Senate receded.

DEFINITIONS

Under the Senate bill to qualify as a "national consensus standard", interested parties had to reach substantial agreement on its adoption after diverse views had been considered. Under the House amendment, a standard qualified if in the process interested parties' views were considered. The House receded.

APPLICABILITY OF ACT

The Senate bill did not provide coverage for Guam. The House amendment did. A House provision excluded from coverage any vessel underway on the Outer Continental Shelf lands. The House receded on the second point, the Senate on the first.

EFFECT ON OTHER LAWS

The Senate bill said the Act should not apply to working conditions with respect to which other Federal agencies exercise statutory authority affecting occupational safety and health, while the House amendment excluded employees whose working conditions were so regulated. The House language had an additional exclusion relating to employees

whose safety and health were regulated by state agencies acting under
section 274 of the Atomic Energy Act of 1954. The House receded on
the first point; the Senate receded on the second.

The Senate bill provided that safety standards under any law
administered by the Secretary of Labor (Walsh-Healy, Service Con-
trac, Act, Construction Safety Act, Arts and Humanities Act, and
Longshore Safety) would be superseded when more effective standards
are ·promulgated under this Act, but until then they were deemed
st nd ds under the present Act. The enforcement process of this Act
was thus added to the enforcement procedures of those other Acts.
The House amendment repealed and rescinded standards under the
Walsh-Healy, the Service Contracts, and the Arts and Humanities
Acts. All construction industry employers were exempted from this
Act and the entire industry brought under the Construction Safety
Act. That Act was amended to make the enforcement provisions of
this Act applicable. Unlike the Senate bill which left the hearing of
contract violation cases with the Secretary, the House amendment
provided the hearing of such cases by the Safety and Health Commission. The House receded.

The conferees intend that the Secretary develop health and safety
standards for construction workers covered by Public Law 91–54
pursuant to the provisions of that law and that he use the same
mechanisms and resources for the development of health and safety
standards for all the other construction workers newly covered by this
Act, including those engaged in alterations, repairs, painting and/or
decorating.

It is understood by the Conferees that in any enforcement proceedings brought under either this Act or under such other Acts, the
principle of collateral estoppel will apply.

DUTIES OF EMPLOYERS AND EMPLOYEES

Employers' Duties.—The Senate bill required workplaces to be free
from "recognized hazards". The House amendment required such
places to be free from "any hazards which are readily apparent and
ar causing or are likely to cause death or serious bodily harm." The
House provision was adopted with the Senate's "recognized hazard"
term replacing the House's "readily apparent hazard."

Employees' Duties.—The Senate bill required each employee to
comply with occupational health and safety standards and the rules,
regulations, and orders issued under this Act. The House amendment
had no comparable provision. The House receded.

THE PROMULGATION OF HEALTH AND SAFETY STANDARDS

Who Should Promulgate.—The Senate bill provided for the promulgation of occupational safety and health standards by the Secretary
of Labor. The House amendment authorized their promulgation by a
National Occupational Safety and Health Board. The House receded.

Interim Standards—Procedure.—Unless it was determined that such
standards would not improve safety or health, both versions of the
bill required the earliest practical promulgation of national consensus
and established Federal standards and permitted use of an informal,
shortened rule-making procedure. Two years were permitted in the
Senate bill, three years in the House amendment. Not contained in

the House amendment was a Senate provision for the promulgation of existing proprietary standards also by a shortened rule-making procedure during the first two years. The Senate receded with respect to the issuance of proprietary standards. The House receded as to the time.

Permanent Standards—Procedure.—In the procedures provided for the establishment and promulgation of standards (other than those mentioned above) there were many similarities in the Senate bill and the House amendment. For instance, both the Secretary and Board were permitted to begin rule-making on their own motion or on the basis of petitions. Some of the procedural differences resulted mainly, however, from the choice of the respective bodies as to who should do the rule-making. The chief difference lay in the fact that the procedure for setting standards in the Senate bill was the informal rule-making procedures of the Administrative Procedure Act and required a hearing only if it was requested. The procedure for setting standards under the House amendment were under the formal rule-making procedures also provided in the Administrative Procedure Act. The House receded on the procedure for promulgating standards.

Once it was decided that a rule should be prescribed, both the Secretary (under the Senate bill) and the Board (under the House amendment) were permitted to appoint an advisory committee to make recommendations. The Senate bill required a report back from the advisory committee within 90 days, which could be extended to 270 days. The House amendment established the normal time to be 270 days, which could be extended to 1 year, 3 months. Both versions permitted the Secretary to prescribe a shorter period.

Under the Senate bill, the Secretary was required to publish a proposed rule promulgating, modifying or remaking a safety or health standard in the Federal Register. This publication had to follow within 60 days the recommendation of an advisory committee or, if they failed to report back, within 60 days of the time set by the Secretary for their recommendations. Publication in the Register permitted interested persons 30 days to submit written data or comments and to ask for a hearing. Within an additional 30 days the Secretary was required to publish any standard which had been objected to and a hearing requested. He had also to set a time and place for a hearing. Sixty days after the expiration of the time permitted for filing written data or comments, or 60 days after completion of the hearing, the Secretary had to issue the rule or determine that a rule should not be issued.

Under the House bill within 4 months after the advisory committee had made its recommendations (or if they failed to do so, 4 months after the time set for them to do so), the Board was required to schedule and give notice of a hearing on the proposal in the Federal Register.

The House provided for issuance of the rule promulgating, modifying, or revoking the standard or declining to do so, within 60 days following completion of the hearings where an advisory committee had acted, 120 days, where no such committee has been appointed. All Senate provisions as to procedure and time limitations were retained.

Effective Date.—Both the Senate bill and the House amendment permitted the Secretary or the Board, respectively, to delay the effective date of a new standard to permit affected employers to familiarize themselves and their employees with its requirements. The House amendment limited that possible delay to 90 days. The Senate bill had no such limitation. The Senate receded.

Development of Standards.—The Senate bill directed the Secretary in setting standards dealing with toxic materials or harmful physical agents to set the standard which assures that no employee will suffer material impairment of health or functional capacity even if he is exposed for all his working life. The Senate bill also provided that (1) standards shall be based on research, demonstrations, experiments, and such other information as may be appropriate; (2) in addition to the attainment to the highest degree of health and safety protection to the employee, other considerations shall be the latest scientific data in the field, the feasibility of these standards, and experience gained under this and other health and safety standards and (3) whenever practicable, the standard promulgated shall be expressed in terms of objective criteria and of the performance desired. The House amendment had no comparable provisions. The House receded with an amendment which provides that employers may petition for a temporary variance from an occupational health or safety standard if they are unable to comply with a standard for the following limited reasons: unavailability of professional or technical personnel or of necessary materials or equipment or because necessary construction or alteration of facilities cannot be completed in time. Economic hardship is not to be a consideration for the qualification for a temporary extension order. Employees are entitled to a hearing on the order. Such an order may be issued for a maximum period of one year and may not be renewed more than twice.

The conference agreement also permits a variance to permit an employer to participate in an approved experiment to demonstrate or validate new techniques to improve employees safety.

Standards—Labels and Warnings.—The Senate bill required standards requiring labels and other warnings to apprise employees of hazards, symptoms, treatments and precautions, etc. The House amendment similarly required the posting of labels and warnings to apprise employees of the existence of hazards and of the suggested methods of avoiding or alleviating them. Such labeling and warning standards were also directed by the Senate bill to be prescribed for protective equipment, control procedures, monitoring methods, and medical examinations. An informal rule-making process was permitted for modifying such labeling, monitoring, and medical examination requirements. The House amendment contained no comparable provision. The House receded.

Both versions required publication of the statement of reasons why an adopted rule would better effectuate the purposes of the Act than a national consensus standard with which it differs. The Senate bill required a publication of the statement in the Federal Register. The House required its publication as part of the rule. The adopted version requires a simultaneous publication of the rule and the statement.

Emergency Temporary Standards.— Emergency temporary standards could be issued under either version of the bill without regard to the normal rule-making requirements and to take immediate effect. The Senate bill permitted such issuances where grave danger results from exposure to toxic substances, harmful physical agents, or new hazards.

The House amendment limited emergency standards to toxic substances, or new hazards "resulting from the introduction of new processes." The House receded.

Standards—Exemption, Variance.—Both the Senate bill and the House amendment permitted an employer limited freedom from a standard promulgated under the Act when he provided equally safe and healthful conditions. The Senate bill characterized this as a "variance" while the House called it an "exemption." The Senate term prevailed

Standards—Pre-enforcement Review.—The Senate bill permitted pre-enforcement judicial review by anyone adversely affected by any standard in his local circuit court of appeals provided he filed within 60 days after the promulgation. Pre-enforcement review was limited by the House amendment to the D.C. Court of Appeals and to within 30 days of issuance. The "substantial evidence" test was the basis of court review in the House amendment; in the Senate bill, the more vigorous standards generally applicable to review of rules would have been applicable. Review in the local Circuit Court of Appeals, the use of the "substantial evidence" test, and a 60-day limitation on the appeal time were accepted by the conferees.

Delegation of Authority.—Under the House amendment the Secretary was authorized to delegate his inspection authority to other agencies of the Federal Government or to agencies of the States with their permission. The Senate bill had no such provision. The House receded.

Advisory Committees—Memberships.—The House amendment made the appointment of employer and employee representatives to Advisory Committees mandatory in standard-setting proceedings. The Senate bill did not. The Senate receded.

Advisory Committees—Meetings.—The House amendment required that Advisory Committee meetings be open to the public, whereas the Senate bill did not. The Senate receded.

National Advisory Committee.—The Senate bill provided that the National Advisory Committee should have twenty members, the House amendment provided for twelve. The Senate bill specifically provided for representation on the Committee of the occupational safety and health professions. The House amendment did not. The House language was adopted but modified to provide for representation of the safety and health professions.

INSPECTIONS, INVESTIGATIONS, AND RECORDKEEPING

Inspections.—The House amendment required that an inspector's entry into a workplace be permitted "without delay," which was not specified in the Senate bill. The Senate bill specified that the inspector could "privately" question employers, owners, agents and employees, the House amendment did not. The Senate receded on the first point, the House on the second. The Senate receded also to the House on its version of the provision authorizing compulsory process for witnesses and the production of evidence.

Inspections—Record Keeping.—The Senate bill permitted the Secretary to require record-keeping not only to insure compliance but also for the collection of research information. The House amendment limited his authority to the former purpose. The House receded.

Self-Inspection and Protection.—The Senate bill permitted the Secretary to require periodic self-inspections by the employer and certification of the results. There was no such provision in the House amendment. The House receded, with an amendment, deleting the language with respect to the certification of results. A Senate bill provision, without a House amendment counterpart, permitting the Secretary to require the posting of notices to keep employees informed of the protections of the Act, was retained.

Employer Reports.—A Senate bill provision without a counterpart in the House amendment permitted the Secretary to require an employer to keep records and make reports on "all work-related deaths, injuries and illnesses." The House receded with an amendment limiting the reporting requirement to injuries and illnesses other than of a minor nature, with a specific definition of what is not of a minor nature.

Employee Exposure Records.—The Senate bill, but not the House amendment, required the recording of employee exposures to potentially toxic or harmful materials required to be monitored or measured under Sections 6 (standards) or 19 (research). The House receded with an amendment which required recording only of those substances required to be monitored or measured under Section 6.

The Senate bill provided and the House amendment did not, for employee access to the monitoring process and for an employee's right to be notified when he had been exposed to *potentially* toxic substances. The House receded with the deletion of the word "potentially."

Information Required of Employers.—Both the Senate bill and the House amendment provided that the federal information requirement imposed on employers be as light as possible with duplication kept to a minimum. The House amendment, in addition, placed a similar stricture on State agencies operating under this Act. The Senate receded.

Labor-Management Aid of Inspection.—The Senate bill required that both a management and an employee representative be given an opportunity to accompany an inspector conducting an inspection of the workplace. Where there is no employee representative the Senate bill required consultation with a reasonable number of employees about safety in the workplace. The House amendment did not require such an opportunity for either the employer or the employee representative but provided that if the employer accompanied the Secretary during the conduct of an inspection the employee representative would also be given the opportunity. The House receded with the understanding that the provision in itself does not confer authority on the Secretary to prescribe regulations with respect to representation questions in a collective bargaining context.

Special Inspections.—A special inspection was required by the Senate bill as soon as practicable where an employee alleges the violation of a standard in writing, and the Secretary finds probable cause to believe that a violation exists. In case of a refusal to conduct an inspection or if any inspection results in a finding that no violation exists, a notification of that decision must be provided the employee in writing. The House receded. Where during any inspection or prior to a scheduled inspection an employee alleges a violation in writing, the Senate bill required a written explanation of a negative finding. An informal review process was in the latter instance also provided for.

There were no comparable provisions in the House amendment. The House receded with amendments requiring the employer to be given notice of the request for an inspection and deleting the requirement that failure to find a violation be explained in writing.

CITATIONS FOR VIOLATIONS

The Senate bill provided that if, upon inspection or investigation, the Secretary or his authorized representative "determines" that an employer has violated mandatory requirements under the Act, he shall "forthwith" issue a citation. The House amendment provided that if on the basis of an inspection or investigation the Secretary "believes" that an employer has violated such requirements, he shall issue a citation to the employer. The conference report provides that if the Secretary "believes" that an employer has violated such requirements he shall issue the citation with reasonable promptness. In the absence of exceptional circumstances any delay is not expected to exceed 72 hours from the time the violation is detected by the inspector.

The Senate bill kept separate the proceedings for the issuance of the citation from those with respect to the imposition of penalties for violations. The House amendment combined proposed penalties with the issuance of the citation. The conference report follows the provisions of the Senate bill in this respect.

The Senate bill provided for a notice in lieu of citations in de minimis cases. The House amendment did not require a citation in de minimis cases. The conference report follows the provisions of the Senate bill.

The House amendment permitted a citation to be issued no later than 90 days following the occurrence of a violation. There was no comparable Senate provision. The House receded.

Both versions required the posting of citations at or near the place of violation, but the Senate bill expressly provided that posting regulations should be issued by the Secretary. The conference report contains the provisions of the Senate bill.

The House amendment prohibited issuance of a citation more than three months after the occurrence of any violation. The Senate bill had no such statute of limitations. The Senate receded with an amendment changing the three months to six months.

Under the Senate bill the Secretary had to notify the employer within a reasonable time after a citation of the amount of a penalty. The employer had to give notice of his intention to contest the citation or penalty with fifteen days of the notice or the penalty was to be final. Under the House amendment the employer had similar rights. He was to notify the Secretary of his intention to appeal. The Secretary was to notify the Appeals Commission which had to give him a hearing. The House receded.

The Senate bill specified procedures to be followed when there was a failure to correct a violation within the time provided in a citation. The House amendment contained no such provision. The House receded.

The Senate bill gave employees the right to appeal the time allowed for abatement of a violation and provided that the Commission should prescribe rules of procedure giving employees the opportunity to participate as parties. The House amendment restricted the right of appeal in such cases to the employer. The House receded with an amendment which provides that the employer shall have a right to reopen the proceedings for a re-hearing in the event it is impossible to comply with the abatement requirements within the period provided for in the citation.

JUDICIAL PROCEEDINGS

Both the Senate bill and the House amendment provided for judicial review of Commission decisions. The Senate bill provided appeal rights to any person adversely affected or aggrieved by an order of the Commission. The House amendment limited appeal rights to the employer and the Secretary. The House amendment provided for judicial review in the Court of Appeals for the circuit where the violation occurred or where the employer had his principal office. The Senate bill also permitted review in the D.C. Court of Appeals. The House receded.

Under the Senate bill all Commission orders became final fifteen days after issuance unless stayed by the Court of Appeals. Under the House amendment the filing of a petition for review automatically stays a Commission order. The Senate bill, but not the House amendment, permitted uncontested orders of the Commission to be entered as orders of the Court of Appeals. The House receded with an amendment providing for the finality of Commission orders thirty days after issuance unless stayed by the court.

The Senate bill provided for assessment of penalties in contempt proceedings to enforce a Court of Appeals decree. The House bill had no comparable provision. The House receded.

The Senate bill did not contain a provision which was in the House amendment authorizing a district court suit to collect civil penalties. The Senate receded.

The Senate bill provided for administrative action to obtain relief for an employee discriminated against for asserting rights under this Act, including reinstatement with back pay. The House bill contained no provision for obtaining such administrative relief; rather it provided civil and criminal penalties for employers who discriminate against employees in such cases. With respect to the first matter, the House receded with an amendment making specific the jurisdiction of the district courts for proceedings brought by the Secretary to restrain violations and other appropriate relief. With respect to the second matter dealing with civil and criminal penalties for employers, the House receded.

OCCUPATIONAL SAFETY AND HEALTH APPEALS COMMISSION

The Occupational Safety and Health Review Commission in the Senate bill and the Occupational Safety and Health Appeals Commission in the House amendment are composed of three members in each instance, with terms under the Senate bill of five years and under the House amendment of six years. In other respects, though differing in actual language, both bills were alike in legal effect. With respect to the terms of office the Senate receded. But in the other respects, the conference report uses the language in the Senate bill.

The Senate bill provided that all members of the Appeals Commission were to receive the same salary at Executive Level 4. The House amendment gave the Chairman a higher salary at Executive Level 3. The Senate receded. The House amendment provided that the Commission might appoint hearing examiners without regard to any statutory limitations on grades GS–16 and above. The Senate receded.

PROCEDURES TO COUNTERACT IMMINENT DANGERS

The Senate bill authorized the Secretary to seek a court order to remove or correct an imminent danger and require the withdrawal of endangered persons other than "those necessary to correct the danger, maintain the operating capacity of a continuous process operation or permit a safe and orderly shutdown." The Senate bill contained no limitation on the duration of such a temporary restraining order, although the 10-day limit in the F.R.C.P. was applicable. The Senate bill permitted the Secretary to issue an administrative imminent danger shutdown order where there was insufficient time to obtain a court order. The House amendment authorized the Secretary to seek court orders to restrain conditions or practices which caused imminent dangers. A temporary restraining order under the House amendment was to remain in effect only five days. The House amendment contained no provision permitting the Secretary to issue an administrative imminent danger order. The Senate receded with an amendment adopting with minor changes the limitations on court authority mentioned in the quotation above.

The Senate bill provided that if the Secretary arbitrarily or capriciously failed to issue or seek an imminent danger order, employees might seek a writ of mandamus against him. The House amendment provided that where the Secretary unreasonably failed to seek an order an employee injured thereby might bring an action for damages in the Court of Claims. The House receded.

The House amendment provided that where an injunction was issued the court must set a sum for the payment of damages if the injunction is eventually found to have been in error. There was no comparable provision in the Senate bill. The House receded.

REPRESENTATION IN CIVIL LITIGATION

The Senate bill and the House amendment contained comparable provisions for the Solicitor of Labor to appear for and represent the Secretary in any civil litigation brought under the Act, but the House amendment unlike the Senate bill made specific reference to the Attorney General's authority to represent the United States in the Court of Claims. The Senate receded. The conferees expect that the Solicitor of Labor will represent the Department of Labor in proceedings before the Review Commission.

CONFIDENTIALITY OF TRADE SECRETS

Provision was made in both versions of the bill for the protection of trade secrets. The House amendment provided that in proceedings arising under the Act such information should be presented off the public record and preserved separarely. The Senate bill provided that the court or the Secretary should issue appropriate orders to preserve confidentiality. The House receded.

VARIATIONS, TOLERANCES AND EXEMPTIONS

Both bills provided that variations, tolerances and exemptions shall not be in effect more than six months without notification to employees and an opportunity for a hearing. In addition, the House bill also provided that variations, tolerances, and exemptions may not be granted in the first instance without notice and an opportunity for a hearing. The Senate receded.

PENALTIES

The Senate bill provided that there shall be assessed a civil penalty of not more than $1,000 for each violation. The House amendment was similar unless the violation was determined not to be of a serious nature in which case a civil penalty of up to $1,000 was discretionary. The Senate bill provided for civil penalties of not more than $1,000 for each day in which an imminent danger order or final order of the Commission was violated. The House amendment also provided for a penalty of up to $1,000 for each day in which an order which has become final was violated. The Senate receded on each point.

Both bills permitted mitigation, compromise, or settlement of penalties. The House amendment required publication in the Federal Register whenever the Secretary mitigated, compromised, or settled any penalty. Both bills contained similar provisions which specify the factors to be considered in assessing a penalty. The Senate receded.

The Senate bill provided criminal penalties for wilful violations (not more than $10,000 and/or six months doubled after first conviction). The House amendment provided for a civil penalty of up to $10,000 for wilful or repeated violations. The Senate receded on civil penalties and the House receded on criminal penalties with an amendment which requires that the wilful violation of the standard or the rule, regulation or order result in death to an employee, for the employer to be subject to the criminal penalties provided in the subsection.

The House amendment provided no penalty for giving advanced notice of any inspection to be conducted under the Act. The Senate bill provided a fine not to exceed $1,000 and imprisonment for not more than six months or both for giving advanced notice. The House receded.

The Senate bill contained a provision providing penalties for false statements, representations, or certifications. The House amendment contained no comparable provision. The House receded.

Both bills provided identical penalties for any person who assaults, intimidates, or interferes with federal investigators and inspectors in the performance of their duties, though the bills took different approaches. The Senate bill extended to such investigators and inspectors the basic statutory protection contained in section 1114 of Title 18 of the United States Code. The House amendment set forth the prohibited activities and the penalties in the Act. The Conference Report contains the language of the Senate bill to which has been added language from the House amendment providing that a person who kills a person while engaged in or on account of the performance of his duties under the Act shall be punished by imprisonment for any term of years or for life.

The Senate bill, unlike the House amendment, did not specifically provide a penalty for violation of posting requirements. The Senate receded.

The House amendment contained a provision specifying the factors to be considered in the assessment of penalties. The Senate receded with an amendment which struck from the provision specified authority for the Commission to collect the penalties as well as to assess them.

The House amendment, unlike the Senate bill, contained a provision setting forth certain factors under which a serious violation shall be deemed to exist. The Senate receded.

STATE JURISDICTION AND STATE PLANS

Both versions of the bill provided for court review of a decision of the Secretary to reject or withdraw approval of a State plan. The Senate bill applied a "substantial evidence" standard of review and the House amendment applied an "arbitrary and capricious" standard. The House receded.

Both versions of the bill allowed agreements between the Secretary and a State whereby the State could continue enforcement of its health and safety standards pending final action on the State plan. The Senate bill limited such agreements to standards which were not in conflict with Federal standards. The Senate bill also provided that a State standard which was more stringent than a Federal standard was not to be regarded as one in conflict with that Federal standard. The Senate receded.

FEDERAL AGENCY SAFETY PROGRAMS AND RESPONSIBILITIES

Annual reports to the Congress with respect to progress of Federal agency safety programs were required in both the Senate bill and the House amendment. The Senate bill specified that the President should forward to the Congress a summary or digest of the reports submitted to him by the Secretary, whereas the House bill required the President to submit a report of the activities of Federal agencies in this regard. The Senate receded.

RESEARCH AND RELATED ACTIVITIES

Both bills required the Secretary of HEW to consult with the Secretary of Labor to develop a research plan in order to develop criteria to assist in setting standards. The Senate bill specified that criteria dealing with toxic materials and harmful physical agents should be developed to demonstrate the exposure levels at which the worker would experience no impairment of health function or life expectancy, whereas the House bill did not. The House amendment required annual publication of the criteria developed by the Secretary of HEW, whereas the Senate bill did not. The House receded on these provisions with an amendment to require the development of such criteria dealing with toxic materials and harmful physical agents and substances which will describe exposure levels that are safe for various periods of employment, including but not limited to the exposure levels at which no employee will suffer impaired health or functional capacity or diminished life expectancy as a result of his work experience.

The Senate bill authorized the Secretary of HEW for research purposes to establish medical examinations for such employees and to require any employer to measure, monitor, and make reports on the exposure of his employees to potentially toxic or harmful agents. With regard to the latter, on the request of any such employer the Secretary was required to defray the added cost incurred by that employer. There was no comparable House provision. The House receded with the understanding that regulations issued by the Secretary of HEW pursuant to this subsection requiring employer measurement, recording, and reporting will be limited to those instances in which there is a reasonable probability of developing information on toxic substances or harmful physical agents.

The House amendment authorized appropriations of such sums as Congress deems necessary to enable the Secretary of Labor to purchase monitoring equipment for all employers required by any standard, rule or regulation to measure the exposure of employees to unhealthy environments for the protection of the employee and to establish compliance with such standards, rules or regulations. There was no comparable Senate provision. The House receded.

Both the Senate bill and the House amendment required the Secretary of HEW to publish on an annual basis a list of toxic substances. The Senate bill required only the publication of those toxic substances which are "used or found in the work place" whereas the House amendment did not contain such a limitation. The Senate receded.

Both the Senate bill and the House amendment provided for the determination of toxicity when requested by any employer or employee. The Senate bill provided that the Secretary of HEW make such a determination on "written request" which specified with "reasonable particularity" the grounds on which the request was being made. Under the Senate bill, if toxicity was determined and no applicable standard was in effect, the Secretary of Labor was to be so advised. There was no such requirement in the House amendment. Further, under the House amendment, the determination of toxicity was to be made by the Board and there was no requirement that the request be particularized or in writing. The House receded on these provisions.

The Senate bill required the Secretary of HEW to conduct and publish annually industrywide studies of the effects of chronic and low level exposure to industrial materials, processes, and stresses on the potential for illness, disease, or loss of functional capacity in aging adults. There was no comparable House provision. The House receded.

NATIONAL INSTITUTE

The Senate bill directed the delegation of HEW functions where feasible to a National Institute for Occupational Safety and Health established by the Senate bill. There were no comparable provisions in the House amendment. The Conference agreement provides for the creation of the National Institute and requires the delegation provided for in the Senate bill.

STATISTICS

Both versions of the bill provided for the collection, compilation and publishing of occupational safety and health statistics. The House amendment but not the Senate bill authorized such efforts for all employments whether or not they were covered by this Act, so long as they are included within the geographical authority of the Act. The Senate receded with an amendment to require the Secretary of Labor to consult with the Secretary of HEW in the carrying out of this statistical program, and specifying the types of injuries on which statistics must be collected.

The House amendment but not the Senate bill explicitly provided that any existing agreements between the Labor Department and the States for the collection of statistics remain in effect until superseded by new arrangements under this Act. The Senate receded.

AUDITS

Both versions of the bill authorized the Secretary of Labor to require grantees under the Act to maintain such records and accounts as deemed necessary. The Senate bill but not the House amendment provided the same authority to the Secretary of HEW. The House receded.

Both versions of the bill required all grantees to provide access to their books and records to the Secretary of Labor and the Comptroller General. The Senate bill also provided the Secretary of HEW with such access. The House receded.

COMMISSION ON WORKMEN'S COMPENSATION LAWS

The Senate bill established a National Commission on State Workmen's Compensation Laws to undertake an effective study and objective evaluation of State Workmen's Compensation laws. The Commission was required to report its findings, conclusions and recommendations to the President and the Congress no later than February 1, 1972. The House receded with an amendment changing the reporting date to July 31, 1972.

ADDITIONAL ASSISTANT SECRETARY OF LABOR

The Senate bill provided for an additional Assistant Secretary of Labor to be known as the "Assistant Secretary of Labor for Occupational Safety and Health." The House amendment did not. The House receded.

ADDITIONAL POSITIONS

To carry out responsibilities under the Act the Senate bill but not the House amendment provided for additional supergrade positions for the Department of Labor and the Review Commission. The House receded.

EMERGENCY LOCATOR BEACONS

The Senate bill, but not the House amendment, amended the Federal Aviation Act to require emergency locator beacons on aircraft. The House receded.

EFFECTIVE DATE

The conference agreement provides that the Act should take effect 120 days after the date of enactment as provided in the House amendment rather than in 30 days after the enactment as provided in the Senate bill.

TITLE

The conference adopted the title contained in the House bill which reads as follows: "An Act to assure safe and healthful working conditions for working men and women; by authorizing enforcement of the standards developed under the Act; by assisting and encouraging the States in their efforts to assure safe and healthful working conditions; by providing for research, information, education, and training in the field of occupational safety and health; and for other purposes."

CARL D. PERKINS,
EDITH GREEN,
FRANK THOMPSON Jr.,
JOHN H. DENT,
DOMINICK V. DANIELS,
JAMES G. O'HARA,
AUGUSTUS F. HAWKINS,
WILLIAM D. FORD,
WILLIAM D. HATHAWAY,
LLOYD MEEDS,
PHILLIP BURTON,
JOSEPH M. GAYDOS,
WILLIAM H. AYRES,
ALBERT H. QUIE,
JOHN N. ERLENBORN,
MARVIN L. ESCH,
EDWIN D. ESHLEMAN,
WM. A. STEIGER,
Managers on the Part of the House.

O

TEXT OF HOUSE EDUCATION AND LABOR COMMITTEE'S REPORT

91st Congress 2d Session	HOUSE OF REPRESENTATIVES	Report No. 91–1291

OCCUPATIONAL SAFETY AND HEALTH ACT

July 9, 1970.—Committed to the Committee of the Whole House on the State of the Union and ordered to be printed

Mr. Perkins, from the Committee on Education and Labor, submitted the following

REPORT

[To accompany H.R. 16785]

The Committee on Education and Labor, to whom was referred the bill (H.R. 16785) to assure safe and healthful working conditions for working men and women; by authorizing enforcement of the standards developed under the act; by assisting and encouraging the States in their efforts to assure safe and healthful working conditions; by providing for research, information, education, and training in the field of occupational safety and health; and for other purposes; having considered the same, report favorably thereon with an amendment and recommend that the bill as amended do pass.

The amendment is as follows:

Strike out all after the enacting clause and insert the following:

That this Act may be cited as the "Occupational Safety and Health Act".

CONGRESSIONAL FINDINGS AND PURPOSE

Sec. 2. (a) The Congress finds that personal injuries and illnesses arising out of work situations impose a substantial burden upon, and are a hindrance to, interstate commerce in terms of lost production, wage loss, medical expenses, and disability compensation payments.

(b) The Congress declares it to be its purpose and policy, through the exercise of its powers to regulate commerce among the several States and with foreign nations and to provide for the general welfare, to assure so far as possible every working man and woman in the Nation safe and healthful working conditions and to preserve our human resources—

(1) by encouraging employers and employees in their efforts to reduce the number of occupational safety and health hazards at their places of employment, and to stimulate employers and employees to institute new and to perfect existing programs for providing safe and healthful working conditions;

(2) by building upon advances already made through employer and employee initiative for providing safe and healthful working conditions;

139

(3) by providing for research in the field of occupational safety and health, including the psychological factors involved, and by developing innovative methods, techniques and approaches for dealing with occupational safety and health problems;

(4) by exploring ways to discover latent diseases, establishing causal connections between diseases and work in environmental conditions, and conducting other research relating to health problems, in recognition of the fact that occupational health standards present problems often different from those involved in occupational safety;

(5) by providing for training programs to increase the number and competence of personnel engaged in the field of occupational safety and health;

(6) by providing for the development, promulgation, and effective enforcement of occupational safety and health standards;

(7) by encouraging the States to assume the fullest responsibility for the administration and enforcement of their occupational safety and health laws by providing grants to the States to assist in identifying their needs and responsibilities in the area of occupational safety and health, to develop plans in accordance with the provisions of this Act, to improve the administration and enforcement of State occupational safety and health laws, and to conduct experimental and demonstration projects in connection therewith;

(8) by providing for appropriate accident and health reporting procedures which will help achieve the objectives of this Act and accurately describe the nature of the occupational safety and health problem; and

(9) by encouraging joint labor-management efforts to reduce injuries and disease arising out of employment.

DEFINITIONS

SEC. 3. For the purposes of this Act—

(1) The term "Secretary" means the Secretary of Labor.

(2) The term "commerce" means trade, traffic, commerce, transportation, or communication among the several States, or between a State and any place outside thereof, or within the District of Columbia, or a possession of the United States (other than a State as defined in paragraph (6) of this subsection), or between points in the same State but through a point outside thereof.

(3) The term "person" means one or more individuals, partnerships, associations, corporations, business trusts, legal representatives, or any organized group of persons.

(4) The term "employer" means a person engaged in a business affecting commerce who has employees, but does not include the United States or any State or political subdivision of a State, except that it does include a public authority which is subject to the jurisdiction of more than one State, whether or not subsidized with public funds, which has employees engaged in the administration or maintenance of a bridge or tunnel.

(5) The term "employee" means an employee of an employer who is employed in a business of his employer which affects commerce.

(6) The term "State" includes a State of the United States, the District of Columbia, Puerto Rico, the Virgin Islands, American Samoa, Guam, and the Trust Territory of the Pacific Islands.

(7) The term "occupational safety and health standard" means a standard which requires conditions, or the adoption or use of one or more practices, means, methods, operations, or processes, reasonably necessary or appropriate to provide safe or healthful employment and places of employment.

(8) The term "national consensus standard" means any occupational safety and health standard or modification thereof which (A) has been adopted and promulgated by a nationally recognized standards-producing organization under procedures whereby it can be determined by the Secretary, that persons interested and affected by the scope or provisions of the standard have reached substantial agreement on its adoption, (B) was formulated in a manner which afforded an opportunity for diverse views to be considered, and (C) has been designated as such a standard by the Secretary, after consultation with other appropriate Federal agencies.

(9) The term "established Federal standard" means any operative occupational safety and health standard established by any agency of the United States and presently in effect, or contained in any Act of Congress in force on the date of enactment of this Act.

APPLICABILITY OF ACT

SEC. 4. (a) This Act shall apply only with respect to employment performed in a workplace in a State, Wake Island, Outer Continental Shelf lands defined in the Outer Continental Shelf Lands Act, Johnston Island, or the Canal Zone. The Secretary of the Interior shall, by regulation, provide for judicial enforcement of this Act by the courts established for areas in which there are no Federal district courts having jurisdiction.

(b)(1) Nothing in this Act shall be deemed to repeal or modify any other Federal law prescribing safety or health requirements or the standards, rules, or regulations promulgated pursuant to such law.

(2) The safety and health standards promulgated under the Walsh-Healy Public Contracts Act (41 U.S.C. 35 et seq.), the Service Contract Act (41 U.S.C. 351 et seq.), Public Law 91-54, Act of August 9, 1969 (83 Stat. 96, 40 U.S.C. 333), and the National Foundation on Arts and Humanities Act (20 U.S.C. 951 et seq.), are deemed replaced on the effective date of corresponding standards promulgated under this Act, as determined by the Secretary of Labor to be corresponding standards.

(3) The Secretary shall, within three years after the effective date of this Act, report to the Congress his recommendations for legislation to avoid unnecessary duplication and to achieve coordination between this Act and other Federal laws.

DUTIES OF EMPLOYERS

SEC. 5. Each employer—
(1) shall furnish to each of his employees employment and a place of employment which is safe and healthful, and
(2) shall, except as provided in section 17, comply with occupational safety and health standards and with interim standards which are promulgated under this Act.

INTERIM SAFETY AND HEALTH STANDARDS

SEC. 6. The Secretary shall, as soon as practicable during the period beginning with the effective date of this Act and ending two years after such date, by rule promulgate as an interim standard, any national consensus standard, any established Federal standard then in effect (not limited to its present area of application), and any standard proposed by a nationally recognized standards-producing organization by other than a consensus method, unless he determines that the promulgation of such a standard as an interim standard would not result in improved safety or health for specifically designated employees. In the event of conflict among any such standards, the Secretary shall promulgate the standard which assures the greatest protection of the safety or health of the affected employees. No such standard shall be promulgated without a public hearing with respect thereto at which interested persons are afforded an opportunity to express their views, but in other respects section 553 of title 5, United States Code, shall be applicable in carrying out this section. Each interim standard shall stay in effect until superseded by another interim standard or until superseded pursuant to a rule issued and in effect under section 7. The Secretary shall commence (by appointing an advisory committee) a proceeding under section 7 for the promulgation of an occupational safety and health standard dealing with the same subject matter as each interim standard or standards, and any additional occupational safety or health issues he deems relevant, within ninety days after he promulgates such interim standard.

OCCUPATIONAL SAFETY AND HEALTH STANDARDS

SEC. 7. (a) The Secretary may, by rule, promulgate, modify, or revoke any occupational safety and health standard in the following manner:
(1) Whenever the Secretary upon the basis of information submitted to him in writing by an interested person, a representative of an organization of employers or employees, a nationally recognized standards-producing organization, the Secretary of Health, Education, and Welfare, a State, or a political subdivision of a State, or on the basis of information otherwise available to him, determines that such a rule should be prescribed in order to serve the objectives of this Act, and whenever he is required to do so by section 6, the Secretary shall appoint an advisory committee under section 8(b) of this Act, which shall submit to him its recommendations regarding the rule to be prescribed which will carry out the

purposes of this Act, which recommendations shall be published by him in the Federal Register, either as part of a subsequent notice of proposed rulemaking or separately. The recommendations of an advisory committee shall be submitted to the Secretary within two hundred and seventy days from its appointment, or within such longer or shorter period as may be prescribed by the Secretary, but in no event may he prescribe a period which is longer than one year and three months.

(2) After the submission of such recommendations, the Secretary shall, as soon as practicable and in any event within four months, schedule and give notice of a hearing on the recommendations of the advisory committee and any other relevant subjects and issues. In the event that the advisory committee fails to submit recommendations with two hundred and seventy days from its appointment (or such longer or shorter period as the Secretary has prescribed) the Secretary shall make a proposal relevant to the purpose for which the advisory committee was appointed, and shall within four months schedule and give notice of hearing thereon. In either case, notice of the time, place, subjects, and issues of any such hearing shall be published in the Federal Register thirty days prior to the hearing and shall contain the recommendations of the advisory committee or the proposal made in absence of such recommendation. Prior to the hearing interested persons shall be afforded an opportunity to submit comments upon any recommendations of the advisory committee or other proposal. Only persons who have submitted such comments shall have a right at such hearing to submit oral arguments, but nothing herein shall be deemed to prevent any person from submitting written evidence, data, views, or arguments.

(3) Upon the entire record before him, including the advisory committee recommendations and any evidence, data, views, and arguments submitted in connection with the hearing, the Secretary shall within sixty days after completion of the hearing issue a rule promulgating, modifying, or revoking an occupational safety and health standard or make a determination that a rule should not be issued. Such a rule may contain a provision delaying its effective date for such period (not in excess of ninety days) as the Secretary determines may be appropriate to insure that affected employers and employees will be informed of the existence of the standard and of its terms and that employers affected are given an opportunity to familiarize themselves and their employees with the requirements of the standard.

(4) The Secretary, in promulgating standards under this subsection, shall set the standard which most adequately assures, on the basis of the best available professional evidence, that no employee will suffer any impairment of health or functional capacity, or diminished life expectancy even if such employee has regular exposure to the hazard dealt with by such standard for the period of his working life. Wherever practicable, such standard shall be expressed in terms of objective criteria and in terms of the performance desired.

(b) Any affected employer may apply to the Secretary for a rule or order for an exemption from clause (2) of section 5. Affected employees shall be given notice of each such application and an opportunity to participate in a hearing. The Secretary shall issue such rule or order if he determines on the record, after an opportunity for an inspection and a hearing, that the proponent of the exemption has demonstrated by a preponderance of the evidence that the conditions, practices, means, methods, operations, or processes used or proposed to be used by an employer will provide employment and places of employment to his employees which are as safe and healthful as those which would prevail if he complied with the standard. The rule or order so issued shall prescribe the conditions the employer must maintain, and the practices, means, methods, operations, and processes which he must adopt and utilize to the extent they differ from the standard in question. Such a rule or order may be modified or revoked upon application by an employer, employees, or by the Secretary on his own motion in the manner prescribed for its issuance under this subsection at any time after six months after its issuance and at six month intervals thereafter.

(c)(1) The Secretary shall determine, as soon as possible after a special inspection, but in any event within 90 days of any such inspection, whether or not to promulgate, on an emergency temporary basis, an occupational safety and health standard to take effect thirty days after publication in the Federal Register. Such standard shall be promulgated if the Secretary finds (A) that employees are exposed to grave danger from exposure to substances determined to be toxic or to new hazards and (B) that such emergency standard is necessary to protect employees from such grave danger.

(2) Such standard shall be effective for a period not to exceed six months unless, prior to the expiration of such period a proceeding under paragraph (3) of this subsection has been commenced and is pending, but shall then be effective only until the termination of that proceeding.

(3) Upon publication of such standard in the Federal Register the Secretary shall commence a hearing in accordance with sections 556 and 557 of title 5, United States Code, and the standard as published shall also serve as a proposed rule for the hearing.

(d) Whenever the Secretary promulgates any standard, makes any rule, order, decision, grants any exemption or extension of time, or compromises, mitigates, or settles any penalty assessed under this Act, he shall include a statement of the reasons for such action, and such statement shall be published in the Federal Register.

ADMINISTRATION; ADVISORY COMMITTEES

SEC. 8. (a) In carrying out his responsibilities under this Act, the Secretary is authorized to—

(1) use, with the consent of any Federal agency, the services, facilities, and employees of such agency with or without reimbursement, and with the consent of any State or political subdivision thereof, accept and use the services, facilities, and employees of the agencies of such State or subdivision with reimbursement; and

(2) employ experts and consultants or organizations thereof as authorized by section 3109 of title 5, United States Code, except that contracts for such employment may be renewed annually; compensate individuals so employed at rates not in excess of the rate specified at the time of service for grade GS–18 in section 5332 of title 5, United States Code, including traveltime; and allow them while away from their homes or regular places of business, travel expenses (including per diem in lieu of subsistence) as authorized by section 5703 of title 5, United States Code, for persons in the Government service employed intermittently, while so employed.

(b) The Secretary shall appoint advisory committees to recommend occupational safety and health standards under section 7(a) of this Act before the commencement of proceedings thereunder. Each such advisory committee shall consist of not more than fifteen members and shall include as a member one or more designees of the Secretary of Health, Education, and Welfare, and shall include among its members an equal number of persons qualified by experience and affiliation to present the viewpoint of the employers involved, and of persons similarly qualified to present the viewpoint of the workers involved, as well as one or more representatives of health and safety agencies of the States. An advisory committee may also include such other persons as the Secretary may appoint who are qualified by knowledge and experience to make a useful contribution to the work of the committee, including one or more representatives of professional organizations of technicians or professionals specializing in occupational safety or health, and one or more representatives of nationally recognized standards-producing organizations, but the number of persons so appointed to any advisory committee shall not exceed the number appointed to such committee as representatives of Federal and State agencies. Persons appointed to advisory committees from private life shall be compensated in the same manner as consultants or experts under subsection (a)(2) of this section. The Secretary shall pay to any State which is the employer of a member of the committee who is a representative of the health or safety agency of that State, reimbursement sufficient to cover the actual cost to the State resulting from such representative's membership on the committee. Any meeting of the committee shall be open to the public and an accurate record shall be kept and made available to the public. No member of the committee (other than representatives of employers and employees) shall have an economic interest in any proposed rule.

(c)(1) The Secretary and the Secretary of Health, Education, and Welfare shall appoint a National Advisory Committee on Occupational Safety and Health (hereafter in this subsection referred to as the "Committee"). The Committee shall consist of twenty members appointed without regard to the civil service laws and composed equally of representatives of management, labor, occupational safety and occupational health professions, and of the public. The Secretary shall appoint all members of the Committee except for occupational health representatives who shall be appointed by the Secretary of Health, Education, and Welfare. The Secretary shall designate one of the public members as Chairman. The members shall be selected upon the basis of their experience and competence in the field of occupational safety and health.

(2) The Committee shall advise, consult with, and make recommendations to, the Secretaries of Labor and Health, Education, and Welfare on matters relating to the implementation of this Act. The Committee shall hold no fewer than two meetings during each calendar year. All meetings of the Committee shall be open to the public and a transcript shall be kept and made available for public inspection.

(3) The members of the Committee shall be compensated in accordance with the provisions of subsection (a)(2) of this section.

(4) The Secretary shall furnish to the Committee an executive secretary and such secretarial, clerical, and other services as are deemed necessary to the conduct of its business.

INSPECTIONS, INVESTIGATIONS, AND REPORTS

SEC. 9. (a) In order to carry out the purposes of this Act, the Secretary, upon presenting appropriate credentials to the owner, operator, or agent in charge, is authorized—

(1) to enter upon at reasonable times any workplace where work is performed to which this Act applies; and

(2) to inspect and investigate during regular working hours and at other reasonable times, and within reasonable limits and in a reasonable manner, any such place and all pertinent conditions, structures, machines, apparatus, devices, equipment, and materials therein, and to question any such employer, owner, operator, agent or employee.

(b) For the purposes of any investigation provided for in this title, the provisions of sections 9 and 10 (relating to the attendance of witnesses and the production of books, papers, and documents) of the Federal Trade Commission Act of September 16, 1914 (15 U.S.C. 49, 50), are hereby made applicable to the jurisdiction, powers, and duties of the Secretary or any officers designated by him.

(c) Each employer shall make, keep, and preserve, and make available to the Secretary such record of his activities concerning the requirements of this Act, and shall make reports therefrom to the Secretary, as he may prescribe by regulation or order as necessary or appropriate for the enforcement of this Act. The Secretary shall also make such regulations as may be necessary to assure that employers keep their employees continuously informed of their rights, privileges, and obligations under this Act. The Secretary in cooperation with the Secretary of Health, Education, and Welfare shall make regulations requiring employers to keep records of all work-related injuries, diseases, and ailments which arise from conditions present in the working environment.

(d) Any information obtained by the Secretary, the Secretary of Health, Education, and Welfare, or a State agency under this Act shall be obtained with a minimum burden upon employers, especially those operating small businesses. Unnecessary duplication of efforts in obtaining information shall be reduced to the maximum extent feasible.

(e) A representative of the employer and a representative authorized by his employees shall be given an opportunity to accompany any person who is making an inspection under subsection (a) of any workplace.

CITATIONS FOR VIOLATIONS

SEC. 10. (a) If, upon inspection or investigation, the Secretary determines that an employer has violated clause (2) of section 5, any rule or order issued under section 7(b), or any regulation prescribed under section 9(c), and that a serious danger exists by reason of any such violation, he shall issue a citation forthwith to the employer for such violation. Each such citation shall (1) be in writing, (2) describe with particularity the nature of the violation, including a reference to the provision of the standard, rule, order, or regulation alleged to have been violated, and (3) the period of time within which it must be corrected.

(b) If, upon inspection or investigation, the Secretary determines that an employer has violated clause (1) of section 5 and a serious danger exists, or has violated any regulation prescribed under section 9(c) or any rule or order issued under section 7(b), but that no serious danger exists by reason of such violation, he shall issue a citation forthwith to the employer for such violation. Each such citation shall (1) be in writing, (2) describe with particularity the nature of the violation, including a reference to the provision of the standard, duty, rule, order, or regulation alleged to have been violated, and (3) the period of time within which it must be corrected. For purposes of this subsection, an employer shall not be deemed to have violated a citation issued for a violation of clause (1) of section 5 where a serious danger exists if the employer is in compliance with an applicable interim standard, occupational health or safety standard, promulgated under this Act or under a State plan applicable under section 17(c).

(c) If, upon inspection or investigation, the Secretary determines that an employer has violated clause (1) or (2) of section 5, and specifically determines, together with his reasons, that no serious danger exists by reason of such violation, he shall issue a citation forthwith to the employer for such violation. Each such citation shall (1) be in writing, (2) describe with particularity the nature of the violation, including a reference to the provision of the standard, rule, order, duty, or regulation alleged to have been violated.

(d) Where a citation is issued under subsection (a) or (b) for a violation which might cause cumulative or latent ill effects, such citation shall specify, where feasible, a period during which employers shall accurately measure the exposure of employees to such danger.

(e) Each citation issued under this section or a copy or copies thereof shall be prominently posted (as prescribed in regulations made under section 9(c)) at or near each place a violation referred to in the citation occurred.

(f) For purposes of this Act a "serious danger" shall be deemed to exist in a place of employment if there is a substantial probability that at any time death or serious physical harm could result from a condition which exists, or from one or more practices, means, methods, operations, or processes which have been adopted or are in use, in such place of employment.

PROCEDURES FOR ENFORCEMENT

SEC. 11. (a) If, after an inspection or investigation, the Secretary issues a citation under section 10 (a) or (b), the Secretary shall, within ten working days of the termination of such inspection or investigation, notify the employer by certified mail of the penalty, if any, proposed to be assessed under section 15 and that he has fifteen working days within which to notify the Secretary that he wishes to contest the citation or proposed assessment of penalty. If such notice is not issued by the Secretary within such ten-day period then such citation and proposed assessment of penalty shall be void. If, within fifteen working days from the receipt of such a notice, the employer fails to notify the Secretary that he intends to contest the citation or proposed assessment of penalty, the citation and the assessment, as proposed, shall be final and not subject to review by any court or agency, and for purposes of subsection (c) shall be considered an order issued by the Secretary under subsection (b).

(b) If an employer notifies the Secretary that he intends to contest a citation issued under section 10 (a) or (b) or proposed assessment of penalty or if the Secretary determines an employer has failed to correct a violation for which such a citation has been issued within the period permitted for its correction (which period shall not begin to run until the termination of proceedings under this subsection), the Secretary shall afford an opportunity for a hearing (in accordance with section 554 of title 5, United States Code, but without regard to subsection (a)(3) of such section), and shall, if he determines such citation is valid, issue an order, based on findings of fact, confirming, denying, or modifying the citation or assessment of penalty, or, if he determines the employer has failed to correct such violation within such period, issue such orders, based on findings of fact, as may be necessary for the correction of the violation for which the citation was issued, and for the assessment and collection of any penalty under section 15 (a), (b), or (c). The Secretary shall give such person the information required by section 554(b) of such title at least fifteen days prior to hearing. In proceedings under this subsection, the Secretary shall consider, among other things, the validity of any standard, rule, order, or regulation alleged to have been violated, and the reasonableness of the period of time permitted for the correction of the violation.

(c) The Secretary shall have power, upon issuance of an order under subsection (b), to petition any United States district court within the district where a violation is alleged to have occurred or where the employer has its principal office for appropriate relief. The United States district courts shall have jurisdiction to enforce (by restraining order, injunction, or otherwise) any order of the Secretary issued under subsection (b). Except in the case of an order which has become final under section 11(a), any person adversely affected or aggrieved by an order of the Secretary issued under subsection (b) may obtain review of such order by the United States district court for the district where the violation is alleged to have occurred or where the employer has its principal office by filing in such court within thirty days following the issuance of such order a petition praying that the action of the Secretary be modified or set aside in whole or in part. Review by the court shall be in accord with the provisions of section 706 of title 5, United States Code. A petition for review by the court shall not stay an order of the Secretary under subsection (b) unless otherwise provided by the court.

PROCEDURES TO COUNTERACT IMMINENT DANGERS

SEC. 12. (a) If an inspection or investigation of a place of employment discloses that imminent danger exists in such place of employment, the Secretary may issue an order prohibiting the employment or presence of any individuals in locations or under conditions where such an imminent danger exists, except to correct or remove it. Such order may remain in effect for not more than five days from the date of its issuance.

(b) If, upon inspection or investigation of a place of employment, the Secretary determines that an imminent danger exists in such place of employment, the Secretary may bring a civil action in the United States district court for the district where the imminent danger exists or where the employer has its principal office for a temporary restraining order or injunction prohibiting the employment or presence of any individual in locations or under conditions where such an imminent danger exists, except to correct or remove it. An action may be brought under this subsection while an order of the Secretary under subsection (a) is in effect. If, in a proceeding under section 11, it is finally determined that any condition which existed, or any practice, means, method, operation, or process which was adopted or in use in a place of employment did not violate section 5, and it was upon the basis of the existence of such condition or the adoption of such practice, means, method, operation, or process that an order was issued under this subsection, then such order shall no longer be in effect.

(c) If the Secretary arbitrarily or capriciously issues or fails to issue an order under subsection (a) and any person is injured thereby either physically or financially by reason of such order or failure to issue such order, such person may bring an action against the United States in the Court of Claims in which he may recover the damages he has sustained, including reasonable court costs and attorneys' fees.

(d) For purposes of this section an imminent danger shall be deemed to exist in a place of employment if such danger could reasonably be expected to cause death or serious physical harm before the imminence of such danger can be eliminated.

REPRESENTATION IN CIVIL LITIGATION

SEC. 13. Except as provided in section 518(a) of title 28, United States Code, relating to litigation before the Supreme Court and the Court of Claims, the Solicitor of Labor may appear for and represent the Secretary in any civil litigation brought under this Act but all such litigation shall be subject to the direction and control of the Attorney General.

CONFIDENTIALITY OF TRADE SECRETS

SEC. 14. All information reported to or otherwise obtained by the Secretary or his representative in connection with any inspection or proceeding under this Act which contains or which might reveal a trade secret referred to in section 1905 of title 18 of the United States Code shall be considered confidential for the purpose of that section, except that such information may be disclosed to other officers or employees concerned with carrying out this Act or when relevant in any proceeding under this Act.

PENALTIES

SEC. 15. (a) Any employer who (1) receives a citation under section 10(a), (2) fails to correct a violation for which a citation has been issued under section 10(a) within the period permitted for its correction (which period shall not begin to run until the termination of any proceedings under section 11(b)), or (3) violates an order issued under section 12(a), shall be assessed by the Secretary, pursuant to an order issued under section 11(b), a civil penalty of not more than $1,000 for each violation. Each violation shall be a separate offense. When the violation is of a continuing nature, each day during which it continues after a reasonable time specified in an initial decision following the hearing held under section 11(b) shall constitute a separate offense except during the time a review of the order under section 11(b) may be taken, or such review is pending and during the time allowed in the order under section 11(b) for correction. The Secretary may compromise, mitigate, or settle any claim for civil penalties. In assessing the penalty consideration shall be given to the appropriateness of the penalty, to the size of the business of the person charged, to the gravity of the violation, to the history of previous violations, and to the good faith of the employer.

(b) Any employer who receives a citation under section 10(b), or fails to correct a violation for which a citation has been issued under section 10(b) within the time prescribed for its correction (which period shall not begin to run until the termination of any proceedings under section 11(b)), may be assessed by the Secretary, pursuant to an order issued under section 11(b), a civil penalty of not more than $1,000 for each violation. Each violation shall be a separate offense. When the violation is of a continuing nature, each day during which it continues after a reasonable time specified in an initial decision following the hearing held under section 11(b) shall constitute a separate offense except during the time a review of the order under section 11(b) may be taken, or such review is pending and during the time allowed in the order under section 11(b) for correction. The Secretary may compromise, mitigate, or settle any claim for civil penalties. In assessing the penalty consideration shall be given to the appropriateness of the penalty, to the size of the business of the person charged, to the gravity of the violation, to the history of previous violations, and to the good faith of the employer.

(c) Any employer who willfully violates any standards promulgated under sections 6 and 7 of this Act may be assessed by the Secretary, pursuant to an order issued under section 11 of this Act, a civil penalty of not more than $10,000 for each violation. In assessing the penalty, consideration shall be given to the appropriateness of the penalty to the size of the business of the person charged, to the gravity of the violation, to the history of previous violations, and to the good faith of the employer.

(d) Any person who forcibly assaults, resists, opposes, impedes, intimidates, or interferes with any person while engaged in or on account of the performance of inspections or investigatory duties under this Act shall be fined not more than $5,000 or imprisoned not more than three years, or both. Whoever, in the commission of any such acts, uses a deadly or dangerous weapon, shall be fined not more than $10,000 or imprisoned not more than ten years or both. Whoever kills any person while engaged in or on account of the performance of inspecting or investigating duties under this Act shall be punished by imprisonment for any term of years or for life.

(e) Advance notice may be given of investigations necessary for the Secretary and the Secretary of Health, Education, and Welfare to effectively obtain, utilize, or disseminate information relating to health or safety conditions, the causes of accidents, diseases, and physical impairments; however, any person who gives advance notice of any inspection to be conducted under this Act shall be fined not more than $1,000 or imprisoned not more than one year, or both.

(f) Any person who discriminates against any employee because of any action such employee has taken on behalf of himself or others, to secure the protection afforded by this Act shall be fined not more than $1,000 or imprisoned not more than one year, or both.

VARIATIONS, TOLERANCES, AND EXEMPTIONS

SEC. 16. The Secretary may provide such reasonable limitations and may make such rules and regulations allowing reasonable variations, tolerances, and exemptions to and from any or all provisions of this Act as he may find necessary and proper to avoid serious impairment of the national defense. Such action shall not be in effect for more than six months without notification to affected employees and an opportunity being afforded for a hearing.

STATE JURISDICTION AND STATE PLANS

SEC. 17. (a) Nothing in this Act shall prevent any State agency or court from asserting jurisdiction under State law over any occupational safety or health issue with respect to which no standard is in effect under section 6 or 7.

(b) Any State which, at any time, desires to assume responsibility for development and enforcement therein of occupational safety and health standards relating to any occupational safety or health issue with respect to which a Federal standard has been promulgated under section 7 shall submit a State plan for the development of such standards and their enforcement.

(c) The Secretary shall approve the plan submitted by a State under subsection (b), or any modification thereof, if such plan in his judgment—

(1) designates a State agency or agencies as the agency or agencies responsible for administering the plan throughout the State,

(2) provides for the development and enforcement of safety and health standards relating to one or more safety or health issues, which standards (and the enforcement of which standards) are or will be at least as effective in providing safe and healthful employment and places of employment as the standards promulgated under section 7 which relate to the same issues,

(3) provides for a right of entry and inspection of all workplaces subject to the Act which is at least as effective as that provided in section 9(a), (c), (d), and (e), and includes a prohibition on advance notice of inspections,

(4) contains satisfactory assurances that such agency or agencies have or will have the legal authority and qualified personnel necessary for the enforcement of such standards,

(5) gives satisfactory assurances that such State will devote adequate funds to the administration and enforcement of such standards,

(6) makes all standards included under the plan applicable to all employees of public agencies of the State and its political subdivisions,

(7) requires employers in the State to make reports to the Secretary in the same manner and to the same extent as if the plan were not in effect, and

(8) provides that the State agency will make such reports to the Secretary in such form and containing such information, as the Secretary shall from time to time require.

(d) If the Secretary rejects a plan submitted under subsection (b), he shall afford the State submitting the plan, due notice and opportunity for a hearing before so doing.

(e) After the Secretary approves a State plan submitted under subsection (b), he may, but shall not be required to, exercise his authority under sections 9, 10, 11, and 15 with respect to comparable standards promulgated under section 7, for the period specified in the next sentence. The Secretary may exercise the authority referred to above until he determines, on the basis of actual operations under the State plan, that the criteria set forth in subsection (c) are being applied, but he shall not make such determination for at least three years after the plan's approval under subsection (c). Upon making the determination referred to in the preceding sentence, the provisions of sections 5(2), 9 (except for purpose of carrying out subsection (f)), 10, 11, and 15 and standards promulgated under section 7 of this Act, shall not apply with respect to any occupational safety or health issues covered under the plan, but the Secretary may retain jurisdiction under the above provisions in any proceeding commenced under section 10 or 11 before the date of determination.

(f) The Secretary shall, on the basis of reports submitted by the State agency and his own inspections make a continuing evaluation of the manner in which each State having a plan approved under this section is carrying out such plan. Whenever the Secretary finds, after affording due notice and opportunity for a hearing, that in the administration of the State plan there is a failure to comply substantially with any provision of the State plan (or any assurance contained therein), he shall notify the State agency of his withdrawal of approval of such plan and upon receipt of such notice such plan shall cease to be in effect, but the State may retain jurisdiction in any case commenced before the withdrawal of the plan in order to enforce standards under the plan whenever the issues involved do not relate to the reasons for the withdrawal of the plan.

(g) The State may obtain a review of a decision of the Secretary withdrawing approval of or rejecting its plan by the United States court of appeals for the circuit in which the State is located by filing in such court within thirty days following receipt of notice of such decision a petition praying that the action of the Secretary be modified or set aside in whole or in part. A copy of such petition shall forthwith be served upon the Secretary, and thereupon the Secretary shall certify and file in the court the record upon which the decision complained of was issued as provided in section 2112 of title 28, United States Code. Unless the court finds that the Secretary's decision in rejecting a proposed State plan or withdrawing his approval of such a plan to be arbitrary and capricious, the court shall affirm the Secretary's decision. The judgment of the court shall be subject to review by the Supreme Court of the United States upon certiorari or certification as provided in section 1254 of title 28, United States Code.

FEDERAL AGENCY SAFETY PROGRAMS AND RESPONSIBILITIES

SEC. 18. (a) It shall be the responsibility of the head of each Federal agency to establish and maintain an effective and comprehensive occupational safety and health program which is consistent with the standards promulgated under section 7. The head of each agency shall (after consultation with representatives of the employees thereof)—

(1) provide safe and healthful places and conditions of employment, consistent with the standards set under section 7;

(2) acquire, maintain, and require the use of safety equipment, personal protective equipment, and devices reasonably necessary to protect employees;

(3) keep adequate records of all occupational accidents and illnesses for proper evaluation and necessary corrective action; and

(4) make an annual report to the Secretary with respect to occupational accidents and injuries and the agency's program under this section. Such report shall include any report submitted under section 7902(e)(2) of title 5, United States Code.

(b) The Secretary shall report to the President a summary or digest of reports submitted to him under subsection (a)(4) of this section, together with his evaluation of and recommendations derived from such reports. The President shall transmit annually to the Senate and House of Representatives a report of the activities of Federal agencies under this section.

(c) Section 7902(c)(1) of title 5, United States Code is amended by inserting after "agencies" the following: "and of labor organizations representing employees".

RESEARCH AND RELATED ACTIVITIES

SEC. 19. (a)(1) The Secretary of Health, Education, and Welfare, after consultation with the Secretary and with other appropriate Federal departments or agencies, shall conduct (directly or by grants or contracts) research, experiments, and demonstrations relating to occupational safety and health, including studies of psychological factors involved, and relating to innovative methods, techniques, and approaches for dealing with occupational safety and health problems.

(2) The Secretary of Health, Education, and Welfare shall from time to time consult with the Secretary in order to develop specific plans for such research, demonstrations, and experiments as are necessary to produce criteria enabling the Secretary to meet his responsibility for the formulation of safety and health standards under this Act; and the Secretary of Health, Education, and Welfare, on the basis of such research, demonstrations, and experiments and any other information available to him, shall develop and publish at least annually such criteria which if applied will assure that no employee will suffer diminished health or life expectancy as a result of his work experience.

(3) The Secretary of Health, Education, and Welfare shall also conduct special research, experiments, and demonstrations relating to occupational safety and health as are necessary to explore new problems, including those created by new technology in occupational safety and health, which may require ameliorative action beyond that which is otherwise provided for in the operating provisions of this Act. The Secretary of Health, Education, and Welfare shall also conduct research into the motivational and behavioral factors relating to the field of occupational safety and health.

(4) The Secretary, in conjunction with the Secretary of Health, Education, and Welfare, shall as soon as practicable develop procedures to assure that all exposure to substances, conditions, or processes he has determined or reasonably believes will result in dangers to health or safety is accurately measured and recorded by employers.

In complying with the provisions of this paragraph—

(A) If such substance, condition, or process is not covered by a standard promulgated by the Secretary, or criteria established by the Secretary of Health, Education, and Welfare as provided under section 19(a)(2) of this Act, the employer may be required by the Secretary or the Secretary of Health, Education, and Welfare to measure or record concentrations or exposures to employees only upon a determination that the health or safety of workers may be in danger and further information is necessary to determine the existence of that danger and the steps necessary for correction.

(B) If such substance, condition, or process is covered by criteria issued by the Secretary of Health, Education, and Welfare as provided by section 19(a)(2), the Secretary may, if he finds it necessary to meet the purposes of this Act, require an employer to measure or record the particular substance.

(C) If such a substance, condition, or process is covered by a standard promulgated by the Secretary and if the employer is found not to be in compliance with the standard, he shall be required to measure and record the particular substances, as provided by regulation, for the period deemed necessary by the Secretary to assure future compliance with such standard.

(D) Any required measurement or recording under this subsection shall be required only where such measurement is technologically feasible and the equipment is available at reasonable cost, and shall be recorded and shall comply with section 9(c) of this Act.

(5) The Secretary of Health, Education, and Welfare shall publish within six months of enactment of this Act and thereafter as needed but at least annually a ist of all known or potentially toxic substances and the concentrations at which such toxicity is known to occur; and shall determine following a request by any employer or authorized representative of any group of employees whether any substance normally found in the working place has potentially toxic or harmful effects in such concentration as used or found; and shall submit such determination both to employers and affected employees as soon as possible. Within sixty days of such determination by the Secretary of Health, Education, and Welfare of potential toxicity of any substance, an employer shall not require any employee to be exposed to such substance designated above in toxic or greater concentrations unless it is accompanied by information, made available to employees, by label or other appropriate means, of the known hazards or toxic or long-term ill effects, the nature of the substance, and the signs, symptoms, emergency treatment, and proper conditions and precautions of safe use, and personal protective equipment is supplied which allows established work procedures to be performed with such equipment, or unless such exposed employee may absent himself from such risk of harm for the period necessary to avoid such danger without loss of regular compensation for such period.

(b) The Secretary of Health, Education, and Welfare is authorized to make inspections and question employers and employees as provided in section 9 of this Act in order to carry out his functions and responsibilities under this section.

(c) The Secretary is authorized to enter into contracts, agreements, or other arrangements with appropriate public agencies or private organizations for the purpose of conducting studies related to the establishing and applying of occupational safety and health standards under section 7 of this Act. In carrying out his responsibilities under this subsection, the Secretary and the Secretary of Health, Education, and Welfare shall cooperate in order to avoid any duplication of efforts under this section.

(d) The Secretary, after consultation with the Secretary of Health, Education, and Welfare, and with the appropriate official in each State as duly designated by such State, shall establish such accident and health reporting systems for employers and for the States as he deems necessary to carry out his responsibilities under this Act.

(e) Information obtained by the Secretary and the Secretary of Health, Education, and Welfare under this section shall be disseminated by the Secretary to employers and employees and organizations thereof.

TRAINING AND EMPLOYEE EDUCATION

Sec. 20. (a) The Secretary of Health, Education, and Welfare, after consultation with the Secretary of Labor and with other appropriate Federal departments and agencies, shall conduct, directly or by grants or contracts (1) education programs to provide an adequate supply of qualified personnel to carry out the purposes of this Act, and (2) informational programs on the importance of and proper use of adequate safety and health equipment.

(b) The Secretary is also authorized to conduct (directly or by grants or contracts) short-term training of personnel engaged in work related to his responsibilities under this Act.

(c) The Secretary, in consultation with the Secretary of Health, Education. and Welfare, shall provide for the establishment and supervision of programs for the education and training of employers and employees in the recognition, avoidance, and prevention of unsafe or unhealthful working conditions in employments covered by this Act, and to consult with and advise employers and employees, and organizations representing employers and employees as to effective means of preventing occupational injuries and illnesses.

GRANTS TO THE STATES

SEC. 21. (a) The Secretary is authorized, during the fiscal year ending June 30, 1971, and the two succeeding fiscal years, to make grants to the States which have designated a State agency under section 17(c) to assist them (1) in identifying their needs and responsibilities in the area of occupational safety and health, (2) in developing State plans under section 17, or (3) in developing plans for—

(A) establishing systems for the collection of information concerning the nature and frequency of occupational injuries and diseases;

(B) increasing the expertise and enforcement capabilities of their personnel engaged in occupational safety and health programs; or

(C) otherwise improving the administration and enforcement of State occupational safety and health laws, including standards thereunder, consistent with the objectives of this Act.

(b) The Secretary is authorized, during the fiscal year ending June 30, 1971, and the two succeeding fiscal years, to make grants to the States for experimental and demonstration projects consistent with the objectives set forth in subsection (a) of this section.

(c) The Governor of the State shall designate the appropriate State agency, or agencies, for receipt of any grant made by the Secretary under this section.

(d) Any State agency, or agencies, designated by the Governor of the State, desiring a grant under this section shall submit an application therefor to the Secretary.

(e) The Secretary shall review the application, and shall, after consultation with the Secretary of Health, Education, and Welfare, approve or reject such application.

(f) The Federal share for each State grant under subsection (a) or (b) of this section may be up to 90 per centum of the State's total cost. In the event the Federal share for all States under either such subsection is not the same, the differences among the States shall be established on the basis of objective criteria.

(g) The Secretary is authorized to make grants to the States to assist them in administering and enforcing programs for occupational safety and health contained in State plans approved by the Secretary pursuant to section 17 of this Act. The Federal share for each State grant under this subsection may be up to 50 per centum of the State's total cost. The last sentence of subsection (f) shall be applicable in determining the Federal share under this subsection.

(h) Prior to June 30, 1973, the Secretary shall, after consultation, with the Secretary of Health, Education, and Welfare, transmit a report to the President and to Congress, describing the experience under the program and making any recommendations he may deem appropriate.

EFFECT ON OTHER LAWS

SEC. 22. (a) Nothing in this Act shall be construed or held to supersede or in any manner affect any workmen's compensation law or to enlarge or diminish or affect in any other manner the common law or statutory rights, duties, or liabilities of employers and employees under any law with respect to injuries, occupational or other diseases, or death of employees arising out of, or in the course of, employment.

(b) Nothing in section 5 of this Act shall apply to working conditions of employees with respect to whom any Federal agency exercises statutory authority to prescribe or enforce standards or regulations affecting occupational safety and health.

AUDITS

SEC. 23. (a) Each recipient of a grant under this Act shall keep such records as the Secretary shall prescribe, including records which fully disclose the amount and disposition by such recipient of the proceeds of such grant, the total cost of the project or undertaking in connection with which such grant is made or used, and the amount of that portion of the cost of the project or undertaking supplied by other sources, and such other records as will facilitate an effective audit.

(b) The Secretary and the Comptroller General of the United States, or any of their duly authorized representatives, shall have access for the purpose of audit and examination to any books, documents, papers, and records of the recipients of any grant under this Act that are pertinent to any such grant.

REPORTS

SEC. 24. Within one hundred and twenty days following the convening of each regular session of each Congress, the Secretary and the Secretary of Health, Education, and Welfare shall each prepare and submit to the President for transmittal to the Congress a report upon the subject matter of this Act, the progress concerning the achievement of its purposes, the needs and requirements in the field of occupational safety and health, and any other relevant information, and including any recommendations to effectuate the purposes of this Act.

APPROPRIATIONS

SEC. 25. There are authorized to be appropriated to carry out this Act for each fiscal year such sums as the Congress shall deem necessary.

EFFECTIVE DATE

SEC. 26. This Act shall take effect on the first day of the first month which begins more than thirty days after the date of it enactment.

SEPARABILITY

SEC. 27. If any provision of this Act, or the application of such provision to any person or circumstance, shall be held invalid, the remainder of this Act, or the application of such provision to persons or circumstances other than those as to which it is held invalid, shall not be affected thereby.

PURPOSE

The purpose of H.R. 16785 is to reduce the number and severity of work-related injuries and illnesses which in spite of current efforts continue at high levels, and which result in human misery and economic waste.

The bill would achieve its purposes by providing needed Federal-State cooperation and by developing and extending Federal support in the field of industrial safety and health. Aid is given specifically in the areas of research, education, training and regulation.

BACKGROUND

More and more nationwide activities are focusing on the "Environmental Crisis"—the pollution of air and water and the destruction of natural resources. Unfortunately, national attention given to environmental problems fails to give sufficient recognition to the pertinent question of occupational safety and health. Our environment is not solely the air we breathe traveling to and from work. It is also the air we breath at work. The issue of the health and safety of the American working man and woman is the most crucial one in the whole environmental question, because it is out of the workplace that the problem of pollution arises; and over 80 million workers spend one-third of their day in that environment.

The on-the-job health and safety crisis is the worst problem confronting American workers, because each year as a result of their jobs over 14,500 workers die. In only four years time, as many people have died because of their employment as have been killed in almost a decade of American involvement in Vietnam. Over two million workers are disabled annually through job-related accidents.

The economic impact of occupational accidents and diseases is overwhelming. Over $1.5 billion is wasted in lost wages, and the annual loss to the Gross National Product is over $8 billion. Ten times as many man-days are lost from job-related disabilities as from strikes, and days of lost productivity through accidents and illnesses are ten times greater than the loss from strikes.

The Committee recognizes the enormity of the problems of occupational safety and health, and its hearings disclosed that these problems seem to be getting worse, not better.

In 1966–67, the Surgeon General of the United States studied six metropolitan areas, examining 1,700 industrial plants which employed 142,000 workers. The study found that 65 percent of the people were potentially exposed to toxic materials or harmful physical agents, such as severe noise or vibration. The Surgeon General further examined controls that were in effect to protect workers from toxic agents and found that only 25 percent of the workers were adequately covered.

California, a state with vigorous occupational safety and health reporting procedures, showed 27,000 occupational diseases in 1964, a rate of 4.8 per 1,000 workers. Projected nationally, there were 336,000 estimated cases of occupational diseases that year, a figure which by all indications continues to grow. In support of this, the U.S. Public Health Service now shows 390,000 new cases of occupational diseases annually.

Studies of specific industries have also given clear warning of the magnitude of the problem. One study showed that about 3.5 million workers are exposed to some extent to asbestos fibers. In addition, another researcher gathered statistics on asbestos insulation workers for 20 years and found seven times more pulmonary cancer among this group than among the general population.

The chemical betanaphthylamine is so toxic that there is no safe limit of exposure to it. Any exposure at all is likely to result in the employee developing bladder cancer over a period of years. The Commonwealth of Pennsylvania discovered this extreme effect of betanaphthylamine and banned its use, manufacture, storage or handling in the state, but production of this lethal chemical has begun in another state where legislation is inadequate. The exposure of workers to betanaphthylamine continues today.

Clearly, the life of a worker in one state is as important as a worker's life in another state, and uniform standards must be required to protect all workers from dangerous substances. Despite this obvious need, state response has been minimal. Federal leadership and assistance are necessary to change this record of inaction.

It cannot be claimed that industry is too diverse for Government programs to be effective in lowering accident rates, when it is a fact that in the states with good occupational safety and health programs the accident rate is 19 per 100,000 workers, and in states with poor programs it is 110 per 100,000 workers—or over 500 percent higher.

However, the Committee recognizes the problem of comparing the health and safety records of one state with another. States with effective safety programs have as a part of their requirements comprehensive reporting of industrial accidents. While efforts have been made to standardize the form of accident and disease reporting, to date there is no uniform system. As a result, states with the least effective programs may appear to have a more favorable accident record. Accurate, uniform reporting standards are an evident Federal responsibility.

Citing technological progress as a mixed blessing in a message to Congress on August 6, 1969, President Nixon urged the passage of a comprehensive occupational safety and health bill. The President stated:

> The same new method or new product which improves our lives can also be the source of unpleasantness and pain. For man's capacity to innovate is not always matched by his ability to understand his innovations fully, to use them properly, or to protect himself against unforeseen consequences of the changes he creates.
>
> The side effects of progress present special dangers in the workplaces of our country. For the working man and women, the by-products of change constitute an especially serious threat. Some efforts to protect the safety and health of the American worker have been made in the past both by private industry and by all levels of government. But new techniques have moved even faster to create newer dangers. Today we are asking our workers to perform far different tasks from those they performed five or fifteen or fifty years ago. It is only right that the protection we give them is also up to date.

COMMITTEE ACTION

The Select Subcommittee on Labor held 13 days of hearings in Washington, D.C. on September 24, 25, 30; October 9, 15, 16, 29, 30; November 5, 6, 12, 13, 18, 1969. Two hearings were held in San Francisco, California, on November 21 and 22, 1969. The bills considered were H.R. 843, H.R. 3809, H.R. 4294, and H.R. 13373.

Testimony was presented by the Honorable George P. Shultz, Secretary of Labor, and Dr. Roger O. Egeberg Assistant Secretary of the Department of Health, Education, and Welfare for Health and Scientific Affairs. Numerous public witnesses also appeared.

On March 25, 1970, H.R. 16785, a clean bill, was reported by the Subcommittee after five Executive Sessions.

Following two days of consideration, the full Committee on Education and Labor reported this bill as amended to the House for approval.

MAJOR PROVISIONS

INTERIM STANDARDS

H.R. 16785 would require every employer as defined in the bill to comply with interim occupational safety and health standards promulgated by the Secretary of Labor under Section 6. Interim standards may be promulgated for a maximum period of two years from the effective date of this Act. They may be national consensus standards, established Federal standards in effect, or standards produced by a nationally-recognized organization by other than a consensus method. In the event of conflict among standards, the Secretary shall promulgate the one which assures the greatest protection of affected employees. Before standards are promulgated, a public hearing must be afforded to interested parties. Each interim standard shall stay in effect until superseded by a rule issued under Section 7, procedures for formal standards-setting. Ninety days after promulgating interim standards, the Secretary must begin procedures for setting permanent ones.

The intent of this Interim Standards provision is to give the Secretary of Labor a speedy mechanism to promulgate standards with which industry is familiar. These might not be as effective or as current as the permanent standards promulgated under formal procedures, but they will be useful for immediately providing a nation-wide minimum level of health and safety.

Two private organizations are the major sources of consensus standards: the American National Standards Institute, Inc., and the National Fire Protection Association. The standards they produce are the only ones we have in many areas. These two groups together produce only about 13 percent of all safety standards but have done very little in the way of developing occupational health standards.

The Committee believes the Secretary should also be able to use proprietary standards for interim regulation. A considerable number of these are produced by various industries, professional societies and associations. Included are such well-known and respected groups as the American Conference of Governmental Industrial Hygienists, the Manufacturing Chemists Association, and the Associated General Contractors. Policy in this group is determined by a straight membership vote, not by consensus.

Although proprietary standards are voluntary, they have gained wide acceptance by American industry. Recognition of proprietary standards, as well as consensus standards, is significant because the Committee realizes that Federal legislation should not ignore experience gained in the private sector.

Section 6 states that Federal standards in effect on the date of enactment of this Act may be used as interim standards to cover additional employees who are not under the jurisdiction of another Federal safety law.

The Committee believes that business should be readily able to adapt itself to Federal standards since many voluntary industrial standards have been incorporated by reference into numerous Federal safety laws. Present Federal standards are applicable to at least 25 million workers.

OCCUPATIONAL SAFETY AND HEALTH STANDARDS

Section 7 provides that the Secretary may by rule, promulgate, modify, or revoke any occupational safety and health standard. The Secretary shall institute proceedings under this Section upon application in writing by an interested person, a representative of an organization of employers or employees, the Secretary of Health, Education and Welfare, or a state or a political subdivision of a state. The Secretary himself may determine that a rule should be prescribed in order to serve the objectives of the Act or if he is required to do so under Section 6.

When the Secretary intends to exercise the provisions of Section 7, he appoints a 15-man advisory committee which must submit recommendations to him within 9 months or such longer or shorter period as the Secretary may prescribe. But in no event may this period be any longer than one year and three months. After the submission of recommendations, the Secretary shall as soon as practicable, but not later than four months, schedule a hearing on the recommendations of the advisory committee and on any other relevant issues. If the advisory committee should fail to submit recommendations, the Secretary shall publish his own proposals and then begin public hearings. All interested persons who have previously submitted comments may be heard at the proceedings.

Within sixty days after completing the hearings, the Secretary must promulgate a rule based upon the entire record before him. If he determines a rule should not be issued, he must also publish his reasons in the Federal Register. The rule issued may contain a provision which would delay its effective date for ninety days, so that affected employees and employers may familiarize themselves with the requirements.

The Committee feels it is vital that when the Secretary sets an occupational health standard he do so on the basis of the best available professional evidence; it is not intended that the Secretary be paralyzed by debate surrounding diverse medical opinions. The Secretary's occupational health standard should insure that no employees will suffer any impairment of health, functional capacity or diminished life expectancy from regular exposure to a hazard. It is the Committee's intent that religious rights of those who maintain their health solely by spiritual means shall be given consideration in any regulations promulgated. Whenever practicable, standards shall be expressed in terms of objective criteria and in terms of desired performance.

During the hearings, the Committee considered the degree to which it would rely upon the use of national consensus standards in the administration of an Occupational Safety and Health Act. It determined that these standards could not be given preferential treatment, since their credibility is suspect on two grounds: first, a private organization is susceptible to the pressures of commercial trade association interests, and second, consensus standard organizations have been slow in the development and updating of present safety standards.

Testimony presented to the Committee called attention to a report to the Secretary of Labor's Committee on Industrial Safety, written by Mr. David Swankin, former Director of the Labor Standards Bureau of the Wage and Labor Standards Administration. It revealed that over 60 percent of USASI safety standards were out of date and needed serious revision.

Voluntary standards set by the consensus method represent the lowest common denominator of change in the status quo that is necessary to achieve acceptance. Now that we have chosen the force of law to command acceptance of safety and health regulations, this method should not apply.

The Committee considered and unequivocally rejected any provision for a National Occupational Safety and Health Board to promulgate standards. Among the arguments supporting the concept of a Safety Board are these:

(1) The Board would represent expertise in the field, and
(2) The Board would represent a separation of power with respect to standards-setting and enforcement.

The Committee agrees that professional and technical information must precede the decision to establish a standard, but experts would be used in an advisory capacity with decision-making as part of the Secretary's authority. In this way, the focal point of responsibility is more easily identified.

Some arguments were made that the development of standards should be separated from their enforcement and that the Board accomplished this. Actually, the effect of a Board whould be to divide up the administrative responsibility of the Act into such small parts that cohesive administration would be difficult if not impossible. Federal departments and regulatory agencies uniformly have both rulemaking and enforcement powers without abuse of any rights. The separation of powers concept is not so much whether the Secretary should be separated from the power to set standards, but whether he should be separated from the power to act effectively.

The Committee realizes that boards and commissions have been used in the past as a common technique to avoid making decisions, even where most of the information with which they deal has been readily available for direct Congressional action or administrative regulation.

A Board whose members are appointed to serve for fixed terms could not be held accountable to anyone for reasonable and consistent establishment of standards. Indeed, it would be far better to place the authority in the one appointee whose primary obligation is to protect the legitimate interests of the workers and to enforce public policy in these areas as given to him by Congress and the President.

For an even greater assurance of prompt decision-making in setting safety and health standards, a time frame has been placed into this Act which will guarantee that procedures for developing criteria and promulgating regulations will proceed swiftly. The intent of specific time periods is not to suggest the necessary length of these proceedings, but to indicate that they should be completed as soon as possible, but not longer than the prescribed periods.

Section 7(b) provides that any affected employer may apply to the Secretary for a rule or order for an exemption from standards set pursuant to clause (2) of Section 5. Affected employees must be notified of the hearing. To receive an exemption the proponent must demonstrate by a preponderance of evidence that he will provide to his employees employment and places of employment which are as safe and healthful as those which would prevail if he complied with the standard.

There are many dangerous areas of contamination to workers which are under constant study. Current health research is aimed at problems we know or believe to exist. Criteria in these areas are needed as fast as they can be developed. To gain this end, research efforts are in progress, supported by the National Institutes of Health and other agencies in the Department of Health, Education, and Welfare, which deal with environmental contaminants both in the workplace and outside it.

However, workers are in daily contact with literally hundreds of new chemicals and formulations about which little is known. As occupational health research becomes more sophisticated, there is every indication that the toxicity of the fumes, gases and chemicals to which workers are exposed will be discovered by researchers.

Because of the obvious need for quick response to new health and safety findings, Section 7(c)(1) mandates the Secretary to promulgate temporary emergency standards if he finds that (A) employees are in grave danger from exposure to substances determined to be toxic or to new hazards, and that (B) such emergency standard is necessary to protect employees from this grave danger. Upon publication of the standard in the Federal Register the Secretary shall begin a hearing in accordance with Sections 556 and 557 of the Administrative Procedure Act. The standard shall be effective for a period not to exceed six months, but shall continue in effect beyond the six months until the determination of the administrative hearing.

The Committee feels it is critical that there be full public disclosures under this Act. Whenever the Secretary promulgates any standard, makes any rule, order, decision, grants any exemption of time, or compromises, mitigates or settles any penalty, or determines not to make such a decision, he shall include a statement of the reasons for his actions which shall be published in the Federal Register.

ADVISORY COMMITTEES

Two kinds of advisory committees are established. Most important is the ad hoc advisory committee appointed by the Secretary to assist in the development of each standard.

Section 8(b) provides that each advisory committee shall consist of not more than fifteen members and *shall* include one or more designees of the Secretary of Health, Education, and Welfare, an equal number of persons qualified by experience and affiliation to present the employers' and employees' views, as well as one or more representatives of professional organizations specializing in occupational safety and health, including licensed health-care practitioners, and one or more representatives from nationally recognized consensus organizations. In order to insure a balanced view between governmental and non-governmental members and to preserve the guarantee of a public interest orientation, the number of persons appointed to any advisory committee shall not exceed the number of representatives of Federal and state agencies who are appointed.

All meetings of the committee are open to the public and an accurate record is to be kept and made available to the public. This is to insure a full exchange between members of the advisory committee, to preserve a record of what they do, and to avoid undue secrecy on vital matters. No member of the committee other than representatives of employers and employees shall have an economic interest in any proposed rule so that members will be free from economic or psychological coercion in their decision-making.

Standards ought to be judged objectively as to whether they do, in fact, give maximum and reasonable protection to the health and safety of workers. Industry wants to be assured that it will be heard and its technical input properly evaluated. Other interested persons also wish to make effective presentations. Public hearings before the technical advisory committees will better accomplish this since the openness of meetings imposes an extra duty of preparation and rebuttal.

In addition to the ad hoc advisory committees, the Secretary and the Secretary of Health, Education, and Welfare shall appoint without regard to the Civil Service laws a National Advisory Committee of 20 members divided between representatives of management, labor and occupational safety and occupational health professions. The Secretary shall appoint all members to the committee except for the occupational health representatives who are to be appointed by the Secretary of Health, Education, and Welfare. The Advisory Committee has an important role to perform in bringing continuing public attention and interest to bear on the Act and on the Secretary's program. Its membership should be chosen with great care and be widely representative.

GENERAL DUTY

Under principles of common law, individuals are obliged to refrain from actions which cause harm to others. Courts often refer to this as a general duty to others. Statutes usually increase but sometimes modify this duty. The Committee believes that employers are equally bound by this general and common duty to bring no adverse effects to the life and health of their employees throughout the course of their employment. Employers have primary control of the work environment and should insure that it is safe and healthful. Section 5(1) merely restates that each employer shall furnish this degree of care. There is a long-established statutory precedent in both Federal and state law to require employers to provide a safe and healthful place of employment. Over 36 states have these provisions, and at least four Federal laws contain similar clauses, including the Walsh-Healey Public Contracts Act, the Service Contract Act, the Longshoremen's and Harbor Workers' Act, and the Federal Employers' Liability Act.

An employer's duty under Section 5(1) is not an absolute one. It is the Committee's intent that an employer exercise care to furnish a safe and healthful place to work and to provide safe tools and equipment. This is not a vague duty, but is protection of the worker from preventable dangers.

Governor Howard Pyle, President of the National Safety Council, testified before the Select Subcommittee on Labor on November 5, 1969, in strong support of such a "general obligation" clause:

> If national policy finally declares that all employees are entitled to safe and healthful working conditions, then all employers would be obligated to provide a safe and healthful workplace rather than only complying with a set of promulgated standards. The absence of such a "general obligation" provision would mean the absence of authority to cope with a hazardous condition which is obvious and admitted by all concerned for which no standard has been promulgated.

There is no Constitutional impediment to a general duty provision.

The authority granted by this provision is no more far reaching than that granted by other Federal statutes. Indeed, in other Federal safety acts, the Congress has delegated comparable authority to Federal administrative officials, while in this provision the Congress is acting directly.

Violations of the bill's general duty clause do not subject the employer to mandatory penalties. Whereas, uncorrected serious violations of standards bring mandatory civil penalties under Section 15(a), uncorrected violations of the general duty clause do not bring automatic penalties under Section 15(b).

Bearing in mind the fact that there is no automatic penalty for violation of the general duty, this clause enables the Federal Government to provide for the protection of employees who are working under such *unique* circumstances that no standard has yet been enacted to cover this situation.

The general obligation clause is necessary in order to encourage compliance with the Congressional intent set forth in Section 2(b), "To assure as far as possible every working man and woman in the nation safe and healthful working conditions."

INSPECTIONS AND INVESTIGATIONS

To implement a national occupational safety and health program, it is necessary for Federal and state personnel to have the right of entry in order to appraise any safety or health hazard. Thus, Section 9(a) authorizes the Secretary, upon presenting appropriate credentials, to enter at reasonable times the premises of any workplace where work is performed to which this Act applies, and to inspect and investigate within reasonable limits all pertinent conditions and also to question owners, operators, agents or employees.

The Committee is aware of widespread concern that under present safety and health legislation, the results of a Federal or state inspection are never revealed to the workers and that much potential benefit from an inspection is never realized. If an inspector determines that a danger to health and safety exists, he should be able to advise a worker's representative or be able to question workers, who ought to be permitted to disclose their concern with an alleged dangerous work area.

Correspondingly, an employer should be entitled to accompany an inspector on his tour. The employer's presence should be helpful to the inspector and educational to the employer. For these reasons, H.R. 16785 provides that a representative of the employer and a representative authorized by his employees shall be given an opportunity to accompany any person who is making an inspection of any workplace under subsection 9(a).

Although questions may arise as to who would be considered a duly authorized representative of employees, the Committee expects the Secretary of Labor to determine this question by promulgating regulations to act as guidelines for an inspector.

Since the Federal Government is moving for the first time into an area of broad national responsibility, corresponding authority must be delegated to the Secretary in order that he may carry out this responsibility. The Committee intends that the Secretary should initially use this authority in those industries or occupations where the need for safeguarding worker safety and health appears to be the greatest. In addition, Section 9(b) grants the Secretary of Labor a subpoena power of books, records and witnesses—a power which is customary and necessary for the proper administration and regulation of an occupational safety and health statute.

Protecting the safety and health of workers certainly will be the Secretary's primary responsibility under this bill, but the Committee wishes to emphasize a strong caveat to the Secretary that illusory safety or health issues should never be used as an excuse to intervene in a labor-management dispute.

CITATIONS FOR VIOLATIONS

Section 10 provides that if the Secretary after an inspection determines that an employer has violated certain provisions of the Act, he shall issue a citation.

Section 10 is closely related to Section 15, the Penalties provision. The issuance of a 10(a) citation may bring about a 15(a) mandatory penalty, while the issuance of a 10(b) citation may bring about a 15(b) discretionary penalty. A 10(c) violation is not subject to a penalty. The Committee desired to categorize types of violations and to attach mandatory and discretionary penalties to each type according to the degree of culpability.

Section 10(a) provides that if the Secretary after an inspection determines that an employer has violated an occupational safety and health standard or an interim standard, an exemption order or a reporting requirement, and that a serious danger exists by reason of such violation, he shall issue a 10(a) citation.

Section 10(b) provides that if the Secretary after an inspection determines that an employer has violated the duty to provide a safe and healthful workplace, and a serious danger exists, or that there is a violation of a reporting requirement under Section 9(c) and no serious danger exists, the Secretary is required to issue a 10(b) citation.

The philosophy underlying H.R. 16785 is not based on the assumption that American industry can be made safe and healthful by simply enacting a Federal law which emphasizes penalties, because even large ones can become mere license fees. Therefore, the Committee believed there was an inherent need for a 10(c) violation, which serves to warn as well as educate both the employer and his workers. In effect, Section 10(c) recognizes that specific violations, even of objective standards based on performance, can be more technical than real. So, it states that if an employer has either violated the duty to maintain a safe and healthful workplace or an occupational safety and health standard, and no serious danger will result, a civil or criminal penalty shall not be levied.

Each citation must be in writing and must describe the nature of the violation. In cases where a citation is issued under section 10 (a) or (b) for a violation which might cause cumulative or latent ill effects, this citation shall specify, were feasible, a period during which employers must accurately measure the exposure of their employees to such danger.

Death and disability prevention is the primary intent of this bill. Although possible penalties for violations may be an important deterrent, they are only a partial solution. If we are to reduce disabilities and fatalities, it is essential that we guarantee adequate warning of possible hazards. For this reason, the Committee provides for the prominent posting of a citation at or near the place of violation in accordance with regulations made under 9(c).

Section 10(f) defines serious danger as a substantial probability that at any time death or serious physical harm could result from a condition which exists in a place of employment.

The words, "at any time," recognize the nature of occupational health problems as different from that of occupational safety. Safety hazards are often immediately apparent, and resulting accidents usually show a clear cause and effect. Diseases resulting from occupational health hazards may not become known until years of continuous exposure have elapsed. This is certainly true in industries with a high risk of dust diseases of the lungs, such as silicosis from coal mining, asbestosis from construction work, and byssinosis from textile production. Since there is a long latent period between dust exposure and most diseases resulting from such exposure, standards which are enforced by the Secretary today will be of great benefit to workers 20 years from now. In two decades it is likely that an employee will be working in similar employment but for another employer. Therefore, uniform national standards must be promulgated and enforced to assure equal protection to both workers and employers. Otherwise, an employer investing in current occupational health precautions would receive no future benefits, not even in the reduction of workmen's compensation costs. He might be paying for the past neglect of another employer. Uniform enforcement will also reduce or eliminate the disadvantage that a conscientious employer might experience where inter-industry or intra-industry competition is present.

PROCEDURES FOR ENFORCEMENT

After a citation is issued by the Secretary for a 10 (a) or (b) violation, he must notify the employer of the proposed assessed penalty, if any, within ten working days of the inspection or investigation. Otherwise, the citation is deemed void. The employer then has 15 working days during which he must notify the Secretary whether or not he wishes to contest the citation or proposed assessment. If the employer fails to notify the Secretary that he intends to contest, the citation or penalty would become final and would not be subject to review. For purposes of enforcement they would be considered orders issued by the Secretary under Section 11(b). However, employers will not be deemed to have violated the Section 5(1) duty if they are in compliance with an applicable standard or a state plan which is in effect.

If an employer decides to contest a citation or penalty, or if the Secretary believes an employer has not corrected a violation within the prescribed period, the Secretary will afford an opportunity for a hearing governed by the Administrative Procedure Act. Based upon the hearing record, the Secretary shall issue an order confirming, denying or modifying the citation or penalty, or issue an order for the correction of the violation for which the citation was issued and for the assessment and collection of any penalty.

In these proceedings, the Secretary is to adjudicate, among other things, the validity of the standard, rule, order, or regulation alleged to have been violated and the reasonableness of the time permitted for the correction of the violation.

Upon issuance of an order under 11(b), the Secretary has the power to petition the U.S. District Court to enforce any order of the Secretary issued under 11(a). Except in the case of an order which became final under 11(a), any person aggrieved by an order of the Secretary under 11(b) may obtain judicial review by the U.S. District Court by filing for review within 30 days of the issuance of the order.

PROCEDURES TO COUNTERACT IMMINENT DANGER

According to H.R. 16785, the Secretary has the authority to issue immediate cease and desist orders when there is real and immediate danger. The time consumed in unnecessary legal steps may be the difference between life and death. In most cases, employers will recognize the gravity of the danger and will voluntarily close down a machine or a process. Where this is not done, it is imperative that the Secretary retain this important authority.

The Committee believes that the causes of safety and the public interest would best be served by allowing immediate remedies for extremely serious situations. The Committee was also aware of the very critical issue involved in closing a plant or shutting down an operation. The testimony of New York State Industrial Commissioner M. P. Catherwood was very persuasive on this point:

> In emergency situations the Secretary should be able to take effective action at least for a limited period pending opportunity for appeal or for adoption of some other approach.
>
> In New York the Department of Labor has the power to "tag" dangerous machinery, equipment and areas. This power is used sparingly but significantly. A person who is affected by such "tagging" has the right of review before the Board of Standards and Appeals within 72 hours.

Modeled after the principles of the New York State health and safety code, Section 12(a) states that the Secretary may issue an order prohibiting employment in a place where an imminent danger exists for not more than 5 days from the date of issuance.

Section 12(b) provides that if the Secretary determines that an imminent danger exists, he may bring a civil action in the U.S. District Court to obtain a temporary restraining order or injunction prohibiting the employment or the presence of individuals where the imminent danger exists. An action may be brought under this subsection while an order of the Secretary under subsection (a) is in effect. A court order under this section becomes ineffective if it is determined by other provisions of the Act that no violation exists.

For the purposes of this section, an imminent danger shall be said to exist in a workplace if such danger could reasonably be expected to cause death or serious physical harm before the imminence of such danger can be eliminated. This section is intended to include the restraining of a specific industrial operation in which lethal substances or conditions are present and exposure to these will cause irreversible harm, even though the resulting physical disability may not manifest itself at once.

In addition to the opportunity for judicial review of the Secretary's enforcement orders, an important form of relief is given in Section 12(c). If the Secretary arbitarily issues or fails to issue an order, any person who is damaged by his action can bring suit in the U.S. Court of Claims for recovery of damages, reasonable costs and attorneys' fees.

The Committee advises that the word "person" under 12(c) should be broadly construed. Employers, employees, employers' customers and other non-employees injured as a result of the Secretary's action or failure to act under Section 12(a) should have recourse in the U.S. Court of Claims.

PENALTIES

A national occupational safety and health program raises the valid question of how great an emphasis shall be placed on seeking out employers who do not follow safe practices and on quickly enforcing the law against them. No matter what priority is given to voluntary compliance, companies which operate in a reckless manner should be dealt with firmly and effectively so that this cause of industrial injury can be eliminated.

American industry cannot be made safe and healthful solely by enacting a Federal law which emphasizes punishment. Nevertheless, this measure recognizes that effective enforcement and sanctions are necessary for serious cases.

Any employer who receives a citation under 10(a), or fails to correct a violation of a 10(a) citation, or violates an order issued under 12(a), shall be subject to a mandatory penalty, which is to be assessed by the Secretary. The secretary's action is subject to a full hearing under the Administrative Procedure Act.

Any employer who receives a citation under 10(b) or fails to correct a violation for which such a citation is issued within a prescribed time, may be subject to a penalty at the discretion of the Secretary.

Each violation shall subject the offender to a possible civil fine of $1,000, and each constitutes a separate offense. When the violation is of a continuing nature, each day it continues after a reasonable limit, specified in an initial decision following a hearing, shall constitute a separate offense, except during the time a review of the order may be taken, or such review is pending, and during the time allowed in the order for correction.

H.R. 16785 does not contain any criminal penalties for violations of standards. Yet, an employer who willfully violates any promulgated standard becomes subject to a possible $10,000 fine for each violation.

Except in the case of willful violations, by not attaching a penalty to 10(c) violations the Committee is reaffirming its belief that if employers are warned of potential danger, they will remedy a deterioration in working conditions.

Other than willful violations, the violator's intent should not be a pertinent factor in the original assessment of penalties where there is a failure to comply with standards and regulations. In mitigating penalties, however, other circumstances are germane. The employer's good faith and his past record, which may include 10(c) violations, should be considered, as well as the appropriateness of the fine in relation to the size of the business and to the gravity of the violation.

Criminal penalties are levied in certain instances. Anyone who forcibly resists a person in the performance of his duties is subject to a $5,000 fine or imprisonment of not more than three years or both. The use of a dangerous weapon or murder of a person in the performance of his duties subjects one to felony charges.

Essential to the effective enforcement of this Act is the premise that employers will not be forewarned of inspections of their plants. Experience under the Walsh-Healey Act has indicated that the practice of advance notice to an employer has been a prime cause of the breakdown in that statute's enforcement provisions. Therefore, Section 15(e) provides a criminal penalty of $1,000 fine or one year's imprisonment or both for advance notice of any inspection. Notice will be given when the Secretary and the Secretary of Health, Education and Welfare conduct necessary investigations or make visits to disseminate information relating to health and safety conditions.

Experience also has shown that workers are quite reluctant to report Walsh-Healey violations because of the fear that they will lose their jobs. This leads to speculation on how many actual violations are never reported. To protect those who exercise their rights under this Act, Section 15(f) provides that any person who discriminates against any employee because of an action that employee has taken on behalf of himself or others to secure the protection afforded by the Act, is subject to one year's imprisonment or $1,000 fine or both.

RESEARCH AND RELATED ACTIVITIES

The House hearings illustrated for the first time both the wide scope of occupational safety and health problems and the small allocation of Federal, state and local research resources to find solutions to these problems. Many states have no ongoing research programs, and many other states have merely made a token effort.

As a result, much of the conclusive research has come from nongovernmental associations whose memberships are often composed of employees of private businesses which have donated time and money to this work. They have earned the gratitude of working men and women and have an important future role to play.

Many safety and health recommendations incorporate new insights based on research. These recommendations, if implemented, may require changes that cost substantial sums of money. This fact alone creates a potential conflict of interest between management and labor.

In view of this, it is expected that wherever the Secretary enters into contracts with nongovernmental organizations and institutions for the purpose of conducting research he should take advance precautions to determine that said organization or institution is, wherever possible, wholly free from any real or potential conflict of interest.

The public interest orientation of governmental research efforts should be aided by the statutory definitions of both Secretaries' responsibilities. This should also help to assure freedom from even a theoretical conflict of responsibilities.

To implement these goals, Section 19(a) (1), (2), (3), and (5) delegates specific authority to the Department of Health, Education, and Welfare to undertake the necessary research in this area. This Section of the bill also mandates the Secretary of Health, Education, and Welfare to develop the criteria which the Secretary of Labor needs to formulate standards. The Committee recognizes the need to have these criteria developed as rapidly as possible and has required the Secretary of Health, Education, and Welfare to publish these criteria at least annually.

To eliminate administrative confusion, the Committee felt it should define what is meant by the term "criteria" as used in the Act.

Criteria are scientifically determined conclusions based on the best available medical evidence; they are commonly presented in

the form of recommendations describing medically acceptable tolerance levels of exposure to harmful substances or conditions over a
period of time. They may also include medical judgments on methods
and devices used to control exposure or its effects.

Standards, on the other hand, will be developed by the Secretary of
Labor and while they will reflect the criteria described above, they
may be modified by practical considerations such as feasibility,
means of implementation and the like. They will specify the conditions that will be required to be present in the working place.

The criteria developed by the Secretary of Health, Education
and Welfare should be as useful and specific as possible. To this
end, they should make explicit all of their accompanying assumptions,
particularly those which relate to the duration of time of worker
exposure. Any recommended criteria should presume that workers
will be exposed to these hazards for the entire period of th ir work
experience—a period which may be only a few years for a deep sea
diver, or up to 47 years for a teenager who may be under a hazard
until he is 65 years old. In developing criteria, the Secretary should
not assume, regardless of existing practice, that any emp oyee will
move from an exposure after a given period of time. The criteria
then retain their integrity as purely medical conclu ions, free from
practical considerations, which, when translated into effective standards, will prevent diminished life expectancy or the loss of health
even if maximum exposure occurs.

In promulgating standards, the Secretary of Labor may prescribe
specific conditions under which such standards may be temporarily
exceeded. Such conditions would be based upon actions of employers
which limited possible exposure of workers, and should require a
showing, for example, that a worker must change exposures and jobs
at specified times and that this will obviate the proscribed dangers of
loss of health or life expectancy.

Since the definitions of "health" and "life expectancy" will be
applied to new workplaces and new dangers, the committee expects
that the Secretary of Health, Education and Welfare will develop
adequate enough information to assure, to the greatest extent possible,
that his criteria will allow wise anticipatory investments by businessmen to obviate workplace dangers. Thus the initial criteria should be
construed broadly enough to encompass such impairments as loss of
functional capacity, hearing, or any illness which the Department of
Health, Education, and Welfare believes will result from this work
experience.

Section 19, subsection (a)(4) directs the Secretary of Labor and the
Secretary of Health, Education, and Welfare to "develop procedures"
to assure that dangerous working conditions are measured by employers. Four separate circumstances are described in paragraphs
(A) (B) (C) (D) under which monitoring requirements are limited to
showing degrees of need, based on the circumstances involved. This
section recognizes that the potential manpower required to send inspectors into plants on a case-by-case basis would effectively defeat
the goal of accurate data on possible dangers. Moreover, if the Secretary of Labor or the Secretary of Health, Education, and Welfare were
to rely exclusively on measurements taken with his own instruments,
implementation of this section would be subject to delay, inattention
and lack of funding. Thus, the employer's effective control of the

situs and means of production should include the requirement to measure that environment when there is a demonstration that it can or will produce damage to workers.

Section 19, subsection (a)(5), is a response to the many problems caused by the continued presence and use of carcinogenic and toxic substances and processes in the workplace. Evidence from state inspections and disease statistics, from unions and from Federal witnesses has substantiated the uncontrolled existence of these dangers. In addition, the hearings gathered testimony which showed that over 600 new substances are introduced into the work environment every year with no assurances of their safety. Today's laws and practices allow workers to receive thousands of cases of occupational disease and illness without any effective protection.

Basically, the worker needs to have adequate advance knowledge of hazards in order to protect himself from damaging exposures. He needs proper protective equipment and the information necessary to treat emergencies if they arise. He should not be economically coerced into a hazardous job. Since inadvertent exposure to unknown products or processes often causes severe and immediate reactions, the exposed worker must know what type of exposure he has suffered in order to use proper treatment. The worker especially needs this information in cases of toxic substances which have delayed or latent ill effects.

For all of these problems, any remedy must be relatively self-enforcing in order to apply equally to the hundreds of thousands of affected workplaces. To provide for a few of these situations, subsection (a)(5) requires that the Secretary of Health, Education and Welfare must give information about known substances with toxic or potentially toxic effects to employees. Since human susceptibility to toxic substances is known to vary, the phrase "potentially toxic" is used to assure coverage when evidence is not completely conclusive and to protect more than the most resistant workers. This subsection also provides that certain information about these toxic substances should be provided to exposed workers by means of "label or other appropriate means" together with necessary protective devices. If the protective equipment should fail, the worker or hospital can take appropriate corrective action and should eliminate "unknown poisoning." This labeling requirement should help alleviate the inability, testified to by some workers, to take the necessary corrective action immediately.

Subsection (a)(5) also recognizes that some of the 600 new substances per year may not manifest their danger to employees until it is too late. The range of remedial actions is wide but not promising. A requirement for the proof of the safety of such substances before their introduction into the workplace would be desirable if it could be achieved without undue burdens on commerce from initial delays in obtaining approval, or if it could be implemented selectively. This still provides inadequate protection, since early testing might not anticipate the many combinations of substances and environments which often create the most dangerous exposures. Mandatory pre-clearance of substances while applicable in the field of drug marketing, may offer more promise than performance. Alternatively, exclusive reliance on site-by-site Federal inspection of three million workplaces for correction would also be imperfect.

Because any workable solution to covering new substances would have to be fast-acting and self-enforcing, the Committee adopted a two-step process whereby workers or employers could submit unknown substances to the Department of Health, Education and Welfare for a determination of their toxicity. Only after the Department of Health, Education and Welfare made a determination that a substance was toxic would employees have a right to information about these substances, a right to necessary protective equipment, if any. To assure these rights, the bill guarantees that employees may not be forced to work without these safeguards. There is still a real danger that an employee may be economically coerced into self-exposure in order to earn his livelihood, so the bill allows an employee to absent himself from that specific danger for the period of its duration without loss of pay. However, the Committee intends that the danger cannot be deliberately caused by the employee. The Department of Labor will implement this intent. Nothing herein restricts the right of the employer, except as he is obligated under other agreements, to assign a worker to other nonprohibited work during this time. This should eliminate possible abuse by allowing the employer to avoid payment for work not performed.

REPORTS AND REPORTING

Adequate information is the precondition for responsive administration of practically all sections of this bill. However, at the present time, the Federal Government and most of the states have inadequate information on the incidence, nature, or causes of occupational injuries and deaths. For diseases, the information gap is even larger. Thus, the first action of both the Federal and State Governments should be to remedy these gaps with the institution of adequate statistical programs. The long-standing charade of the Z.16 standard is specifically recognized and rejected by the language of the Committee bill which requires that all deaths, injuries and ailments should be recorded at least once.

To assure the completeness of data, Section 9(c) directs the Secretary of Labor to cooperate with the Secretary of Health, Education and Welfare in devising regulations which implement this goal. The Committee recognizes the fact that some work-related injuries or ailments may involve only a minimal loss of work time or perhaps none at all, thus these might not be of enough value to the Governmental bodies to require record-keeping thereof. However, the Committee was not offered any statutory language which was not subject to the greater peril of allowing under-reporting. The Committee therefore intends that its language of "all work-related injuries, diseases and ailments" should be treated as a minimum floor which includes such conditions as work-related loss of consciousness, treatment by a physician (even if the treatment occurs only once and subsequent treatment is by a nurse or medical technician), and records of diseases which are incurred from work exposure (such as asbestosis and silicosis) and which may not be known to an employer until after an employee retires and applies for medical benefits under his retirement plan. These latter records may be available or known only to state officials and not to the employer, and thus the employer would have no such record-keeping responsibility; however, in such case, the Committee expects that the Secretary of Labor and the Secretary of Health, Education and Welfare will develop other means by which the Government can carry out their explicit responsibilities to report the incidence of these problems accurately.

At the same time, the Committee recognizes the need to assure employers that they will not be subject to unnecessary or duplicative record-keeping requests and has specifically stated this intent in Section 9(d). To that end, the Committee intends that wherever possible, reporting requirements should be satisfied by having an employer report relevant data only to one Governmental agency and that other Governmental agencies, if any, should then acquire their information from the original agency.

The Committee also intends that the annual reports of both the Department of Labor and the Department of Health, Education and Welfare should contain comprehensive presentations of all this data, together with an analysis thereof so that this Committee and others in Congress may review the adequacy of progress and the possible need for further legislation.

TRAINING AND EMPLOYEE EDUCATION

The Committee judges that one of the key contributions Government can make to the occupational safety movement is through education by the dissemination of safety information and by the training of employers and employees.

The primary goal of any safety act is to prevent accidents and illnesses. Yet, if an effective law is enacted, it will fail to achieve this goal unless proper resources for safety training and education are appropriated.

Both Federal and state safety and health inspectors are severely inadequate in number. There are only 1,600 state safety inspectors and fewer than 100 Federal inspectors. Some states purport to cover all or most wage-earning workers under their rule-making, but have few inspectors to enforce the codes. Only three states have over 100 inspectors; about half have fewer than 25 inspectors; 16 have a dozen or less; four states have no inspection personnel whatsoever. Only three states have inspectors who are trained in the field of occupational health and hygiene. Ironically, there are twice as many fish and game wardens in the United States as there are safety and health inspectors. The hearings revealed a dearth of occupational health experts in this country.

The Committee recognizes that a substantial increase in manpower with professional competence is needed to bring about a successful program. To remedy this situation, certain provisions in the bill are designed to expand significantly the number of properly trained personnel to work in the field of occupational safety and health. Section 20 authorizes the Secretary of Health, Education and Welfare, after consultation with the Secretary of Labor, to conduct education and preparation of safety and health personnel.

In order to promote a greater awareness of safety in the workplace, the bill also provides for employee training to be conducted by the Secretary of Labor. Special emphasis is to be placed on technical assistance to both labor and management for the adoption of sound safety and health practices.

The Secretary of Labor, working with the Civil Service Commission, will continue to establish qualifications for Federal occupational safety personnel which have a meaningful relationship to any standards promulgated under this Act. It is absolutely essential that all who are carrying out duties under this Act will be fully qualified to do so.

As a substantial number of Federal standards are adopted over a period of time, states will have an opportunity to demonstrate that their legislation and administration meet certain criteria, and that their plan is at least as effective in assuring safe and healthful conditions as the Federal standards promulgated under Sections 6 and 7 of this Act.

Whenever a state wishes to assume responsibility for developing and enforcing standards in an area where the Secretary has issued a standard, the state may submit a plan to him. It must contain assurances that the state will develop and enforce a standard at least as effective as that developed by the Secretary, that the state will have the legal authority, the personnel and the funds necessary to do the job, and that the right of entry into workplaces subject to the Act is provided. The plan must contain additional assurances that the state agency will report accidents and injuries to the Secretary in the same form and to the same extent as if the plan were not in effect.

On the basis of reports submitted by the state agencies, the Secretary shall, after an opportunity for a hearing, withdraw his approval if he finds that in actual operation there has been a failure to comply substantially with the plan or with the assurances stated in it. If the state plan ceases to be in effect, the Secretary may reassert his full authority under the Act. H.R. 16785, in addition to providing a hearing before the Secretary can reject a plan, assures judicial review of the Secretary's action. It should be noted that a state's program need not be all-encompassing; it may restrict itself to a particular hazard or industry. However, any industries or hazards not covered by the plan will continue to be under Federal jurisdiction.

The Committee calls attention to the requirement making standards promulgated under the plan applicable to all employees of public agencies of the state and its political subdivisions. This provision was endorsed by countless witnesses including the National Safety Council. In advocating that state and local governments be covered by this Act, this group stated:

> As a matter of principle, the National Safety Council believes that the occupational safety and health program under consideration should be applicable to all employees involved in interstate commerce and to all employees of Federal, state or local governments or agencies, excluding only the working conditions of employees covered by other Federal agencies having jurisdiction.

If a state presents such a plan and it is in full compliance with the requirements of this Section, the Secretary shall approve the plan. His standards-setting and enforcement authority is suspended in that state to the extent that the plan covers the field. The Secretary's authority still exists to the extent that the plan is silent about other occupational safety and health issues and to the extent that the Secretary has acted. The Secretary retains the right to inspect workplaces subject to approved state plans, but only in pursuance of his obligation to maintain a continuing evaluation of the manner in which each plan is operating.

As an encouragement for state action, the bill provides Federal financial support to assist them in assuming their own program for worker safety. Planning grants with up to 90 percent Federal participation, and program grants with up to 50 percent Federal participation are provided.

The 90 percent grant is designed to induce the states in identifying needs, developing state plans and programs for collecting statistical data, increasing personnel capabilities and improving administration and enforcement.

The Secretary may also authorize grants to assist states in administering and enforcing programs for occupational safety and health contained in their plans. The Federal share may be up to 50 percent of the total costs. In the event that the Federal share for all states is not the same, the difference among the states is to be determined on the basis of objective criteria.

The three-year concept of these grants is designed with the belief that in the next few years practically all states will need Federal financial assistance to provide quality programs of occupational safety and health.

FEDERAL AGENCY SAFETY PROGRAMS AND RESPONSIBILITIES

H.R. 16785 contains coverage for approximately three million employees of the Federal Government. Section 18 requires Federal agencies to promulgate safety and health standards consistent with those developed by the Secretary of Labor for private industry. This Section also amends Section 7902(c)(1) of Title 5, U.S. Code, to permit labor organizations to serve on the President's Federal Safety Council.

During the past 25 years, there has been considerable improvement in the safety record of the Federal Government, but if it is to serve as a model employer, there must be a continuous effort to achieve the ideal. Less than a substantial yearly reduction in injuries and illnesses would not be satisfactory.

In February 1965, President Johnson launched the Mission Safety–70 in an effort to dramatically reduce injuries among Federal employees. The plan envisioned a 30 percent reduction in the frequency rate of disabling injuries during the life of the program. Four years have elapsed since the plan was initiated. Today the Government has progressed only eight percent toward the goal. Clearly, there is a margin of improvement yet to be achieved.

In order to create a more effective safety program, the bill directs each Federal agency to purchase and maintain safety devices and to require their use. Agencies must also keep adequate records and make an annual report on occupational accidents and injuries to the Secretary.

The above requirements will clearly establish primary responsibility for the Federal Government's internal safety effort by giving it a more active role in coordinating the multiplicity of safety programs devised by various agencies. Congress also will be offered an opportunity to learn of current health and safety conditions through annual reports.

COVERAGE, APPLICABILITY, AND RELATIONS WITH STATE LAWS AND OTHER FEDERAL STATUTES AND AGENCIES

This bill applies to all employment performed in interstate commerce at a workplace in a state, Wake Island, the Outer Continental

Shelf lands, Johnston Island and the Canal Zone. A state is deemed to be a state of the United States, the District of Columbia, Puerto Rico, the Virgin Islands, American Samoa, Guam, and the Trust Territories of the Pacific.

Nothing in the bill should be construed as repealing or modifying in any way other Federal laws prescribing safety and health requirements. In addition, nothing is intended to affect state or Federal workmen's compensation laws, or the rights, duties, or liabilities of employers and employees under them.

The Committee does not wish the Secretary of Labor to assert his statutory authority under this bill where another agency or department is actually exercising its authority. Section 22(b) expressly states that nothing in Section 5 of this Act shall apply to the working conditions of employees where any Federal agency exercises statutory authority to prescribe or enforce standards or regulations affecting occupational safety and health.

To further reduce duplication of coverage between this bill and other Federal laws, the safety and health standards promulgated under the Walsh-Healey Public Contracts Act, the Service Contract Act, the Construction Safety Act and the National Foundation on Arts and Humanities Act are deemed replaced by standards promulgated under H.R. 16785, which are determined by the Secretary to be corresponding standards. The Committee intends that "corresponding standards" implies that these standards will be at least as effective as those replaced.

It is the intent of the Committee that the Secretary will develop health and safety standards for construction workers covered by Public Law 91-54 pursuant to the provisions of that law and that the Secretary will utilize the same mechanisms and resources for the development and enforcement of health and safety objectives for construction workers newly covered by this Act. The use of the term "corresponding" in Section 4(b)(2) is not intended to affect any reduction in the health and safety afforded construction workers.

Although the Committee has taken care to avoid probable areas of duplication, some questions may arise after enactment. Thus, within three years after the effective date of this Act, the Secretary must report to Congress his recommendations to achieve coordination between this Act and other Federal laws.

APPROPRIATIONS AUTHORIZED

There are authorized to be appropriated to carry out this Act such sums as the Congress shall deem necessary for each Fiscal Year.

While the Administration has given no indication of the cost of a comprehensive occupational safety and health program, obviously a large sum will be required to recruit, train and maintain the many individuals needed for the administration and enforcement of this law. It has been estimated that one-half of one percent of the projected loss from occupational accidents over the next three years would be about $118 million. No less an appropriation for the same time period would be reasonable.

It will take substantial sums of money to produce a concerted effort to improve health and safety. A diluted effort may be worse than no effort at all, since expectations without fulfillment may not evoke the voluntary compliance which is necessary to the success of the program.

Therefore, if Congress gives its consent to this legislation, it is hoped that adequate funding will be authorized to achieve maximum benefits from all aspects of this bill.

CONCLUSION

If you have taken one hour to read and study this report, in that time at least eight workers will have been killed and approximately 1,100 workers will have been disabled by job-related injuries.

Without this legislation, we are faced with the dim prospect that three out of every four teenagers now entering the work force will sustain a disabling injury during their working career.

Must we always have mass disasters to pass safety legislation? Even the price of one life is too expensive when a meaningful occupational safety and health law could save many lives.

Is the price of progress the death of 14,500 workers annually?

Is the price of an expanding economy 2.2 million disabled workers each year?

As a nation, we simply have not faced up to the truth: our men, women and children are being killed needlessly; they are being maimed, injured, disabled and infected on the job by largely preventable injuries and diseases.

It is not accurate for those who oppose occupational safety and health legislation at the Federal level to state: "We are doing better." For in the past ten years the total number of deaths and disabling injuries has in fact increased, and this upward trend shows no signs of change.

Most states are not doing a creditable job in administering occupational safety and health programs when some of them annually spend as little as two cents per worker in job safety enforcement. State experience refutes the claim that industry is too diverse for Government programs to be effective in lowering accident rates. In fact, states with good occupational safety and health programs have an accident rate of 19 per 100,000 workers, and in those states with the poorest programs it is 110 per 100,000 workers, or over 550 percent higher.

We can no longer blame what happens to us on some remote or uncontrollable force. Modern logic will not permit the deliberate condoning of death, disease or injury when the causes are identifiable or preventable.

1970 brings a new and challenging decade. In the last ten years we have made great progress in realizing our social responsibility to all citizens. Our efforts must not diminish. The well-being of every American working man and woman is an essential human right which we can no longer deny.

SECTION-BY-SECTION ANALYSIS

SEC. 1—SHORT TITLE

This section provides that the act may be cited as the "Occupational Safety and Health Act."

SEC. 2—CONGRESSIONAL FINDINGS AND PURPOSE

This section finds that personal injuries and illnesses arising out of work impose a substantial burden upon interstate commerce; and that it is the policy of Congress to assure as far as possible every working man and woman safe and healthful working conditions in the following manner—

(1) Encouraging employers and employees to institute new and to perfect existing programs for providing safe and healthful working conditions;

(2) Building on advances made through employer and employee initiative;

(3) Providing research, including research into psychological factors, and developing innovative methods;

(4) Exploring means for early detection of latent diseases, causal connections between diseases and work environment, and conducting research in health problems, recognizing the differences between occupational health problems and safety problems;

(5) Providing training programs to increase the number and competence of personnel;

(6) Providing development, promulgation, and effective enforcement of occupational safety and health standards;

(7) Encouraging States to assume responsibility for administration and enforcement, and to conduct experimental and demonstration projects by providing grants to States;

(8) Providing accident and health reporting procedures;

(9) Encouraging joint labor-management efforts.

SEC. 3—DEFINITIONS

This section defines the terms "Secretary," "commerce," "person," "employee," and "State." In addition, of particular significance are the provisions which define the term "occupational safety and health standard" as a standard which requires conditions or the adoption or use of one or more practices, means, methods, operations, or processes, reasonably necessary to provide safe or healthful employment and places of employment, and the term "national consensus standard" as any occupational safety and health standard or modification which (A) has been adopted and promulgated by a national, standards-producing organization under procedures whereby it can be determined by the Secretary that persons affected have reached substantial agreement on its adoption (B) and formulated after an opportunity for consideration of diverse views (C) and designated as such a standard by the Secretary, after consultation with other appropriate Federal agencies. The term "established Federal standard" is defined to mean any operative occupational safety and health standard established by any agency of the United States and presently in effect, or contained in any act of Congress in force on the date of enactment. The term "employer" is defined to exclude the United States and States and their political subdivisions, but to include any public authority which is subject to the jurisdiction of more than one State and has employees engaged in the administration or maintenance of a bridge or tunnel.

SEC. 4—APPLICABILITY OF ACT

(a) Designates geographic application of act and provides that in areas where there are no Federal district courts having jurisdiction, the Secretary of the Interior shall provide for judicial enforcement.

(b)(1) Provides that this act shall not be deemed to repeal other Federal laws prescribing safety or health requirements or rules or regulations promulgated pursuant to such law.

(2) Provides that standards promulgated under this Act will replace any corresponding standards promulgated under certain listed laws relating to safety and health of employees.

(3) Requires the Secretary to report his recommendations to the Congress for legislation to avoid unnecessary duplication between this act and other Federal laws within 3 years after the effective date of the act.

SEC. 5—DUTIES OF EMPLOYERS

Each employer—

(1) Has a *duty* to provide his employees with a safe and healthful workplace.

(2) Must comply with occupational health and safety standards and with interim standards promulgated under this act, except as provided in Sec. 17 (relating to State jurisdiction and State plans)

SEC. 6—INTERIM SAFETY AND HEALTH STANDARDS

This section provides that the Secretary shall by rule promulgate interim standards during the 2-year period from the effective date of this act.

These standards may be—

any national consensus standard;

established Federal standard (not limited to its present area of application);

standards proposed by a nationally recognized standards-producing organization by other than a consensus method— unless promulgation would not result in improved health or safety for employees. In the event of conflict among standards the one which offers the greatest protection of the safety and health of affected employees will be promulgated.

This section also provides for a public hearing and for the application of section 553 of title 5, United States Code (Rule-making provisions of the Administrative Procedure Act).

The Secretary must commence a proceeding under section 7 for promulgation of an occupational safety and health standard within 90 days concerning the same subject matter dealt with by an interim standard or any additional matter which the Secretary deems relevant within 90 days after the interim standard is promulgated.

Each interim standard shall stay in effect until superseded by another interim standard or superseded pursuant to a rule issued under section 7.

SEC. 7—OCCUPATIONAL SAFETY AND HEALTH STANDARDS

(a)(1) Provides procedures for the Secretary to promulgate, modify, or revoke any occupational safety and health standard by which he will commence appointing an advisory committee under section 8(b). The advisory committee shall submit its recommendations within 270 days (or longer or shorter if the Secretary prescribes). These recommendations are printed in the Federal Register as notice of proposed rule-making. This section also provides that the Secretary can extend the life of the advisory committee for an additional 6-month period after the expiration of 270 days.

(2) Provides that within 4 months after submission of advisory committee recommendations or the Secretary's proposals (made where an advisory committee has failed to submit recommendations), the Secretary shall give notice of a hearing. Such notice (including time, place, subjects, issues, and recommendations) is to be published in the Federal Register 30 days prior to the hearing. Only those who have submitted comments prior to the hearing shall have a right to submit oral evidence at the hearing but nothing shall prevent anyone from submitting written views for consideration.

(3) Provides that within 60 days after completion of a hearing on the record the Secretary shall issue a rule promulgating, modifying, or revoking an occupational safety and health standard or make a determination that a rule should not be issued. Such rule may contain a provision delaying the effective date up to 90 days to permit familiarization of employees and employers with the standard and its terms.

(4) Requires the Secretary in setting standards to set the standard which assures, on the basis of the available professional evidence, that employees will not suffer impairment of health, functional capacity, or diminished life expectancy with exposure throughout their working lives.

(b) Provides for an exemption procedure from section 5(2) (Standards). If after an opportunity for a formal hearing and an opportunity for an inspection by the Secretary the proponent has demonstrated by a preponderance of the evidence that the variation is as safe and healthful as if the proponent complied with the standard. The rule or order must state the conditions and practices the employer must utilize and the extent to which they differ from a section 5(2) standard.

Affected employees shall be given notice of an application for exemption.

Such rule may be modified or revoked at any time after at least 6 months after issuance upon application by an employer, employees, or by the Secretary on his motion.

(c) Requires the Secretary to determine as soon as possible (but not more than 90 days) after a special inspection whether to promulgate an occupational health and safety standard on an emergency temporary basis. Such a standard would take effect 30 days after its publication in the Federal Register. A standard will be promulgated under this authority if the Secretary finds that employees are exposed to grave danger from exposure to substances determined to be toxic or to new hazards, and that the emergency standard is necessary to protect employees from the grave danger. These standards will be effective for up to six months or until the termination of a proceeding for the issuance of a permanent standard. Such a proceeding will utilize the procedures of sections 556 and 557 of title 5, United States Code, and the emergency standard will serve as a proposed rule in the proceeding.

(d) Provides that whenever the Secretary promulgates any standard, makes any rule, order, decision, grants any exemption or extension of time, or mitigates any penalty under this act, he shall include a statement of the reasons for such action, and such statement shall be published in the Federal Register.

SEC. 8—ADMINISTRATION; ADVISORY COMMITTEES

(a)(1) Permits the Secretary to use the services, facilities, or personnel of another Federal agency, or of a State or its political subdivision.

(2) Permits the Secretary to employ experts and consultants.

(b) This subsection directs the Secretary to appoint an advisory committee not to exceed 15 members to commence section 7 proceedings and designates specific representatives to serve, as well as other public members qualified by knowledge and experience, but the number of persons so appointed to any advisory committee shall not exceed the number appointed to such committee as representatives of Federal and State agencies.

This subsection also provides for the compensation of advisory committee members but forbids one to serve as a committee member (other than representatives of employers and employees) who has an economic interest in any proposed rule.

All committee meetings are to be open and an accurate record is to be kept.

(c) Provides for a National Advisory Committee composed equally of representatives of management, labor, occupational safety and health professions, and of the public. Occupational health representatives to be appointed by Secretary of HEW; others by Secretary of Labor. Provides for consultation with the Secretaries of Labor and Health, Education, and Welfare and at least two open meetings annually.

SEC. 9—INSPECTIONS, INVESTIGATIONS AND REPORTS

(a) The Secretary, upon presenting appropriate credentials, is authorized—

> (1) to enter premises at reasonable times of any work place where work is performed to which this act applies;
>
> (2) to make reasonable inspections and investigations of conditions in workplaces and to question owners, operators, agents or employees.

(b) Provides the Secretary of Labor with a subpena power of books, records, and witnesses.

(c) Provides that employers shall keep such records as the Secretary requires and provides that the Secretary shall make such regulations as may be necessary so that employers keep employees informed of their rights and privileges under this act. This section also requires the Secretary, in cooperation with the Secretary of HEW, to keep records of all work-related injuries and diseases which arise from the working environment.

(d) Provides that employers should have minimum burden for recordkeeping, especially small businesses.

(e) A representative of the employer and an authorized representative of employees shall be given an opportunity to accompany any person making an inspection under (a).

SEC. 10—CITATIONS FOR VIOLATIONS

(a) Provides that if the Secretary, after inspection, determines that an employer has violated—

> Section 5(2) (occupational safety and health standards (including emergency standards) or interim standards);

Section 7(b) (exemption order);

Section 9(c) (reporting requirement);

and that a *serious danger* exists by reason of any such violation, the Secretary shall issue a citation to the employer for such violation—

    (1) in writing,

    (2) describing the specific nature of the violation and the specific standard violated,

    (3) and the time for correction.

    (b) Provides that if the Secretary after inspection determines that an employer has violated—

Section 5(1) (Duty) and *a serious danger exists;*

Section 9(c) (reporting requirement) and *no serious danger exists*—

the Secretary shall issue a citation to the employer for such violation—

    (1) in writing,

    (2) describing the specific nature of the violation and the specific standard violated,

    (3) the period of time within which it must be corrected.

Employers will not be deemed to have violated a citation issued for a violation of section 5(1) (duty) if they are complying with an applicable standard or a State plan which is in effect.

    (c) Provides that the Secretary after inspection determines that an employer has violated—

Section 5(1)—Duty

Section 5(2)—Standards—

and specifically determines that *no serious danger exists,* he shall issue a citation—

    (1) in writing,

    (2) describing the nature of the violation.

(*The Act does not provide a penalty for this citation, except in the case of a willful violation.*)

    (d) Provides where citation is issued under subsection (a) or (b) for a violation which might cause cumulative or latent ill effects, such citation shall specify, where feasible, a period during which employers shall accurately measure the exposure of employees to such danger.

    (e) Provides for prominent posting of a citation at or near place of violation in accordance with regulations made under 9(c).

    (f) Defines "serious danger potential" as a substantial probability that at any time death or serious physical harm could result from a condition which exists in a place of employment.

SEC. 11—PROCEDURES FOR ENFORCEMENT

    (a) If the Secretary issues a citation under section 10 (other than subsection (c)), he shall within 10 working days of the inspection or investigation notify the employer of the penalty, if any, proposed to be assessed under section 15. The employer then has 15 working days to notify the Secretary whether he wishes to contest the citation or proposed assessment. If he fails to give such notice, the citation and the proposed assessment will be final and not subject to review. For purposes of enforcement it would be considered an order issued by the Secretary under subsection (b).

    (b) If an employer decides to contest a citation or proposed assessment, or where the Secretary believes an employer has not corrected a violation within the prescribed period, the Secretary will after affording an opportunity for a hearing, and on the basis of findings of fact, issue an order confirming, denying, or modifying the citation or assessment, or issue an order for the correction of the violation for which the citation was issued and for the assessment and collection of any penalty under section 15. In these proceedings the Secretary will adjudicate, among other things, the validity of the standard, rule, order, or regulation alleged to have been violated, and the reasonableness of the time permitted for the correction of the violation.

(c) Upon issuance of an order under subsection (b), the Secretary is empowered to petition the U.S. district court. The court has the jurisdiction to enforce (by restraining order, injunction, or otherwise) any order of the Secretary issued under subsection (b). Except in the case of an order which becomes final under section 11(a), any person aggrieved by an order of the Secretary issued under subsection (b) may obtain review by the U.S. district court in accordance with section 706 of title 5, U.S.C., by filing for review within 30 days of the issuance of the order.

SEC. 12—PROCEDURES TO COUNTERACT IMMINENT DANGERS

(a) This section provides the Secretary of Labor may issue an order prohibiting employment in a place where an imminent danger exists for not more than 5 days from date of issuance.

(b) Provides that if the Secretary determines that an imminent danger exists, he may bring a civil action in the U.S. district court for a temporary restraining order or injunction prohibiting employment or presence of individuals where the imminent danger exists. An action may be brought under this subsection while an order of the Secretary under subsection (a) is in effect.

A court order under this section becomes ineffective if it is determined under other provisions of the act that no violation exists.

(c) This subsection provides that where the Secretary acts arbitrarily or capriciously in issuing or failing to issue a 12(a) administrative order, any person injured thereby either physically or financially may bring an action in the Court of Claims.

(d) Defines "imminent danger" as a danger which could reasonably be expected to cause death or serious physical harm before the imminence of such danger can be eliminated.

SEC. 13—REPRESENTATION IN CIVIL LITIGATION

Provides that the Solicitor of Labor may appear and represent the Secretary in civil litigation subject to the direction of the Attorney General.

SEC. 14—CONFIDENTIALITY OF TRADE SECRETS

This section deals with the confidentiality of trade secrets.

SEC. 15—PENALTIES

(a) Any employer who—
    (1) receives a citation under 10(a),
    (2) fails to correct a violation which a citation has been issued under 10(a) within the period permitted for its correction,
    (3) violates an order issued under 12(a)—
shall be assessed a penalty by the Secretary pursuant to a section 11(b) order, a civil penalty of not more than $1,000 for each violation. Each

violation is a separate offense, except when the violation is of a continuing nature after a reasonable time specified in an initial decision following the hearing under 11(b), or during the time allowed in the order under 11(b) for correction, or during the time a review is pending. The Secretary may mitigate civil penalties under certain criteria.

(b) Any employer who receives a citation under section 10(b) or fails to correct a violation for which such a citation is issued within the time prescribed, *may* be assessed by the Secretary, pursuant to an 11(b) order, a civil penalty of not more than $1,000 for each violation.

Each violation is a separate offense except when the violation is a continuing one after a reasonable time specified following the hearing under 11(b), or during the time allowed in the order under 11(b) for correction or during the time a review is pending.

The Secretary may mitigate civil penalties under certain criteria.

(c) Provides for assessment of penalties as above, for any willful violation of an interim standard or occupational health and safety standard.

(d) Provides any person who forcibly resists a person in the performance of his duties under this act is subject to a $5,000 fine or imprisonment of not more than 3 years or both. The use of a dangerous weapon or murder of a person in the performance of his duties subjects one to felony charges.

(e) Provides criminal penalty of 1 year or $1,000 for advance notice of any inspection, except where the Secretary and the Secretary of HEW conduct necessary investigations to utilize or disseminate information relating to health or safety conditions.

(f) Provides a criminal penalty of imprisonment for up to one year or a fine of up to $1,000, or both, for discriminating against an employee because he has sought to use the protection of this Act.

SEC. 16—VARIATIONS, TOLERANCES AND EXEMPTIONS

The Secretary may provide reasonable limitations, variations, and tolerances to avoid serious impairment of the national defense; to be effective for no more than 6 months unless notice and opportunity for hearing is afforded affected employees.

SEC. 17—STATE JURISDICTION AND STATE PLANS

(a) Provides that a State may assert jurisdiction under State law over any occupational safety or health issue with respect to which no standard is in effect under section 6 (interim standards) or section 7 (occupational safety and health standards).

(b) Provides that States can submit a state plan for the development and enforcement of standards relating to occupational safety or health issues that have been dealt with in standards promulgated under section 7.

(c) Provides that the Secretary shall approve the plan submitted by a State under subsection (b) or any modification thereof, if—

    (1) a State agency (or agencies) is designated for administering a plan throughout the State;

    (2) it provides for the development and enforcement of standards which are or will be at least as effective as section 7 standards;

    (3) it provides for the effective right of entry and inspection of all workplaces subject to the act at least as effective as provided in section 9 (a), (c), (d), and (e), and includes a prohibition on advance notice of inspections;

    (4) it contains assurances of legal authority and qualified State personnel;

    (5) it contains assurances of adequate State funds for administration and enforcement;

    (6) it makes all standards included under the plan applicable to all employees of public agencies of the State and its political subdivisions;

    (7) it requires employers in the State to make reports in the same manner and extent as if the plan were not in effect;

    (8) it provides that the State agency will make reports to the Secretary in such form as the Secretary shall from time to time require.

(d) Provides that if the Secretary rejects a plan, he shall afford a State due notice and opportunity for a hearing.

(e) Provides after approval of a State plan, the Secretary may exercise his authority under sections 9, 10, 11, and 15 with respect to comparable standards promulgated under section 7 for at least 3 years after the plan's approval under subsection (c). After State plan approval, provisions of sections 5(2), 9 (except for the purposes of carrying out subsection (f)), 10, 11 and 15 shall not apply, but the Secretary may retain jurisdiction under the above provisions in any proceeding commenced under sections 10 and 11 before the date of determination.

(f) Provides that the Secretary continually evaluate a State plan. The Secretary has the power to withdraw approval of a State plan if he finds a failure to comply substantially with any provision of the State plan.

(g) The State may obtain review of withdrawal of approval or rejection in the U.S. Court of Appeals. The Secretary's decision shall be sustained unless the court finds that the Secretary's decision is arbitrary and capricious. This subsection provides for further appeal to the Supreme Court.

SEC. 18—FEDERAL AGENCY SAFETY PROGRAMS AND RESPONSIBILITIES

(a) Provides that each Federal agency shall maintain a comprehensive occupational safety and health program consistent with standards promulgated under section 7. The head of each agency, after consultation with representatives of employees, shall provide—

    (1) standards consistent with standards under section 7;

    (2) acquire and maintain and require the use of safety devices to protect its personnel;

    (3) keep adequate records;

    (4) make an annual report to the Secretary with respect to occupational accidents and injuries.

(b) Provides that the Secretary shall submit a summary of reports submitted to him under subsection (a)(4) to the President. The President shall transmit annually to the Senate and House of Representatives a report of the activities of Federal agencies under this section.

(c) Amends section 7902(c)(1) of title 5, United States Code, by permitting labor organizations representing employees to serve on the President's Federal Safety Council.

SEC. 19—RESEARCH AND RELATED ACTIVITIES

(a)(1) Provides the Secretary of Health, Education, and Welfare, after consultation with the Secretary of Labor and other appropriate Federal agencies, shall conduct research (directly or by grant or contract) into relating to occupational safety and health, including innovative methods of dealing with occupational safety and health problems.

(2) Provides that the Secretary of Health, Education, and Welfare shall consult with the Secretary of Labor to develop specific plans for research necessary to produce criteria enabling the Secretary to formulate safety and health standards under this act. The Secretary of Health, Education, and Welfare is also required to develop and publish at least annually criteria which would, if applied, protect employees from diminished health or life expectancy because of their work experiences.

(3) Provides that the Secretary of HEW shall conduct special research to explore new problems created by technology in occupational safety and health. The Secretary of HEW shall also conduct research into motivational and behavioral factors.

(4) Requires the Secretary, in conjunction with the Secretary of Health, Education, and Welfare, to develop procedures for accurately measuring and recording exposure to substances, conditions, or processes which he believes will endanger safety or health. In carrying out this requirement, the Secretary or the Secretary of Health, Education, and Welfare may require employers to measure or record concentrations or exposures to employees where he determines their health or safety may be in danger and that further information is necessary and the substance, condition, or process is not covered by an occupational safety and health standard or a criteria established by the Secretary of Health, Education, and Welfare. If the substance, condition, or process is covered by a criteria issued by the Secretary of Health, Education, and Welfare, then the Secretary may, where necessary, require employers to measure or record particular substances. If the substance, condition, or process is covered by an occupational safety and health standard, and an employer is not in compliance with it, he shall be required to measure and record the particular substances for as long as the Secretary deems necessary to assure future compliance. The above requirements are applicable only where the measurement is technologically feasible and necessary equipment is available at reasonable cost. Authority of section 9(c) is to be used in carrying out this paragraph.

(5) Within 6 months of enactment, and annually thereafter, the Secretary of HEW shall publish a list of all known or potentially toxic substances and concentrations at which toxicity occurs, and shall if requested by an employer or authorized representative of employees apprise those affected of the findings. Within 60 days of such determination, an employer shall not require any employee to be exposed to such toxic substance unless it is accompanied by information made available to employees by label or other appropriate means of the hazards and proper conditions and precautions for safe use and emergency treatment, and personal protective equipment is supplied or unless such exposed employee may absent himself from such risk of harm for the period necessary to avoid danger without loss of compensation.

(b) Provides that the Secretary of HEW is authorized to make inspections and question employees as provided in section 9.

(c) Provides that the Secretary is authorized to enter into contracts or arrangements with public agencies or private organizations for the purpose of conducting studies related to establishing and applying standards under section 7. Provides for cooperation between the Secretary and the Secretary of HEW to avoid duplication of effort under this section.

(d) Provides that the Secretary and the Secretary of HEW and an appropriate State official shall establish health and accident reporting systems for employers and the States as the Secretary deems necessary.

(e) Provides for the dissemination of information by the Secretary and the Secretary of HEW to employers and employees and organizations.

SEC. 20—TRAINING AND EMPLOYEE EDUCATION

(a) Authorizes the Secretary of HEW, after consultation with the Secretary of Labor and with other Federal agencies, to conduct directly or by grant or contract, programs—

(1) to educate and train personnel;

(2) to provide informational programs.

(b) Authorizes the Secretary to conduct directly or by grants or contracts short-term training of personnel.

(c) Provides that the Secretary together with the Secretary of HEW shall educate and train employers and employees in the recognition and avoidance of accidents, and consult and advise employers and employees as to means of preventing injuries and illnesses.

SEC. 21—GRANTS TO THE STATES

(a) Provides that the Secretary, during fiscal year 1971, and the 2 succeeding fiscal years, make grants to State agencies designated under section 17(c) to assist—

(1) in identifying needs;

(2) in developing plans under section 17;

(3) in developing plans for—

(a) collecting statistical data;

(b) increasing personnel capabilities;

(c) improving administration and enforcement, including standards.

(b) Provides that the Secretary, commencing in fiscal year 1971, and the 2 succeeding fiscal years, shall make experimental and demonstration grants.

(c) Provides that the Governor of a State shall designate the State agency to receive a grant.

(d) Provides that the State agency designated by the Governor shall submit grant application to the Secretary.

(e) The Secretary, after review with the Secretary of HEW, shall accept or reject the application for grant.

(f) The Federal share for each State grant under (a) or (b) of this section may be up to 90 percent. Different percentage distribution among the States shall be established on the basis of objective criteria.

(g) Authorizes the Secretary to make grants to States to assist them in administering and enforcing programs for occupational safety and health contained in State plans. The Federal share may be up to 50 percent of the total cost. Differential in allotments to the States must be based on objective criteria.

(h) The Secretary must make a report after consultation with the Secretary of HEW to the President and the Congress prior to June 30, 1973.

SEC. 22—EFFECT ON OTHER LAWS

(a) This provision makes it clear that this law will not supersede or affect any workmen's compensation law or enlarge, diminish, or affect common law or statutory rights, duties, or liabilities under any law related to injuries, occupational or other diseases, or death of employees arising out of, or in the course of, employment.

(b) This subsection provides that section 5 shall not apply to working conditions of employees with respect to whom a Federal agency exercises statutory authority to prescribe or enforce standards or regulations affecting occupational safety and health.

SEC. 23—AUDITS

(a) This provision provides audit procedures for recipients of grants under this act.

SEC. 24—REPORTS

This section requires the Secretary and the Secretary of Health, Education, and Welfare to make annual reports to the President for transmittal to the Congress.

SEC. 25—APPROPRIATIONS

This section authorizes the appropriations necessary to carry out the Act.

SEC. 26—EFFECTIVE DATE

This section provides that the Act will become effective at the beginning of the first month which begins more than 30 days after its enactment.

SEC. 27—SEPARABILITY

This section contains the usual separability provision.

CHANGES IN EXISTING LAW MADE BY THE BILL, AS REPORTED

In compliance with clause 3 of rule XIII of the Rules of the House of Representatives, changes in existing law made by the bill, as reported, are shown as follows (new matter is printed in italic, existing law in which no change is proposed is shown in roman):

SECTION 7902(c)(1) OF TITLE 5, UNITED STATES CODE

§ 7902. Safety programs

     *   *   *   *   *   *   *

(c) The President may—
(1) establish by Executive order a safety council composed of representatives of the agencies *and of labor organizations representing employees* to serve as an advisory body to the Secretary in furtherance of the safety program carried out by the Secretary under subsection (b) of this section; and
(2) undertake such other measures as he considers proper to prevent injuries and accidents to employees of the agencies.

MINORITY VIEWS ON H.R. 16785

We had every confidence that in this session of Congress we would see the enactment of effective Federal legislation to bring about safe and more healthful working conditions in this country. That confidence was born of the fact of President Nixon's having recommended this legislation in three separate messages to Congress, including a special one devoted exclusively to the urgent and unique problems of job safety and health.

Our hope was sustained over the months by clear indications from majority members that while reasonable men might differ, any differences could be worked out so that we might achieve the goal of enacting a genuinely effective law to reduce job hazards. These indications of apparent willingness to overcome differences even led us to offer a completely new bill as a substitute for the Administration's original bill. And we were willing to reach further accord with the majority up until the final moments before the Committee reported out its bill.

Unfortunately, our efforts were in vain. In retrospect, the majority's willingness to work out disputed points proved to be illusory. In sum, the Committee had rejected the original Administration bill which had been carefully drafted to take account of the harsh but well deserved lessons learned from the 90th Congress' experience with occupational safety and health legislation. The Committee then rejected the Administration's substitute; and finally, spurning even our eleventh hour endeavors to produce a viable piece of legislation, the Committee reported out a bill which we had to vote against.

The measure as reported by the Committee is unacceptable because in rejecting the concept of an independent Board to set standards, the bill would create a monopoly of functions in the Secretary of Labor. Such a monopoly not only ignores the element of fairness to those required to comply with the Act, but also fails to resolve the jurisdictional division between HEW's responsibility for health and the Labor Department's for safety. In addition, the Committee bill does not overcome the widespread objection to permitting an inspector to close down a plant in imminent-danger situations. We regard this as a serious shortcoming. Lastly, the Committee bill contains a sweeping general duty requirement that employers maintain safe and healthful working conditions. This broad mandate is grossly unfair to employers who may be penalized for situations which they have no way of knowing are in violation of the Act.

I. GENERAL DIFFERENCES

The single most important difference between the Committee bill and the substitute is where and how, each would place the prime responsibility for providing safe and healthful working conditions.

The Committee bill follows the stock approach of placing all responsibility in the Secretary of Labor. He would set standards through a time-consuming and complicated procedure involving *ad hoc* advisory committees; he would enforce the standards, prosecute violations before Labor Department hearing examiners; and he again, would be the one to issue corrective orders along with assessing civil penalties.

The substitute bill, on the other hand, refocuses responsibility for job safety and health by distributing these functions. In an effort to stress the importance and non-partisan nature of occupational safety and health, the substitute bill would create a new, top-echelon independent National Occupational Safety and Health Board to set standards composed of five members who would be appointed by the President solely because they are high-calibre professionals in the field of occupational safety and health. The members would serve at the pleasure of the President so that the independent Board does not become the captive of any special interest and remains responsible to the President.

The fact that the proposed legislation is concerned with working men and women is not sufficient reason for placing the standard-setting function under the Department of Labor. The Federal Mediation and Conciliation Service, the National Mediation Board, and the National Labor Relations Board, for example, are wholly concerned with matters pertaining to labor—nevertheless, thay are entirely independent of the Department of Labor. Thus, there is ample statutory precedent for our proposed independent Safety and Health Board.

But even more significant is this. The members of the Board will not be appointed because they are Democrats or Republicans, pro-labor or pro-management, an approach which unfortunately has too often been followed in the making of appointments to Federal positions. The problems to be dealt with are not political, they are not primarily economic, they do not involve issues where there are deep differences concerning policy. To the contrary, these problems are almost entirely technical and technological. The appointment of an independent Board whose members must be highly competent professional experts in a field where the subject matter is almost wholly objective and susceptible to genuinely scientific and technical analysis, judgment, and decision, would inspire the utmost confidence in every segment of the American public.

And finally, the creation of a Board of this kind would more than meet the recommendations for a national advisory commission or for such a Board itself, which were made by the leading professional organizations in the safety and health fields, such as the National Safety Council, the American Industrial Hygiene Association, the American Academy of Occupational Medicine, the Industrial Medical Association, the American Society of Safety Engineers, and several of the State health or industrial safety agencies which testified in the hearings held during the present or immediately preceding Congress.

Aimed at providing both fair and uncomplicated procedures, the substitute bill would thus have the Board set standards, simply using the familiar procedures under the Administrative Procedure Act (APA). The Secretary of Labor would conduct inspections, and in violation cases, he would seek enforcement in the Safety and Health Commission created by the substitute and United States appellate courts in accordance with procedures which would provide appropriate equity remedies and assess civil penalties.

II. SPECIFIC SIGNIFICANT DIFFERENCES

1. *Standards*

The Administration's substitute bill provides very simply that the Board set standards according to the formal procedures of the APA. This means that a full hearing will be held so that a wide variety of views can be aired; and standards will be based on substantial evidence with an opportunity to cross-examine.

However, the substitute bill also recognizes that out-of-the-ordinary situations will arise in which the Board has to act quickly and should not have to go through a hearing before it can respond to these situations. Therefore, section 6(b) of the substitute bill provides that where it is *essential* to protect the health or safety of employees, national consensus standards or established Federal standards can go into effect *immediately* on publication in the Federal Register, and they will remain in effect until later superseded by standards promulgated through formal APA hearings.

Also, section 6(i) of the substitute bill provides that where employees are exposed to *grave* danger from exposure either to toxic substances or to hazards resulting from new processes, then thte Board may issue new "emergency temporary standards". These too would go into effect immediately on publication but would remain in effect until superseded by standards promulgated pursuant to formal APA proceedings. The substitute requires the Board to start formal APA proceedings by publishing the temporary standard as the notice of proposed rule making, as soon as the emergency temporary standards are published. The Board is required to promulgate such standard within six months after the publication of the temporary standard.

The substitute bill provides that where an applicable national consensus standard, or an established Federal standard exists, then the Board would begin with those standards as the proposed rules for the hearings used to set permanent standards. If the standard as finally promulgated by the Board differs from the original proposed rule, then the Board must state its reasons for departing from the original.

The Committee bill would also set permanent standards through formal APA hearings, but before these hearings even begin, it would be necessary to go through an intricate maze of procedures involving assorted advisory committees. Whenever the Secretary wanted to set a standard under the Committee bill, he would have to appoint an advisory committee This advisory committee has up to nine months to submit its recommendations to the Secretary and the Secretary may not begin any hearings until he has afforded the advisory committee the prescribed time to submit its recommendations Although the Secretary may shorten this period, the Committee bill also provides that he may lengthen it; but there is an outside time limit of one year and three months

After this excessive length of time, the Secretary has an additional four-month time period before he is required to hold a formal hearing on the advisory committee's recommendations

If the committee does not submit recommendations on time (bearing in mind this can be up to well over a year), the Secretary may wait up to four more months before he has to schedule a hearing; the hearing begins 30 days after scheduling.

By simple arithmetic, we compute that under the Committee's bill, the Secretary of Labor might well have to wait close to two years before a formal hearing begins. This means that it may take him all that time just to catch up to the starting point of the Board's standard-setting procedure under the substitute bill.

It is understandable that the Committee bill would have to provide these excessive preliminary time lags. After all, it is going to take time to set up an array of *ad hoc* committees and more time still for each of them to undertake and complete their required assignments before they will be in any position to make their recommendations. However, no such time periods are needed under the substitute bill since a full-time, top professional National Board would be continually involved in standards-development and therefore needs only to commence a formal APA hearing when it seeks to set permanent standards.

2. Enforcement

The Committee bill's enforcement provisions are as complicated as its standard-setting procedures, but the enforcement provisions present uniquely serious problems because due process is a matter of grave personal concern where enforcement is involved.

Under the Committee bill, the Secretary of Labor conducts inspections, holds hearings before Labor Department hearing examiners, and it is also the Labor Department which issues corrective orders and assesses civil penalties.

Unlike the Committee bill the substitute provides for an *effective* and *fair* method of enforcement. The Secretary of Labor would continue to be responsible for making inspections and investigations. However, a special permanent three-member administrative Occupational Safety and Health Appeals Commission would be appointed to conduct formal hearings on alleged violations which were discovered by the Secretary; and the Commission would issue any necessary corrective orders, as well as assess penalties. The Commission would utilize hearing examiners whose decisions would become final unless an appeal is made to the Commission.

3. General Safety and Health Requirement

We strongly object to the Committee bill's sweeping general requirement that employers furnish safe and healthful working conditions. This was one of the first provisions which this Committee struck when it reported an occupational safety and health bill in the 90th Congress. Why it has not done so again is beyond our comprehension. The argument used in support of the Committee bill's general requirement is that a similar provision is found in the Walsh-Healey Act, the Service Contract Act, the Maritime Safety Act, and in the laws of some 35 States. This argument does not persuade us.

The Walsh-Healey and Service Contract Acts deal with the duties of those who contract with the Government. If a person freely contracts with the Government, then he assumes the responsibility for maintaining safe and sanitary working conditions as provided for in those two-procurement-related statutes. While the language of the requirement in those two laws may be general, its application could hardly be described as "general" since coverage under those Acts extends only to those circumstances to which the supply and service contracts themselves apply. Moreover, we understand that the general safety and health requirements of those two Acts have never been enforced in the absence of specified standards.

In the case of the Maritime Safety Act, the term "general" safety and health requirement is also a misnomer. The Maritime Safety Act applies to a single industry, so by force of circumstances, that Act does not contain a so-called general requirement like the one in the Committee bill which would apply to the whole spectrum of American industry.

States also do not have general safety and health requirements in the same sense as the Committee bill does. Not only do none of the States provide the wide and varied coverage of the Committee bill, but many State laws apply only to limited areas of activity such as boiler and elevator safety.

The objection to the very broad general safety and health requirement is not, of course, that there are no valid arguments to justify it. The offensive feature of such a provision is that it is essentially unfair to employers to require compliance with a vague mandate applied to highly complex industrial circumstances. Under such a mandate, the employer will simply have no way of knowing whether he is complying with the law or not, nor will the inspector have any concrete criteria, either statutory or administrative, to guide him in finding a violation.

On the one hand, the Committee bill recognizes this industrial complexity by providing for specific standards to be developed through the use of any number of advisory committees and public hearings. But the Committee does a turnabout, and requires the employer to follow a mandate which is almost as broad as "do good and avoid evil." We seriously doubt that the Committee bill could be enforced on the basis of this broad requirement; but if it could, we would be faced with the serious problem that there would be no incentive to develop any standards where such a broad mandate exists.

We recognize, however, that specific standards could not be fashioned to cover every conceivable situation. We would be remiss in our duty, if any worker were killed or seriously injured on the job merely because there was no particular standard applicable to a dangerous situation which was apparent to an employer. Hence, in addition to requiring employers to comply with the specific standards promulgated by the Board, and applicable to them, the substitute bill also requires each covered employer to furnish his employees employment and a place of employment which are free from any hazards which are readily apparent and are causing or are likely to cause death or serious physical harm to his employees.

III. CONCLUSION

Despite our criticism of various provisions of the Committee bill, we do not wish to convey the impression that we object to the bill in its entirety; quite the contrary. Many provisions of the Committee bill are in large part, satisfactory and comparable provisions are found in our substitute. Some examples are the State grants section, the provisions for State participation through the submission of plans, the carefully circumscribed employer-exemption provisions, and the Federal employee safety program. A few provisions, in addition to those discussed herein, are more questionable. Several other provisions of the Committee bill would be acceptable if they were modified.

However, we regard the establishment of an independent Board to promulgate standards and due process as essential provisions which cannot be omitted from any bill which genuinely purports to have the best interests of employees and employers as the basis for its enactment. Hence, we intend to offer our own proposal, which was rejected by the Committee's majority, as a substitute for H.R. 16785 as reported by the Committee.

WILLIAM H. AYRES.
ALBERT H. QUIE.
JOHN M. ASHBROOK.
JOHN N. ERLENBORN.
WILLIAM J. SCHERLE.
JOHN DELLENBACK.
MARVIN L. ESCH.
EDWIN D. ESHLEMAN.
WILLIAM A. STEIGER.
JAMES M. COLLINS.
EARL F. LANDGREBE.
ORVAL HANSEN.
EARL B. RUTH.

ADDITIONAL MINORITY VIEWS OF REPRESENTATIVES SCHERLE, ASHBROOK, ESHLEMAN, COLLINS, LAND-GREBE, AND RUTH

There are few matters of greater importance to both employers and working people than that of on-the-job safety and health. Yet, regrettably, for the second year now, the members of this committee have failed to reach public agreement on this vital issue.

The situation has not been helped by the excessive emotion generated mostly by people with little knowledge or practical experience in these fields. This emotionalism has brought us to the verge of making this issue a partisan one. That is unfortunate.

In our view, it is wrong to imply that accidents will end or substantially diminish if only Congress would pass a law. Poor safety laws can and have done more harm than good. Mistakes we make now will have a serious impact on workers and on the state of our economy.

We must also recognize that this legislation will affect nearly every aspect of the employment relationship. The federal government will be called on to regulate such diverse matters as the height of railings, the amount of dust in the air, noise levels and the type of equipment to be used to perform a particular task. Potentially, regulations could be adopted fixing the number of hours employees should work, the qualifications needed to perform a job and the size of crews thought necessary for safe work performance.

Because of the importance of these subjects to both employers and employees, great care must be taken by us. For that reason we have decided to expand on the minority views.

The goal of any occupational safety and health bill can be stated simply: we must foster improved standards of health and safety for American workers and do it in a way that is reasonable and fair. We have little patience with those who believe that to be effective we must destroy fair trial procedures and due process. Neither justice nor safety will be achieved by that kind of approach. We will, therefore, oppose H.R. 16785. It is a penalty oriented bill that does little to build upon and encourage what has already been done by private employer and employee groups in the field of occupational safety and health. It also raises several serious constitutional problems.

Some of the specific defects in H.R. 16785 are as follows:

No Separation of Powers.—The committee bill vests all authority to write, police and enforce standards in the Secretary of Labor. This procedure is contrary to the basic constitutional theory of separation of powers. It is tantamount to having the chief of police, in addition to his regular duties, also write criminal laws and then act as judge and jury.

In order to provide for effective safety standards, provision must be made for the establishment of an independent, impartial board of experts to develop, on the basis of facts and upon their knowledge and experience, regulations in this field.

Undefined Obligations.—Although H.R. 16785 requires compliance with all interim, permanent and emergency standards promulgated by the Secretary, it also imposes an additional *general duty* upon employers to keep a safe and healthful work place. A penalty of $1,000 per day can be imposed on violators of this catch-all provision. The Supreme Court has ruled that statutes must designate the standard of conduct expected so that affected parties can govern their actions in order to avoid violations. (See: *International Harvester* v. *Kentucky*, 243 U.S. 216; *U.S.* v. *Pennsylvania Railroad Company* 242 US 208). It seems inconceivable for anyone to suggest that we pass a law prohibiting the doing of wrong to anyone. Yet, in effect, that is what Congress has been asked to do by the sponsors of H.R. 16785. The ruling of the Supreme Court makes good sense. We should heed its wisdom here.

Full Protection of the Administrative Procedures Act Denied.—When Congress passed the Administrative Procedures Act we recognized the importance of requiring government agencies to follow uniform procedures that preserved the effectiveness of the laws to be enforced and at the same time compelled fair methods of developing and enforcing regulations. H.R. 16785 departs from the provisions of the APA in at least two important respects.

First, Section 7 permits adoption of administrative regulations based upon "views and arguments" rather than solely on probative evidence. No reason has been offered justifying this deviation from regular and fair procedures. The requirements that administrative decisions be based upon facts and sound reasons mean little when a loophole of this type is included in a statute.

Second, the bill also authorizes the establishment of an extensive measurement, accident and health reporting system (See Section 19 (a)(4)(C) and Section 19 (a)(5)(D)).

Regulations under these provisions are a matter of great importance to employees and also will have a substantial financial impact on employers—particularly in the health field where regular psychological studies and medical examinations are obviously contemplated.

Yet, the validity of any regulations developed in this area could not be tested in court pursuant to the normal appeals procedures of Section 10 of the Administrative Procedures Act. This is so, because administrative action by the specific language of the bill is committed to the *discretion* of the Secretary. (See *Attorney General Manual* on the Administrative Procedures Act at page 94.)

No Assistance to Employers—During the hearing estimates were made indicating that between 12 and 16 thousand consensus codes alone have been developed by businessmen themselves. These codes now are intended as non-mandatory guides. Shortly after this legislation is adopted, however. they will in all likelihood become a matter of law.

Experience with other safety regulations shows that some employers will have considerable financial difficulty in obtaining necessary funds to comply with the new mandatory regulations. H.R. 16785 makes no provision for federal assistance to these individuals. Certainly a federally insured loan program should be made available in order to protect against forced business close-downs and against the unemployment that will follow.

Ill-advised inspections provisions.—H.R. 16785 authorizes searches of employer establishments for safety and health violations. Such searches may be conducted without a warrant and individuals who are not government officials may participate in the search. Evidence so obtained may be used in a criminal prosecution. Anyone who gives advance notice of, or who forceably resists such a search may be subject to criminal prosecution.

These provisions, in our view, indicate the unfortunate direction of this bill. The major approach is penal. It is more concerned with cathing employers at some wrong doing than with obtaining safe and healthful working conditions.

The fourth amendment of our constitution was designed to safeguard the privacy and security of individuals against arbitrary invasions and searches by government officials. (*Norman See* v. *City of Seattle* 387 US 541; *Camera* v. *Municipal Court* 387 US 523). The amendment is a concrete expression of a right that is basic to a free society. (*Wolf* v. *Conorado*, 338 US 25, 27). As a general rule, a search of private property must be decided by "a judicial official, not by a police or government enforcement agent." (*Johnson* v. *US* 333 US 10, 14).

Yet, instead of limiting this extraordinary power to government agents acting in carefully restricted circumstances the bill provides for participation in the search by non-government personnel. Even the use of advance notice of intention to search, relied on by some jurists to justify non-warrant inspections in some limited circumstances, is prohibited by the bill. (*See* v. *Seattle* 387 US 541, 549). Advance notice of inspection should obviously be permitted not only to satisfy constitutional consideration but also to permit appropriate company officials to be present in order to immediately correct any violation found.

Lastly, it should be noted that the only way an employer may test the constitutional validity of the search provided for by this legislation is by risking a conviction for forceably resisting the effort to inspect.

We do not oppose inspections designed to protect the public or employees from unsafe and unhealthy working conditions. But we believe that the penal and other provisions that accompany the search procedures provided for in H.R. 16785 are untenable and unnecessary.

Imminent Danger Procedures.—It is equally distressing to note that H.R. 16785 is replete with potentially disruptive intrusions into harmonious labor-management relations.

The procedures to counteract imminent dangers, for example, contained in Section 12 of the bill, simply stated call for giving a federal safety inspector the power to issue an order closing down a place of employment if he discovers what he believes to be an "imminent danger. "An imminent danger" is defined as a danger which could reasonably be expected to cause death or serious physical harm before the imminence of such danger can be eliminated.

The stated purpose of giving this extreme power to one person was that the federal safety inspector would be able to protect employees in case a roof was about to collapse or a boiler about to explode. The prospect of a federal inspector happening upon a scene of imminent disaster is highly unlikely, at best. Nor would any federal safety inspector be needed to point out such situation to an employer; no employer would continue operating if such were actually the case.

More realistically, the all powerful inspector would become a pawn in labor disputes.

The great potential for misuse that would be created if this power were put into the hands of an inspector in the field was amply demonstrated during the public hearings. The testimony reflected fears that pressure would be brought to bear upon federal inspectors to shut down plants in cases other than *bona fide* imminent danger situations. Thus, this unrestricted power in one person would realistically find itself in the middle of labor-management disputes. It would be far simpler for a disgruntled employee to pass by established labor-management grievance procedures and complain to a federal safety inspector that unsafe conditions existed when the real basis of a dispute was properly a labor-management problem, to be settled by established collective bargaining methods.

One witness citing examples of experience in his industry stated:

"The following incidents are noted for the purpose of illustrating how the cause of safety and safety legislation has been invoked for other purposes.

"(1) In a Texas refinery, the union workers went out on strike at 2:00 a.m. on a Sunday morning. The unions gave the company only a few minutes notice of the impending strike and walked out leaving the refinery units unattended. The refinery, which had a contract with the Federal Government to supply jet fuel to the Air Force, was able to keep the plant operating with management personnel.

"The union sent a complaint to the Secretary of Labor (and published it in the local newspaper) charging that the plant was unsafe because it was not being operated by a full crew. It asked the Secretary to use his authority under the Walsh-Healey Act to find that the operation of the plant was not safe.

"The union issued a strike bulletin to its members stating that it was going to see that a safety investigation would follow so that the company's Government contracts would be cancelled. This plant had two safety inspections under the Walsh-Healey Act earlier the same year. Furthermore, its safety record during the strike period was considerably better than its average during the normal operation."

This example and others reflected in the record indicate that giving a federal safety inspector complete authority over operations of a business enterprise would certainly subject the inspector to intimidation pressures to act, and in many cases, he would be requested to inspect a plant simply to harass or intimidate employers. In essence, the exercise of this shut-down power amounts to summary punishment which is contrary to our established standards of law.

This is not to say, of course, that the Government should not have the power to abate a *bona fide* potential disaster. This is an inherent power of the Government, both Federal and Local. What is objectionable here is the method outlined in H.R. 16785, which has no safeguards or guidelines and realistically would lend itself to misuse.

Clearly, any Occupational Safety and Health Bill should recognize the possibility of disaster potential situations, and provide means for dealing with them. The appropriate means to this end would be through Courts. If a federal safety inspector comes upon what he believes to be an imminent danger situation, he should first notify the employer in an attempt to abate or clarify the situation. Then the Government official should seek injunctive relief in the Federal Courts.

This method would act as a safeguard against possible misuse of power or possible error on the part of the inspector, and more important, with the swift and ready access to our Federal Courts, a bona fide potential disaster situation could be dealt with in short measure. Thus, the health and safety of employees on the job could be reasonably safeguarded, while at the same time, the rights of the employer and the viability of the collective bargaining process would be assured.

A Better Bill.—A better bill than H.R. 16785 is obviously needed. The above are just some of what we believe are valid objections to this measure. There are other important problems, such as: the inequities of the posting requirements and the inadequate protection of trade secrets. The cumulative effects of all of these defects indicate that improvement of this legislation by amendment is not feasible. A complete substitute is necessary. A number of committee members are planning to take this step and we urge that their efforts be given support.

There are other matters developed during the hearing that need decisions.

Safety in America Today.—During the hearings we became deeply concerned over the status of safety in America today. Charges of "on the job slaughter" of the American worker were alleged. Businessmen were portrayed as villains, reaping profits through the abuse of employees.

The facts do not support this picture.

Statistics gathered by the National Safety Council show that the average American is safer at his workplace than he is at home, on the highway, or at play. This is directly attributable to the fact that, for many decades, businessmen have worked hard to improve industrial safety and health conditions. They know they are dealing with the lives and limbs of other human beings. Moreover, they know that operating a safe shop is good business; production losses and medical and insurance costs are expensive by-products of on-the-job accidents, whereas accident prevention programs boost employee morale and promote efficiency.

The results of business' voluntary and continuing dedication to provide a safe workplace are dramatic. In 1912, an estimated 18,000 to 21,000 workers' lives were lost while producing $100 billion worth of gross national product. In 1968, *in a workforce more than double in size and producing over eight times as much,* there were only 14,300 work deaths. The following chart traces the steady decline in the death rate over the years

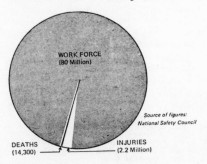

Source of figures:
National Safety Council

(Source: for statistics, National Safety Council, chart: Nation's Business, May 1970)

Likewise, during the last 40 years the frequency and severity rates of injuries have been drastically reduced. And while there has been some plateauing of industry's accident frequency record in recent years, it is generally conceded that this is to be expected during periods of highly increasing productivity and employment. Significantly, during the last two decades alone productivity has risen by 93.7 percent and employment has also been up sharply.

Finally, a look at the most recent year for which full statistics are available—1968—provides equally dramatic evidence as to why the safety record of American business has no equal anywhere in the world.

In 1968, there were 14,300 occupational fatalities and 2,200,000 occupational injuries (some were serious, but most were of a temporary nature) *out of a total labor force of nearly 80 million people.* *

The drawing below provides a visual illustration of how small the portions of the workforce injured or killed on the job in 1968 were:

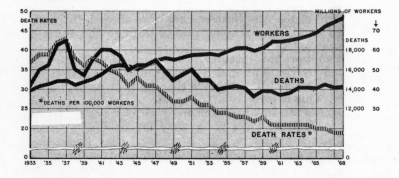

(Source: <u>Accident</u> <u>Facts</u>, 1969 Edition)

Statistically, these injury and fatality experiences figure out, respectively, to an extremely low .0275 and an incredibly low .00018.

One accident, of course, is one too many. Greater improvements can and must be made. But these figures make it abundantly clear that American business owes no apology for its safety record, and deserves to be treated fairly in any legislation adopted.

A FEDERAL ROLE IS NEEDED

Notably, too, our present system is based on state-determined standards adapted to local needs, consensus codes voluntarily agreed to by employers, education and cooperation. This pluralistic system has stimulated individual and local commitments and has been largely

----

*There were a total of 115,000 accidental deaths in the United States in 1968. Fourteen thousand three hundred were job-related, and of this amount approximately 20 percent were caused by motor vehicles and 11 percent involved government employees. If accidents attributable to occupations already covered by federal regulations, i.e. mining, government contract employers and transportation, are excluded, the total number of industrial accidents affected by this legislation becomes less than 10 percent.

responsible for the splended achievements to date. Logically, then, the most prudent and constructive way to attain still greater improvements would be to provide additional encouragement and support for these state, local and voluntary efforts. The federal role, in other words, should be a helping hand, rather than a stiff-arm. The value of such an approach was underscored for the Committee by many industrial safety experts. As a result of extensive personal experiences, these men know that safety cannot be legislated. Their testimony made clear that the cause of occupational injuries is some type of "people failure," rather than inadequate equipment or facilities. All too often the worker himself rebels at wearing safety shoes or hard hats, ignores the warning signs, and tries to beat the machine guards or removes them because they "get in the way."

Nor can we afford to close our eyes to the fact that authoritarian federalization of job safety may well have the opposite effect of that intended.

In Europe, for example, safety programs are nationalized. Yet the safety performance of American industry is far better. A British safety expert who compared the record of the United States to that of the United Kingdom found that the accident frequency rate of U.S. firms in each of the 17 industrial groupings compared was better than the accident rate in his own country. The record of our chemical companies, for example, was seven times better than that of similar British firms; and in the steel industry the accident frequency rate of U.S. firms was ten times better.

CONCLUSION

All of these considerations clearly seem to mandate that any federal legislation be a cautious and reasonable effort genuinely tailored to strengthen our present safety system through incentives and cooperation.

Recognition of this, significantly, was mirrored in the message President Nixon sent to the Congress on August 6, 1969 with his own proposal:

> . . . The comprehensive Occupational Safety and Health Act . . . will correct some of the important deficiencies of earlier approaches . . . It will separate the function of setting safety and health standards from the function of enforcing them. Appropriate procedures to guarantee due process of law and the right to appeal will be incorporated. The proposal will also provide a flexible mechanism which can reach quickly to the new technologies of tomorrow.
>
> Under the suggested legislation, maximum use will be made of standards established through a voluntary consensus of industry, labor, and other experts. No standard will be set until the views of all interested parties have been heard. This proposal would also encourage stronger efforts at the State level, sharing enforcement responsibility with states which have adequate programs. Greater emphasis will also be given to research and education, for the effects of modern technologies on the physical well-being of workers are complex and poorly understood . . .

(This legislation) . . . can do much to improve the environment of the American worker. But it will take much more than new government efforts if we are to achieve our objectives. Employers and employees alike must be committed to the prevention of accident and disease and alert to every opportunity for promoting that end. Together the private and public sectors can do much that we cannot do separately.

Regrettably, this philosophy has been rejected by the majority members of the Committee in favor of the authoritarian, penalty-oriented, "bull-in-the-china-shop" approach of H.R. 16785.

Admittedly, industrial accidents are tragic.

But to those who cherish constitutional due process—to those who know from long experience that job-safety and health programs developed in an uncoerced, cooperative context hold the best hope for continued progress—and to those who believe that American working men and women deserve more than an unworkable legislative deception—the Committee's action in approving H.R. 16785 is a tragedy without equal.

For these reasons, and the reasons set forth in the minority report, we must oppose H.R. 16785.

BILL SCHERLE.
JOHN M. ASHBROOK.
EDWIN D. ESHLEMAN.
JAMES M. COLLINS.
EARL F. LANDGREBE.
EARL B. RUTH.

SEPARATE AND CONCURRING VIEWS OF MR. BURTON

This bill represents a long-overdue significant additional recognition that working men and women need Federal assistance to secure their inalienable right to earn their living free from the ravages of job-caused death, disease and injury. This bill is also a testimonial to this Committee's faith that the formalization of standards and standard setting, coupled with enforcement, will bring a reduction in the high level of death, disease, and injury.

While I share the conviction that standard-setting and enforcement is an appropriate Federal responsibility, I am gravely concerned that this bill may not go far enough to reach and remove the root causes of the macabre facts of life in the working place. More specifically, I am convinced that most of the diseases and a substantial portion of deaths and injuries are not the result of worker carelessness, but are avoidable by management's exercise of preventative measures. Unfortunately, the costs of the necessary preventative measures appear, even in 1970, to exceed the costs to employers from the employee injuries which may occur without these expenditures. Therefore, until and unless the basic economics of these disasters are changed, nothing in the working place may change. Thus, with today's low level of Workmen's Compensation, preventative expenditures for better health and safety are often the employer's most expensive and uneconomic choice. In short, today's Workmen's Compensation laws and associated laws offer an economic incentive to many corporations to forbear from preventative expenditures because they have concluded that the costs of employee death and injury (potentially higher Workmen's Compensation, Health Insurance premiums, etc.) are often less than the costs of accident and disease prevention.

I believe that employers in every state should be able to invest in better safety and health and know that they are saving money for every death and injury which is prevented. At the very least, I believe that any employers who choose to spend funds for preventative safety and health measures should not be economically penalized for that decision. Employers in states with the higher levels of Workmen's Compensation payments should not be at an economic disadvantage with reference to employers obligated to pay far lower levels. Without this equality, and without a higher value on human life and health from higher Workmen's Compensation standards, an uncertain and unnecessary number of deaths and injuries will be occurring each year.

To achieve the goals of making safety and health economic and effective, the state levels of workmen's compensation should be adequate and relatively uniform. National, uniform, minimum standards of benefits, universal coverage, and comprehensive medical and related benefits appear to be the minimum initial commitment which working men and women should have as a matter of right. More specifically, any levels of workmen's compensation should be sufficient to adequately sustain a widowed spouse or family otherwise incapable of support. The actual level of many State Workmen's Compensation payment programs portrays an obviously inadequate program both in terms of benefits and coverage. However, this portrayal is only the vague outline of the hundreds of thousands of cases of uncompensated loss to working men and women each year. Such losses are staggering in amount—both in their aggregate size and in their actual impact on workers' families. Such losses are particularly harsh when they fall on the majority of men and women who work without the benefit of a union and an adequate compensatory health plan. Such losses are unconscionable when they are the result of negligence by the employer for which the worker has no legal remedy in court.

I believe this bill must rapidly eliminate the source of these wrongs in the workplace by significantly lowering the incidence of death, disease, and injury. I will be reviewing the record of this progress carefully. If such a decrease in death, disease and injury does not rather rapidly take place and continue, *and* if the character of other rights of working men and women is not raised to a humane level by the states, then I believe this committee must adopt the additional, alternative, and more basic economic solutions I have suggested above.

PHILLIP BURTON.

O

APPENDIX D

THE BILL AS AMENDED BY THE HOUSE

The House Education and Labor Committee bill did not survive House floor debate. On November 24, a measure introduced by Congressmen William A. Steiger (R-Wis) and Robert L. Sikes (D-Fla), as an amendment to the committee bill, was accepted as a substitute.

The Steiger-Sikes substitute was developed as a compromise between legislation originally proposed by the Administration and the Committee bill.

The Steiger-Sikes substitute, as passed by the House, follows.

House
11-24-70
pp. 10693-10701

The SPEAKER. The Clerk will report the amendment on which a separate vote has been demanded.

The Clerk read as follows:

Amendment: strike out all after the enacting clause and insert:

That this Act may be cited as the "Occupational Safety and Health Act".

CONGRESSIONAL FINDINGS AND PURPOSE

SEC. 2. (a) The Congress finds that personal injuries and illnesses arising out of work situations impose a substantial burden upon, and are a hindrance to, interstate commerce in terms of lost production, wage loss, medical expenses, and disability compensation payments.

(b) The Congress declares it to be its purpose and policy, through the exercise of its powers, to regulate commerce among the several States and with foreign nations and to provide for the general welfare, to assure so far as possible every working man and woman in the Nation safe and healthful working conditions and to preserve our human resources—

(1) by encouraging employers and employees in their efforts to reduce the number of occupational safety and health hazards at their places of employment, and to stimulate employers and employees to institute new and to perfect existing programs for providing safe and healthful working conditions;

(2) by providing that employers and employees have separate but dependent responsibilities and rights with respect to achieving safe and healthful working conditions;

(3) by creating a National Occupational Safety and Health Board to be appointed by the President for the purpose of setting mandatory occupational safety and health standards applicable to businesses affecting interstate commerce, and by creating an Occupational Safety and Health Appeals Commission for carrying out adjudicatory functions under the Act;

(4) by building upon advances already made through employer and employee initiative for providing safe and healthful working conditions;

(5) by providing for research in the field of occupational safety and health, including the psychological factors involved, and by developing innovative methods, techniques, and approaches for dealing with occupational safety and health problems;

(6) by exploring ways to discover latent diseases, establishing causal connections between diseases and work in environmental conditions, and conducting other research relating to health problems, in recognition of the fact that occupational health standards present problems often different from those involved in occupational safety;

(7) by providing medical criteria which will assure insofar as practicable that no employee will suffer diminished health, functional capacity, or life expectancy as a result of his work experience;

(8) by providing for training programs to increase the number and competence of personnel engaged in the field of occupational safety and health;

(9) by providing for the development and promulgation of occupational safety and health standards;

(10) by providing an effective enforcement program which shall include a prohibition against giving advance notice of any inspection and sanctions for any individual violating this prohibition;

(11) by encouraging the States to assume the fullest responsibility for the administration and enforcement of their occupational safety and health laws by providing grants to the States to assist in identifying their needs and responsibilities in the area of occupational safety and health, to develop plans in accordance with the provisions of this Act, to improve the administration and enforcement of State occupational safety and health laws, and to conduct experimental and demonstration projects in connection therewith;

(12) by providing for appropriate reporting procedures with respect to occupational safety and health which procedures will help achieve the objectives of this Act and ac-

201

curately describe the nature of the occupational safety and health problem;

(13) by encouraging joint labor-management efforts to reduce injuries and disease arising out of employment.

DEFINITIONS

SEC. 3. For the purposes of this Act—

(1) The term "Secretary" means the Secretary of Labor.

(2) The term "Safety and Health Appeals Commission" means the Occupational Safety and Health Appeals Commission established under section 12 of this Act.

(3) The term "Board" means the National Occupational Safety and Health Board established under section 8 of this Act.

(4) The term "commerce" means trade, traffic, commerce, transportation, or communication among the several States, or between a State and any place outside thereof, or within the District of Columbia, or a possession of the United States (other than a State as defined in paragraph (8) of this subsection), or between points in the same State but through a point outside thereof.

(5) The term "person" means one or more individuals, partnerships, associations, corporations, business trusts, legal representatives, or any organized group of persons.

(6) The term "employer" means a person engaged in a business affecting commerce who has employees, but does not include the United States or any State or political subdivision of a State.

(7) The term "employee" means an employee of an employer who is employed in a business of his employer which affects commerce.

(8) The term "State" includes a State of the United States, the District of Columbia, Puerto Rico, the Virgin Islands, American Samoa, Guam, and the Trust Territory of the Pacific Islands.

(9) The term "occupational safety and health standard" means a standard which requires conditions, or the adoption or use of one or more practices, means, methods, operations, or processes, reasonably necessary or appropriate to provide safe or healthful employment and places of employment.

(10) The term "national consensus standard" means any occupational safety and health standard or modification thereof which (a) has been adopted and promulgated by a nationally recognized public or private standards-producing organization possessing technical competence and under a consensus method which involves consideration of the views of interested and affected parties, and (b) has been designated by the Board, after consultation with other appropriate Federal agencies.

(11) The term "established Federal standard" means any operative occupational safety and health standard established by any agency of the United States and presently in effect, or contained in any Act of Congress in force on the date of enactment of this Act.

APPLICABILITY OF ACT

SEC. 4. This Act shall apply only with respect to employment performed in a workplace in a State, Wake Island, Outer Continental Shelf lands defined in the Outer Continental Shelf Lands Act, Johnston Island, or the Canal Zone, except that this Act shall not apply to any vessel underway on the Outer Continental Shelf lands. The Secretary of the Interior shall, by regulation, provide for judicial enforcement of this Act by the courts established for areas in which there are no Federal district courts having jurisdiction.

DUTIES OF EMPLOYERS

SEC. 5. Each employer—

(a) shall furnish to each of his employees employment and a place of employment which are free from any hazards which are readily apparent and are causing or are likely to cause death or serious physical harm to his employees;

(b) shall comply with occupational safety and health standards promulgated under this Act.

OCCUPATIONAL SAFETY AND HEALTH STANDARDS

SEC. 6. (a) The National Occupational Safety and Health Board established under section 8 of this Act is authorized to promulgate rules prescribing occupational safety and health standards in accordance with sections 556 and 557 of title 5, United States Code.

(b) Without regard to the provisions of sections 553, 556, and 557, title 5, United States Code, the Board shall, as soon as practicable, but in no event later than three years after the date of enactment of this Act, by rule promulgate as an occupational safety and health standard, any national consensus standard or any established Federal standard, unless it determines that the promulgation of such a standard as an occupational safety and health standrd would not rseult in improved sfety or health for affected employees. In the event of conflict among such standards, the Board shall promulgate the standard which assures the greatest protection of the safety or health of the affected employees. Such national consensus standard or established Federal standard shall take effect immediately upon publication and remain in effect until superseded by a rule promulgated pursuant to subsection (a) of this section.

(c) (1) Whenever the Board promulgates any standard, makes any rule, order, decision, grants any exemption or extension of time, it shall include a statement of the reasons for such action, and such statement shall be published in the Federal Register; and

(2) Whenever a rule issued by the Board differs substantially from an existing national consensus standard, the Board shall include in the rule issued a statement of the reasons why the rule as adopted will better effectuate the purposes of this Act than the national consensus standard.

(d) Any agency may participate in the rulemaking under this section.

(e) The Secretary of Labor (with respect to safety issues) or the Secretary of Health, Education, and Welfare (with respect to health issues) may submit a request to the Board at any time to establish or modify occupational safety and health standards indicated in the request. Within sixty days from the receipt of the request, the Board shall commence proceedings under this section.

(f) Any interested person may also submit a request in writing to the Board at any time to establish or modify occupational safety and health standards. The Board shall give due consideration to such request and may commence proceedings under this section on the basis of such request.

(g) If, prior to the publication of the rule, an interested person or agency which submitted written data, views, or arguments makes application to the Board for leave to adduce additional data, views, or arguments and such person or agency shows to the satisfaction of the Board that additions may materially affect the result of the rulemaking procedure and that there were reasonable grounds for failure to adduce such additions earlier, the Board may receive and consider such additions.

(h) In determining the priority for establishing standards under this section, the Board shall give due regard to the need for mandatory safety and health standards for particular industries, trades, crafts, occupations, businesses, workplaces or work environments. The Board shall also give due regard to the recommendations of the Secretary and the Secretary of Health, Education, and Welfare regarding the need for mandatory standards in determining the priority for establishing such standards.

(i)(1) The Board shall provide without regard to requirements of Ch. 5, title 5, United States Code, for an emergency temporary standard to take immediate effect upon publication in the Federal Register if it determines (A) that employees are exposed to grave danger from exposure to substances determined to be toxic or from new hazards resulting from the introduction of new processes, and (B) that such emergency standard is necessary to protect employees from such danger.

(2) Such standard shall be effective until superseded by a standard promulgated in accordance with the procedures prescribed in paragraph (3) of this subsection.

(3) Upon publication of such standard in the Federal Register the Board shall commence a hearing in accordance with sections 556 and 557 of title 5, United States Code, and the standard as published shall also serve as a proposed rule for the hearing. The Board shall promulgate a standard under this paragraph no later than six months after publication of the emergency temporary standard as provided in paragraph (2) of this subsection.

(j)(1) Whenever the Board upon the basis of information submitted to it in writing by an interested person (including a representative of an organization of employers or employees, or a nationally recognized standards-producing organization) or by the Secretary or the Secretary of Health, Education, and Welfare, a State or a political subdivision of a State, or on the basis of information otherwise available to it, determines that a rule should be prescribed under subsection (a) of this section, the Board may appoint an advisory committee as provided for in section 7(e) of this Act, which shall submit recommendations to the Board regarding the rule to be prescribed which will carry out the purposes of this Act, which recommendations shall be published by the Board in the Federal Register, either as part of a subsequent notice of proposed rulemaking or separately. The recommendations of an advisory committee shall be submitted to the Board within two hundred and seventy days from its appointment, or within such longer or shorter period as may be prescribed by the Board, but in no event may the Board prescribe a period which is longer than one year and three months.

(2) After the submission of such recommendations, the Board shall, as soon as practicable and in any event within four months, schedule and give notice of a hearing on the recommendations of the advisory committee and any other relevant subjects and issues. In the event that the advisory committee fails to submit recommendations within two hundred and seventy days from its appointment (or such longer or shorter period as the Board has prescribed) the Board shall make a proposal relevant to the purpose for which the advisory committee was appointed, and shall within four months schedule and give notice of hearing thereon. In either case, notice of the time, place, subjects, and issues of any such hearing shall be published in the Federal Register thirty days prior to the hearing and shall contain the recommendations of the advisory committee or the proposal made in absence of such recommendation. Prior to the hearing interested persons shall be afforded an opportunity to submit comments upon any recommendations of the advisory committee or other proposal. Only persons who have submitted such comments shall have a right at such hearing to submit oral arguments, but nothing herein shall be deemed to prevent any person from submitting written evidence, data, views, or arguments.

(k) The Board shall within sixty days (where an advisory committee is utilized) or one hundred and twenty days (where no advisory committee is utilized) after completion of the hearing held pursuant to section 6(a) issue a rule promulgating, modifying, or revoking an occupational safety and health standard or make a determination that a rule should not be issued. Such a rule may contain a provision delaying its effective date for such period (not in excess of ninety days) as the Board determines may be appropriate to insure that affected employers are given an opportunity to familiarize themselves and their employees with the requirements of the standard.

(1) Any affected employer may apply to the Board for a rule or order for an exemption from the requirements of section 5(b) of this Act. Affected employees shall be given notice by the employer of each such applica-

tion and an opportunity to participate in a hearing. The Board shall issue such rule or order if it determines on the record, after an opportunity for an inspection and a hearing, that the proponent of the exemption has demonstrated by a preponderance of the evidence that the conditions, practices, means, methods, operations, or processes used or proposed to be used by an employer will provide employment and places of employment to his employees which are as safe and healthful as those which would prevail if he complied with the standard. The rule or order so issued shall prescribe the conditions the employer must maintain, and the practices, means, methods, operations, and processes which he must adopt and utilize to the extent they differ from the standard in question. Such a rule or order may be modified or revoked upon application by an employer, employees, or by the Board on its own motion in the manner prescribed for its issuance at any time after six months after its issuance.

(m) Standards promulgated under this section shall prescribe the posting of such labels or warnings as are necessary to apprise employees of the nature and extent of hazards and of the suggested methods of avoiding or ameliorating them.

ADVISORY COMMITTEES

SEC. 7. (a) There is hereby established a National Advisory Committee on Occupational Safety and Health (hereafter in this section referred to as the "Committee") consisting of twelve members appointed by the Secretary, four of whom are to be designated by the Secretary of Health, Education, and Welfare, without regard to the civil service laws and composed equally of representatives of management, labor and the public. The Secretary shall designate one of the public members as Chairman. The members shall be selected upon the basis of their experience and competence in the field of occupational safety and health.

(b) The Committee shall advise, consult with, and make recommendations to the Secretary and the Secretary of Health, Education, and Welfare on matters relating to the administration of the Act. The Committee shall hold no fewer than two meetings during each calendar year. All meetings of the Committee shall be open to the public and a transcript shall be kept and made available for public inspection.

(c) The members of the Committee shall be compensated in accordance with the provisions of subsection 8(g) of this Act.

(d) The Secretary shall furnish to the Committee an executive secretary and such secretarial, clerical, and other services as are deemed necessary to the conduct of its business.

(e) An advisory committee which may be utilized by the Board in its standard-setting functions under section 6 of this Act shall consist of not more than fifteen members and shall include as a member one or more designees of the Secretary of Health, Education, and Welfare, and also as a member one or more designees of the Secretary of Labor and shall include among its members an equal number of persons qualified by experience and affiliation to present the viewpoint of the employers involved, and of persons similarly qualified to present the viewpoint of the workers involved, as well as one or more repersentatives of health and safety agencies of the States. An advisory committee may also include such other persons as the Board may appoint who are qualified by knowledge and experience to make a useful contribution to the work of such committee, including one or more representatives of professional organizations of technicians or professionals specializing in occupational safety or health, and one or more representatives of nationally recognized standards-producing organizations, but the number of persons so appointed to any advisory committee shall not exceed the number appointed to such committee as representatives of Federal and State agencies. Persons appointed to advisory committees from private life shall be compensated in the same manner as consultants or experts under section 8(g) of this Act. The Board shall pay to any State which is the employer of a member of such committee who is a representative of the health or safety agency of that State, reimbursement sufficient to cover the actual cost to the State resulting from such representative's membership on such committee. Any meeting of such committee shall be open to the public and an accurate record shall be kept and made available to the public. No member of such committee (other than representatives of employers and employees) shall have an economic interest in any proposed rule.

NATIONAL OCCUPATIONAL SAFETY AND HEALTH BOARD

SEC. 8. (a) The National Occupational Safety and Health Board is hereby established. The Board shall be composed of five members, having a background either by reason of previous training, education, or experience in the field of occupational safety or health, who shall be appointed by the President, by and with the consent of the Senate, and shall serve at the pleasure of the President. One of the five members may be designated at any time by the President to serve as Chairman of the Board.

(b) Subchapter II (relating to Executive Schedule pay rates) of chapter 53 of title V of the United States Code is amended as follows:

(1) Section 5314 (5 U.S.C. 5314) is amended by adding at the end thereof the following: "(54) Chairman, National Occupational Safety and Health Board.".

(2) Section 5315 (5 U.S.C. 5315) is amended by adding at the end thereof the following: "(92) Members, National Occupational Safety and Health Board.".

(c) The principal office of the Board shall be in the District of Columbia. The Board shall have an official seal which shall be judicially noticed and which shall be preserved in the custody of the Secretary of the Board.

(d) The Chairman of the Board shall, without regard to the civil service laws, appoint and prescribe the duties of a Secretary of the Board.

(e) The Chairman shall be responsible on behalf of the Board for the administrative operations of the Board, and shall appoint, in accordance with the civil service laws, such officers, hearing examiners, agents, attorneys, and employees as are deemed necessary and to fix their compensation in accordance with the Classification Act of 1949, as amended.

(f) Three members of the Board shall constitute a quorum.

(g) The Board is authorized to employ experts, advisers, and consultants or organizations thereof as authorized by section 3109 of title 5, United States Code, and allow them while away from their homes or regular places of business, travel expenses (including per diem in lieu of subsistence) as authorized by section 5703(b) of title 5, United States Code, for persons in the Government service employed intermittently, while so employed.

(h) To carry out its functions under this Act, the Board is authorized to issue subpenas for the attendance and testimony of witnesses and the production of relevant papers, books, and documents and administer oaths. Witnesses summoned before the Board shall be paid the same fees and mileage that are paid witnesses in the courts of the United States.

(i) The Board may order testimony to be taken by deposition in any proceeding pending before it at any stage of such proceeding. Reasonable notice must first be given in writing by the Board or by the party or his attorney of record, which notice shall state the name of the witness and the time and place of the taking of his deposition. Any person may be compelled to appear and depose, and to produce books, papers, or documents, in the same manner as witnesses may be compelled to appear and testify and produce like documentary evidence before the Board, as provided in subsection (j) of this section. Witnesses whose depositions are taken under this subsection, and the persons taking such depositions, shall be entitled to the same fees as are paid for like services in the courts of the United States.

(j) In the case of contumacy by, or refusal to obey a subpena served upon any person under this section, the Federal district court for any district in which such person is found or resides or transacts business, upon application by the United States, and after notice to such person and hearing, shall have jurisdiction to issue an order requiring such person to appear and produce documents before the Board, or both; and any failure to obey such order of the court may be punished by such court as a contempt thereof.

(k) The Board is authorized to make such rules as are necessary for the orderly transaction of its proceedings.

DUTIES OF THE SECRETARY

Inspections, Investigations, and Reports

SEC. 9. (a) In order to carry out the purposes of this Act, the Secretary, upon presenting appropriate credentials to the owner, operator, or agent in charge, is authorized—

(1) to enter without delay and at reasonable times any factory, plant, establishment, construction site, or other area, workplace or environment where work is performed by an employee of an employer; and

(2) to question any such employee and to inspect and investigate during regular working hours and at other reasonable times and within reasonable limits and in a reasonable manner, any such area, workplace, or environment, and all pertinent conditions, structures, machines, apparatus, devices, equipment, and materials therein.

(b) If the employer, or his representative, accompanies the Secretary or his designated representative during the conduct of all or any part of an inspection, a representative authorized by the employees shall also be given an opportunity to do so.

(c) Each employer shall make, keep, and preserve for such period of time, and make available to the Secretary such record of his activities concerning the requirements of this Act as the Secretary may prescribe by regulation or order as necessary or appropriate for carrying out his duties under this Act.

(d) In making his inspections and investigations under this Act the Secretary may require the attendance and testimony of witnesses and the production of evidence under oath. Witnesses shall be paid the same fees and mileage that are paid witnesses in the courts of the United States. In case of contumacy, failure, or refusal of any person to obey such an order, any district court of the United States or the United States courts of any territory or possession, within the jurisdiction of which such person is found, or resides or transacts business, upon the application by the Secretary, shall have jurisdiction to issue to such person an order requiring such person to appear to produce evidence if, as, and when so ordered, and to give testimony relating to the matter under investigation or in question; and any failure to obey such order of the court may be punished by said court as a contempt thereof.

(e) In carrying out his responsibilities under this Act, the Secretary is authorized to—

(1) use, with the consent of any Federal agency, the services, facilities, and employees of such agency with or without reimbursement, and with the consent of any State or political subdivision thereof, accept and use the services, facilities, and employees of the agencies of such State or subdivision with or without reimbursement; and

(2) employ experts and consultants or organizations thereof as authorized by section 3109 of title 5, United States Code, except that contracts for such employment may be renewed annually; compensate individuals so employed at rates not in excess of the rate specified at the time of service for grade GS–18 in section 5332 of title 5, United States Code, including travel-time, and allow them while away from their homes or regular

places of business, travel expenses (including per diem in lieu of subsistence) as authorized by section 5703 of title 5, United States Code, for persons in the Government service employed intermittently, while so employed.

(3) delegate his authority under subsection (a) of this section to any agency of the Federal Government with or without reimbursement and with its consent and to any State agency or agencies designated by the Governor of the State and with or without reimbursement and under conditions agreed upon by the Secretary and such State agency or agencies.

(f) Any information obtained by the Secretary, the Secretary of Health, Education, and Welfare, or a State agency under this Act shall be obtained wth a minimum burden upon employers especially those operating small businesses. Unnecessary duplication of efforts in obtaining information shall be reduced to the maximum extent feasible.

(g) The Secretary shall prescribe such rules and regulations as he may deem necessary to carry out his responsibilities under this Act, including rules and regulations dealing with the inspection or an employer's establishment.

(h) There are hereby authorized to be appropriated such sums as the Congress shall deem necessary to enable the Secretary to purchase equipment which he determines as necessary to measure the exposure of employees to working environments which might cause cumulative or latent ill effects.

CITATIONS AND SAFETY AND HEALTH APPEALS COMMISSION HEARINGS

SEC. 10. (a) If, upon the basis of an inspection or investigation, the Secretary believes that an employer has violated the requirements of sections 5, 6, or 9(c) of this Act, or subsection (e) of this section, or regulations prescribed pursuant to this Act, he shall issue a citation to the employer unless the violation is de minimis. The citation shall be in writing and describe with particularity the nature of the violation, including a reference to the requirement, standard, rule, order, or regulation alleged to have been violated.

(b) In addition, the citation shall include—

(1) the amount of any proposed civil penalties; and

(2) a reasonable time within which the employer shall correct the violation.

(c) The Secretary shall issue each citation within forty-five days from the concurrence of the alleged violation but for good cause the Secretary may extend such period up to a maximum of ninety days from such occurrence.

(d) If an employer notifies the Secretary that he intends to contest a citation issued under this section, the Secretary shall notify the Safety and Health Appeals Commission of the employer's intention and the Safety and Health Appeals Commission shall afford the employer an opportunity for a hearing as provided in section 11 of this Act. However,

if the employer fails to notify the Secretary within fifteen days after the receipt of the citation of his intention to contest the citation issued by the Secretary, the citation shall, on the day immediately following the expiration of the fifteen-day period, become a final order of the Safety and Health Appeals Commission.

(e) Each employer who receives a citation under this section shall prominently post such citation or copy thereof at or near each place a violation referred to in the citation occurred.

(f) No citation may be issued under this section after the expiration of three months following the occurrence of any violation.

(g) Whenever the Secretary compromises, mitigates, or settles any penalty assessed under this Act, he shall include a statement of the reasons for such action, and such statement shall be published in the Federal Register.

OCCUPATIONAL SAFETY AND HEALTH APPEALS COMMISSION

SEC. 11. A. ORGANIZATION AND JURISDICTION—

(1) STATUS.—The Occupational Safety and Health Appeals Commission is hereby established as an independent agency in the Executive Branch of the Government. The members thereof shall be known as the Chairman of the Commission and the Commissioners of the Occupational Safety and Health Appeals Commission.

(2) JURISDICTION.—The Commission shall have such jurisdiction as is conferred on it by this Act.

(3) MEMBERSHIP.—(a) The Commission shall be composed of three Commissioners, appointed by the President, by and with the advice and consent of the Senate, solely on the grounds of fitness to perform the duties of the office.

(b) The salary of the Chairman of the Commission shall be equal to that provided for the executive level in section 5314, title 5, United States Code, and the salary of the remaining two Commissioners shall be in accordance with the executive level as provided in section 5315, title 5, United States Code.

(c) The terms of office of the Commissioners shall be as follows: one Commissioner shall be appointed for a term of two years, one Commissioner shall be appointed for a term of four years, and the remaining Commissioner for a term of six years, respectively. Their successors shall be appointed for terms of six years each, except that vacancy caused by death, resignation, or removal of a member prior to the expiration of the term for which he was appointed shall be filled only for the remainder of such unexpired term. A Commissioner may be removed by the President for inefficiency, neglect of duty, or malfeasance in office.

(d) A Commissioner removed from office in accordance with the provisions of this section shall not be permitted at any time to practice before the Commission.

(4) ORGANIZATION.—(a) The Commission

shall have a seal which shall be judicially noticed.

(b) The President may at any time designate one of the three Commissioners to serve as Chairman of the Commission.

(c) A majority of the Commissioners shall constitute a quorum for the transaction of the Commission's business. A vacancy shall not impair its powers nor affect its duties.

(d) The principal office of the Commission shall be in the District of Columbia, but it may sit at any place within the United States giving due consideration to the expeditious conduct of its proceedings and the convenience of the parties.

(5) HEARING EXAMINERS.—(a) The Commission may appoint hearing examiners to conduct such business as the Commission may require. Each hearing examiner shall be an attorney at law and shall be selected from the Civil Service Commission list of individuals eligible for selection as administrative hearing examiners.

(b) Except as otherwise provided in this Act, the hearing examiners shall be subject to the laws governing employees in the classified civil service, except that appointments shall be made without regard to 5 U.S.C. 5108. Each hearing examiner shall receive compensation at a rate not less than the GS–16 level.

B. PROCEDURE—

(1) REPRESENTATION OF PARTIES.—The Secretary or his delegate shall be represented by the Solicitor of Labor or his delegate before the Commission. The respondent shall be represented in accordance with the rules of practice prescribed by the Commission.

(2) RULES OF PRACTICE, PROCEDURE, AND EVIDENCE.—The proceedings of the Commission shall be conducted in accordance with such rules of practice and procedure (other than rules of evidence) as the Commission may prescribe and in accordance with the rules of evidence applicable in trials without a jury in the United States District Court of the District of Columbia.

(3) SERVICE OF PROCESS.—The mailing by certified mail or registered mail of any pleading, decision, order, notice or process in respect of proceedings before the Commission shall be held sufficient service of such pleading, decision, order, notice or process.

(4) ADMINISTRATION OF OATHS AND PROCUREMENT OF TESTIMONY.—For the efficient administration of the functions vested in the Commission any Commissioner of the Commission, the clerk of the Commission, or any other employee of the Commission designated in writing for the purpose by the Chairman of the Commission, may administer oaths, and any Commissioner may examine witnesses and require, by subpena ordered by the Commission and signed by the Commissioner (or by the Secretary of the Commission or by any other employee of the Commission) when acting under authority from the Secretary of the Commission—

(a) The attendance and testimony of witnesses, and the production of all necessary books, papers, documents, correspondence, and other evidence, from any place in the United States at any designated place of hearing, or

(b) The taking of a deposition before any designated individual competent to administer oaths under this title. In the case of a deposition the testimony shall be reduced to writing by the individual taking the deposition or under his direction and shall then be subscribed by the deponent.

(5) WITNESS FEES.—(a) Any witness summoned or whose deposition is taken shall receive the same fees and mileage as witnesses in courts of the United States.

(b) Such fees and mileage and the expenses of taking any such deposition shall be paid as follows:

(A) In the case of witnesses for the Secretary or his delegate, such payments shall be made by the Secretary or his delegate out of any moneys appropriated for the enforcement of this Act and may be made in advance.

(B) In the case of any other witnesses, such payments shall be made, subject to rules prescribed by the Commission, by the party at whose instance the witness appears or the deposition is taken.

(6) HEARINGS.—Notice and opportunity to be heard upon any proceeding instituted before the Commission shall be given to the respondent and the Secretary or his delegate. If an opportunity to be heard upon the proceedings is given before a hearing examiner of the Commission, neither the respondent nor the Secretary nor his delegate shall be entitled to notice and opportunity to be heard before the Commission upon review, except upon a specific order of the Chairman of the Commission. Hearings before the Commission shall be open to the public, and the testimony, and, if the Commission so requires, the argument, shall be stenographically reported. The Commission is authorized to contract for the reporting of such hearings, and in such contract to fix the terms and conditions under which transcripts will be supplied by the contractor to the Commission and to others and agencies.

(7) REPORTS AND DECISIONS.—(a) A report upon any proceeding instituted before the Commission and a decision thereon shall be made as quickly as practicable. The decision shall be made by a Commissioner in accordance with the report of the Commission, and such decision so made shall, when entered, be the decision of the Commission.

(b) It shall be the duty of the Commission to include in its report upon any proceeding its findings of fact or opinion or memorandum opinion. The Commission shall report in writing all its findings of fact, opinions, and memorandum opinions.

(c) A decision of the Commission dismissing the proceeding shall be considered as its decision.

(8) PROCEDURES IN REGARD TO THE HEARING EXAMINERS.—(a) A hearing examiner shall hear, and make a determination upon, any proceeding instituted before the Commission and any motion in connection therewith, assigned to such hearing examiner by the Chairman of the Commission, and shall

make a report of any such determination which constitutes his final disposition of the proceeding.

(b) The report of the hearing examiner shall become the report of the Commission within thirty days after such report by the hearing examiner unless within such period any Commissioner has directed that such report shall be reviewed by the Commission. Any preliminary action by a hearing examiner which does not form the basis for the entry of the final decision shall not be subject to review by the Commission except in accordance with such rules as the Commission may prescribe. The report of a hearing examiner shall not be a part of the record in any case in which the Chairman directs that such report shall be reviewed by the Commission.

(9) Publicity of Proceedings.—All reports of the Commission and all evidence received by the Commission, including a transcript of the stenographic report of the hearings, shall be public records open to the inspection of the public; except that after the decision of the Commission in any proceeding which has become final the Commission may, upon motion of the respondent or the Secretary or his delegate, permit the withdrawal by the party entitled thereto of originals of books, documents, and records, and of models, diagrams, and other exhibits, introduced in evidence before the Commission; or the Commission may, on its own motion, make such other disposition thereof as it deems advisable.

(10) Publication of Reports.—The Commission shall provide for the publication of its reports at the Government Printing Office in such form and manner as may be best adapted for public information and use, and such authorized publication shall be competent evidence of the reports of the Commission therein contained in all courts of the United States and of the several States without any further proof or authentication thereof. Such reports shall be subject to sale in the same manner and upon the same terms as other public documents.

(11) Upon issuance of a citation and notification of the Commission, pursuant to section 10, the Commission shall afford an opportunity for a hearing, and shall issue such orders, and make such decisions, based upon findings of fact, as are deemed necessary to enforce the Act.

C. Miscellaneous Provisions.—

(1) Employees.—(a) Appointment and Compensation. The Commission is authorized in accordance with the civil service laws to appoint, and in accordance with the Classification Act of 1949 (63 Stat. 954; 5 U.S.C. chapter 21), as amended to fix the compensation of such employees, including a Secretary to the Commission, as may be necessary to efficiently execute the functions vested in the Commission.

(b) Expenses for Travel and Subsistence. The employees of the Commission shall receive their necessary traveling expenses, and expenses for subsistence while traveling on duty and away from their designated stations, as provided in the Travel Expense Act of 1949 (63 Stat. 166; 5 U.S.C., chapter 16.

(2) Expenditures.—The Commission is authorized to make such expenditures (including expenditures for personal services and rent at the seat of Government and elsewhere, and for law books, books of reference, and periodicals), as may be necessary to efficiently execute the functions vested in the Commission. All expenditures of the Commission shall be allowed and paid, out of any moneys appropriated for purposes of the Commission, upon presentation of itemized vouchers therefor signed by the certifying officer designated by the Chairman.

(3) Disposition of Fees.—All fees received by the Commission shall be covered into the Treasury as miscellaneous receipts.

(4) Fee for Transcript of Record.—The Commission is authorized to fix a fee, not in excess of the fee fixed by law to be charged and collected therefor by the clerks of the district courts, for comparing, or for preparing and comparing, a transcript of the record, or for copying any record, entry, or other paper and the comparison and certification thereof.

PROCEDURES TO COUNTERACT IMMINENT DANGERS

Sec. 12. (a) The United States district courts shall have jurisdiction, upon petition of the Secretary, to restrain any conditions or practices in any place of employment which are such that a danger exists which could reasonably be expected to cause death or serious physical harm immediately or before the imminence of such danger can be eliminated through the enforcement procedures otherwise provided by this Act.

(b) Upon the filing of any such petition the district court shall have jurisdiction to grant such injunctive relief or temporary restraining order pending the outcome of an enforcement proceeding pursuant to section 11 of this Act. The proceeding shall be as provided by Rule 65 of the Federal Rules, Civil Procedure, except that no temporary restraining order issued without notice shall be effective for a period longer than five days.

(c) Whenever and as soon as an inspector concludes that conditions or practices described in subsection (a) exist in any place of employment, he shall inform the affected employees and employers of the danger and that he is recommending to the Secretary that relief be sought.

(d) If the Secretary unreasonably fails to petition the court for appropriate relief under this section and any employee is injured thereby either physically or financially by reason of such failure on the part of the Secretary, such employee may bring an action against the United States in the Court of Claims in which he may recover the damages he has sustained, including reasonable court costs and attorney's fees.

(e) In any case where a temporary restraining order is obtained under this section by the Secretary, the court which grants such relief shall set a sum which it deems proper for the payment of such costs, damages, and attorney's fees as may be incurred or suffered by any employer who is found to have been wrongfully restrained or enjoined. In no case shall any employer wrongfully restrained or enjoined be entitled to a recovery for costs, damages, and attorney's fees in excess of the sum set by the court.

JUDICIAL PROCEEDINGS

SEC. 13. (a) (1) Any employer required by an order of the Commission to comply with the standards, regulations, or requirements under this Act, or to pay a penalty, may obtain judicial review of such order by filing a petition for review, within sixty days after service of such order, in the United States court of appeals for the circuit wherein the violation is alleged to have occurred or wherein the employer has its principal office. A copy of the petition shall forthwith be transmitted by the clerk of the court to the Commission and to the Secretary.

(2) The Secretary may also obtain judicial review or enforcement of a decision of the Commission as provided in subsection (1) of this section.

(3) Until the record in a case shall have been filed in a court, as herein provided, the Commission may at any time, upon reasonable notice and in such manner as it shall deem proper, modify or set aside, in whole or in part any finding, order, or rule made or issued by it.

(4) Upon the filing of a petition for review under this section, such court shall have jurisdiction of the proceeding and shall have power to affirm the order of the Commission, or to set aside, in whole or in part, temporarily or permanently, and to enforce such order to the extent that it is affirmed. To the extent that the order of the Commission is affirmed, the court shall thereupon issue its own order requiring compliance with the terms of the order of the Commission. The commencement of proceedings under this paragraph shall not, unless specifically ordered by the court, operate as a stay of the order of the Commission.

(5) No objection to the order of the Commission shall be considered by the court unless such objection was urged before the Commission or unless there were reasonable grounds for failure to do so. The findings of the Commission as to the facts, if supported by substantial evidence on the record considered as a whole, shall be conclusive, but the court, for good cause shown, may remand the case to the Commission for the taking of additional evidence in such manner and upon such terms and conditions as the court may deem proper, in which event the Commission may make new or modified findings and shall file such findings (which, if supported by substantial evidence on the record considered as a whole, shall be conclusive) and its recommendation, if any, for the modification or setting aside of its original order, with the return of such additional evidence.

(6) The judgment of the court affirming or setting aside, in whole or in part, any order under this subsection shall be final, subject to review by the Supreme Court of the United States upon certiorari or certification as provided in section 1254 of title 28, United States Code.

(7) An order of the Commission shall become final under the same conditions as an order of the Federal Trade Commission under section 45(g) of title 15, United States Code.

(b) Any interested person affected by the action of the Board in issuing a standard under section 6 may obtain review of such action by the United States Court of Appeals for the District of Columbia by filing in such court within thirty days following the publication of such rule a petition praying that the action of the Board be modified or set aside in whole or in part. A copy of such petition shall forthwith be served upon the Board and thereupon the Board shall certify and file in the court the record upon which the action complained of was issued as provided in section 2112 of title 28, United States Code. Review by the court shall be in accordance with the provisions of section 706 of title 5, United States Code. The court, for good cause shown, may remand the case to the Board to take further evidence, and the Board may thereupon make new or modified fiindings of fact and may modify its previous action and shall certify to the court the record of the further proceedings. The remedy provided by this subsetcion for reviewing a standard or rule shall be exclusive. The judgment of the court shall be subject to review by the Supreme Court of the United States upon certiorari or certification as provided in section 1254 of title 28, United States Code. The commencement of a proceeding under this subsection shall not, unless specifically ordered by the court, delay the application of the Board's standards.

(c) Civil penalties owed under this Act shall be paid to the Secretary for deposit into the Treasury of the United States and shall accrue to the United States and may be recovered in a civil suit in the name of the United States brought in the Federal district court in the district where the violation is alleged to have occurred or where the employer has its principal office.

(d) The Federal district courts shall have jurisdiction of actions to collect penalties prescribed in this Act and may provide such additional relief as the court deems appropriate to carry out the order of the Occupational Safety and Health Appeals Commission.

REPRESENTATION IN CIVIL LITIGATION

SEC. 14. Except as provided in section 518(a) of title 28, United States Code, relating to litigation before the Supreme Court and the Court of Claims, the Solicitor of Labor may appear for and represent the Secretary in any civil litigation brought under this Act but all such litigatilon shall be subject to the direction and control of the Attorney General.

CONFIDENTIALITY OF TRADE SECRETS

SEC. 15. All information reported to or otherwise obtained by the Secretary or his representative in connection with any inspection or proceeding under this Act which contains or which might reveal a trade secret referred to in section 1905 of title 18 of the United States Code shall be considered confidential for the purpose of that section, except that such information may be disclosed to other officers or employees concerned with carrying out this Act or when essential in any proceeding under this Act. However, any such information shall be recorded and presented off the official public record, and shall be kept and preserved separately.

VARIATIONS, TOLERANCES, AND EXEMPTIONS

SEC. 16. The Board, on the record, after notice and opportunity for a hearing may provide such reasonable limitations and may make such rules and regulations allowing reasonable variations, tolerances, and exemptions to and from any or all provisions of this Act as it may find necessary and proper to avoid serious impairment of the national defense. Such action shall not be in effect for more than six months without notification to affected employees and an opportunity being afforded for a hearing.

PENALTIES

SEC. 17. (a) Any employer who willfully or repeatedly violates the requirements of section 5 of this Act, any standard or rule promulgated pursuant to section 6 of this Act, or regulations prescribed pursuant to this Act, may be assessed a civil penalty of not more than $10,000 for each violation.

(b) Any citation for a serious violation of the requirements of section 5 of this Act, of any standard or rule promulgated pursuant to section 6 of this Act, or of any regulations prescribed pursuant to this Act, shall include a proposed penalty of up to $1,000 for each such violation.

(c) Any employer who violates the requirements of section 5 of this Act, any standard or rule promulgated pursuant to section 6 of this Act, or regulations prescribed pursuant to this Act, and such violation is specifically determined by the Secretary not to be of a serious nature, the Secretary may include in the citation issued for such violation a proposed penalty of up to $1,000 for each such violation.

(d) Any employer who violates any order or citation which has become final in accordance with the provision of section 10 of this Act may be assessed a penalty of up to $1,000 for each such violation. When such violation is of a continuing nature, each day during which it continues shall constitute a separate offense for the purpose of assessing the penalty except where such order or citation is pending review under section 11 of this Act.

(e) Any person who forcibly assaults, resists, opposes, impedes, intimidates, or interferes with any person while engaged in or on account of the performance of inspections or investigatory duties under this Act shall be fined not more than $5,000 or im-

prisoned not more than three years, or both. Whoever, in the commission of any such acts, uses a deadly or dangerous weapon, shall be fined not more than $10,000 or imprisoned not more than ten years or both. Whoever kills a person while engaged in or on account of the performance of inspecting or investigating duties under this Act shall be punished by imprisonment for any term of years or for life.

(f) Any employer who violates any of the posting requirements, as prescribed under the provisions of this Act, shall be assessed by the Commission a civil penalty of up to $1,000 for each such violation.

(g) Any person who discharges or in any other manner discriminates against any employee because such employee has filed any complaint or instituted or caused to be instituted any proceeding under or related to this Act, or has testified or is about to testify in any such proceeding, shall be assessed a civil penalty by the Commission of up to $10,000. Such person may also be subject to a fine of not more than $10,000 or imprisonment of a period not to exceed ten years or both.

(h) The Commission shall have authority to assess and collect all penalties provided in this section, giving due consideration to the appropriateness of the penalty with respect to the size of the business being charged, the gravity of the violation, the good faith of the employer, and the history of previous violations.

(i) For purposes of this section a serious violation shall be deemed to exist in a place of employment if there is a substantial probability that death or serious physical harm could result from a condition which exists, or from one or more practices, means, methods, operations, or processes which have been adopted or are in use, in such place of employment unless the Secretary determines that the employer did not, and could not with the exercise of reasonable diligence, know of the presence of the violation.

STATE JURISDICTION AND STATE PLANS

SEC. 18. (a) Nothing in this Act shall prevent any State agency or court from asserting jurisdiction under State law over any occupational safety or health issue with respect to which no standard is in effect under section 6.

(b) Any State which, at any time, desires to assume responsibility for development and enforcement therein of occupational safety and health standards relating to any occupational safety or health issue with respect to which a Federal standard has been promulgated under section 6 shall submit a State plan for the development of such standards and their enforcement.

(c) The Secretary shall approve the plan submitted by a State under subsection (b), or any modification thereof, if such plan in his judgment—

(1) designates a State agency or agencies as the agency or agencies responsible for administering the plan throughout the State,

(2) provides for the development and en-

forcement of safety and health standards relating to one or more safety or health issues, which standards (and the enforcement of which standards) are or will be at least as effective in providing safe and healthful employment and places of employment as the standards promulgated under section 6 which relate to the same issues, and which standards, when applicable to products which are distributed or used in interstate commerce, are required by compelling local conditions and do not unduly burden interstate commerce,

(3) provides for a right of entry and inspection of all workplaces subject to the Act which is at least as effective as that provided in section 9(a)(1), and includes a prohibition on advance notice of inspections,

(4) contains satisfactory assurances that such agency or agencies have or will have the legal authority and qualified personnel necessary for the enforcement of such standards,

(5) gives satisfactory assurances that such State will devote adequate funds to the administration and enforcement of such standards,

(6) contains satisfactory assurances that such State will, to the extent permitted by its law, establish and maintain an effective and comprehensive occupational safety and health program applicable to all employees of public agencies of the State and its political subdivisions, which program is as effective as the standards contained in an approved plan,

(7) requires employers in the State to make reports to the Secretary in the same manner and to the same extent as if the plan were not in effect, and

(8) provides that the State agency will make such reports to the Secretary in such form and containing such information, as the Secretary shall from time to time require.

(d) If the Secretary rejects a plan submitted under subsection (b), he shall afford the State submitting the plan due notice and opportunity for a hearing before so doing.

(e) After the Secretary approves a State plan submitted under subsection (b), he may, but shall not be required to, exercise his authority under sections 9, 10, 11, and 12 with respect to comparable standards promulgated under section 6, for the period specified in the next sentence. The Secretary may exercise the authority referred to above until he determines, on the basis of actual operations under the State plan, that the criteria set forth in subsection (c) are being applied, but he shall not make such determination for at least three years after the plan's approval under subsection (c). Upon making the determination referred to in the preceding sentence, the provisions of section 5(b), 9 (except for the purpose of carrying out subsection (c)), 10, 11, and 12, and standards promulgated under section 6 of this Act, shall not apply with respect to any occupational safety or health issues covered under the plan, but the Secretary may retain jurisdiction under the above provisions in

any proceeding commenced under section 10 or 11 before the date of determination.

(f) The Secretary shall, on the basis of reports submitted by the State agency and his own inspections make a continuing evaluation of the manner in which each State having a plan approved under this section is carrying out such plan. Whenever the Secretary finds, after affording due notice and opportunity for a hearing, that in the administration of the State plan there is a failure to comply substantially with any provision of the State plan (or any assurance contained therein), he shall notify the State agency of his withdrawal of approval of such plan and upon receipt of such notice such plan shall cease to be in effect, but the State may retain jurisdiction in any case commenced before the withdrawal of the plan in order to enforce standards under the plan whenever the issues involved do not relate to the reasons for the withdrawal of the plan.

(g) The State may obtain a review of a decision of the Secretary withdrawing approval of or rejecting its plan by the United States court of appeals for the circuit in which the State is located by filing in such court within thirty days following receipt of notice of such decision a petition praying that the action of the Secretary be modified or set aside in whole or in part. A copy of such petition shall forthwith be served upon the Secretary, and thereupon the Secretary shall certify and file in the court the record upon which the decision complained of was issued as provided in section 2112 of title 28, United States Code. Unless the court finds that the Secretary's decision in rejecting a proposed State plan or withdrawing his approval of such a plan to be arbitrary and capricious, the court shall affirm the Secretary's decision. The judgment of the court shall be subject to review by the Supreme Court of the United States upon certiorari or certification as provided in section 1254 of title 28, United States Code.

(h) The Secretary may enter into an agreement with a State under which the State will be permitted to continue to enforce one or more occupational health and safety standards in effect in such State until final action is taken by the Secretary with respect to a plan submitted by a State under subsection (b) of this section, or two years from the date of enactment of this Act, whichever is earlier.

FEDERAL AGENCY SAFETY PROGRAMS AND RESPONSIBILITIES

SEC. 19. (a) It shall be the responsibility of the head of each Federal agency to establish and maintain an effective and comprehensive occupational safety and health program which is consistent with the standards promulgated under section 6. The head of each agency shall (after consultation with representatives of the employees thereof)—

(1) provide safe and healthful places and conditions of employment, consistent with the standards set under section 6;

(2) acquire, maintain, and require the use of safety equipment, personal protective equipment, and devices reasonably necessary to protect employees;

(3) keep adequate records of all occupational accidents and illnesses for proper evaluation and necessary corrective action;

(4) consult with the Secretary with regard to the adequacy as to form and content of records kept pursuant to subsection (a)(3) of this section; and

(5) make an annual report to the Secretary with respect to occupational accidents and injuries and the agency's program under this section. Such report shall include any report submitted under section 7902(a)(2) of title 5, United States Code.

(b) The Secretary shall report to the President a summary or digest of reports submitted to him under subsection (a)(5) of this section, together with his evaluations of and recommendations derived from such reports. The President shall transmit annually to the Senate and the House of Representatives a report of the activities of Federal agencies under this section.

(c) Section 7902(c)(1) of title 5, United States Code, is amended by inserting after "agencies" the following: "and of labor organizations representing employees".

(d) The Secretary shall have access to records and reports kept and filed by Federal agencies pursuant to subsections (a) (3) and (5) of this section unless those records and reports are specifically required by Executive order to be kept secret in the interest of the national defense or foreign policy, in which case the Secretary shall have access to such information as will not jeopardize national defense or foreign policy.

TRAINING AND EMPLOYEE EDUCATION

SEC. 20. (a) The Secretary of Health, Education, and Welfare, after consultation with the Secretary of Labor, the Board, and with other appropriate Federal departments and agencies, shall conduct, directly or by grants or contracts (1) education programs to provide an adequate supply of qualified personnel to carry out the purposes of this Act, and (2) informational programs on the importance of and proper use of adequate safety and health equipment.

(b) The Secretary is also authorized to conduct (directly or by grants or contracts) short-term training of personnel engaged in work related to his responsibilities under this Act.

(c) The Secretary, in consultation with the Secretary of Health, Education, and Welfare, shall provide for the establishment and supervision of programs for the education and training of employers and employees in the recognition, avoidance, and prevention of unsafe or unhealthful working conditions in employments covered by this Act, and to consult with and advise employers and employees, and organizations representing employers and employees as to effective means of preventing occupational injuries and illnesses.

GRANTS TO THE STATES

SEC. 21. (a) The Secretary is authorized, during the fiscal year ending June 30, 1971, and the two succeeding fiscal years, to make grants to the States which have designated a State agency under section 18(c) to assist them (1) in identifying their needs and responsibilities in the area of occupational safety and health, (2) in developing State plans under section 18, or (3) in developing plans for—

(A) establishing systems for the collection of information concerning the nature and frequency of occupational injuries and diseases;

(B) increasing the expertise and enforcement capabilities of their personnel engaged in occupational safety and health programs; or

(C) otherwise improving the administration and enforcement of State occupational safety and health laws, including standards thereunder, consistent with the objectives of this Act.

(b) The Secretary is authorized, during the fiscal year ending June 30, 1971, and the two succeeding fiscal years, to make grants to the States for experimental and demonstration projects consistent with the objectives set forth in subsection (a) of this section.

(c) The Governor of the State shall designate the appropriate State agency, or agencies, for receipt of any grant made by the Secretary under this section.

(d) Any State agency, or agencies, designated by the Governor of the State, desiring a grant under this section shall submit an application therefor to the Secretary.

(e) The Secretary shall review the application, and shall, after consultation with the Secretary of Health, Education, and Welfare, approve or reject such application.

(f) The Federal share for each State grant under subsection (a) or (b) of this section may be up to 90 per centum of the State's total cost. In the event the Federal share for all States under either such subsection is not the same, the differences among the States shall be established on the basis of objective criteria.

(g) The Secretary is authorized to make grants to the States to assist them in administering and enforcing programs for occupational safety and health contained in State plans approved by the Secretary pursuant to section 18 of this Act. The Federal share for each State grant under this subsection may be up to 50 per centum of the State's total cost. The last sentence of subsection (f) shall be applicable in determining the Federal share under this subsection.

(h) Prior to June 30, 1973, the Secretary shall, after consultation with the Secretary of Health, Education, and Welfare, transmit a report to the President and to Congress, describing the experience under the program and making any recommendations he may deem appropriate.

ECONOMIC ASSISTANCE TO SMALL BUSINESSES

SEC. 22. (a) Section 7(b) of the Small Business Act, as amended, is amended—

(1) by striking out the period at. the end of "paragraph (5)" and inserting in lieu thereof "; and"; and

(2) by adding after paragraph (5) a new paragraph as follows:

"(6) to make such loans (either directly or in cooperation with banks or other lending institutions through agreements to participate on an immediate or deferred basis) as the Administration may determine to be necessary or appropriate to assist any small business concern in affecting additions to or alterations in the equipment, facilities, or methods of operation of such business in order to comply with the applicable standards promulgated pursuant to section 6 of the Occupational Safety and Health Act or standards adopted by a State pursuant to a plan approved under section 18 of the Occupational Safety and Health Act, if the Administration determines that such concern is likely to suffer substantial economic injury without assistance under this paragraph."

(b) The third sentence of section 7(b) of the Small Business Act, as amended, is amended by striking out "or (5)" after "paragraph (3)" and inserting a comma followed by "(5) or (6)".

(c) Section 4(c)(1) of the Small Business Act, as amended, is amended by inserting "7(b) (6)," after "7(b) (5),".

(d) Loans may also be made or guaranteed for the purposes set forth in section 7(b)(6) of the Small Business Act, as amended, pursuant to the provisions of section 202 of the Public Works and Economic Development Act of 1965, as amended.

RESEARCH AND RELATED ACTIVITIES

SEC. 23. (a)(1) The Secretary of Health, Education, and Welfare, after consultation with the Secretary, the Board, and with other appropriate Federal departments or agencies, shall conduct (directly or by grants or contracts) research, experiments, and demonstrations relating to occupational safety and health, including studies of psychological factors involved, and relating to innovative methods, techniques, and approaches for dealing with occupational safety and health problems.

(2) The Secretary of Health, Education, and Welfare shall from time to time consult with the Board in order to develop specific plans for such research, demonstrations, and experiments as are necessary to produce criteria, including criteria identifying toxic substances, enabling the Board to meet its responsibility for the formulation of safety and health standards under this Act; and the Secretary of Health, Education, and Welfare, on the basis of such research, demonstrations, and experiments and any other information available to him, shall develop and publish at least annually such criteria as will effectuate the purposes of this Act.

(3) The Secretary of Health, Education, and Welfare shall also conduct special research, experiments, and demonstrations relating to occupational safety and health as are necessary to explore new problems, including those created by new technology in occupational safety and health, which may require ameliorative action beyond that which is otherwise provided for in the operating provisions of this Act. The Secretary of Health, Education, and Welfare shall also conduct research into the motivational and behavioral factors relating to the field of occupational safety and health.

(4) The Secretary of Health, Education, and Welfare shall publish within six months of enactment of this Act and thereafter as needed but at least annually a list of all known toxic substances by generic family or other useful grouping, and the concentrations at which such toxicity is known to occur.

(5) The Board shall respond, as soon as possible, to a request by any employer or employee for a determination whether or not any substance normally found in a working place has toxic or harmful effects in such concentration as used or found.

(b) The Secretary of Health, Education, and Welfare is authorized to make inspections and question employers and employees as provided in section 9 of this Act in order to carry out his functions and responsibilities under this section.

(c) The Secretary is authorized to enter into contracts, agreements, or other arrangements with appropriate public agencies or private organizations for the purpose of conducting studies relating to his responsibilities under this Act. In carrying out his responsibilities under this subsection, the Secretary and the Secretary of Health, Education, and Welfare shall cooperate in order to avoid any duplication of efforts under this section.

(d) Information obtained by the Secretary, the Board, and the Secretary of Health, Education, and Welfare under this section shall be disseminated by the Secretary to employers and employees and organizations thereof.

STATISTICS

SEC. 24. (a) In order to further the purposes of this Act, the Secretary shall develop and maintain an effective program of collection, compilation, and analysis of occupational safety and health statistics. Such program may cover all employments whether or not subject to any other provisions of this Act but shall not cover employments excluded by section 4 of the Act.

(b) To carry out his duties under subsection (a) of this section, the Secretary may:

(1) Promote, encourage, or directly engage in programs of studies, information and communication concerning occupational safety and health statistics.

(2) Make grants to States or political subdivisions thereof in order to assist them in developing and administering programs dealing with occupational safety and health statistics.

(3) Arrange, through grants or contracts, for the conduct of such research and investi-

gations as give promise of furthering the objectives of this section.

(c) The Federal share for each State grant under subsection (b) of this section may be up to 50 per centum of the State's total cost.

(d) The Secretary may, with the consent of any State or political subdivision thereof, accept and use the services, facilities, and employees of the agencies of such State or political subdivision, with or without reimbursement, in order to assist him in carrying out his functions under this section.

(e) On the basis of the records made and kept pursuant to section 9(c) of this Act, employers shall file such reports with the Secretary as he shall prescribe by regulation, as necessary to carry out his functions under this Act.

(f) Agreements between the Department of Labor and the States pertaining to the collection of occupational safety and health statistics already in effect on the effective date of this Act shall remain in effect until superseded by grants or contracts made under this Act.

EFFECT ON OTHER LAWS

SEC. 25. (a) Nothing in this Act shall be construed or held to supersede or in any manner affect any workmen's compensation law or to enlarge or diminish or affect in any other manner the common law or statutory rights, duties, or liabilities of employers and employees under any law with respect to injuries, occupational or other diseases, or death of employees arising out of, or in the course of, employment.

(b) Nothing in this Act shall apply to working conditions of employees with respect to whom other Federal agencies, and State agencies acting under section 274 of the Atomic Energy Act of 1954, as amended (42 U.S.C. 2021) exercise statutory authority to prescribe or enforce standards or regulations affecting occupational safety or health.

(c) The safety and health standards promulgated under the Walsh-Healey Public Contracts Act (41 U.S.C. 35 et seq.) the Service Contract Act (41 U.S.C. et seq.), and the National Foundation on Arts and Humanities Act (20 U.S.C. 951 et seq.), are deemed repealed and rescinded on the effective date of corresponding standards promulgated under this Act, as determined by the Secretary of Labor to be corresponding standards.

(d) Nothing in this Act shall apply to any employer who is a contractor or subcontractor for construction, alteration, and/or repair of buildings or works, including painting or decorating in the regular course of his business.

(e) The Secretary shall, within three years after the effective date of this Act, report to the Congress his recommendations for legislation to avoid unnecessary duplication and to achieve coordination between this Act and other Federal laws.

(f) Section 2 of the Act of August 9, 1969 (Public Law 91–54; 83 Stat. 96), is hereby amended to read as follows:

"SEC. 2. The first section and section 2 of the Act of August 13, 1962, are each amended by inserting 'and Construction Safety and Health' before 'standards' each time it appears."

(g) Subsection 107 of Public Law 91–54 (83 Stat. 96) is amended to read as follows:

"SEC. 107. (a) (1) It shall be a condition of each contract which is entered into under legislation subject to Reorganization Plan Numbered 14 of 1950 (64 Stat. 1267), and is for construction, alteration, and/or repair, including painting and decorating, that no contractor or subcontractor contracting for any part of the contract work shall require any laborer or mechanic employed in the performance of the contract to work in surroundings or under working conditions which are unsanitary, hazardous, or dangerous to his health or safety, as determined under construction safety and health standards promulgated by the Secretary by regulation based on proceedings pursuant to section 553 of title 5, United States Code, provided that such proceedings include a hearing of the nature authorized by said section. The Secretary of Labor shall consult with the Advisory Committee on Construction Safety and Health created by subsection (f) and shall give due regard to the Committee's recommendations and information in framing proposed rules or subjects and issues in setting standards in accordance with section 443 of title 5, United States Code.

"(2) Each employer as defined in section 3(6) of the Occupational Safety and Health Act who is a contractor or subcontractor for construction, alteration, and/or repair of buildings or works, including painting and decorating in the regular course of his business, shall comply with construction safety and health standards promulgated under this section."

(h) Subsection (b) of section 107 of Public Law 91–54 (83 Stat. 96) is amended to read as follows:

"(b)(1) The Secretary is authorized to make inspections and investigations pursuant to sections 9 (a), (c), and (d) of the Occupational Safety and Health Act. If upon the basis of inspection or investigation, the Secretary believes that an employer subject to the provisions of section 107(a)(2) has violated any health of safety standard promulgated under section 107(a) of this Act, or has violated the condition required of any contract to which subsection (a) of this section applies, the Secretary shall issue a citation to the employer unless the violation is de minimis. The provisions of section 10 (except subsection (c) thereof) of the Occupational Safety and Health Act shall apply to citations issued under this Act. In issuing citations under this Act, the Secretary shall issue each citation at the earliest possible time from the occurrence of the alleged violation but in no event later than forty-five days from the occurrence of the alleged violation except that for good cause the Secretary may extend such period up to a maximum of ninety days from such occurrence. The provisions of section 12 of the Occupational Safety and Health Act shall also apply to this Act.

"(2) If, after notice and opportunity for hearing, the Commission determines that a violation has occurred of any condition prescribed by this section for a contract of the type described in clause (1) or (2) of section 103(a) of this Act, the governmental agency for which the contract work is done shall have the right to cancel the contract, and to enter into other contracts for the completion of the contract work, charging any addiional cost to the original contractor. If, after notice and opportunity for hearing, the Commission determines that a violation has occurred of any condition prescribed by this section for a contract of the type described in clause 3 of section 103(a), the governmental agency by which financial guarantee, assistance, or insurance for the contract work is provided shall have the right to withhold any such assistance attributable to the performance of the contract. Section 104 of this Act shall not apply to the enforcement of this section."

(i) Subsection (c) of section 107 of Public Law 91-54 (83 Stat. 96) is hereby repealed and subsection (d) of that section is redesignated as subsection "(c)" and is amended to read as follows:

"(c)(1) If the Commission determines on the record after an opportunity for hearing that by repeated willful or grossly negligent violations of this Act, a contractor or subcontractor has demonstrated that the provisions of subsection (b) of this section and actions by the Secretary under paragraph (3) of this subsection are not effective to protect the safety and health of his employees, the Commission shall make a finding to that effect and shall, not sooner than thirty days after giving notice of the findings to all interested persons, transmit the name of such contractor or subcontractor to the Comptroller General.

"(2) The Comptroller General shall distribute each name so transmitted to him to all agencies of the Government. Unless the Commission otherwise recommends, no contract subject to this section shall be awarded to such contractor or subcontractor or to any person in which such contractor or subcontractor has a substantial interest until three years have elapsed from the date the name is transmitted to the Comptroller General. If, before the end of such three-year period, the Commission, after affording interested persons due notice and opportunity for hearing, is satisfied that a contractor or subcontractor whose name he has transmitted to the Comptroller General will thereafter comply responsibly with the requirements of this section, the Commission shall terminate the application of the preceding sentence to such contractor or subcontractor (and to any person in which the contractor or subcontractor has a substantial interest); and when the Comptroller General is informed of the Commission's action he shall inform all agencies of the Government thereof.

"(3) Any person aggrieved by an action of the Commission under subsections (b) or (c) of this section may seek a review of such action in the appropriate United States Court of Appeals pursuant to the provisions of section 13(a) of the Occupational Safety and Health Act. The Secretary may also obtain judicial review or seek enforcement as provided in sections 13(a) and 13 (c) and (d), and section 14 of the Occupational Safety and Health Act."

(j) Section 107 of Public Law 91-54 (83 Stat. 96) is amended by adding a new subsection "(d)" immediately after the new section "(c)". Subsection (e) of section 107 of Public Law 91-54 (83 Stat. 96) is hereby redesignated as subsection "(f)" and subsection (f) of section 107 of Public Law 91-54 (83 Stat. 96) is accordingly redesignated as subsection "(g)". The new subsection "(d)" shall read as follows:

"(d) (1) Any employer who willfully or repeatedly violates the standards promulgated by the Secretary under section 107(a) of this Act, may be assessed a civil penalty of not more than $10,000 for each violation.

"(2) Any citation for a serious violation of the standards promulgated by the Secretary under section 107(a) of this Act shall include a proposed penalty of up to $1,000 for each such violation.

"(3) Any employer who violates the standards promulgated by the Secretary under section 107(a) of this Act and such violation is specifically determined by the Secretary not to be of a serious nature, the Secretary may include in the citation issued for such a violation a proposed penalty of up to $1,000 for each such violation.

"(4) Any employer who violates any order or citation which has become final in accordance with the provisions of section 10 of the Occupational Safety and Health Act may be assessed a penalty of up to $1,000 for each such violation. When such violation is of a continuing nature, each day during which it continues shall constitute a separate offense for the purpose of assessing the penalty except where such order or citation is pending review under section 11 of the Occupational Safety and Health Act.

"(5) Any employer who violates any of the posting requirements, as prescribed in section 10(e) of the Occupational Safety and Health Act, shall be assessed by the Commission a civil penalty of up to $1,000 for each such violation.

"(6) Any person who discharges or in any other manner discriminates against any employee because such employee has filed any complaint or instituted or caused to be instituted any proceeding under or related to this Act, or has testified or is about to testify in any such proceeding, shall be assessed a civil penalty by the Commission of up to $10,000. Such person may also be subject to a fine of not more than $10,000 or imprisonment of a period not to exceed ten years, or both.

"(7) Any person who forcibly assaults, resists, opposes, impedes, intimidates, or interferes with any person while engaged in or on account of the performance of inspections or investigatory duties under this Act shall be fined not more than $5,000 or imprisoned not more than three years, or both. Whoever, in the commission of any such acts, uses a deadly or dangerous weapon, shall be fined not more than $10,000 or imprisoned not more than ten years or both. Whoever kills a person while engaged in or on account of the performance of inspecting or investigating duties under this Act shall be punished by imprisonment for any term of years or for life.

"(8) The Commission shall have authority to assess and collect all penalties provided in this section, giving due consideration to the appropriateness of the penalty with respect to the size of the business being charged, the gravity of the violation, the good faith of the employer, and the history of previous violations.

"(9) For the purpose of this subsection a serious violation shall be deemed to exist in a place of employment if there is a substantial probability that death or serious physical harm could result from a condition which exists, or from one or more practices, means, methods, operations, or processes which have been adopted or are in use, in such place of employment unless the Secretary determines that the employer did not, and could not with the exercise of reasonable diligence, know of the presence of the violation."

AUDITS

Sec. 26. (a) Each recipient of a grant under this Act shall keep such records as the Secretary shall prescribe, including records which fully disclose the amount and disposition by such recipient of the proceeds of such grant, the total cost of the project or undertaking in connection with which such grant is made or used, and the amount of that portion of the cost of the project or undertaking supplied by other sources, and such other records as will facilitate an effective audit.

(b) The Secretary and the Comptroller General of the United States, or any of their duly authorized representatives, shall have access for the purpose of audit and examination to any books, documents, papers, and records of the recipients of any grant under this Act that are pertinent to any such grant.

REPORTS

Sec. 27. Within one hundred and twenty days following the convening of each regular session of each Congress, the Secretary and the Secretary of Health, Education, and Welfare shall each prepare and submit to the President for transmittal to the Congress a report upon the subject matter of this Act, the progress concerning the achievement of its purposes, the needs and requirements in the field of occupational safety and health, and any other relevant information, and including any recommendations to effectuate the purposes of this Act.

OBSERVANCE OF RELIGIOUS BELIEFS

Sec. 28. Nothing in this Act shall be deemed to authorize or require medical examination, immunization, or treatment for those who object thereto on religious grounds, except where such medical examination, immunization, or treatment is necessary for the protection of the health or safety of others.

APPROPRIATIONS

Sec. 29. There are authorized to be appropriated to carry out this Act for each fiscal year such sums as the Congress shall deem necessary.

EFFECTIVE DATE

Sec. 30. This Act shall take effect one hundred and twenty days after the date of its enactment.

SEPARABILITY

Sec. 31. If any provision of this Act, or the application of such provision to any person or circumstance, shall be held invalid, the remainder of this Act, or the application of such provision to persons or circumstances other than those as to which it is held invalid, shall not be affected thereby.

The SPEAKER. The question is on the amendment.

Mr. PERKINS. Mr. Speaker, on that I demand the yeas and nays.

The yeas and nays were ordered.

The question was taken; and there were—yeas 220, nays 172, not voting 42, as follows:

TEXT OF SENATE LABOR AND PUBLIC WELFARE COMMITTEE'S REPORT

91st Congress	SENATE	Report
2d Session		No. 91-1282

OCCUPATIONAL SAFETY AND HEALTH ACT OF 1970

OCTOBER 6 –(legislative day, OCTOBER 5), 1970.—Ordered to be printed

Mr. WILLIAMS of New Jersey, from the Committee on Labor and Public Welfare, submitted the following

REPORT

together with

INDIVIDUAL AND MINORITY VIEWS

[To accompany S. 2193]

The Committee on Labor and Public Welfare, to which was referred the bill (S. 2193) to authorize the Secretary of Labor to set standards to assure safe and healthful working conditions for working men and women, to assist and encourage States to participate in efforts to assure such working conditions, to provide for research, information, education, and training in the field of occupational safety and health, and for other purposes, having considered the same, reports favorably thereon with an amendment (in the nature of a substitute) and recommends that the bill (as amended) do pass.

PURPOSE

The purpose of S. 2193 is to reduce the number and severity of work-related injuries and illnesses which, despite current efforts of employers and government, are resulting in ever-increasing human misery and economic loss.

The bill would achieve its purpose through programs of research, education and training, and through the development and administration, by the Secretary of Labor, of uniformly applied occupational safety and health standards. Such standards would be developed with the assistance of the Secretary of Health, Education and Welfare, and both their promulgation and their enforcement would be judicially reviewable. Encouragement is given to Federal-state cooperation, and financial assistance is authorized to enable states, under approved plans, to take over entirely and administer their own programs for achieving safe and healthful jobsites for the Nation's workers.

217

Background

The problem of assuring safe and healthful workplaces for our working men and women ranks in importance with any that engages the national attention today.

As former Secretary of Labor Shultz pointed out during the hearings on this bill, 14,500 persons are killed annually as a result of industrial accidents; accordingly, during the past four years more Americans have been killed where they work than in the Vietnam war. By the lowest count, 2.2 million persons are disabled on the job each year, resulting in the loss of 250 million man days of work—many times more than are lost through strikes.

In addition to the individual human tragedies involved, the economic impact of industrial deaths and disability is staggering. Over $1.5 billion is wasted in lost wages, and the annual loss to the Gross National Product is estimated to be over $8 billion. Vast resources that could be available for productive use are siphoned off to pay workmen's compensation benefits and medical expenses.

This "grim current scene", Secretary Shultz further pointed out, represents a worsening trend, for the fact is that the number of disabling injuries per million man hours worked is today 20% higher than in 1958. The knowledge that the industrial accident situation is deteriorating, rather than improving, underscores the need for action now.

In the field of occupational health the view is particularly bleak, and, due to the lack of information and records, may well be considerably worse than we currently know.

Occupational diseases which first commanded attention at the beginning of the Industrial Revolution are still undermining the health of workers. Substantial numbers, even today, fall victim to ancient industrial poisons such as lead and mercury. Workers in the dusty trades still contract various respiratory diseases. Other materials long in industrial use are only now being discovered to have toxic effects. In addition, technological advances and new processes in American industry have brought numerous new hazards to the workplace. Carcinogenic chemicals, lasers, ultasonic energy, beryllium metal, epoxy resins, pesticides, among others, all present incipient threats to the health of workers. Indeed, new materials and processes are being introduced into industry at a much faster rate than the present meager resources of occupational health can keep up with. It is estimated that every 20 minutes a new and potentially toxic chemical is introduced into industry. New processes and new sources of energy present occupational health problems of unprecedented complexity.

Recent scientific knowledge points to hitherto unsuspected cause-and-effect relationships between occupational exposures and many of the so-called chronic diseases—cancer, respiratory ailments, allergies, heart disease, and others. In some instances, the relationship appears to be direct: asbestos, ionizing radiation, chromates, and certain dye intermediaries, among others, are directly involved in the genesis of cancer. In other cases, occupational exposures are implicated as contributory factors. The distinction between occupational and non-occupational illnesses is growing increasingly difficult to define.

In 1966–67, the Surgeon General of the United States studied six metropolitan areas, examining 1,700 industrial plants which employed

142,000 workers. The study found that 65 percent of the people were potentially exposed to harmful physical agents, such as severe noise or vibration, or to toxic materials. The Surgeon General further examined controls that were in effect to protect workers from such hazards, and found that only 25 percent of the workers were adequately covered.

California, a state with more rigorous occupational safety and health reporting procedures than most, showed 27,000 occupational diseases in 1964, a rate of 4.8 per 1,000 workers. Projected nationally, there were an estimated 336,000 cases of occupational diseases that year, a figure which by all indications continues to grow. Based on limited reporting experience, the Public Health Service now indicates that there are 390,000 new occurrences of occupational disease each year.

Studies of particular industries provide specific emphasis regarding the magnitude of the problem. For example, despite repeated warnings over the years from other countries that their cotton workers suffered from lung disease, it is only within the past decade that we have recognized byssinosis as a distinct occupational disease among workers in American cotton mills. Recent studies now show that this illness, caused by the dust generated in the processing of cotton, and resulting in continuous shortness of breath, chronic cough and total disablement, affects substantial percentages of cotton textile workers. In some states as many as 30% of those in the carding or spinning rooms have been affected, and it has been estimated that as many as 100,000 active or retired workers currently suffer from this disease.

Asbestos is another material which continues to destroy the lives of workers. For 40 years it has been known that exposure to asbestos caused the severe lung scarring called asbestosis. Nevertheless, as an eminent physician and researcher, Dr. Irving J. Selikoff, testified during the hearings on this bill:

> It is depressing to report, in 1970 that the disease that we knew well 40 years ago is still with us just as if nothing was ever known.

It has also since been found that manufacturing and construction workers exposed to asbestos suffer disproportionately from pulmonary cancer and mesothelioma. Because nothing has been done about the hazards of asbestos, even after the association of asbestos and lung cancer was first reported in 1935, 20,000 out of the 50,000 workers who have since entered one asbestos trade alone—insulation work— are likely to die of asbestosis, lung cancer or mesothelioma. Nor is the potential hazard confined to these workers, since it is estimated that as many as 3.5 million workers are exposed to some extent to asbestos fibers, as are many more in the general population.

Pesticides, herbicides and fungicides used in the agricultural industry have increasingly become recognized as a particular source of hazard to large numbers of farmers and farmworkers. One of the major classifications of agricultural chemicals—the organophosphates—has a chemical similarity to commonly used agents of chemical and biological warfare, and exposure, depending on degree, causes headache, fever, nausea, convulsions, long-term psychological effects, or death. Another group—the chlorinated hydrocarbons—are stored in fatty tissues of the body, and have been identified as causing mutations, sterilization, and death.

While the full extent of the effect that such chemicals have had upon those working in agriculture is totally unknown, an official of the Department of Health, Education, and Welfare stated, during hearings of the Migratory Labor Subcommittee, that an estimated 800 persons are killed each year as a result of improper use of such pesticides, and another 80,000 injured. Despite the unmistakable danger that these substances present, no effective controls presently exist over their safe use and no effective protections against toxic exposure of farmworkers or others in the rural populace.

Although many employers in all industries have demonstrated an exemplary degree of concern for health and safety in the workplace, their efforts are too often undercut by those who are not so concerned. Moreover, the fact is that many employers—particularly smaller ones—simply cannot make the necessary investment in health and safety, and survive competitively, unless all are compelled to do so. The competitive disadvantage of the more conscientious employer is especially evident where there is a long period between exposure to a hazard and manifestation of an illness. In such instances a particular employer has no economic incentive to invest in current precautions, not even in the reduction of workmen's compensation costs, because he will seldom have to pay for the consequences of his own neglect.

Nor has state regulation proven sufficient to the need. No one has seriously disputed that only a relatively few states have modern laws relating to occupational health and safety and have devoted adequate resources to their administration and enforcement. Moreover, in a state-by-state approach, the efforts of the more vigorous states are inevitably undermined by the shortsightedness of others. The inadequacy of anything less than a comprehensive, nationwide approach has been exemplified by experience with the chemical betanaphthylamine—a chemical so toxic that any exposure at all is likely to cause the development of bladder cancer over a period of years. The Commonwealth of Pennsylvania discovered this extreme effect of betanaphthylamine and banned its use, manufacture, storage or handling in that State, but production of this lethal chemical has begun in another State where legislation is inadequate. The exposure of workers to betanaphthylamine continues today.

In sum, the chemical and physical hazards which characterize modern industry are not the problem of a single employer, a single industry, nor a single state jurisdiction. The spread of industry and the mobility of the workforce combine to make the health and safety of the worker truly a national concern.

Citing technological progress as a mixed blessing in a message to Congress on August 6, 1969, President Nixon urged the passage of a comprehensive occupational safety and health bill. The President stated:

> The same new method or new product which improves our lives can also be the source of unpleasantness and pain. For man's capacity to innovate is not always matched by his ability to understand his innovations fully, to use them properly, or to protect himself against unforeseen consequences of the changes he creates.

The side effects of progress present special dangers in the workplaces of our country. For the working man and woman, the by-products of change constitute an especially serious threat. Some efforts to protect the safety and health of the American worker have been made in the past both by private industry and by all levels of government. But new techniques have moved even faster to create newer dangers. Today we are asking our workers to perform far different tasks from those they performed five of fifteen or fifty years ago. It is only right that the protection we give them is also up to date.

COMMITTEE CONSIDERATION

S. 2193 was introduced on May 16, 1969, by Senator Williams of New Jersey, for himself, Senator Yarborough, Senator Mondale, and Senator Kennedy. An Administration bill, S. 2788, was introduced by Senator Javits on August 6, 1969.

The Subcommittee on Labor held nine days of hearings in Washington, D.C., on September 30, November 4, November 21, November 24, November 26, December 9, December 15, December 16, 1969, and May 5, 1970. In addition, hearings were held in Jersey City, New Jersey, on March 7, 1970; in Duquesne, Pennsylvania, on April 10, 1970; and in Greenville, South Carolina, on April 28, 1970.

Testimony was presented by the then Secretary of Labor, George P. Shultz, and by Dr. Roger G. Edgeberg, Assistant Secretary of the Department of Health, Education, and Welfare for Health and Scientific Affairs. Numerous other witnesses also testified, including industry spokesmen, officials of labor organizations, representatives of professional associations, and individual workers.

S. 2193 was reported by the Subcommittee on Labor, with an amendment in the nature of a substitute, on September 9, 1970, after two executive sessions. Following three executive sessions, the Committee on Labor and Public Welfare ordered the bill reported on September 25, 1970.

MAJOR PROVISIONS OCCUPATIONAL SAFETY AND HEALTH STANDARDS

S. 2193 would require every employer subject to the Act to comply with occupational safety and health standards promulgated by the Secretary of Labor in accordance with procedures provided in section 6. Those procedures are as follows:

Consensus Standards, Established Federal Standards, Proprietary Standards.—Within two years after enactment, the Secretary would be required by section 6(a), to promulgate all national consensus standards and all established Federal standards unless he determines that a standard would not result in improved safety or health for all or some of the affected employees. If there is a conflict among standards, the Secretary shall promulgate that which assures the greatest protection for the affected employees.

During this two-year period, the Secretary has discretion to promulgate any standard which has been adopted by a nationally recognized standards-producing organization by other than a consensus method, provided that such standard has been adopted on or before the enactment of this act.

The purpose of this procedure is to establish as rapidly as possible national occupational safety and health standards with which industry is familiar. These standards may not be as effective or as up-to-date as is desirable, but they will be useful for immediately providing a nationwide minimum level of health and safety.

Two private organizations are the major sources of consensus standards: the American National Standards Institute, Inc., and the National Fire Protection Association. Since, by the Act's definition, a "consensus standard" is one which has been adopted under procedures which have given diverse views an opportunity to be considered and which indicate that interested and affected persons have reached substantial agreement on its adoption, it is appropriate to permit the Secretary to promulgate such standards without regard to the provisions of the Administrative Procedure Act.

The bill also provides for the issuance in similar fashion of those standards which have been issued under other Federal statutes and which under this act may be made applicable to additional employees who are not under the protection of such other Federal laws. Such standards have already been subjected to the procedural scrutiny mandated by the law under which they were issued; such standards, moreover, in large part, represent the incorporation of voluntary industrial standards.

The committee has also concluded that the Secretary should be able to make use of so-called proprietary standards which have been produced by various industrial and professional groups, such as the American Conference of Governmental Industrial Hygienists, the Manufacturing Chemists Association, and the National Electrical Manufacturers Association. Such standards have gained wide acceptance by American industry. However, since they were not adopted by their associations with the same procedural limitations applicable to consensus standards, the committee has provided that the Secretary must afford interested persons an opportunity to participate in the rulemaking through submission of written data, views, or arguments before making such standards effective.

Promulgation, Revision and Revocation of Standards.—The consensus and other standards issued under section 6(a) would provide a sound foundation for a national safety and health program. However, as a recent Department of Labor study has shown, a large proportion of the voluntary standards are seriously out-of-date. Many represent merely the lowest common denominator of acceptance by interested private groups. Accordingly, it is essential that such standards be constantly improved and replaced as new knowledge and techniques are developed. In addition, there are many occupational hazards—particularly those affecting health—which are not covered by any standards at all. Section 6(b) sets forth the procedures by which the promulgation of new standards, and the revision and revocation of adopted standards, are to be accomplished.

The Secretary may initiate such proceedings by the appointment of an advisory committee, which would have 90 days, or such shorter or longer period—not to exceed 270 days—as the Secretary may prescribe, to submit its recommendations. Where an advisory committee has been appointed, publication of proposed standards would be made in the Federal Register within 60 days of receipt of the advisory committee's recommendations.

The Secretary may elect to dispense with an advisory committee—particularly where the subject matter is noncontroversial—and simply begin the procedure by publishing proposed standards in the Federal Register. In either case, the Secretary would afford interested persons a period of 30 days after publication to submit data or comments, and to request a public hearing on any objections.

If written objection is made to the Secretary's proposal, and a hearing requested, the Secretary would then publish a notice specifying the objections made and setting a time and place for hearing. Such hearing would be of the informal type authorized for rulemaking by the Administrative Procedure Act. Within 60 days after completion of any such hearing, the Secretary would issue a rule promulgating, modifying, or revoking a standard or group of standards dealing with the occupational safety or health issue which had been the subject of the proceeding. Under section 6(b)(4), the rule issued may contain a provision delaying its effective date for such a period as the Secretary determines necessary. For example, it may be necessary to delay the effective date of a standard to permit affected employers and employees to familiarize themselves with its requirements. In providing for a delayed effective date, however, the Secretary must be assured of the need to grant such a delay.

Standards promulgated under this procedure would include requirements regarding the use of labels or other forms of warning to alert employees to the hazards covered by the standard and to provide them with necessary information regarding proper methods of use or exposure and appropriate emergency treatment. where appropriate, such standards would also prescribe protective equipment and other control measures, as well as, in the case of toxic substances or harmful physical agents, requirements for monitoring conditions or measuring employee exposure as may be necessary to protect employees' health. In addition, where exposure to potentially toxic substances or harmful physical agents is involved, the standard may prescribe medical examinations of employees when it is necessary to determine whether such exposure is having or is likely to have adverse effects on health.

The committee intends that standards promulgated under section 6(b) shall represent feasible requirements, which, where appropriate, shall be based on research, experiments, demonstrations, past experience, and the latest available scientific data. Such standards should be directed at assuring, so far as possible, that no employee will suffer impaired health or functional capacity, or diminished life expectancy, by reason of exposure to the hazard involved, even though such exposure may be over the period of his entire working life. Insofar as practicable, standards are to be expressed in terms of objective criteria and the performance desired.

Emergency Standards.—Because of the obvious need for quick response to new health and safety findings, section 6(c) mandates the Secretary to promulgate temporary emergency standards if he finds that such a standard is needed to protect employees who are being exposed to grave dangers from potentially toxic materials or harmful physical agents, or from new hazards for which no applicable standard has been promulgated. Upon publication of such an emergency temporary standard, the Secretary must begin a regular standard-setting procedure for such hazard, which proceeding must be completed within six months.

Variances.—Section 6(d) provides that any affected employer may apply to the Secretary for a variance from a standard otherwise applicable to him. Affected employees must be notified of the application and afforded an opportunity to participate in a hearing. To receive a variance, the employer must demonstrate by a preponderance of evidence in the record that he will provide to his employees employment which is as safe and healthful as would prevail if he complied with the standard.

Judicial Review of Standards.—Section 6(f) provides that any person who may be adversely affected by a standard may, within 60 days of its issuance, seek judicial review in an appropriate United States court of appeals. While this would be the exclusive method for obtaining pre-enforcement judicial review of a standard, the provision does not foreclose an employer from challenging the validity of a standard during an enforcement proceeding. Unless otherwise ordered by the court, the filing of the petition would not operate as a stay of the standard.

The Proposal for an Occupational Safety and Health Board.—The committee considered and rejected a proposal to have an independent five-member Board promulgate standards, rather than the Secretary of Labor. The chief arguments supporting this proposal were that (1) the Board would represent expertise in the field of occupational safety and health, and (2) the Board would represent a separation of powers between standards-setting and enforcement.

The committee agrees that professional and technical expertise must be involved in the development and promulgation of a standard, but such expertise would be fully available to the Secretary, both as members of his staff, and as members of advisory committees.

Rather than dividing responsibility by creating yet another agency, the committee believes that a sounder program will result if responsibility for the formulation of rules is assigned to the same administrator. who is also responsible for their enforcement and for seeing that they are workable and effective in their day-to-day application, thus permitting cohesive administration of a total program. In the committee's view, the question of separation of power is not so much one of whether the Secretary should be separated from the power to set standards, but whether he should be separated from the power to administer an integral program, and from the power of the Congress and the public to hold him accountable for the overall implementation of that program.

It should be emphasized that regulatory statutes have customarily accorded the administering agency overall authority for formulating and enforcing regulations—including a number of executive departments or subordinate administrations responsible for other types of safety programs. Indeed, in establishing those existing safety programs which cover the most hazardous occupations, such as mining and longshoring, as well as the various safety programs applicable to Federal contractors, the Congress has placed both standards-setting and enforcement responsibilities in the same agency. The committee believes it equally appropriate that this approach be followed in the present instance.

ADVISORY COMMITTEES

Two kinds of advisory committees are authorized. One is the ad hoc advisory committee which the Secretary may appoint to assist in the development of a standard or group of standards.

Section 7(b) provides that the ad hoc advisory committees shall consist of not more than 15 members, and shall include one or more designees of the Secretary of Health, Education, and Welfare. Such a committee may also include an equal number of persons qualified by experience and affiliation to present the views of employers and of employees, as well as one or more representatives of State health and safety agencies, representatives of professional organizations specializing in occupational health or safety, and representatives of nationally recognized standards-producing organizations. In order to insure a balanced view between government and non-government members and to preserve the guarantee of a public interest orientation, the number of non-government persons appointed to any advisory committee shall not exceed the number of representatives of Federal and State agencies who are appointed.

In addition to the ad hoc advisory committees, the Secretary and the Secretary of Health, Education, and Welfare shall appoint a National Advisory Committee of 20 members divided between representatives of management, labor and occupational safety and health professions. The Secretary shall appoint all members to the committee, except for the occupational health representatives who are to be appointed by the Secretary of Health, Education, and Welfare. The Advisory Committee has an important role to perform in bringing continuing public attention and interest to bear on the act and on its programs. Its membership should be chosen with great care and should be widely representative.

GENERAL DUTY

The committee recognizes that precise standards to cover every conceivable situation will not always exist. This legislation would be seriously deficient if any employee were killed or seriously injured on the job simply because there was no specific standard applicable to a recognized hazard which could result in such a misfortune. Therefore, to cover such circumstances the committee has included a requirement to the effect that employers are to furnish employment and places of employment which are free from recognized hazards to the health and safety of their employees.

The committee has concluded that such a provision is based on sound and reasonable policy. Under principles of common law, individuals are obliged to refrain from actions which cause harm to others. Courts often refer to this as a general duty to others. Statutes usually increase but sometimes modify this duty. The committee believes that employers are equally bound by this general and common duty to bring no adverse effects to the life and health of their employees throughout the course of their employment. Employers have primary control of the work environment and should insure that it is safe and healthful. Section 5(a), in providing that employers must furnish employment "which is free from recognized hazards so as to provide safe and healthful working conditions," merely restates that each employer shall furnish this degree of care.

There is a long-established statutory precedent in both Federal and State law to require employers to provide a safe and healthful place of employment. Over 36 states have provisions of this type, and at least three Federal laws contain similar clauses, including the Wash-Healey Public Contracts Act, the Service Contract Act, and the Longshoremen's and Harbor Workers' Act.

The general duty clause in this bill would not be a general substitute for reliance on standards, but would simply enable the Secretary to insure the protection of employees who are working under special circumstances for which no standard has yet been adopted. Moreover, the clause merely requires an employer to correct recognized hazards after they have been discovered on inspection and made the subject of an abatement order. There is no penalty for violation of the general duty clause. It is only if the employer refuses to correct the unsafe condition after it has been called to his attention and made the subject of an abatement order that a penalty can be imposed. Before that is done, the employer would be entitled to a full administrative hearing, followed by judicial review, if he disagrees that the situation in question is unsafe.

The need for such a clause was strongly urged by Governor Howard Pyle, President of the National Safety Council, in testimony before the Subcommittee on Labor on December 9, 1969. Governor Pyle stated:

> If national policy finally declares that all employees are entitled to safe and healthful working conditions, then all employers would be obligated to provide a safe and healthful workplace rather than only complying with a set of promulgated standards. The absence of such a general obligation provision would mean the absence of authority to cope with a hazardous condition which is obvious and admitted by all concerned for which no standard has been promulgated.

OBLIGATIONS OF EMPLOYEES

The committee recognizes that accomplishment of the purposes of this bill cannot be totally achieved without the fullest cooperation of affected employees. In this connection, Section 5(b) expressly places upon each employee the obligation to comply with standards and other applicable requirements under the act.

It should be noted, too, that studies of employee motivation are among the research efforts which the committee expects to be under-taken under section 18, and it is hoped that such studies, as well as the programs for employee and employer training authorized by section 18(f), will provide the basis for achieving the fullest possible commitment of individual workers to the health and safety efforts of their employers. It has been made clear to the committee that the most successful plant safety programs are those which emphasize employee participation in their formulation and administration; every effort should therefore be made to maximize such participation throughout industry.

The committee does not intend the employee-duty provided in section 5(b) to diminish in anyway the employer's compliance responsibilities or his responsibility to assure compliance by his own employees.

Final responsibility for compliance with the requirements of this act remains with the employer.

INSPECTIONS AND INVESTIGATIONS

In order to carry out an effective national occupational safety and health program, it is necessary for government personnel to have the right of entry in order to ascertain the safety and health conditions and status of compliance of any covered employing establishment. Section 8(a) therefore authorizes the Secretary or his representative, upon presenting appropriate credentials, to enter at reasonable times the premises of any place of employment covered by this act, to inspect and investigate within reasonable limits all pertinent conditions, and also to privately question owners, operators, agents or employees.

During the field hearings held by the Subcommittee on Labor, the complaint was repeatedly voiced that under existing safety and health legislation, employees are generally not advised of the content and results of a Federal or State inspection. Indeed, they are often not even aware of the inspector's presence and are thereby deprived of an opportunity to inform him of alleged hazards. Much potential benefit of an inspection is therefore never realized, and workers tend to be cynical regarding the thoroughness and efficacy of such inspections. Consequently, in order to aid in the inspection and provide an appropriate degree of involvement of employees themselves in the physical inspections of their own places of employment, the committee has concluded that an authorized representative of employees should be given an opportunity to accompany the person who is making the physical inspection of a place of employment under section 9(a). Correspondingly, an employer should be entitled to accompany an inspector on his physical inspection, although the inspector should have an opportunity to question employees in private so that they will not be hesitant to point out hazardous conditions which they might otherwise be reluctant to discuss.

Although questions may arise as to who shall be considered a duly authorized representative of employees, the bill provides the Secretary of Labor with authority to promulgate regulations for resolving this question. Where the Secretary is not able to determine the existence of any authorized representative of employees, section 8(e) provides that the inspector shall consult with a reasonable number of employees concerning matters of health and safety in the workplace. It is expected that such consultation shall be undertaken with a view both to apprising the inspector of all possible hazards to be found in the workplace, as well as to insure that employees generally will be informed of the inspector's presence and the purpose and manner of his inspection.

In order that employees will be informed of any violation found by the inspector, section 10 specifies that citations shall be prominently posted near the place where the violation occurred. In addition, section 8(f)(2) provides that employees or a representative of employees may, before or during an inspection, give written notification to the Secretary or an inspector of any violation which they believe exists, and such employees or representative of employees shall be provided with a written explanation when no citation is issued respecting such alleged violation. The Secretary must also establish informal review procedures for use of employees or employee representatives who wish to question further the refusal to issue a citation.

A further provision, section 8(f)(1), entitles employees or a representative of employees who believe that a health or safety violation exists which threatens physical harm or that an imminent danger exists, to request a special inspection by giving notification to the Secretary, setting forth the basis of the request. If the Secretary determines upon receipt of the notification that there are reasonable grounds to believe that a violation or imminent danger exists, he shall make a special inspection as soon as practicable. If the Secretary determines there are no reasonable grounds to believe that a violation or imminent danger exists he shall so notify in writing those making the request.

By requiring that the special inspection be made "as soon as practicable," the committee contemplates that the Secretary, in scheduling the special inspection, will take into account such factors as the degree of harmful potential involved in the condition described in the request and the urgency of competing demands for inspectors arising from other requests or regularly scheduled inspections.

While the bill provides that a request for a special inspection shall be reduced to writing, the committee intends that notification may first be made by telephone, and that where an immediate harm is threatened, such as in an imminent danger situation, the Secretary should not await receipt through the mail of the written notification before beginning his inspection.

In recognition of the possibility of limited inspection manpower in the earlier phases of the program, the committee expects that the Secretary will initially place emphasis on inspections in those industries or occupations where the need to assure safe and healthful conditions is determined to be the most compelling.

In addition to the inspection authority, Section 8(b) grants the Secretary of Labor a subpoena power over books, records and witnesses—a power which is customary and necessary for the proper administration and enforcement of a statute of this nature.

The committee, bearing in mind that the number of inspections which it would be desirable to have made will undoubtedly, for an unforseeable period, exceed the capacity of the inspection force, has incorporated a further provision, authorizing the Secretary to adopt regulations obliging employers to conduct periodic inspections to determine their own state of compliance with applicable health and safety requirements, and to certify the results of such inspections to the Secretary. Such a procedure could well provide a valuable, and probably indispensable, supplement to the Secretary's own inspections, since it would cause an employer regularly to review conditions in the workplace which might otherwise be ignored between official inspections. False certifications of compliance by the employer would subject the employer to penalties if such falsity were later established.

PROCEDURES TO COUNTERACT IMMINENT DANGERS

When an inspector finds, as the result of an employee complaint or otherwise, that there exists an "imminent danger"—defined in section 11(a) as "a condition or practice which could reasonably be expected to cause death or serious physical harm before such condition or practice can be abated"—delay in taking necessary action can plainly mean the difference between life and death. In almost all such cases, employers recognize the gravity of the danger and voluntarily take the necessary steps, including withdrawing workers from a particular machine or process. Where this is not done, however, it is imperative that there be Governmental authority available to require the appropriate actions.

Section 11(a) provides that in these imminent danger situations, the Secretary may bring action in the appropriate United States district court for a temporary restraining order or an injunction requiring steps to be taken to correct, remove, or avoid the danger, and prohibiting the presence of individuals where the imminent danger exists. However, the bill authorizes the continued presence of individuals necessary to the correction or removal of the danger or to maintain the capacity of a continuous process operation to restart without a complete cessation of operations, and to permit any necessary shutdown of operations to be accomplished in a safe and orderly manner.

Where the Secretary determines that the danger of death or serious harm is so immediate that action must be taken without awaiting the institution of court proceedings, he may order such action to be taken and his order may remain in effect for 72 hours. Section 11(b) specifies that in delegating to an inspector his authority to issue imminent danger orders, the Secretary shall require the inspector to obtain the concurrence of an appropriate regional Labor Department official before such an order is issued. The committee adopted this qualification in order to meet the concern expressed by some that it should not be within the sole judgment of a single inspector to determine whether a hazard is so imminent as to warrant interference with a production operation. The bill now provides that an additional judgment shall be obtained; however, bearing in mind the act's purpose to protect fully employees whose lives and health may be under immediate risk, it is intended that the necessary concurrence may be obtained by telephone consultation rather than more protracted means. In order that difficulties of communication will not thwart the act's purpose by delaying the issuance of an order, it is expected that the Secretary will make suitable provision to insure that persons authorized to provide such concurrence can be reached by telephone at all times. The bill further specifies that once an imminent danger order has been issued, the employer, without postponing its mandatory effect, may obtain expeditious informal reconsideration within the Department of Labor, in accordance with procedures to be prescribed by the Secretary.

The committee believes that objections to authorizing the Secretary of Labor to issue imminent danger orders have been greatly overstated in public discussion of this legislation. The safety laws of at least 35 states authorize administrative officials to deal with imminent danger situations. Such "red tag" or "stop work" provisions typically empower the appropriate state agency to post a notice or issue an order prohibiting the use of machinery, equipment or work areas found to be dangerous, and the committee has learned of no instance in which such provisions have been invoked unreasonably. It may also be noted that similar authority is provided in both the Coal Mine Health and Safety Act of 1969 and the recently passed Railroad Safety Act.

CITATIONS FOR VIOLATIONS

Section 9 provides that if upon inspection or investigation, the Secretary determines that an employer has violated certain provisions of the act, or a rule, regulation or order issued under one of those sections, he shall forthwith issue a citation to the employer. Such citation, which provides the basis for subsequent enforcement procedures, shall be in writing, shall describe the particulars of the violation, and shall fix a reasonable time for abatement of the violation. A copy of the citation shall be posted at or near each place of violation, in accordance with regulations of the Secretary.

It should be made clear that the language of section 9 does not limit the issuance of citations to those violations which the inspector has himself witnessed. It is the committee's intent that if an investigation should disclose that violations have occurred, even though since corrected, a citation may be issued in appropriate cases.

The committee recognizes that many violations will be found on inspection which will not warrant the issuance of a citation or subsequent enforcement proceedings. Accordingly, section 9 provides that the Secretary may prescribe procedures for the issuance of a notice in lieu of a citation when the inspector finds *de minimis* violations which have no direct or immediate relationship to safety or health. The committee intends that the notice given by the Secretary should detail the conditions and circumstances of the violation and prescribe the means for correcting it. However, no penalties would attach to a violation covered by such a notice.

PROCEDURES FOR ENFORCEMENT

Section 10 provides that if the Secretary issues a citation for a violation, he shall, within a reasonable time, notify the employer by certified mail of any penalty (as provided in section 14) proposed to be assessed. It is intended that such notice should be sent as promptly as possible, taking into account the need to give consideration to the various factors required to be weighed in assessing penalties.

The Secretary's notice must also advise the employer that he has 15 working days within which to notify the Secretary that he wishes to contest the citation or proposed assessment of penalty. If the employer does not file such a notice within that time period, the citation and proposed penalty become final.

Similarly, if the Secretary has reason to believe that an employer has failed to correct a violation for which a citation has previously issued, during the time permitted for correction, or has failed to comply with an imminent danger order issued by the Secretary, the Secretary shall notify the employer by certified mail of such failure and of the penalty proposed to be assessed. The employer shall also have 15 days to contest such notification or proposed assessment of penalty, and, if he does not do so, they become final.

If the employer decides to contest a citation or notification, or proposed assessment of penalty, the Secretary must afford an opportunity for a formal hearing under the Administrative Procedure Act. Based upon the hearing record the Secretary shall issue an order confirming, denying, or modifying the citation, notification, or proposed penalty assessment. The procedural rules prescribed by the

Secretary for the conduct of such hearings must make provision for affected employees or their representatives to participate as parties.

Section 10(c) also gives an employee or representative of employees a right, whenever he believes that the period of time provided in a citation for abatement of a violation is unreasonably long, to challenge the citation on that ground. Such challenges must be filed within 15 days of the issuance of the citation, and an opportunity for a hearing must be provided in similar fashion to hearings when an employer contests. The employer is to be given an opportunity to participate as a party.

Any person adversely affected or aggrieved by a final order of the Secretary which is issued after a hearing may obtain review in the appropriate United States court of appeals within sixty days of the service of the Secretary's order. Such judicial review will be based upon the record made in the administrative hearing, and the substantial evidence rule will apply to the Secretary's findings. Provision is also made, in section 10(e), for the Secretary to obtain an automatic court enforcement order when no review has been requested within such 60 day period.

It is anticipated that in many cases an employer will choose not to file a timely challenge to a citation when it is issued, on the assumption that he can comply with the period allowed in the citation for abatement of the violation. In some such cases the employer may subsequently find that despite his good faith efforts to comply, abatement cannot be completed within the time permitted because of factors beyond his reasonable control—for example, where the delivery of necessary equipment is unavoidably delayed. In order to prevent unfair hardship, the bill provides that in such instances the employer may obtain review and modification by the Secretary of the abatement requirements specified in the citation, even though the citation has otherwise become final.

Mention should be made of the proposal offered in committee to establish an independent three-member enforcement panel. Such a panel would hear and decide those cases in which a citation, a notification of failure to abate, or a proposed assessment of penalty is being challenged.

As in the case of the previously discussed proposal for an independent board to promulgate standards, the committee concluded that sounder policy would be to place the responsibility and accountability for administration of the total program in the Secretary of Labor, rather than to establish a new agency and create an unnecessary division of responsibility. While the argument has been made that due process considerations would be better served if the investigative and adjudicative functions were separated between two different agencies, the fact is that the provisions of the Administrative Procedure Act insure that under the bill as reported by the committee there will be a separation of functions within the Department of Labor between those subordinates of the Secretary who are engaged in investigation and prosecution, and those who are engaged in adjudication. The overwhelming majority of other regulatory programs are administered in just this fashion, and the requirements of due process are fully observed.

PENALTIES

Section 14 provides for civil penalties of up to $1000 for each violation for which a citation has issued, or for failure either to correct a violation within the time prescribed, or to comply with an imminent danger order. In the case of a failure to correct a violation, the penalty applies to each day of failure (excluding any period of review proceedings which the employer has initiated in good faith). Section 14(b) specifies that in the assessment of penalties consideration shall be given to the size of the business involved, the gravity of the violation, the history of previous violations, and the good faith of the employer. The Secretary may compromise, mitigate, or settle any claim for such penalties.

The Committee recognizes that given the complexities of modern industry, violations involving the broad range of technical standards do not lend themselves to any simple determination as to the amount of civil penalties to be assessed. Therefore, the Committee believes that within the framework of the Act's penalty provisions, the Secretary should have as much flexibility as possible to enable him to assess the amount of civil penalty which he determines is appropriate to the violation in question. We would expect the Secretary, therefore, to develop an internal manual or guide which would include a set of principles to follow in determining the proper amount of civil penalties to be applied to violations under the Act. The Secretary may compromise, mitigate or settle such penalties through informal procedures without the need of a hearing.

Section 14 also makes it a misdemeanor to willfully violate the requirements of the act; to give advance notice of an inspection without authority from the Secretary; and to make any false statement, representation or certification in any document filed or required to be maintained under the act. The provisions already contained in title 18, United States Code, which make it a crime to kill, assault, or resist certain Federal law enforcement personnel while engaged in the performance of official duties, are extended so as to protect all law enforcement officials of the Departments of Labor and Health, Education and Welfare.

RECORDKEEPING AND REPORTS

Full and accurate information is a fundamental precondition for meaningful administration of an occupational safety and health program. At the present time, however, the Federal government and most of the states have inadequate information on the incidence, nature, or causes of occupational injuries, illnesses, and deaths. Not only are there serious deficiencies in the present data collection procedures, but adherence to the commonly used method of work injury measurement—the Z16.1 standard of the American National Standards Institute—thwarts the collection of information regarding many significant work injuries and occupational illnesses. Thus an essential first action under this bill should be the institution of adequate statistical programs.

Section 8(c) of the bill directs the Secretary of Labor to cooperate with the Secretary of Health, Education and Welfare in devising regulations which will implement the goal of completeness in the recording and reporting of pertinent data.

The committee recognizes the fact that some work-related injuries or ailments may involve only a minimal loss of work time or perhaps none at all, and may not be of sufficient significance to the Government to require their being recorded or reported. However, the committee was also unwilling to adopt statutory language which in practice might result in under-reporting. The committee believes that records and reports prescribed by the Secretary should include such occurrences as work-related injuries and illnesses requiring medical treatment or restriction or reassignment of work activity, as well as work-related loss of consciousness.

The committee also expects that the Secretary of Labor and the Secretary of Health, Education, and Welfare will make every effort, through the authority to issue regulations and other means, to obtain complete data regarding the occurrence of illnesses, including those resulting from occupational exposure which may not be manifested until after the termination of such exposure.

The committee recognizes the need to assure employers that they will not be subject to unnecessary or duplicative record-keeping requests and has specifically stated this intent in section 8(d). To that end the committee intends that, wherever possible, reporting requirements should be satisfied by having an employer report relevant data only to one Governmental agency and that other Governmental agencies, if any, should then acquire their information from the original agency.

The committee also intends that the annual reports of both the Department of Labor and the Department of Health, Education, and Welfare should contain comprehensive presentations of collected data, together with analyses thereof, so that this committee and others in Congress may review the adequacy of progress and the possible need for further legislation.

MONITORING OF HAZARDOUS SUBSTANCES AND PHYSICAL AGENTS

Under Section 8(c) the Secretary of Labor, in cooperation with the Secretary of Health, Education, and Welfare, is to issue regulations specifying the records to be kept by employers who are required to monitor employee exposures to potentially toxic materials or harmful physical agents. Since such exposure is a matter of crucial concern to affected employees, provision is also made for employee observation of such monitoring and for employee access to the records thereof. This section also places upon the employer the burden of promptly notifying any employees who have been or are being exposed to harmful materials or agents in concentrations or at levels above those prescribed in applicable standards, of that fact and of the corrective action being taken.

These provisions serve as essential complements to those contained in section 6, which provide that standards relating to hazardous substances and agents shall prescribe the use of labels or other forms of warning to apprise employees of the symptoms of over-exposure and appropriate emergency treatment, and shall also prescribe medical examinations of employees when necessary to determine whether exposure has been or may be harmful.

FEDERAL-STATE RELATIONS

Section 16 makes clear the intent that no State will be prevented from asserting jurisdiction under state law over any occupational safety or health matter for which no Federal standard has been established under this act.

Moreover, whenever a State wishes to assume responsibility for developing or enforcing standards in an area where standards have been promulgated under this act, the State may do so under a state plan approved by the Secretary of Labor. The plan must contain assurances that the State will develop and enforce standards at least as effective as those developed by the Secretary, that the State will have the legal authority, personnel and funds necessary to do the job, and that a right of entry into workplaces is provided. The plan must contain added assurances that employers will make reports to the Secretary in the same form and to the same extent as if the plan were not in effect. In addition, the plan must contain assurances that the State will, to the extent possible under its law, establish and maintain an occupational safety and health program applicable to all employees of the State and its political subdivisions, and that such program will be as effective as that applicable to provide employers covered by the plan.

On the basis of reports submitted by the State agencies, the Secretary shall withdraw his approval if he finds that in actual operation there has been a failure to comply substantially with the plan or with the assurances stated in it.

The bill provides that an opportunity for a hearing shall be afforded whenever the Secretary rejects a proposed State plan and whenever he withdraws approval previously given. Judicial review of such action by the Secretary is also provided.

It should be noted that a State's program need not be all-encompassing; it may restrict itself to a particular hazard or industry. However, industries or hazards not covered by the plan will continue to be under Federal jurisdiction.

As an encouragement for State action, the bill provides Federal financial support to assist the States in assuming their own programs for worker health and safety. Planning grants with up to 90 percent Federal participation, and program grants with up to 50 percent Federal participation are provided.

The 90 percent grant is designed to aid the States in identifying needs, developing State plans and programs for collecting statistical data, increasing personnel capabilities, and improving administration and enforcement. The 50 percent Federal grant is made available to assist States in carrying out the occupational safety and health programs contained in their plans, as well as programs concerning occupational safety and health statistics.

FEDERAL AGENCY SAFETY PROGRAMS AND RESPONSIBILITIES

S. 2193 provides coverage for the approximately three million employees of the Federal Government. Section 17 requires Federal agencies to promulgate safety and health standards consistent with those developed by the Secretary of Labor for private industry. This section also amends section 7902(c)(1) of title 5, United States Code, to permit representatives of labor organizations to serve on the President's Federal Safety Council.

During the past 25 years, there has been considerable improvement in the safety record of the Federal Government, but if it is to serve as a model employer, there must be an increased effort to achieve this ideal.

In 1965, President Johnson launched the Mission Safety—70 program in an effort to dramatically reduce injuries among Federal employees. The plan envisioned a 30 percent reduction in the frequency rate of disabling injuries during the life of the program. In the first four years after the plan's initiation, the Government progressed only 10.4 percent toward its goal. Clearly, there is a significant margin of improvement yet to be achieved.

In order to create a more effective safety program, the bill directs each Federal agency to purchase and maintain safety devices and to require their use. Agencies must also keep adequate records and make an annual report on occupational accidents and illnesses to the Secretary. The Secretary, in turn, shall annually prepare and submit to the President for transmittal to Congress his evaluations and recommendations of the Federal safety program.

The above requirements are intended to establish clear responsibility for the Federal Government's internal safety and health efforts, and provide the Secretary with an active role in coordinating the multiplicity of programs devised by various agencies. Congress also will be offered an opportunity to learn of current health and safety conditions through annual reports.

RESEARCH AND RELATED ACTIVITIES; THE NATIONAL INSTITUTE FOR OCCUPATIONAL SAFETY AND HEALTH

The hearings on this bill made unmistakably clear the critical inadequacy of past and current research activities to furnish solutions to the problems of occupational health and safety. When we realize that not only do we still have insufficient information regarding many of the threats to health which have long been known to exist in industry, but, in addition, that the modern worker encounters health hazards involving complex, often synergistic, interactions of numerous physical and chemical agents, and that the introduction of such agents into industry is proceeding at a rapid pace, the shortcomings of our present research efforts must necessarily be a matter of utmost concern.

Accordingly, section 18 has placed specific statutory responsibility upon the Secretary of Health, Education, and Welfare to carry on a variety of research activities. These include studies of the psychological factors involved in solving occupational safety and health problems and the development of innovative methods and techniques for dealing with such problems.

In addition, the Secretary of Health, Education, and Welfare is made responsible for producing criteria upon which the Secretary of Labor may promulgate occupational safety and health standards. Such criteria are scientifically determined conclusions, describing medically acceptable tolerance levels of exposure to harmful substances or conditions over a period of time, and may include medical judgments on methods and devices used to control exposure or its effects.

At the present time criteria and standards have been developed for relatively few materials and are continually in need or review and revision. There is a serious deficiency in criteria for a growing number toxic industrial chemicals, as well as such physical hazards as noise, vibration, extremes of temperature and humidity, effects of parts of the electromagnetic spectrum, and extremes of pressure.

In order to carry out his research functions, the Secretar of Health, Education, and Welfare is given authority to require employers to measure and report on employee exposure to substances and physical agents which may be harmful, and to establish programs of medical examinations for determining the incidence of occupational illness and susceptibility of employees to such illness. When such programs of medical examinations are established for research purposes, they may be furnished at the expense of the Government; in addition, provision is made for the Secretary of Health, Education, and Welfare to furnish financial or other assistance to employers in order to defray additional expenses incurred in carrying out programs of measuring and recording exposures for research purposes.

Section 18 further requires the Secretary of Health, Education, and Welfare to publish and regularly maintain a list of all substances used or found in the workplace and known to be potentially toxic, and the concentrations at which toxicity is known to occur. Provision is made for employers or employees to request a determination regarding the potential toxicity of any material normally found in the workplace. Any such determination shall be furnished to those affected, and, if the substance is not covered by an existing standard, the determination shall also be submitted to the Secretary of Labor so that he may take appropriate action.

Section 18 also makes specific provision for studies of the effect of chronic or low-level exposure to industrial materials, processes, and stresses on the potential for illness, disease, or loss of functional capacity in aging adults.

In addition to those types of studies specified in the bill, Section 18 would authorize a wide range of other research projects, which may be conducted directly or through grants. Among those which the committee believes it important to undertake are studies of the toxic effects of exposure to particular combinations of chemical and physical agents; development of appropriate instruments for monitoring the level of environmental hazards in the workplace, including personal monitoring devices to be used by individual workers; studies of mental and personality disorders attributable to occupational stresses; development of reliable tests for identifying and predicting the level of individual tolerance to workplace hazards, and medical surveillance programs to provide early detection of incipient health deterioration; and studies of the potential genetic effects of complex chemicals and other materials in the work environment.

In order to provide occupational health and safety research with the visibility and status it merits, section 19 of the bill establishes within the Department of Health, Education, and Welfare a new Institute, to be known as the National Institute of Occupational Health and Safety. The Institute will be headed by a Director, appointed by the Secretary of Health, Education, and Welfare for a term of six years, and will have the responsibility for conducting research into all phases of occupational health and safety on an in-house and contract basis. It is also authorized to perform all of the research, training, and related activities to be performed by the Secretary of Health, Education, and Welfare under section 18 of the bill, described above.

On the basis of its research the Institute will formulate recommended occupational health and safety standards and transmit them to the Secretaries of Labor and Health, Education, and Welfare for appropriate further action in accordance with the procedures established by section 6 of the bill for the promulgation of mandatory standards.

The new Institute would perform all of the research now conducted by the Bureau of Occupational Health and Safety (BOSH) in the Health Services and Mental Health Administration of the Department. In the past, BOSH, notwithstanding its limited resources, has performed extremely valuable work in the field of occupational health and safety. The establishment of a special Institute to perform the work previously done by BOSH is not intended as any criticism of BOSH, but stems from the need to elevate the status of occupational health and safety research and to increase greatly the funds devoted for that purpose.

The present budget request for BOSH in FY 1971 is $13.6 million with 375 authorized positions. ($5.1 million and 95 positions are for coal mine health research). According to an issue report prepared by an HEW task force, an adequate program for occupational health alone in 1975 would require $49.1 million and 800 positions (Hearings, Pt. 2, p. 1713). A similar conclusion was reached by the National Environmental Health Committee which, in a 1965 report to the Surgeon General, estimated that an adequate national occupational health program would require at least $50 million annually (Hearings, Pt. 2, p. 1770). In light of these estimates the committee seriously questions the adequacy of the budgetary estimate in the range of $7 to $8 million annually submitted to the committee by Administration spokesmen (Hearings, Pt. 1, p. 156).

TRAINING AND EMPLOYEE EDUCATION

One of the essential contributions Government can make to accomplishing the purposes of this act is through the dissemination of vital health and safety information and the development of necessary educational and training programs. For the enactment of an effective law will not achieve its purposes, unless proper resources are directed toward appropriate education and training activities.

Both Federal and state safety and health inspectors are in critically short supply. There are only 1,600 state safety inspectors, and fewer than 100 Federal inspectors. Only three states have over 100 inspectors; about half have fewer than 25 inspectors; 16 have a dozen or less; four states have no inspection personnel whatsoever. Only three states have inspectors who are trained in the field of occupational health and hygiene. Ironically, there are twice as many fish and game wardens in the United States as there are safety and health inspectors. The hearings revealed a dearth of occupational health specialists in this country—probably no more that 700 are available to meet the demands of a national program to provide healthful working conditions.

A substantial increase in manpower with professional competence is plainly needed to bring about a successful program. To help meet this need, certain provisions in the bill are designed to expand significantly the number of properly trained personnel to work in the field of occupational safety and health. Section 18 authorizes the Secretary of Health, Education, and Welfare, after consultation with the Secretary of Labor, to conduct programs for the education of safety and health personnel.

In order to promote a greater awareness of safety in the workplace, the bill also provides for the training of employers and employees in sound safety and health practices.

There is need for the Secretary of Labor, working with the Civil Service Commission, to continue to establish qualifications for Federal occupational safety personnel which have a meaningful relationship to standards promulgated under this act. It is absolutely essential that all who are carrying out duties under this act will be fully qualified to do so.

Coverage, Applicability, and Relationship to Other Laws

This bill applies to all employment performed in a business affecting commerce among the states, as well as employment in the District of Columbia, the Commonwealth of Puerto Rico, the Virgin Islands, American Samoa, the Trust Territory of the Pacific Islands, Wake Island, Outer Continental Shelf lands, Johnston Island and the Canal Zone.

The bill does not affect any Federal or state workmen's compensation laws, or the rights, duties, or liabilities of employers and employees under them. In addition, it does not modify other Federal laws prescribing safety and health standards. The bill does not authorize the Secretary of Labor to assert authority under this bill over particular working conditions regarding which another Federal agency exercises statutory authority to prescribe or enforce standards affecting occupational safety and health.

Section 4(b) of the bill provides that the safety and health standards promulgated under other statutes administered by the Secretary of Labor—the Walsh-Healey Public Contracts Act, the Service Contract Act, the Construction Safety Act, the National Foundation on Arts and Humanities Act, and the Longshoremen's and Harbor Workers' Compensation Act—shall be superseded if corresponding standards are promulgated under this act which are determined by the Secretary to be more effective. Section 4(b) also provides that standards issued under such other statutes shall be deemed to be standards issued under this act. This provision is included in order to make applicable the provisions of this act in administering the other health and safety statutes under the jurisdiction of the Secretary of Labor. Other remedies provided by such statutes, such as the contract remedies contained in most of those statutes, are not modified by this bill.

It is the intent of the committee that the Secretary will develop health and safety standards for construction workers covered by Public Law 91-54 pursuant to the provisions of that law and that the Secretary will utilize the same mechanisms and resources for the development of health and safety standards for other construction workers newly covered by this act.

Although the committee has taken care to avoid probable areas of duplication, some questions may arise after enactment. Thus, within three years after the effective date of this act, the Secretary must report to Congress his recommendations to achieve coordination between this act and other Federal laws.

NATIONAL COMMISSION TO STUDY STATE WORKMEN'S COMPENSATION LAWS

During the hearings and research conducted by the Committee and its staff on the adequacy of State programs to prevent occupational injury and disease, the Committee's attention was, inevitably, also drawn to the nature of State workmen's compensation programs, upon which injured or diseased workers, and their families are frequently wholly dependent for the replacement of lost income, proper medical treatment, and rehabilitation. Testimony received by the Committee, as well as other information available to the Committee, raises serious questions about the present inadequacy of many State workmen's compensation laws.

For example, workmen's compensation benefit levels do not appear to have kept pace with increasing wage levels and the rising cost of living faced by American workers, with the result that benefits usually replace only a small fraction of the income lost due to disabling injury or disease. As the following table shows, between 1940 and 1969 the ratio of maximum benefits to average weekly wages decreased in 44 States:

RATIO OF MAXIMUM WEEKLY BENEFIT FOR TEMPORARY TOTAL DISABILITY TO AVERAGE WEEKLY WAGES, BY STATE (1940 AND 1970)

[In percent]

State	Ratio of maximum temporary total disability benefit for worker, wife, and 2 dependent children to average weekly wage [1]		State	Ratio of maximum temporary total disability benefit for worker, wife, and 2 dependent children to average weekly wage [1]	
	1940	1970		1940	1970
Alabama	94.9	43.9	Montana	79.8	48.9
Alaska	(2)	61.5	Nebraska	63.1	47.8
Arizona	(2)	117.7	Nevada	84.7	57.9
Arkansas	122.2	49.5	New Hampshire	83.8	55.4
California	80.2	59.7	New Jersey	67.9	63.7
Colorado	54.7	47.1	New Mexico	86.5	42.4
Connecticut	85.9	62.9	New York	80.9	63.3
Delaware	50.6	52.9	North Carolina	100.1	47.0
District of Columbia	93.7	50.7	North Dakota	89.6	64.8
Florida	89.5	45.8	Ohio	63.8	43.1
Georgia	112.0	42.9	Oklahoma	71.2	40.8
Hawaii	116.2	88.0	Oregon	87.5	55.2
Idaho	79.4	59.7	Pennsylvania	69.0	45.8
Illinois	67.5	56.3	Puerto Rico	(4)	59.2
Indiana	60.1	41.3	Rhode Island	83.7	70.0
Iowa	63.2	50.0	South Carolina	153.4	47.2
Kansas	78.0	47.4	South Dakota	66.4	49.4
Kentucky	68.2	43.4	Tennessee	78.2	41.6
Louisiana	94.3	38.8	Texas	84.0	39.4
Maine	85.8	66.7	Utah	72.0	51.3
Maryland	81.0	44.0	Vermont	62.3	56.5
Massachusetts	68.2	68.5	Virginia	74.9	54.4
Michigan	55.1	57.8	Washington	51.1	45.5
Minnesota	77.4	53.7	West Virginia	62.1	50.1
Mississippi	(3)	39.0	Wisconsin	73.5	59.9
Missouri	78.4	48.4	Wyoming	88.4	52.8

Source: U.S. Department of Labor.

[1] The percentages in these columns are found by dividing the maximum weekly benefit for a worker, his wife, and 2 dependent children by the average weekly wage as reported under the State unemployment insurance acts. The 1969 benefit is divided by the 1968 average weekly wage as the wage data for 1969 were not available when the ratios were computed.
[2] No maximum weekly benefit for temporary total disability.
[3] No workmen's compensation law.
[4] Average weekly wage not available.

Another matter of serious concern is the failure of many State programs to recognize certain types of occupational disease as compensable. The tragic results of the failure of State programs to recognize one such disease, coal workers' pneumoconiosis—better known as "black Lung"—have already been recognized, and responded to, by Congress in the Coal Mine Health and Safety Act of 1969, title 4 of which provides special federal benefits for black lung victims and requires that State laws provide adequate coverage for them commencing January 1, 1973. According to testimony received by the Committee, equally tragic results have attended the failure of State workmen's compensation programs to recognize as compensable bysinosis, a respiratory disease caused by the inhalation of cotton dust produced during the processing of textiles.

Failure to provide adequate coverage for occupational disease is only one of the gaps in the coverage of existing State laws. Because of exemptions based on type of employment, or number of employees, approximately 20% of all American workers fail to enjoy the protection of workmen's compensation. Among those workers usually excluded are agricultural employees, notwithstanding the fact that today agriculture is one of our most hazardous occupations.

More generally, although for many years the U.S. Department of Labor and the International Association of Industrial Accident Boards and Commissions have published recommended standards for State laws, the overall ratio of compliance with such standards today is less than 50%. Similarly, a model workmen's compensation law, even though developed under the auspices of the Council of State Governments, appears to have been largely ignored.

Given the breadth and seriousness of the problem, and the importance of an adequate workmen's compensation program to assure injured or diseased employees of reasonable and prompt compensation, adequate medical treatment, and rehabilitation, the Committee believes that a comprehensive study and evaluation of State workmen's compensation laws should be undertaken immediately.

Accordingly, section 23 of the bill would establish a 15-member National Commission on State Workmen's Compensation Laws. The function of the Commission would be to study and evaluate existing State laws in order to determine if they provide an adequate, prompt and equitable system of compensation for the victims of occupational injuries and diseases. Members of the Commission would be appointed by the President from among members of State workmen's compensation boards, representatives of insurance carriers, business, labor, physicians having experience in industrial medicine or in workmen's compensation cases, educators specializing in workmen's compensation, and the general public. The Secretaries of Labor, Commerce, and Health, Education, and Welfare would be ex officio members. The final report of the Commission, with its findings, conclusions, and recommendations, would be due on October 1, 1971.

The Commission's attention would be specifically (but not exclusively) directed to the following 16 subjects:

(1) The amount and duration of permanent and temporary disability benefits and the criteria for determining the maximum limitations thereon;

(2) The amount and duration of medical benefits and provisions insuring adequate medical care and free choice of physician;

(3) The extent of coverage of workers, including exemptions based on numbers or type of employment;

(4) Standards for determining which injuries or diseases should be deemed compensable;

(5) Rehabilitation;

(6) Coverage under second or subsequent injury funds;

(7) Time limits on filing claims;

(8) Waiting periods;

(9) Compulsory or elective coverage;

(10) Administration;

(11) Legal expenses;

(12) The feasibility and desirability of a uniform system of reporting information concerning job-related injuries and diseases and the operation of workmen's compensation laws;

(13) The resolution of conflict of laws, extraterritoriality and similar problems arising from claims with multistate aspects;

(14) The extent to which private insurance carriers are excluded from supplying workmen's compensation coverage and the desirability of such exclusionary practices, to the extent they are found to exist;

(15) The relationship between workmen's compensation on the one hand and old-age, disability, and survivors insurance and other types of insurance, public or private, on the other hand;

(16) Methods of implementing the recommendations of the Commission.

The listed subjects include most of the standards for workmen's compensation laws recommended by the U.S. Department of Labor and the International Association of Industrial Accident Boards and Commissions, as well as other matters which the Committee believes deserve particular attention.

The Committee wishes to emphasize that by authorizing this study it is not impliedly recommending federalization of the existing workmen's compensation system or its merger with the O.A.S.D.I. program. Nor is it willing to accept the notion that workmen's compensation would, under any and all circumstances, remain a matter completely within the prerogatives of the States. Just as the federal government has a responsibility to assure that American workers are protected from job-related injury and disease, it also has an interest in insuring that those American workers who do suffer job-related injury or disease are adequately compensated and treated.

Whether, and to what extent, the Federal government should become directly or indirectly involved in assuring the adequacy of workmen's compensation will be one of the matters considered by the Commission in framing its recommendations. Indeed, one of the primary purposes of authorizing this study and report is to provide a basis for an informed decision by Congress of this question in the future.

Section-by-Section Analysis

Section 1—Short title

This section provides that the act may be cited as the "Occupational Safety and Health Act of 1970."

Section 2—Congressional findings and purpose

Under this section Congress finds that personal injuries and illnesses arising out of work impose a substantial burden upon interstate commerce; and declares a Congressional policy to assure as far as possible every working man and woman safe and healthful working conditions in the following manner—

(1) providing development, promulgation and effective enforcement of occupational safety and health standards;

(2) providing for research relating to occupational safety and health;

(3) providing training programs to increase the competence of personnel;

(4) delineating the responsibilities of the Federal Government and States in their activities related to occupational safety and health;

(5) providing grants to States to help them in identifying their needs and responsibilities in the area of occupational safety and health; to develop plans under the Act; and, to conduct experimental and demonstration projects;

(6) providing accident and health reporting procedures to more accurately describe occupational safety and health problems and achieve the Act's objectives.

Section 3—Definitions

Sections 3(a)–3(e).—These subsections define the terms "Secretary," "commerce," "person," "employee," and "employer." The term "employer" is defined to exclude the United States and their political subdivisions.

Section 3(b).—This subsection defines the term "occupational safety and health standard" as a standard which requires conditions or the adoption or use of one or more practices, means, methods, operations, or processes, reasonably necessary to provide safe or healthful employment and places of employment.

Section 3(g).—This subsection defines the term "national consensus standard" as any occupational safety and health standard or modification which (1) has been adopted and promulgated by a nationally recognized standards-producing organization under procedures whereby it can be determined by the Secretary that persons affected have reached substantial agreement on its adoption (2) and formulated after an opportunity for consideration of diverse views (3) and designated as such a standard by the Secretary, after consultation with other appropriate Federal agencies.

Subsection 3(h).—This subsection defines the term "established Federal standard" as any operative occupational safety and health standard established by any agency of the United States and presently in effect, or contained in any act of Congress in force on the date of enactment.

Section 4—Applicability of act

Section 4(a).—This subsection designates geographic application of the act to all of the United States, territories and possessions. It provides that in areas where there are no Federal district courts having jurisdiction, the Secretary of the Interior shall provide for judicial enforcement.

Section 4(b)(1).—This subsection states that this act does not repeal or modify other Federal laws prescribing safety or health requirements or the standards, rules or regulations promulgated pursuant to such law except to the extent such modifications are provided for under subsection 4(b)(2). The subsection also provides that the Act will not apply to working conditions of employees where any Federal agency other than the Secretary of Labor exercises statutory authority to prescribe or enforce standards or regulations affecting occupational safety and health.

Section 4(b)(2).—Under this subsection, standards promulgated under this act and determined by the Secretary to be more effective, will supersede corresponding standards promulgated under certain listed laws relating to safety and health of employees. Standards under the listed laws are deemed to be standards under this act. The provisions of this act apply to the administration of the statutes named in this subsection, but other remedies provided by such statures also apply.

Section 4(b)(3).—This subsection requires the Secretary to report his recommendations to Congress for legislation to avoid unnecessary duplication between this act and other Federal laws within 3 years after the effective date of this act.

Section 4(b)(4).—This subsection provides that the act shall not be deemed to affect workmen's compensation laws or common law or statutory rights, duties or liabilities of employers and employees under any law relating to injuries, diseases or death, stemming from the course of employment.

Section 5—Duties of employers

Section 5(a).—This subsection provides that each employer—

(1) is under a duty to provide his employees with employment and a place of employment free from recognized hazards so as to provide safe and healthful working conditions; and

(2) must comply with occupational health and safety standards and rules, regulations and orders promulgated under this act, except as provided in section 16 (relating to State jurisdiction and State plans).

Section 5(b).—Under this subsection, each employee has the duty of complying with occupational health and safety standards and the rules, regulations and orders issued under this act, except as provided by section 16.

Section 6—Occupational safety and health standards

Section 6(a).—Under this subsection, the Secretary, as soon as practicable after the effective date of the act, and until two years from such date, shall by rule promulgate (without regard to the rule making provisions of the Administrative Procedure Act) as an occupational safety or health standard any national consensus standard or any established Federal standard unless he determines promulgation would not result in improved safety or health for specifically designated employees. The Secretary shall resolve any conflict in standards by promulgating the standard assuring the greatest protection of safety and health to affected employees. The Secretary may also promulgate any standard adopted prior to the date of enactment by a nationally recognized standards-producing organization by other than a consensus method in accordance with section 553 of title 5, United States Code (Rulemaking provisions of the Administrative Procedure Act).

Sections 6(b)(1) to Subsections 6(b)(6).—These subsections contain procedures for the Secretary to promulgate, modify, or revoke any occupational safety and health standard.

Section 6(b)(1) provides that the Secretary may request the recommendations of an advisory committee appointed under section 7 whenever he determines from information submitted in writing by an interested person, a representative of an employer or employee organization, a nationally recognized standard producing organization, the Secretary of Health, Education, and Welfare, the National Institute of Occupational Health and Safety, a State or political subdivision, or on the basis of his own information, that a rule (standard) should be promulgated. Where an advisory committee is appointed, the Secretary must provide such committee with any proposal of his own or of the Secretary of Health, Education, and Welfare as well as any factual information that has been developed. The advisory committee must submit to the Secretary its recommendations within 90 days from the date of its appointment or a longer or shorter period of time prescribed by the Secretary, but no longer than 270 days.

Section 6(b)(2).—Under this subsection, the Secretary is required to publish a proposed rule promulgating, modifying or revoking an occupational safety or health standard in the Federal Register and afford interested persons a period of 30 days after publication to submit written comments. Where an advisory committee is appointed and the Secretary determines that a rule shall be issued, he must publish the proposed rule within 60 days after submission of the advisory committee's recommendations or the expiration of the period prescribed by the Secretary.

Section 6(b)(3).—This subsection permits any interested person to file with the Secretary written objections to the proposed rule and requesting a public hearing on or before the last day of the period provided for in subsection 6(b)(2). Within 30 days after the last day for filing such objections, the Secretary shall publish in the Federal Register a notice specifying the standard objected to and time and place for a hearing.

Section 6(b)(4).—This subsection provides that within 60 days after expiration of the period of notice under subsection 6(b)(2) or within 60 days after completion of a hearing, under subsection 6(b)(3) the Secretary shall issue a rule promulgating, modifying, or revoking an occupational safety and health standard or make a determination that a rule should not be issued. A rule issued may contain a provision delaying the effective date for a period determined by the Secretary.

Section 6(b)(5).—Under this subsection, the Secretary, in promulgating standards, is required to set the standard which most adequately and feasibly assures, on the basis of the best available evidence, that employees will not suffer impairment of health, functional capacity, or diminished life expectancy even if regularly exposed to the hazard throughout their working lives. Development of standards is to be based on research, demonstration, experiment, and other appropriate information. In addition to attainment of the highest degree of safety and health protection for the employee, other considerations shall be the latest available scientific data in the field, the feasibility of the standards and experience gained under this and other health and safety statutes. Wherever practicable, the standard should be expressed in terms of objective criteria and performance desired.

Section 6(b)(6).—Under this subsection, any standard promulgated under subsection 6(b) must prescribe the use of labels or other warnings as are necessary to ensure that employees are apprised of all hazards to which they are exposed, relevant symptoms and appropriate emergency treatment, and proper conditions and precautions of safe use or exposure. A standard, when appropriate, shall prescribe protective equipment, control or technological procedures to be used, and shall provide for monitoring or measuring employee exposure as may be necessary for the protection of the employee. Where appropriate, such standard shall prescribe the type and frequency of medical examination or tests which the employer shall provide, at his cost, in order to determine whether the employee exposed to such hazards is adversely affected by such exposure. The medical examination may be furnished at the expense of the Secretary of Health, Education, and Welfare if he determines them to be in the nature of research. The results of such examinations or tests shall be furnished only to the Secretary, the Secretary of Health, Education, and Welfare and at the employee's request, to his physician. The Secretary, in consultation with the Secretary of Health, Education, and Welfare, may by rule promulgated pursuant to section 553 of title 5, United States Code, modify the foregoing requirement relating to labels, warning, monitoring and medical examination as subsequently acquired experience, information, or medical and technical developments warrant.

Sections 6(c)(1)–6(c)(3).—Contain procedures for the Secretary to promulgate emergency temporary occupational safety and health standards.

Section 6(c)(1).—Under this subsection, where the Secretary determines that employees are being exposed to grave dangers from exposure to substances or agents determined to be toxic or physically harmful or from new hazards and that an emergency standard is necessary to protect the employees, he may promulgate an emergency temporary standard effective upon publication in the Federal Register without regard to the rulemaking procedures of the Administrative Procedure Act.

Section 6(c)(2).—Under this subsection, an emergency temporary standard shall be effective until superseded by a standard promulgated in accordance with the procedures of subsection 6(c)(3).

Section 6(c)(3).—This subsection requires the Secretary to commence a proceeding for promulgating a standard in accordance with section 6(b) upon publication of the emergency temporary standard. The Secretary shall promulgate the permanent standard no later than six months after publication of the emergency temporary standard.

Section 6(d).—This subsection allows an affected employer to apply to the Secretary for a rule for a variance from a standard promulgated under this section. The subsection provides that affected employees shall be given notice of the application and an opportunity to participate in a hearing. The Secretary shall issue such a rule if he determines on the record, after opportunity for an inspection where appropriate, and a hearing, that the proponent of the variance has demonstrated by a preponderance of the evidence, that the conditions, practices, means, methods, operations or processes used or proposed to be used by the employer will provide employment and places of employment at least as safe and healthful as would prevail if he complied with the standard. The rule or order must prescribe the conditions the employer must maintain and the practices he must adopt. Such a rule may be modified or revoked upon application by an employer, employee or by the Secretary in the manner prescribed for its issuance under this subsection at any time after six months after its issuance.

Section 6(e).—This subsection provides that where the Secretary promulgates a standard, makes a rule, order or decision, grants an exemption or extension of time, or compromises, mitigates or settles any penalty, that he include a statement of his reasons for the action and publish it in the Federal Register.

Section 6(f).—Under this subsection, a person adversely affected by a standard issued under this section may, within 60 days of its promulgation, obtain judicial review of such standard by filing a petition challenging the validity of the standard in an appropriate United States Court of Appeals. The filing of a petition shall not stay the standard unless otherwise ordered by the court.

Section 7—Administration; advisory committees

Section 7(a).—This subsection authorizes the Secretary:

> (1) To use with the consent of any Federal agency, the services, facilities, or personnel of such Federal agency, with or without reimbursement, or of a State or its political subdivision with reimbursement;
>
> (2) To employ experts and consultants.

Section 7(b).—This subsection allows the Secretary to appoint advisory committees to recommend standards under section 6(b) proceedings. Each committee, consisting of not more than 15 members, is to include one or more designees of the Secretary of Health, Education, and Welfare, and may include employer and employee representatives in equal numbers, representatives of State and local safety agencies, and other members qualified by knowledge and experience. The number of persons from private organizations appointed to any advisory committee shall not exceed the number appointed to such committee as representatives of Federal and State agencies. This subsection also provides for the compensation of advisory committee members and forbids anyone serving as a committee member (other than representatives of employers and employees) who has an economic interest in any proposed rule.

Section 7(c).—This subsection requires the Secretary and the Secretary of Health, Education, and Welfare to appoint a National Advisory Committee on Occupational Health and Safety. The Committee, with twenty members, is to be composed equally of representatives of management, labor, occupational safety and health professions, and of the public. The Secretary appoints all members and a chairman, except occupational health representatives who are appointed by the Secretary of Health, Education, and Welfare. The Committee is to advise, consult with, and make recommendations to the Secretaries of Labor and Health, Education, and Welfare on matters relating to the act. At least two meetings on the record are required annually. All meetings are to be open. Provision is made for compensation of the members and staff support by the Secretary.

Section 8—Inspections, investigations and reports

Section 8(a).—Under this subsection, the Secretary or his representative, upon presenting appropriate credentials to the owner, operator or agent in charge, is authorized—

> (1) to enter premises at reasonable times of any workplace where work is performed to which this act applies;
> (2) to make reasonable inspections and investigations of conditions in workplaces and to question privately owners, operators, agents or employees.

Section 8(b).—This subsection provides the Secretary of Labor with the investigation and subpoena power relating to books, records, documents and witnesses contained in sections 9 and 10 of the Federal Trade Commission Act.

Section 8(c)(1).—This subsection requires employers to keep such records as the Secretary and the Secretary of Health, Education, and Welfare require by regulation, as necessary or appropriate for enforcement of the act or for developing information relating to occupational accidents and illnesses. The regulations may include provisions requiring employers to conduct periodic inspection to determine their own state of compliance with the act and regulations. The Secretary also must issue regulations requiring, through appropriate means, that employers keep employees informed of their rights, protections and obligations under the act, including provisions of applicable standards.

Section 8(c)(2).—This subsection requires the Secretary in cooperation with the Secretary of Health, Education, and Welfare to prescribe regulations requiring employers to keep records of all work-related injuries and diseases which arise, and make periodic reports. The Secretary is to compile accurate statistics on work injuries and diseases whether or not resulting in loss of time from work.

Section 8(c)(3).—This subsection requires the Secretary, in cooperation with the Secretary of Health, Education, and Welfare, to issue regulations requiring employers to maintain records of employee exposures to potentially toxic materials or harmful physical agents which are required to be monitored under sections 6 and 18. The regulations are to give employees or their representatives an opportunity to observe the monitoring or measuring, and to give employees and former employees access to such records of individual exposure. Employers are to notify employees of overexposure and shall inform overexposed employees of the corrective action being taken.

Section 8(d).—This subsection provides that information from employers should be obtained with a minimum burden on them, especially from employers operating small businesses.

Section 8(e).—Under this subsection, subject to regulations issued by the Secretary, a representative of the employer and an authorized representative of employees shall be given an opportunity to accompany the Secretary or his representative during a physical inspection under subsection 8(a) for the purpose of aiding such inspection. If the Secretary is unable to determine the existence of an authorized employee representative, the Secretary or his representative is to consult with a reasonable number of employees.

Section 8(f)(1).—Under this subsection, an employee or representative of employees who believes that a violation of a safety and health standard exists that threatens physical harm or imminent danger may request an immediate inspection by giving notice to the Secretary of such violation. The notice, which may be by telephone, to be reduced to writing, and signed, and upon request, the name of the person giving notice shall be kept confidential. The Secretary shall make a special inspection as soon as practicable if he determines upon receiving such notification that there are reasonable grounds to believe that such a violation or danger exists. If the Secretary does not find reasonable grounds, he shall give written notice to the employee or employee representative of such determination.

Section 8(f)(2).—Under this subsection, an employee or representative of employees, prior to or during an inspection, may notify the Secretary of a possible violation. The Secretary, if he fails to issue a citation with respect to such an alleged violation, shall furnish the employee or representative of employees a written explanation and must also establish by regulation procedures for informal review of any refusal to issue the citation.

Section 8(g).—This subsection authorizes the Secretary or the Secretary of Health, Education, and Welfare to publish information obtained from reports or information obtained under this section. Release of this information is discretionary, but shall be made available for public inspection to the extent required by the provisions of section 552 of title 5, United States Code (Freedom of Information Act.)

Section 9—Citations for violations

Section 9(a).—Under this subsection, if the Secretary, after inspection, determines that an employer has violated sections 5, 6(d), 8(c), 18 or a rule, regulation or order made pursuant thereto, he shall issue to the employer a citation in writing, describing the violation and giving a reference to the provision of the act, rule, regulation or order alleged to have been violated. The citation must fix a reasonable time for abatement of the violation. The Secretary may prescribe procedures for issuance of a notice in lieu of a citation in the case of de minimus violations not having a direct or immediate relationship to safety or health.

Section 9(b).—This subsection requires the posting of the citation at or near the place of occurrence of the violation.

Section 10—Procedures for enforcement

Section 10(a).—This subsection requires the Secretary, if he issues a citation under section 9(a), within a reasonable time after termination of the inspection or investigation to notify the employer of the penalty, if any, proposed to be assessed under section 14. The employer then has 15 working days to notify the Secretary whether he wishes to contest the citation or proposed assessment. If he fails to give such notice, and no notice is filed by employees or employee representative contesting the time fixed for abatement, the citation and the proposed assessment will be final and not subject to review. For purposes of enforcement under subsection 10(e) it would be considered a final order issued by the Secretary under subsection 10(c).

Section 10(b).—Under this subsection, if the Secretary has reason to believe that an employer has failed to correct a violation for which a citation has been issued within the period of time permitted for its correction (which time does not begin to run until the expiration of administrative and judicial review initiated in good faith), or has failed to comply with an order issued under section 11(b), the Secretary shall notify the employer of such failure and of the penalty proposed to be assessed under section 14. The employer has 15 working days within which to notify the Secretary that he wishes to contest the Secretary's notification. If the employer fails to notify the Secretary, the proposed penalty will be final and for the purposes of enforcement under subsection 10(e), it shall be deemed a final order under subsection 10(c).

Section 10(c).—This subsection contains the procedures for contesting citations and proposed penalties. If an employer decides to contest a citation, notification or proposed penalty, or if within 15 days of the issuance of a citation an employee or employee representative files a notice alleging that the time fixed for abatement is unreasonable, the Secretary shall afford an opportunity for a hearing. The Secretary shall issue an order, based on findings of fact, confirming, denying, or modifying the citation or assessment of penalty. If he determines that an employer has not corrected a violation within the prescribed period, the Secretary shall issue such orders, based on findings of fact, as may be necessary for the correction of the violation and the assessment and collection of penalties. The Secretary shall give the employer or any other person who has filed notice under this subsection the information required under section 554(b) of title 5, United States Code, at least 15 days prior to the hearing. Upon the employer's showing of good faith efforts to comply with an abatement requirement of a citation, and that abatement has not been completed because of factors beyond his reasonable control, the Secretary, after an opportunity for a hearing, shall issue an order affirming or modifying the abatement requirements. Affected employees or their representatives shall have an opportunity to participate as parties in hearings under this subsection.

Section 10(d).—This subsection permits persons adversely affected or aggrieved by a final order of the Secretary, except where the order becomes final under subsection 10(a) or 10(b), to obtain review of such order in a United States Court of Appeals for the Circuit, where the violation is alleged to have taken place, or where the employer has its office, or in the District of Columbia within 60 days after the service of the Secretary's order. The subsection specifies the procedures to be followed after a petition for review is filed, including:

(1) The clerk of the court transmits a copy of the petition to the Secretary.

(2) The Secretary files in court the record in the proceedings pursuant to 28 U.S.C. 2112 at which time the court of appeals has exclusive jurisdiction.

(3) The court of appeals is authorized to grant such temporary relief, restraining order, or other orders as it deems just and proper and may enter a decree enforcing, modifying and enforcing as so modified, or setting aside in whole or in part the order of the Secretary. The findings of fact by the Secretary are conclusive if they are supported by substantial evidence on the record considered as a whole. (*See Universal Camera* v. *Labor Board*, 340 U.S. 474 (1951)).

(4) Any party may apply for leave to adduce additional evidence before the Secretary, who could then modify his original findings. Modified findings would also be conclusive if supported by substantial evidence on the record considered as a whole.

(5) Objections not urged before the Secretary will not be considered by the court unless the failure or neglect to urge such objection is excused because of extraordinary circumstances.

(6) Commencement of proceedings under this subsection would not stay the Secretary's order unless ordered by the court.

(7) The courts of appeals are required to hear petitions expeditiously. This requirement is intended to emphasize to the courts of appeals the need for promptly acting on petitions in order to have speedy resolution of these cases.

(8) The judgment of the court of appeals is final, except that it is subject to review by the Supreme Court as provided in 28 United States Code 1254.

Section 10(e).—This subsection would authorize the Secretary to petition a United States court of appeals for enforcement of his order. The prescribed procedures in the case of petitions for enforcement under this subsection are similar to subsection 10(d), except that no time limit is specified for the enforcement petition by the Secretary. If there is no petition for review filed within 60 days after service of the Secretary's order as provided in subsection 10(d), the Secretary's findings of fact and order would become conclusive in connection with any petition for enforcement filed by the Secretary after the expiration of such 60-day period. In the case of such petitions, as well as in the case of noncontested citations or notices by the Secretary which have become final under subsection (a) or (b), the clerk of the court of appeals would enter a decree enforcing the order of the Secretary and transmit copies to the Secretary and the employer.

In any contempt proceedings brought under this subsection or under subsection (d), the court of appeals may impose penalties as provided in section 14 in addition to other available remedies.

Section 10(f).—This subsection prohibits discharge or discrimination against an employee because of the exercise by the employee, on behalf of himself or others, of any rights under this act. Any employee who believes he has been discharged or discriminated against by any person in violation of this subsection may apply to the Secretary for a review of such discrimination. The Secretary shall investigate and provide the opportunity for a public hearing on the record and in accordance with title 5, United States Code 554 (Administrative Procedure Act). If the Secretary finds a violation, he shall issue a decision and order requiring the person committing the violation to take such affirmative action as may be appropriate to abate the violation, including but not limited to, rehiring or reinstatement with back pay. Judicial review of proceedings under this subsection may be obtained pursuant to subsection 10(d) or (e) of this section.

Section 11—Procedures to counteract imminent dangers

Section 11(a).—Under this subsection, if the Secretary determines that imminent danger exists in a place of employment, he may bring a civil action in a United States District Court for a temporary restraining order or injunction requiring correction of the danger and prohibiting the employment of individuals at the location, except for those whose presence is necessary to correct the danger, to maintain the capacity of a continuous process to restart, or to permit an orderly cessation of operations. The subsection provides that actions may be brought while an order under subsection 11(b) is in effect. "Imminent danger" is defined as a condition or practice which could reasonably be expected to cause death or serious physical harm before such condition or practice can be abated.

Section 11(b).—Under this subsection, if the danger referred to in subsection 11(a) is of a nature such that immediate action is necessary, the Secretary may issue an order requiring the same steps to be taken as in subsection 11(a) to remain in effect not more than 72 hours. The Secretary must issue regulations providing for informal reconsideration by appropriate officials of such order. If the authority to issue orders is delegated by the Secretary, the concurrence of an appropriate regional Labor Department official must be obtained. This concurrence may be obtained by telephone.

Section 11(c).—Under this subsection, if the Secretary arbitrarily or capriciously fails to issue an order or seek relief under this section, any employee or representative of employees who may be injured by such failure, may seek a writ of mandamus in the United States District Court to compel the Secretary to issue an order or for other relief.

Section 12—Representation in civil litigation

This section authorizes the Solicitor of Labor to appear and represent the Secretary in civil litigation under this act subject to the direction and control of the Attorney General.

Section 13—Confidentiality of trade secrets

This section contains procedures for maintaining the confidentiality of trade secrets.

Section 14—Penalties

Section 14(a).—This subsection provides that an employer who violates any standard issued under section 6 or the requirements of 6(d), 8(c), 18 or any rule, regulation or order issued thereunder shall be assessed a civil penalty of not more than $1,000. Any employer who fails to correct a violation for which a citation has been issued under section 9(a) or violates an order under section 11(b), shall be assessed a civil penalty of not more than $1,000 for each day of violation.

Section 14(b).—This subsection permits the Secretary to compromise, mitigate or settle civil penalties using certain criteria specified in the subsection.

Section 14(c).—This subsection provides criminal penalties including fine and imprisonment for willful violation of sections 6, 6(d), 8(c), 18 or rules, regulations or orders issued thereunder.

Section 14(d).—This subsection provides a criminal penalty including fine and imprisonment for any person giving advance notice of an inspection.

Section 14(e).—This subsection provides criminal penalties for any person knowingly making a false statement or representation in any record, report, plan or other document filed under this act.

Section 14(f).—This subsection brings Department of Labor and Department of Health, Education, and Welfare personnel assigned to perform investigative, inspection, or law-enforcement functions under the protection of title 18 of the United States Code.

Section 15—Variations, tolerances and expemptions

This section allows the Secretary to provide reasonable limitations, variations, and tolerances to avoid serious impairment of the national defense, to be effective for no more than six months unless notice and opportunity for hearing is afforded affected employees.

Section 16—State jurisdiction and State plans

Section 16(a).—Under this subsection, a State may assert jurisdiction under State law over any occupational safety or health issue with respect to which no standard is in effect under section 6 (occupational safety and health standards).

Section 16(b).—Under this subsection, a State can submit a State plan for the development and enforcement of standards relating to occupational safety or health issues that have been dealt with in standards promulgated under section 6.

Section 16(c).—This subsection requires the Secretary to approve the plan submitted by a State under subsection 16(b) or any modification thereof, if in his judgment:

(1) a State agency (or agencies) is designated for administering a plan throughout the State;

(2) it provides for the development and enforcement of standards which are or will be at least as effective as section 6 standards;

(3) it provides for a right of entry and inspection of all workplaces subject to the act at least as effective as provided in section 8(a), (c), (d) and (e) and includes a prohibition on advance notice of inspections;

(4) it contains satisfactory assurances that the State agency will have adequate legal authority and qualified personnel necessary for the enforcement of the standards;

(5) it contains satisfactory assurances of adequate State funds for administration and enforcement of standards;

(6) it contains satisfactory assurances that the State, to the extent permitted by law will establish an occupational safety and health program applicable to all employees of public agencies of the State and its political subdivisions over which it has jurisdiction at least as effective as the State plan;

(7) it requires employers in the State to make reports to the Secretary in the same manner and extent as if the plan were not in effect;

(8) it provides that the State agency will make reports to the Secretary in such form as the Secretary shall from time to time require.

Section 16(d).—This subsection provides that if the Secretary disapproves a plan, he shall afford the State notice and opportunity for a hearing.

Section 16(e).—Under this subsection, after approval of a State plan, the Secretary may, but is not required to, exercise his authority under sections 8, 9, 10, and 14 with respect to comparable standards promulgated under section 6 until he determines on the basis of actual operations that the State is following the plan. However, if he exercises the authority, he shall not make the determination for at least three years after the plan's approval under subsection (16c). After State plan approval, provisions of sections 5(a)(2), 8 (except for the purposes of carrying out subsection (c)), 9, 10, and 14 and standards promulgated under section 6, shall not apply, but the Secretary may retain jurisdiction under the above provisions in any proceeding commenced under sections 9 and 10 before the date of determination.

Section 16(f).—This subsection requires the Secretary to continually evaluate State plans. The Secretary has the power to withdraw approval of a State plan if he finds a failure to comply substantially with any provision of the State plan.

Section 16(g).—Under this subsection, the State may obtain review of withdrawal of approval or rejection of a plan in the United States Court of Appeals. The Secretary's decision shall be sustained unless the court finds that the Secretary's decision is arbitrary and capricious. This subsection provides for further appeal to the Supreme Court.

Section 17—Federal agency safety programs and responsibilities

Section 17(a).—This subsection states that the head of each Federal agency shall maintain a comprehensive occupational safety and health program consistent with standards promulgated under section 6. The head of each agency, after consultation with representatives of employees, shall provide—

(1) standards consistent with standards under section 6;

(2) acquire and maintain and require the use of safety devices to protect its personnel;

(3) keep adequate records of occupational accidents and illnesses;

(4) consult with the Secretary as to the adequacy of records; and

(5) make an annual report to the Secretary with respect to occupational accidents and injuries.

Section 17(b).—This subsection requires the Secretary to submit a summary of reports submitted to him under subsection 17(a)(4) to the President. The President shall transmit annually to the Senate and House of Representatives a report of the activities of Federal agencies under this section.

Section 17(c).—This subsection amends section 7902(c)(1) of title 5, United States Code, to permit labor organizations representing employees to serve on the President's Federal Safety Council.

Section 17(d).—This subsection provides that the Secretary shall have access to records and reports kept by Federal agencies pursuant to (a) (3) and (5) of this subsection, unless the reports are required to be kept secret in the interests of national defense.

Section 18—Research training and related activities

(a)(1) Provides the Secretary of Health, Education, and Welfare, after consultation with the Secretary of Labor and other appropriate Federal agencies, shall conduct research (directly or by grant or contract) relating to occupational safety and health, including innovative methods of dealing with occupational safety and health problems.

(2) Provides that the Secretary of Health, Education, and Welfare shall be responsible for producing criteria upon which the Secretary of Labor may formulate occupational safety and health standards under this act. The Secretary of Health, Education, and Welfare is also required to consult with the Secretary of Labor to develop specific plans for research necessary to produce the criteria. The Secretary of Health, Education, and Welfare is also required to develop such criteria which would, if applied, assure that no employee will suffer impaired health or functional capacities, or diminished life expectancy as a result of his work experience.

(3) Provides that the Secretary of Health, Education, and Welfare, in order to meet his responsibilities under (2) and develop needed information regarding toxic substances or harmful physical agents, may prescribe regulations requiring employers to measure, record and report on the exposure of employees to substances and physical agents which may endanger the health and safety of employees. He may also require programs for the physical examination of employees. An exemption from examinations or tests on religious grounds is provided. Upon request, the Secretary of Health, Education, and Welfare shall furnish full financial assistance to defray the expenses incurred by an employer developing this information.

(4) Within six months of enactment, and thereafter at least annually, the Secretary of Health, Education, and Welfare shall publish a list of all known or potentially toxic substances used or found in the workplace and concentrations at which such toxicity is known to occur. If requested by an employer or authorized representative of employees, he shall determine whether any substance found at a workplace has potentially toxic effects and shall so notify the employer and affected employees. Such determination shall be submitted to the Secretary if the substance is not covered by a standard promulgated under section 6.

(5) Provides that the Secretary of Health, Education, and Welfare within two years of enactment and annually thereafter shall conduct industry-wide studies of chronic or low-level exposure to industrial material, processes and stress on the potential for illness, disease, or loss of functional capacity in aging adults.

(6) Provides that the Secretary of Health, Education, and Welfare is authorized to make inspections and question employees as provided in section 8.

(b) Provides that the Secretary is authorized to enter into contracts or arrangements with public agencies or private organizations for the purpose of conducting studies related to establishing and applying standards under section 6. Provides for cooperation between the Secretary and the Secretary of Health, Education, and Welfare to avoid duplication of effort under this section.

(c) Provides that information obtained by the Secretary and the Secretary of Health, Education, and Welfare be disseminated by the Secretary to employers and employees and organizations.

(d) Provides that the Secretary of Health, Education, and Welfare, after consultation with the Secretary, shall conduct directly or by grant or contract educational programs to provide qualified personnel to carry out the act and information on the use of safety and health equipment.

(e) Provides that the Secretary directly or by grant or contract set up short-term training programs for personnel.

(f) Provides for the establishment by the Secretary of training programs for employers and employees in the prevention of unsafe and unhealthful working conditions.

(g) Provides for the delegation of functions, as feasible, by the Secretary of Health, Education, and Welfare to the Director of the National Institute for Occupational Safety and Health established in section 19.

Section 19—National Institute for Occupational Safety and Health

(a) States that the purpose of this section is to establish a National Institute for Occupational Safety and Health in the Department of Health, Education, and Welfare to carry out policy set forth in section 2 and to perform the functions of the Secretary of Health, Education, and Welfare under section 18.

(b) Defines the terms "Director" and "Institute."

(c) Establishes the National Institute for Occupational Safety and Health to be headed by a Director appointed by the Secretary of Health, Education, and Welfare to serve for six years.

(d) Authorizes the Institute to develop and establish recommended occupational safety and health standards and perform the functions of the Secretary of Health, Education, and Welfare.

(e) Authorizes the Director to conduct research and experimental programs for the development of criteria for new or improved standards and make recommendations for such standards. Provides for the forwarding of such standards to the Secretary and the Secretary of Health, Education, and Welfare.

(f) Authorizes the Director to: prescribe regulations, receive money and donations and dispose of them in accordance with paragraph (2), appoint and compensate personnel, obtain the services of experts in accordance with section 3109 of title 5, United States Code, accept voluntary services, enter into grants, contracts, make advance payments, and rent office space.

(g) Provides for an annual report by the Institute to be submitted to the Secretary of Health, Education, and Welfare, the President, and Congress on its operations.

Section 20—Grants to the States: Statistics

(a)(1) Authorizes the Secretary, during fiscal year 1971, and two succeeding fiscal years, to make grants to State agencies designated under section 16(c) to assist—

    (A) in identifying needs;

    (B) in developing plans under section 16;

    (C) in developing plans for—

        (i) collecting statistical data;

(ii) increasing personnel capabilities;

(iii) improving administration and enforcement, including standards.

(2) Provides that the Secretary, commencing in fiscal year 1971, and the two succeeding fiscal years, shall make experimental and demonstration grants.

(3) Provides that the Governor of a State shall designate the State agency to receive a grant.

(4) Provides that the State agency designated by the Governor shall submit grant application to the Secretary.

(5) The Secretary, after review and consultation with the Secretary of Health, Education, and Welfare shall accept or reject the application for grant.

(6) The Federal share for each State grant under (1) or (2) of this section may be up to 90 percent. Different percentage distribution among the States shall be established on the basis of objective criteria.

(7) Authorizes the Secretary to make grants to States to assist them in administering and enforcing programs for occupational safety and health contained in State plans approved under section 16. The Federal share may be up to 50 percent of the total cost. Differential in allotments to the States must be based on objective criteria.

(8) The Secretary must make a report after consultation with the Secretary of Health, Education, and Welfare to the President and the Congress prior to June 30, 1973, on the experience under the grant program.

(b) Provides that the Secretary shall develop a program of collection, compilation and analysis of occupational safety and health statistics. Authorizes the Secretary to make grants to States to assist them in developing programs on such statistics, up to 50 percent of the State's total cost and to use the services of a State. Authorizes the Secretary by contract or grant to conduct research in this area; authorizes the Secretary to prescribe by regulation the necessary records that employers must file with the Secretary.

Section 21—Audits

(a) This provision provides audit procedures for recipients of grants under this act.

Section 22—Annual report

This section requires the Secretary and the Secretary of Health, Education, and Welfare to make annual reports to the President for transmittal to the Congress.

Section 23—National Commission on State Workmen's Compensation Laws

Provides for the establishment of a 15-member commission appointed by the President to study and evaluate State Workmen's compensation laws in order to determine if such laws provide an adequate system of compensation for injury or death arising out of or in the course of employment.

The Commission must report its findings to the President and Congress no later than October 1, 1971.

The Commission is authorized in carrying out its objectives to hold hearings, compensate its members and appoint a staff and compensate them.

This section authorizes the necessary funds to be appropriated to carry out the provisions of this section.

Section 24—Economic assistance to small businesses

Amends the Small Business Act to facilitate loans to small businesses involved in altering their equipment or operations in order to comply with standards issued under section 6 of the Occupational Safety and Health Act.

Section 25—Additional Assistant Secretary of Labor

Provides for the appointment of an Assistant Secretary of Labor for Occupational Safety and Health.

Section 26—Separability

This section contains the usual separability provision.

Section 27—Appropriations

This section authorizes the appropriations necessary to carry out the act.

Section 28—Effective date

This section provides that the act will become effective at the beginning of the first month which begins more than 30 days after its enactment.

CHANGES IN EXISTING LAW

In compliance with subsection (4) of rule XXIX of the Standing Rules of the Senate, changes in existing law made by the bill, as reported, are shown as follows (existing law proposed to be omitted is enclosed in black brackets, new matter is printed in italic, existing law in which no change is proposed is shown in roman):

TITLE 18.—CRIMES AND CRIMINAL PROCEDURE

*   *   *   *   *   *   *

§ 111. Assaulting, resisting, or impeding certain officers or employees.

Whoever forcibly assaults, resists, opposes, impedes, intimidates, or interferes with any person designated in section 1114 of this title while engaged in or on account of the performance of his official duties, shall be fined not more than $5,000 or imprisoned not more than three years, or both.

Whoever, in the commission of any such acts uses a deadly or dangerous weapon, shall be fined not more than $10,000 or imprisoned not more than ten years, or both.

*   *   *   *   *   *   *

§ 1114. Protection of officers and employees of the United States.

Whoever kills any judge of the United States, any United States Attorney, any Assistant United States Attorney, or any United States marshal or deputy marshal or person employed to assist such marshal or deputy marshal, any officer or employee of the Federal Bureau of Investigation of the Department of Justice, any postal inspector, any postmaster, officer, or employee in the field service of the Post Office Department, any officer or employee of the secret service or of the Bureau of Narcotics, any officer or enlisted man of the Coast Guard, any officer or employee of any United States penal or correctional institution, any officer, employee or agent of the customs or of the internal revenue or any person assisting him in the execution of his duties, any immigration officer, any officer or employee of the Department of Agriculture or of the Department of the Interior designated by the Secretary of Agriculture or the Secretary of the Interior to enforce any Act of Congress for the protection, preservation, or restoration of game and other wild birds and animals, any employee of the Department of Agriculture designated by the Secretary of Agriculture to carry out any law or regulation, or to perform any function in connection with any Federal or State program or any program of Puerto Rico, Guam, the Virgin Islands of the United States, or the District of Columbia, for the control or eradication or prevention of the introduction or dissemination of animal diseases, any officer or employee of the National Park Service, any officer or employee of, or assigned to duty, in the field service of the Bureau of Land Management, any employee of the Bureau of Animal Industry of the Department of Agriculture, or any officer or employee of the Indian field service of the United States, or any officer or employee of the National Aeronautics and Space Administration directed to guard and protect property of the United States under the administration and control of the National Aeronautics and Space Administration, any security officer of the Department of State or the Foreign Service, or any officer or employee of the Department of Health, Education, and Welfare [designated by the Secretary of Health, Education, and Welfare to conduct investigations or inspections under the Federal Food, Drug, and Cosmetic Act] *or of the Department of Labor assigned to perform investigative, inspection, or law enforcement functions* while engaged in the performance of his official duties, or on account of the performance of his official duties, shall be punished as provided under sections 1111 and 1112 of this title.

TITLE 5.—GOVERNMENT ORGANIZATION AND EMPLOYEES

*   *   *   *   *   *   *

§ 5315. Positions at level IV.

Level IV of the Executive Schedule applies to the following positions, for which the annual rate of basic pay is $28,750:

*   *   *   *   *   *   *

(20) Assistant Secretaries of Labor [(4).] *(5)*.

*   *   *   *   *   *   *

§ 7902. Safety programs.

(a) For the purpose of this section—

(1) "employee" means an employee as defined by section 8101 of this title; and

(2) "agency" means an agency in any branch of the Government of the United States, including an instrumentality wholly owned by the United States, and the government of the District of Columbia.

(b) The Secretary of Labor shall carry out a safety program under section 941(b)(1) of title 33 covering the employment of each employee of an agency.

(c) The President may—

(1) establish by Executive order a safety council composed of representatives of the agencies *and of labor organisations representing employees* to serve as an advisory body to the Secretary in furtherance of the safety program carried out by the Secretary under subsection (b) of this section; and

(2) undertake such other measures as he considers proper to prevent injuries and accidents to employees of the agencies.

(d) The head of each agency shall develop and support organized safety promotion to reduce accidents and injuries among employees of his agency, encourage safe practices, and eliminate work hazards and health risks.

(e) Each agency shall—

(1) keep a record of injuries and accidents to its employees whether or not they result in loss of time or in the payment or furnishing of benefits; and

(2) make such statistical or other reports on such forms as the Secretary may prescribe by regulation.

*   *   *   *   *   *   *

DEPARTMENT OF LABOR

AN ACT

To establish an office of Under Secretary of Labor, and three offices of Assistant Secretary of Labor, and to abolish the existing office of Assistant Secretary of Labor and the existing office of Second Assistant Secretary of Labor.

*   *   *   *   *   *   *

SEC. 2. There are established in the Department of Labor [four] *five* offices of Assistant Secretary of Labor, which shall be filled by appointment by the President, by and with the advice and consent of the Senate. *One of such Assistant Secretaries shall be an Assistant Secretary of Labor for Occupational Safety and Health.* Each of the Assistant Secretaries of Labor shall perform such duties as may be prescribed by the Secretary of Labor or required by law.

*   *   *   *   *   *   *

SMALL BUSINESS ACT

AN ACT

To amend the Small Business Act of 1953, as amended.

Be it enacted by the Senate and House of Representatives of the United States of America in Congress assembled, That title II of the Act of July 30, 1953 (Public Law 163, Eighty-third Congress), as amended, is hereby withdrawn as a part of that Act and is made a separate Act to be known as the "Small Business Act".

*   *   *   *   *   *   *

SEC. 4.

*   *   *   *   *   *   *

(c)(1) There are hereby established in the Treasury the following revolving funds: (A) a disaster loan fund which shall be available for financing functions performed under sections 636(b)(1), 636(b)(2), 636(b)(4), 636(b)(6), and 636(c)(2) of this title, including administrative expenses in connection with such functions; and (B) a business loan and investment fund which shall be available for financing functions performed under sections 636(a), 636(b)(3), 636(e), and 637(a) of this title, titles III and V of the Small Business Investment Act of 1958, and title IV of the Economic Opportunity Act of 1964, including administrative expenses in connection with such functions.

*   *   *   *   *   *   *

"SEC. 7. * * *

*   *   *   *   *   *   *

"(b) The Administration also is empowered—

*   *   *   *   *   *   *

"*(6) to make such loans (either directly or in cooperation with banks or other lending institutions through agreements to participate on an immediate or deferred basis) as the Administration may determine to be necessary or appropriate to assist any small business concern in affecting additions to or alterations in the equipment, facilities, or methods of operation of such business in order to comply with the applicable standards promulgated pursuant to section 6 of the Occupational Safety and Health Act or standards adopted by a State pursuant to a plan approved under section 18 of the Occupational Safety and Health Act, if the Administration determines that such concern is likely to suffer substantial economic injury without assistance under this paragraph.*"

APPENDIX A

ADMINISTRATIVE PROCEDURE ACT OF 1946, AS CODIFIED IN TITLE 5, UNITED STATES CODE, EXCERPTS

§ 551. Definitions

For the purpose of this subchapter—

(1) "agency" means each authority of the Government of the United States, whether or not it is within or subject to review by another agency, but does not include—

    (A) the Congress;

    (B) the courts of the United States;

    (C) the governments of the territories or possessions of the United States;

    (D) the government of the District of Columbia; or except as to the requirements of section 552 of this title—

    (E) agencies composed of representatives of the parties or of representatives of organizations of the parties to the disputes determined by them;

    (F) courts-martial and military commissions;

    (G) military authority exercised in the field in time of war or in occupied territory; or

    (H) functions conferred by sections 1738, 1739, 1743, and 1744, of title 12; chapter 2 of title 41; or sections 1622, 1884, 1891–1902, and former section 1641(b)(2), of title 50, appendix;

(2) "person" includes an individual, partnership, corporation, association, or public or private organization other than an agency;

(3) "party" includes a person or agency named or admitted as a party, or properly seeking and entitled as of right to be admitted as a party, in an agency proceeding, and a person or agency admitted by an agency as a party for limited purposes;

(4) "rule" means the whole or a part of an agency statement of general or particular applicability and future effect designed to implement, interpret, or prescribe law or policy or describing the organization, procedure, or practice requirements of an agency and includes the approval or prescription for the future of rates, wages, corporate or financial structures or reorganizations thereof, prices, facilities, appliances, services or allowances therefor or of valuations, costs, or accounting, or practices bearing on any of the foregoing;

(5) "rule making" means agency process for formulating, amending, or repealing a rule;

(6) "order" means the whole or a part of a final disposition, whether affirmative, negative, injunctive, or declaratory in form, of an agency in a matter other than rule making but including licensing;

(7) "adjudication" means agency process for the formulation of an order;

(8) "license" includes the whole or a part of an agency permit, certificate, approval, registration, charter, membership, statutory exemption or other form of permission;

(9) "licensing" includes agency process respecting the grant, renewal, denial, revocation, suspension, annulment, withdrawal, limitation, amendment, modification, or conditioning of a license;

(10) "sanction" includes the whole or a part of an agency.—

(A) prohibition, requirement, limitation, or other condition affecting the freedom of a person;

(B) withholding of relief;

(C) imposition of penalty or fine;

(D) destruction, taking, seizure, or withholding of property;

(E) assessment of damages, reimbursement, restitution, compensation, costs, charges, or fees;

(F) requirement, revocation, or suspension of a license; or

(G) taking other compulsory or restrictive action;

(11) "relief" includes the whole or a part of an agency—

(A) grant of money, assistance, license, authority, exemption, exception, privilege, or remedy;

(B) recognition of a claim, right, immunity, privilege, exemption, or exception; or

(C) taking of other action on the application or petition of, and beneficial to, a person;

(12) "agency proceeding" means an agency process as defined by paragraphs (5), (7), and (9) of this section and

(13) "agency action" includes the whole or a part of an agency rule, order, license, sanction, relief or the equivalent, or denial thereof, or failure to act.

§ 553. Rule making

(a) This section applies, according to the provisions thereof, except to the extent that there is involved—

(1) a military or foreign affairs function of the United States; or

(2) a matter relating to agency management or personnel or to public property, loans, grants, benefits, or contracts.

(b) General notice of proposed rule making shall be published in the Federal Register, unless persons subject thereto are named and either personally served or otherwise have actual notice thereof in accordance with law. The notice shall include—

(1) a statement of the time, place, and nature of public rule making proceedings;

(2) reference to the legal authority under which the rule is proposed; and

(3) either the terms or substance of the proposed rule or a description of the subjects and issues involved.

Except when notice or hearing is required by statute this subsection does not apply—

(A) to interpretative rules, general statements of policy, or rules of agency organization, procedure, or practice; or

(B) when the agency for good cause finds (and incorporates the findings and a brief statement of reasons therefor in the rules issued) that notice and public procedure thereon are impracticable, unnecessary, or contrary to the public interest.

(c) After notice required by this section, the agency shall give interested persons an opportunity to participate in the rule making through submission of written data, views, or arguments with or without opportunity for oral presentation. After consideration of the relevant matter presented, the agency shall incorporate in the rules adopted a concise general statement of their basis and purpose. When rules are required by statute to be made on the record after opportunity for an agency hearing, sections 556 and 557 of this title apply instead of this subsection.

(d) The required publication or service of a substantive rule shall be made not less than 30 days before its effective date, except—

    (1) a substantive rule which grants or recognizes an exemption or relieves a restriction;

    (2) interpretative rules and statements of policy; or

    (3) as otherwise provided by the agency for good cause found and published with the rule.

(e) Each agency shall give an interested person the right to petition for the issuance, amendment, or repeal of a rule.

§ 554. Adjudications

(a) This section applies, according to the provisions thereof, in every case of adjudication required by statute to be determined on the record after opportunity for an agency hearing, except to the extent that there is involved—

    (1) a matter subject to a subsequent trial of the law and the facts de novo in a court;

    (2) the selection or tenure of an employee, except a hearing examiner appointed under section 3105 of this title;

    (3) proceedings in which decisions rest solely on inspections, tests, or elections;

    (4) the conduct of military or foreign affairs functions;

    (5) cases in which an agency is acting as an agent for a court; or

    (6) the certification of worker representatives.

(b) Persons entitled to notice of an agency hearing shall be timely informed of—

    (1) the time, place, and nature of the hearing;

    (2) the legal authority and jurisdiction under which the hearing is to be held; and

    (3) the matters of fact and law asserted.

When private persons are the moving parties, other parties to the proceeding shall give prompt notice of issues controverted in fact or law; and in other instances agencies may by rule require responsive pleading. In fixing the time and place for hearings, due regard shall be had for the convenience and necessity of the parties or their representatives.

(c) The agency shall give all interested parties opportunity for—

    (1) the submission and consideration of facts, arguments, offers of settlement, or proposals of adjustment when time, the nature o the proceeding, and the public interest permit; and

    (2) to the extent that the parties are unable so to determine a controversy by consent, hearing and decision on notice and in accordance with sections 556 and 557 of this title.

(d) The employee who presides at the reception of evidence pursuant to section 556 of this title shall make the recommended decision or initial decision required by section 557 of this title, unless he becomes unavailable to the agency. Except to the extent required for the disposition of ex parte matters as authorized by law, such an employee may not—

    (1) consult a person or party on a fact in issue, unless on notice and opportunity for all parties to participate; or

    (2) be responsible to or subject to the supervision or direction of an employee or agent engaged in the performance of investigative or prosecuting functions for an agency.

An employee or agent engaged in the performance of investigative or prosecuting functions for an agency in a case may not, in that or a factually related case, participate or advise in the decision, recommended decision, or agency review pursuant to section 557 of this title, except as witness or counsel in public proceedings. This subsection does not apply—

    (A) in determining applications for initial licenses;

    (B) to proceedings involving the validity or application of rates, facilities, or practices of public utilities or carriers; or

    (C) to the agency or a member or members of the body comprising the agency.

(e) The agency, with like effect as in the case of other orders, and in its sound discretion, may issue a declaratory order to terminate a controversy or remove uncertainty.

§ 555. Ancillary matters

(a) This section applies, according to the provisions thereof, except as otherwise provided by this subchapter.

(b) A person compelled to appear in person before an agency or representative thereof is entitled to be accompanied, represented, and advised by counsel or, if permitted by the agency, by other qualified representative. A party is entitled to appear in person or by or with counsel or other duly qualified representative in an agency proceeding. So far as the orderly conduct of public business permits, an interested person may appear before an agency or its responsible employees for the presentation, adjustment, or determination of an issue, request, or controversy in a proceeding, whether interlocutory, summary, or otherwise, or in connection with an agency function. With due regard for the convenience and necessity of the parties or their representatives and within a reasonable time, each agency shall proceed to conclude a matter presented to it. This subsection does not grant or deny a person who is not a lawyer the right to appear for or represent others before an agency or in an agency proceedings.

(c) Process, requirement of a report, inspection, or other investigative act or demand may not be issued made, or enforced except as authorized by law. A person compelled to submit data or evidence is entitled to retain or, on payment of lawfully prescribed costs, procure a copy or transcript thereof, except that in a nonpublic investigatory proceeding the witness may for good cause be limited to inspection of the official transcript of his testimony.

(d) Agency subpenas authorized by law shall be issued to a party on request and, when required by rules of procedure, on a statement or showing of general relevance and reasonable scope of the evidence sought. On contest, the court shall sustain the subpena or similar process or demand to the extent that it found to be in accordance with law. In a proceeding for enforcement, the court shall issue an order requiring the appearance of the witness or the production of the evidence or data within a reasonable time under penalty of punishment for contempt in case of contumacious failure to comply.

(e) Prompt notice shall be given of the denial in whole or in part of a written application, petition, or other request of an interested person made in connection with any agency proceeding. Except in affirming a prior denial or when the denial is self-explanatory, the notice shall be accompanied by a brief statement of the grounds for denial.

§ 556. Hearings; presiding employees; powers and duties; burden of proof; evidence; record as basis of decision

(a) This section applies, according to the provisions thereof, to hearings required by section 553 or 554 of this title to be conducted in accordance with this section.

(b) There shall preside at the taking of evidence—

    (1) the agency;

    (2) one or more members of the body which comprises the agency; or

    (3) one or more hearing examiners appointed under section 3105 of this title.

This subchapter does not supersede the conduct of specified calsses of proceedings, in whole or in part, by or before boards or other employees specially provided for by or designated under statute. The functions of presiding employees and of employees participating in decisions in accordance with section 557 of this title shall be conducted in an impartial manner. A presiding or participating employee may at any time disqualify himself. On the filing in good faith of a timely and sufficient affidavit of personal bias or other disqualification of a presiding or participating employee, the agency shall determine the matter as a part of the record and decision in the case.

(c) Subject to published rules of the agency and within its powers employees presiding at hearings may—

    (1) administer oaths and affirmations;

    (2) issue subpenas authorized by law;

    (3) rule on offers of proof and receive relevant evidence;

    (4) take depositions or have depositions taken when the ends of justice would be served;

    (5) regulate the course of the hearing;

    (6) hold conferences for the settlement or simplification of the issues by consent of the parties;

    (7) dispose of procedural requests or similar matters;

    (8) make or recommend decisions in accordance with section 557 of this title; and

    (9) take other action authorized by agency rule consistent with this subchapter.

(d) Except as otherwise provided by statute, the proponent of a rule or order has the burden of proof. Any oral or documentary evidence may be received, but the agency as a matter of policy shall provide for the exclusion of irrelevant, immaterial, or unduly repetitious evidence. A sanction may not be imposed or rule or order issued except on consideration of the whole record or those parts thereof cited by a party and supported by and in accordance with the reliable, probative, and substantial evidence. A party is entitled to present his case or defense by oral or documentary evidence, to submit rebuttal evidence, and to conduct such cross-examination as may be required for a full and true disclosure of the facts. In rule making or determining claims for money or benefits or applications for initial licenses an agency may, when a party will not be prejudiced thereby, adopt procedures for the submission of all or part of the evidence in written form.

(e) The transcript of testimony and exhibits, together with all papers and requests filed in the proceeding, constitutes the exclusive record for decision in accordance with section 557 of this title and, on payment of lawfully prescribed costs, shall be made available to the parties. When an agency decision rests on official notice of a material fact not appearing in the evidence in the record, a party is entitled, on timely request, to an opportunity to show the contrary.

§ 557. Initial decisions; conclusiveness; review by agency; submissions by parties; contents of decisions; record

(a) This section applies according to the provisions thereof, when a hearing is required to be conducted in accordance with section 556 of this title.

(b) When the agency did not preside at the reception of the evidence, the presiding employee or, in cases not subject to section 554 (d) of this title, an employee qualified to preside at hearings pursuant to section 556 of this title, shall initially decide the case unless the agency requires, either in specific cases or by general rule, the entire record to be certified to it for decision. When the presiding employee makes an initial decision, that decision then becomes the decision of the agency without further proceedings unless there is an appeal to, or review on motion of, the agency within time provided by rule. On appeal from or review of the initial decision, the agency has all the powers which it would have in making the initial decision except as it may limit the issues on notice or by rule. When the agency makes the decision without having presided at the reception of the evidence, the presiding employee or an employee qualified to preside at hearings pursuant to section 556 of this title shall first recommend a decision, except that in rule making or determining applications for initial licenses—

(1) instead thereof the agency may issue a tentative decision or one of its responsible employees may recommend a decision; or

(2) this procedure may be omitted in a case in which the agency finds on the record that due and timely execution of its functions imperatively and unavoidably so requires.

(c) Before a recommended, initial, or tentative decision, or a decision on agency review of the decision of subordinate employees, the parties are entitled to a reasonable opportunity to submit for the consideration of the employees participating in the decisions—

(1) proposed findings and conclusions; or

(2) exceptions to the decisions or recommended decisions of subordinate employees or to tentative agency decisions; and

(3) supporting reasons for the exceptions or proposed findings or conclusions.

The record shall show the ruling on each finding, conclusion, or exception presented. All decisions, including initial, recommended, and tentative decisions, are a part of the record and shall include a statement of—

(A) findings and conclusions, and the reasons or basis therefor, on all the material issues of fact, law, or discretion presented on the record; and

(B) the appropriate rule, order, sanction, relief, or denial thereof.

§ 558. Imposition of sanctions; determination of applications for licenses; suspension, revocation, and expiration of licenses

(a) This section applies, according to the provisions thereof, to the exercise of a power or authority.

(b) A sanction may not be imposed or a substantive rule or order issued except within jurisdiction delegated to the agency and as authorized by law.

(c) When application is made for a license required by law, the agency, with due regard for the rights and privileges of all the interested parties or adversely affected persons and within a reasonable time, shall set and complete proceedings required to be conducted in accordance with sections 556 and 557 of this title or other proceedings required by law and shall make its decision. Except in cases of willfulness or those in which public health, interest, or safety requires otherwise, the withdrawal, suspension, revocation, or annulment of a license is lawful only if, before the institution of agency proceedings therefor, the license has been given—

(1) notice by the agency in writing of the facts or conduct which may warrant the action; and

(2) opportunity to demonstrate or achieve compliance with all lawful requirements.

When the licensee has made timely and sufficient application for a renewal or a new license in accordance with agency rules, a license with reference to an activity of a continuing nature does not expire until the application has been finally determined by the agency.

§ 559. Effect on other laws; effect of subsequent statute

This subchapter, chapter 7, and sections 1305, 3105, 3344, 4301(2) (E), 5362, and 7521, and the provisions of section 5335 (a)(B) of this title that relate to hearing examiners, do not limit or repeal additional requirements imposed by statute or otherwise recognized by law. Except as otherwise required by law, requirements or privileges relating to evidence or procedure apply equally to agencies and persons. Each agency is granted the authority necessary to comply with the requirements of this subchapter through the issuance of rules or otherwise. Subsequent statute may not be held to supersede or modify this subchapter, chapter 7, sections 1305, 3105, 3344, 4301(2)(E), 5362, or 7521, or the provisions of section 5335(a)(B) of this title that relate to hearing examiners, except to the extent that it does so expressly.

INDIVIDUAL VIEWS OF MR. JAVITS

The bill reported herewith is the most important piece of legislation affecting American workers to be considered by Congress in many years. Each year over 14,000 Americans are killed at work, more than 2,000,000 suffer disabling injuries, and uncounted thousands fall victims to occupational diseases such as silicosis, asbestosis, bysinosis, pesticide and chemical poisoning, lung and bladder cancer, and other horrible byproducts of our industrial progress.

There is no dispute that a strong Federal occupational health and safety program is necessary if we are to achieve a real diminution in this industrial carnage. The statistics on occupational injury, disease and death show all too clearly that private industry and the States are not doing an adequate job of insuring health and safety in the workplace. Nor is there any dispute that the Federal program should include promulgation and enforcement of Federal standards, and substantial aid to those States willing to operate an occupational health and safety program that meets Federal standards.

Yet, despite the substantial agreement which exists as to the objective of this legislation, the most bitter labor-management political fight in years has erupted over the means to achieve that objective. The lines have hardened around the so-called Daniels bill, reported out by the House Education and Labor Committee (H.R. 16785) and the Administration bill, introduced by Congressmen Steiger and Sikes in the House (H.R. 19200), and by Senator Dominick in the Senate (S. 4404). All efforts to work out a fair and moderate compromise have been so far rebuffed.

In this Committee, most of the differences between the Daniels bill and the Administration bill were resolved—frequently through the adoption of amendments offered by the minority. As I shall point out below, in the wide areas where the Committee was able to reach such agreement, the provisions of the Committee bill are, in my view, clearly superior to corresponding provisions of either the Daniels or the Administration bill.

Unfortunately, the Committee was unable to resolve all the differences. The key issue which remains, and the one which has polarized labor and management, is whether the Secretary of Labor should, in addition to his functions as prosecutor shall also be given the power to promulgate standards and adjudicate enforcement cases. The Committee bill reported herewith, and the Daniels bill, would give the Secretary all of these powers, as urged by spokesmen for organized labor; the Administration bill would separate them by giving the quasi-legislative power to promulgate standards to a five-man board and the quasi-judicial power of adjudication to an independent three-man Panel, as urged (or at least acquiesced in) by spokesmen for the business community. The members of the Board and the Panel would be Presidentially appointed with the advice and consent of the Senate.

It is most regrettable that the dispute over this issue should have become so bitter as to jeopardize seriously the prospects for enactment of this bill during this session of Congress, especially since either approach has both merits and demerits. I, for one, believe that in the light of over 30 years of utterly dismal performance by the Department of Labor of its safety and health responsibilities under the Walsh-Healey Act, labor has little reason to expect, or business any reason to fear, overly energetic administration of this Act by the Secretary of Labor or disregard by him of the legitimate concerns of business. Justice Holmes' famous aphorism, "The life of the law has not been logic: it has been experience.", applies as much to the process of shaping legislation as it does to deciding questions of common law.

Conversely, our experience with multimember independent administrative agencies (e.g. the National Labor Relations Board), especially in the area of quasi-judicial adjudication, has been neither so uniformly bad nor so uniformly good, or favorable to business, as compared to our experience with administration by cabinet-level officials, that we can assume that the use of such an agency would seriously weaken (or strengthen) this legislation. Cabinet-level officials are, it is true, more sensitive to political influences and can be held accountable for the failure of their Departments, but political influences are, at best, a two-edged sword, and completely improper, in any event, where adjudication is concerned.

Attempts at Compromise of the Basic Issue

In an attempt to resolve this obstacle to agreement by the Committee on a bill, I suggested a compromise amendment under which the Secretary of Labor would promulgate standards and a three-man independent Panel (similar to that provided in the Administration bill) would adjudicate enforcement cases. Unfortunately the Committee, after first expressing interest, rejected the compromise by a vote of 10 to 7. Since the same issue may well arise again when this bill is considered by the Senate, I believe a brief statement concerning my compromise amendment is appropriate.

In the area of adjudication, there are several reasons for preferring an independent panel approach, especially in the form proposed by the Administration and embodied in my amendment.

First, under the procedures established by the amendment, speed of enforcement would be greatly increased. In most contested cases, between six months and two years would be saved under the provisions which provide for true self-enforcing orders and discretionary review of trial examiner decisions.

Under the Committee bill, no enforceable order to correct a violation would issue until the completion of all administrative and judicial review proceedings. This would involve, at a minimum in a contested case, (1) hearings by a trial examiner, (2) mandatory review of the decision by the Secretary or his designee, and (3) review by a Court of Appeals. It is doubtful that this process could be completed in less than 18 months (two years would be a more realistic estimate) in a seriously contested case.

Under my amendment, an enforceable order would issue at the end of the administrative review stage, rather than after judicial review (unless the Court of Appeals issued a stay). Furthermore, the administrative review stage itself would be shortened by three to six months in many cases by making review by the Panel of trial examiners' decisions discretionary. If review were denied, the trial examiners' decision would automatically become the final order of the Panel and enforceable as such.

Second, hearing and determination of enforcement cases by an independent panel more closely accords with traditional notions of due process than would hearing and determination by the Secretary. In the latter case the Secretary is essentially acting as prosecutor and judge. Any finding by the Secretary in favor of a respondent would be essentially a repudiation by the Secretary of his own Department's employees. While this type of enforcement has been used in connection with other statutes, is contemplated by the Administrative Procedures Act, and is not jurisdictionally defective on due process grounds, the awkward mechanics it imposes upon heads of Departments who wish to exercise their adjudicatory power personally in order to preserve due process has not generally been appreciated. What happens is that one official of the Department (e.g. the Deputy Solicitor) will take the position of prosecutor and another official (e.g. the Solicitor) will take the position of a neutral in order to advise the Secretary.

More important, because of the awkwardness of this procedure and the heavy burden of personally reviewing hundreds of enforcement cases, it is highly likely that the Secretary of Labor will not even exercise his power under the Committee bill personally, but will delegate it to a panel of officials within the Department. That is precisely what the Secretary of Interior has done under the Coal Mine Health and Safety Act of 1969. The net result will be enforcement by a panel anyway, but not one which is independent, and without the benefit of the shortened procedures which my amendment would provide.

These considerations, it seems to me, outweigh any possible benefits which might be gained from the better "coordination" which would allegedly occur if the adjudicatory power, as well as the prosecutorial and standards setting powers were given to the Secretary. Such coordination as is necessary would seem just as readily attainable with a Panel as with the Secretary. It is the prosecutors upon whom this burden will primarily fall and under either approach they will be under the Secretary's control.

In short, the adjudicatory scheme of the Committee bill can be made to work, and due process can be preserved under it, but the independent Panel approach would do the same job faster, preserve due process more easily, and thereby instill much more confidence in the whole program in workers and businessmen alike.

Imminent Danger Orders

The other issue upon which the Committee was unable to reach agreement is the procedure for dealing with imminent dangers. The Committee rejected an amendment which would have required the Secretary to obtain a court order to secure prompt relief against an imminent danger. The Committee bill (properly, in my view) permits remedial orders to be issued by the Secretary for 72 hours in the case of an imminent danger. However, the Committee did adopt amendments proposed by Senator Schweiker designed to guard against abuse of discretion in the exercise of this extraordinary power. The amendments provide (a) that such orders are to be issued by the Secretary or his representative only if there is not sufficient time, in light of the nature and imminence of the danger to seek and obtain a court order, (b) that no such order may be issued without the concurrence of an appropriate regional official of the Labor Department, and (c) that the Secretary must provide appropriate procedures to permit employers to obtain expeditious, informal reconsideration of such orders. None of these safeguards is contained in the Daniels bill.

Resolution of Other Issues—Minority Amendments

On the numerous other issues involved in this legislation the Committee was able to reach virtually complete agreement. Many of the more difficult problems were resolved, and the bill thereby strengthened, through the adoption of amendments offered by members of the minority. Among the more important of these amendments are the following:

JAVITS AMENDMENTS

1. *National Institute of Occupational Health and Safety.*—This amendment would establish a new institute, to be known as the National Institute of Occupational Health and Safety in the Department of Health, Education, and Welfare. The establishment of this institute will elevate the status of occupational health and safety research to place it on an equal footing with the research conducted by HEW into other matters of vital social concern, particularly in the health area. Such an institute will be able to attract the qualified personnel necessary to engage in occupational health and safety research if we are to make any real progress in reducing job-related injury and disease under the Act, and will much more easily attract the substantial increase in funding which will be necessary to achieve the purposes of this act.

Equally important, the research and recommendations of the institute will be of critical importance in continually improving occupational health and safety standards promulgated under this act. The primary source of these standards at this time are the various consensus and proprietary organizations such as the American National Standards Institute and the American Conference of Governmental and Industrial Hygienists. Without in any way denigrating the substantial contributions to occupational health and safety which such organizations have already made, and which they will undoubtedly continue to make, it is apparent that the government must develop a capacity for developing these standards which will operate independently of self interest groups.

2. *National Commission on Workmen's Compensation.*—The Committee bill includes provisions establishing a broadly based fifteen member national commission on State workmen's compensation laws. As this report points out elsewhere, serious questions have been raised concerning the adequacy of existing State workmen's compensation programs. The study and recommendations of this commission will be of invaluable assistance in upgrading these programs and in determining what, if any, further action by the federal government should be taken in this area.

3. *Economic Assistance to Small Business (with Senators Dominick and Saxbe).*—This amendment authorizes loans to small businesses adversely affected by the need to comply with this act. Similar provisions are included in both the Administration and the Daniels bills.

4. *Feasibility of Standards.*—As a result of this amendment the Secretary, in setting standards, is expressly required to consider feasibility of proposed standards. This is an improvement over the Daniels bill, which might be interpreted to require absolute health and safety in all cases, regardless of feasibility, and the Administration bill, which contains no criteria for standards at all.

5. *Modification of General Duty.*—As the result of this amendment the general duty of employers was clarified to require maintenance of a workplace free from "recognized" hazards. This is a significant improvement over the Administration bill, which requires employers to maintain the workplace free from "readily apparent" hazards. That approach would not cover non-obvious hazards discovered in the course of inspection. It is also better than the corresponding provision of the Daniels bill which embraces all hazards. In addition, the provisions of the Committee bill which provide a penalty only for failure to correct a violation of the general duty requirement are better than the provisions of the Administration bill which impose a penalty on an employer for his initial violation of the duty, as well as his failure to correct it.

6. *Confidentiality of Inspection Reports and Other Material.*—Under this amendment publication of ordinarily confidential matter, such as inspection reports, is left to the discretion of the Secretary, rather than required, as is the case under the Daniels bill.

DOMINICK AMENDMENTS

1. *Modification of State plan provisions to exclude employees of political subdivisions not subject to the jurisdiction to the States.*—This amendment removed what might operate as a substantial impediment to the ability of the States to adopt plans meeting federal requirements by limiting the States' responsibility to adopt a safety program for State and local employees only to those employees over which they have jurisdiction and authority in this respect.

2. *Protection of trade secrets.*—This amendment provided protection against disclosure of trade secrets in enforcement proceedings by requiring the Secretary or the court to issue appropriate orders for the protection of the confidentiality of trade secrets.

3. *Reopening of abatement order.*—Under this amendment the language of the bill was modified to make it clear that in the event of factors beyond the employers' control preventing him, in good faith, from complying with an abatement order which has previously become final, he may apply for modification of the order to the Secretary. No such provision is contained in either the Daniels bill or the Administration bill.

SAXBE AMENDMENTS

1. *Right of employees and their representatives to accompany inspectors.*—As a result of this amendment the provisions of both the Administration and the Daniels bills permitting authorized representatives of employees to accompany inspectors have been clarified and protected from abuse by provisions making such right clearly subject to

regulations of the Secretary, defining the purpose of such accompaniment as aid of the inspection, and extending mandatory consultation rights to a reasonable number of employees where there is no "authorized" represenative of employees. In the absence of such provisions the Secretary might well find himself required to resolve union organizing issues which have no relationship to this legislation.

2. *Limitation on use of shortened procedures for adoption of proprietary standards.*—Under this amendment the use of somewhat shortened procedures (a hearing would be discretionary) for promulgation of proprietary standards is limited to proprietary standards adopted prior to the date of enactment of this act. This will avoid the possibility of proprietary groups adopting or modifying standards because of the possibility that they can be more easily adopted under this act. The discretionary provisions of the Committee bill concerning the adoption of such standards are much better than those of the Administration bill, which does not provide any shortened procedure for the adoption of such standards, and those in the Daniels bill which require the adoption of virtually all such standards.

3. *Inspections on demand.*—As a result of this amendment the provisions of the bill requiring an inspection to be conducted by the Secretary as soon as possible upon receipt of a notice from employees alleging a violation of standards or imminent danger were modified to require such an inspection as soon as practicable only if the Secretary determines there are reasonable grounds to believe that an alleged violation or danger exists. This will ensure that inspections are not required in response to groundless complaints, and will permit the Secretary to schedule such inspections more flexibly.

4. *Payment by the government of the cost of research and medical examinations.*—These amendments provided for the furnishing of assistance by the federal government to employers for additional expenses incurred by them in conducting monitoring and measuring required by the Secretary of Health, Education, and Welfare for research purposes, and for payment by the government of the costs of medical examinations required by standards where such examinations are in the nature of research.

JACOB K. JAVITS.

INDIVIDUAL VIEWS OF MR. SAXBE

I too favored and voted for the independent board approach to the promulgation and enforcement of occupational health and safety standards. The concentration of power within the Department of Labor as proposed by the reported bill would not promote the stated objectives of the legislation. These objections are more fully stated in the minority views.

I voted in favor of reporting the committee bill, however, because I believe legislation on this subject should be considered by the Senate. Each year more than 14,000 people are killed as a result of occupational accidents. More than 2,000,000 persons are disabled. 250,000 days of labor are lost each year. The problem is not improving.

I also agree with the minority objection to the imminent danger provision permitting an inspector, upon consultation with regional personnel to issue an order for immediate remedial action including closing of a plant or department. Although the Committee accepted an amendment which required consultation with regional personnel, I still believe that an inspector finding a hazardous condition should seek injunctive relief in the courts.

WILLIAM B. SAXBE.

MINORITY VIEWS OF MESSRS. DOMINICK AND SMITH OF ILLINOIS

I. THE NEED FOR LEGISLATION

The need for occupational safety and health legislation is well-recognized in this Nation today. Over and over again the statistics relating to injury, death, and disease in American industry have been brought to the attention of Congress. The need has also been recognized by the President of the United States in three separate messages.

It is our belief that all members of Congress are in accord with the President in his desire to provide a legislative answer to the safety and health problems of our Nation's workforce. The law which we provide must call for the promulgation of strong standards to insure occupational health and safety. The bill we pass must be workable and effective. This means the bill must establish realistic mechanisms which call not only for the development and enforcement of strong standards but will also be fair and accord all parties, including employers subject to regulation, due process.

We do not believe that the Committee bill provides the mechanisms which will meet these objectives. The narrow, single-minded approach of the bill fails to provide due process to those subject to regulation. The procedures it provides are unworkable and not truly effective. The bill also fails to adequately utilize all resources available to combat the problem and hence fails to meet the needs of our workforce. Indeed, the bill is opposed by the Administration, employers, State occupational health and safety agencies, and by national standards producing organizations while its primary support comes from the leadership of large unions. Therefore, we are unable to support the bill in its present form and urge the consideration of the alternatives discussed below.

The basic scheme of the bill, as reported, is this: All authority for action is concentrated in the office of the Secretary of Labor. He will promulgate the standards of safety and health. He will conduct inspections and investigations to detect violations of the standards. He will charge those he believes have violated the standards by citation and penalty assessments. Upon any challenge of penalty assessment or issuance of a citation, the Secretary or his agent must defend the penalty or citation against the challenge. The Secretary is also responsible for hearing any such challenge and issuing an order affirming, denying, or modifying the original penalty or citation. Finally, the Secretary will be authorized to defend his order or seek its enforcement in the Court of Appeals. All functions, including standard setting, investigation, prosecution, adjudication, and review are settled in the hands of the Secretary.

The philosophy of this approach by the Majority is clear. All power and authority must be centralized in the hands of a single person—

the Secretary of Labor. Few safeguards or restrictions are to be placed on the authority of the Secretary.

In one sense, the concentration of power into the hands of a single person is obviously more efficient—provided that person exercises that power in accord with the wishes of those who concentrate the power. The concentration of power also simplifies the problems of those who wish to persuade the Secretary to accept a particular point of view.

While the concentration of authority may lead to more efficient action in line with a particular point of view, it also raises the sceptre of abuse. A single man is easier to harass than an independent standards board or quasi-judicial panel. With the concentration of power in the hands of one man, he will be subject to intense political pressure to act a particular way. If he fails to act in accord with the wishes of a particular group, he may be subjected to court action for tort liability.

The concentration of authority in the hands of the Secretary necessarily precludes the utilization of other approaches to achieve compliance. The scheme of enforcement established by the bill effectively discourages positive State and private initiative.

Private initiative is encouraged only through the strong negative incentive program. Employers are faced with swift inspections, swift penalties and virtually self-enforcing orders. The punitive powers of the Secretary are the keystone of the enforcement process. The Secretary issues the citation and the assessment of penalty prior to any hearing. Only through an appeal can the employer challenge the administrative determination of a violation. And then, under the bill, the appeal is to the Secretary for relief. This approach does not encourage voluntary compliance. It does not place emphasis on cooperation between employers, employees and the regulatory agent. Its focus is on motivation through "the stick" rather than through "the carrot." Indeed, this approach is apparently based on the erroneous assumption that most employers are actively and maliciously seeking to avoid safety and health responsibilities.

The role of state governments in the regulatory scheme is also limited. A state may assume responsibility for regulation only on the submission of a stringent state plan. The Secretary must monitor the plan and has authority to revoke it if he finds it does not meet the strict requirements of the plan.

However, while we find the scheme advanced by the bill as reported to be objectionable, we believe that the broad objectives of the bill can be achieved. We believe that the need for regulation and the need for procedural safeguards can be reconciled. We urge the consideration of alternatives which will achieve the desired substantive regulation yet will supply the procedural safeguards necessary for fair determination of rights, responsibilities, and obligations of all parties.

II. ALTERNATIVES

As noted above, the concentration of all authority in the hands of the Secretary of Labor is the great failing of the bill as reported. There are two alternatives which will cure this objection.

First, the bill should provide for an Occupational Safety and Health Board. The Board would be composed of five members, appointed by the President, who would designate the Chairman from among the Board Members. A background in the field of occupational health and safety would be required for at least three members.

The Board approach is the soundest approach to standard-promulgation for several reasons.

One, the development of occupational health and safety standards involves technical and complex problems requiring professional expertise and competence. Establishing a separate Board of competent professional experts will bring far greater expertise to the job of establishing standards than the Secretary of Labor with all of this other job functions can achieve.

Two, since the standards to be established under this Act involve both health and safety, the resources of HEW as well as the Labor Department must be closely coordinated. The independent Board assures that both aspects are given equal consideration and that their policies and practices in this area are uniform.

Three, the establishing of an independent Board for standard-promulgation will separate the quasi-legislative function from the enforcement function of the Secretary. The Board can be held responsible for the development of standards. It can concentrate on using the expertise of its members to develop the technological rules necessary to maintain health and safety. The Secretary will not be placed in the intolerable position of being called to task for rule-making responsibilities and enforcement responsibilities. Further, as is usual in administrative agency situations, there will be no difficulty in telling who is wearing what hat when. A separate Board whose members are professional experts will achieve a far greater degree of public confidence than a Secretary of Labor who combines the roles of rule-maker, inspector, prosecutor, and adjudicator of violations.

In addition to the separation of the quasi-legislative function from the inspection and prosecution functions, the quasi-judicial function should be removed from the hands of the Secretary and placed in an independent panel. After investigation and inspection, the Secretary issues a citation which sets forth the violation and the order necessary to correct the violation.

At this point, under the bill, the party aggrieved by such an order must appeal to the Secretary. We believe that traditional concepts of due process dictate that this function be carried out by a panel independent of the Secretary. This will obviate the inevitable conflict which arises when the Secretary must review his own actions as carried out by the various subordinate levels of the Department.

In addition to the two key provisions mentioned above, there are other provisions of the committee bill which we feel are contrary to a proper balance between the need for regulation and the need for safeguards. These provisions carry a potential for abuse which may lead to a lack of confidence in the enforcement of this important legislation. They also follow the single-minded punitive approach of the Majority rather than seeking true compliance with the objectives of this bill. These provisions include:

(1) The imminent danger provision permitting an inspector, upon consultation with Regional personnel, to issue an order for immediate remedial action including closing of a plant or department.

(2) The so-called walk-around provision which requires an inspector to permit an authorized representative of employees to

accompany the inspector on any physical tour of a plant or business operation.

Therefore, we respectfully urge that consideration be given to modifying the committee bill to remedy the deficiencies. We believe that a compromise which adequately balances the need for regulation with the concerns which we have expressed must be reached. The modifications we have suggested do not destroy the essential elements of the regulatory process. The bill provides for standard-setting, inspection, and investigation, enforcement and adjudication. However, these functions will be carried out within a framework of due process and all interests will be properly balanced.

PETER H. DOMINICK,
RALPH TYLER SMITH.

○

APPENDIX F

COMPARATIVE ANALYSIS

A comparison of the House and Senate bills with the conference bill approved by both Houses was prepared by the House Labor Committee. The comparison shows where the House receded (H.R.), where the Senate receded (S.R.), and where either receded with an amendment made in the final bill rather than taking the exact provision of either earlier one (H.R. or S.R. w/am.).

THE OCCUPATIONAL SAFETY AND HEALTH ACT

ITEM	HOUSE BILL	SENATE BILL	CONFERENCE REPORT
Standards —Issued By	National Occupational Safety and Health Board.	Secretary of Labor.	**H.R.** Secretary of Labor (Section 6 (a)).
—Procedures for Setting Standards.	Formal rule-making procedures of Administrative Procedure Act.	Informal rule-making procedures of the Administrative Procedure Act.	**H.R.** Informal rule-making procedures of the Administrative Procedure Act. (Section 6 (b) (2) and (3).)
—Hearings.	Hearing on a proposed rule mandatory.	Hearing required only when requested by any interested persons.	**H.R.** Hearing required only when requested by any interested persons. (Section 6 (b) (3).)
—Proprietary Standards.	No provision for shortened rule-making procedure for issuance of existing proprietary standards.	Presently existing proprietary standards may be used during 2-year period utilizing informal APA rule-making procedures.	**S.R.** No provision for shortened rule-making procedure for issuance of existing proprietary standards.
—Development of Standards.	In the development of standards, the House bill did not require that the feasibility of a standard be considered.	Required that when in the development of standards consideration be given to the feasibility of the standard and experience gained under this Act and other health and safety laws.	**H.R. w/am.** Contains the Senate language with the Javits Variance addition—under which employers may petition for a temporary order granting a variance from a standard. Such an order is only to be granted if the employer shows he is unable to comply with a standard for the following limited reasons: unavailability of professional or

—Emergency Temporary Standards.	Limited to standards on toxic substances or new hazards "resulting from the introduction of new processes."	Issued when it is determined employees are exposed to grave danger from toxic substances, harmful physical agents, or new hazards.	technical personnel or of necessary materials or equipment or because necessary construction or alteration of facilities cannot be completed in time. Employees are entitled to a hearing on the order. Such an order may be issued for a maximum period of one year and may not be renewed more than twice. (Section 6(b)) **H.R.** Issued when it is determined employees are exposed to grave danger from toxic substances, harmful physical agents, or new hazards.
—Pre-enforcement Review.	Limited to review in D.C. Court of Appeals within *30 days* of issuance of standard. Court review of standards would be on the basis of a *substantial evidence test.*	Provides for review in circuit where employee does business *within 60 days* after date of issuance. Court review of standards was on the basis of *arbitrary and capricious test.*	**S.R. w/am.** Provides for review in circuit where employer does business *within 60 days* after date of issuance but with a *substantial evidence test.*
Inspections —Self Inspections.	No provision.	Secretary could require periodic self inspections by the employer and certification of the results.	**H.R. w/am.** Self inspection may be required but no certification of results.
—Walk Around.	A representative authorized by the employee had to be given an opportunity to accompany an inspector if the employer or his representative accompanied the inspector.	Both a management and employee representative had to be given opportunity to accompany an inspector.	**H.R.** Both a management and employee representative have to be given opportunity to accompany an inspector.

ITEM	HOUSE BILL	SENATE BILL	CONFERENCE REPORT
Citations —Issuance.	If upon the basis of an inspection or investigation, the Secretary *believes* that an employer has violated requirements — of this Act, he shall issue a citation to the employer.	If upon an inspection or investigation, the Secretary—determines that an employer has violated—he shall issue *forthright* a citation to the employer.	**H.R. w/am.** When the Secretary *believes* that an employer has violated—he shall issue a citation with *reasonable promptness*. It is the understanding of the Managers that unless there is exceptional circumstance, delay in issuance of citation is not expected to exceed 72 hours.
—Statute of Limitations.	Prohibited the issuance of a citation more than *3 months* after the occurrence of any violation.	No statute of limitations.	**S.R. w/am.** Prohibits issuance of a citation more than *6 months* after the occurrence of a violation.
—Appeal.	The right to appeal the time allowed for abatement of a violation was provided to the employer only.	Employees as well as employers have a right to appeal.	**H.R. w/am.** Employees are given right to appeal as well as employers. In addition, employer shall have right to reopen the proceedings for a rehearing in the event it is impossible to comply with the abatement requirements within the period provided for in the citation.
Judicial Proceedings —Rights.	Limited right of appeal to the employer or the Secretary within 60 days of Commission's orders.	Any person adversely affected or aggrieved has a right to appeal.	**H.R.** Any person adversely affected or aggrieved has a right to appeal.
—Court.	Review in Court of Appeals in the circuit where violation occurs or where employer has principal office.	Review in Court of Appeals in the circuit where violation occurs or where employer has principal office, or the D.C. Court of Appeals.	**H.R.** Review in Court of Appeals in the circuit where violation occurs or where employer has principal office, or the D.C. Court of Appeals.

Employees Discriminated Against.	Civil and criminal penalties for employers who discriminate against employees.	Administrative remedies to obtain relief for an employee discriminated against —including reinstatement with backpay.	Judicial remedy by Secretary for **reinstatement** and backpay as well as criminal penalties.
Imminent Danger —Administrative Order.	Not authorized.	Permitted the Secretary to issue an administrative imminent danger shutdown order where there was insufficient time to obtain a court order for 72 hours.	**S.R.** No authority for administrative imminent danger shutdown.
—Court Action.	Authorized Secretary to seek court orders to restrain conditions or practices which cause imminent danger. Temporary restraining order was to remain in effect only 5 days.	Authorizes Secretary to seek court order to **remove** or correct imminent danger together with withdrawal of endangered persons other than "those necessary to correct the danger, maintain the operating capacity of the continuous process operation or permit a safe or orderly shutdown." No time limit on the duration of a temporary restraining order.	**S.R. w/am.** Secretary is authorized to seek court order to restrain conditions or practices which cause imminent danger; such order may not, however, provide for the withdrawal of persons "whose presence is necessary to avoid, correct or remove imminent danger or to maintain capacity for the continuous process operation, to resume normal operations without a complete cessation of operations." Temporary restraining order in effect only 5 days.
—Failure to Act.	Where the Secretary unreasonably failed to seek relief, an employee injured could bring an action for damages in the Court of Claims.	If the Secretary arbitrarily or capriciously failed to act, employee was authorized to seek a writ of mandamus.	**H.R.** If the Secretary arbitrarily or capriciously fails to act, employee is authorized to seek a writ of mandamus.

ITEM	HOUSE BILL	SENATE BILL	CONFERENCE REPORT
Penalties —Civil Penalties	Shall be fined an amount of not more than $1,000 unless violation is deemed not to be of a serious nature in which case a fine of up to $1,000 was discretionary.	Not more than $1,000 for each violation.	S.R. Not more than $1,000 unless violation is deemed not to be of a serious nature in which case a fine of up to $1,000 is discretionary.
—Continuing Penalties.	Penalty of up to $1,000 for each day during which an order which has become final has been violated.	Penalty of not more than $1,000 for each day in which an imminent danger order or final order was violated.	S.R. Penalty of up to $1,000 for each day in which an order which has become final is violated.
—Wilful Penalties	Civil penalty of up to $10,000.	Criminal penalty of not more than $10,000 and/or 6 months imprisonment for first conviction, and $20,000 and/or one year imprisonment after first conviction.	H.R. w/am. Criminal penalty of not more than $10,000 and/or 6 months imprisonment for first conviction, and $20,000 and/or one year imprisonment after first conviction, *but only if the violation results in death to an employee.*
—Advance Notice.	No provision.	Provided a fine not to exceed $1,000 and imprisonment of not more than 6 months for giving advance notice of any inspection.	H.R. Provided a fine not to exceed $1,000 and imprisonment of not more than 6 months for giving advance notice of any inspection.
Effect on Other Laws —Construction Safety.	Construction industry employees were exempt from this Act. Entire construction industry brought un-	Standards under Construction Safety Act were deemed standards under this Act.	H.R. Safety standards of Construction Safety Act are deemed standards under this Act, with the understanding as stated by the Managers that the Secretary will be bound by

	der Construction Safety Act. Enforcement provisions of this Act were made applicable to Construction Safety Act.		principle of collateral estoppel in any enforcement proceedings. (Section 4)
—Others.	Repealed and rescinded Walsh-Healy, Service Contracts, and Arts and Humanities Act standards.	Standards under Walsh-Healy, Service Contracts, Arts and Humanities, and Longshoreman Safety were deemed standards under this Act.	H.R. Standards under Walsh-Healy, Service Contracts, Arts and Humanities, and Longshoreman Safety are deemed standards under this Act. (Section 4)
Duties of Employers.	Employers were required to furnish places of employment "free from any hazards which are *readily apparent and are causing or are likely to cause death or serious physical harm*".	Employers were required to furnish places of employment "free from *recognized hazards* so as to provide safe and helpful working conditions".	S.R. w/am. Employers are required to furnish places of employment free from *recognized hazards that are causing or likely to cause death or serious physical harm*. (Section 5(a)(1))
Duties of Employees.	No provisions.	Required each employee to comply with Occupational Safety and Health standards.	H.R. Requires each employee to comply with Occupational Safety and Health standards. (Section 5 (b))

EXPLANATION OF CHANGES MADE BY CONFERENCE BILL

The conference report was agreed to by the Senate on December 16 and by the House the following day. Chairman Perkins (D-Ky) of the House Labor Committee and Congressman Steiger (R-Wis), sponsor of the Administration safety bill that originally passed the House, inserted in the Congressional Record (Vol. 116) more extensive statements on the measure than they had time to make orally during House debate on the conference report.

Congressman Perkins presented a summary of the differences in the two bills and what the conferees came up with. Congressman Steiger explained what some of the bill's provisions mean and how he thought they were to be applied.

Perkins Explanation
House
12-17-70
pp. 11893-11894

Mr. PERKINS. * * *

Mr. Speaker, I shall review the major differences resolved in the conference report.

THE PROMULGATION OF STANDARDS

A major concession on the part of the managers representing the House of Representatives was with respect to the procedure to be used in the development and promulgation of the health and safety standards. The Members of this body will recall that the Senate bill provided for promulgation of these standards by the Secretary of Labor. The House amendment authorized their promulgation by a National Occupational Safety and Health Board. In the procedures provided for the establishment and promulgation of standards there were many similarities in the Senate bill and the House amendment. For instance, both the Secretary and Board were permitted to begin rulemaking on their own motion or on the basis of petitions. Some of the procedural differences resulted mainly, however, from the choice of the respective bodies as to who should do the rulemaking. The chief difference lay in the fact that the procedure for setting standards under the House amendment were under the formal rulemaking procedures also provided in the Administrative Procedure Act. The House receded on the procedure for promulgating standards. We accepted the Secretary of Labor as the promulgator of the standards and we adopted the informal rule-making procedures which the Senate bill authorized.

We accepted a provision that hearings should be required only when requested by interested parties, and did not require a hearing on every proposed standard as the House amendment would have required. There were important Senate concessions even in this area, however. The Senate receded with respect to a provision in their bill which would have permitted a shortened rulemaking procedure for the issuance of existing proprietary standards. In addition, in adopting the Senate language the House insisted on an amendment under which employers may petition for a temporary order granting a variance from a standard promulgated by the Secretary. Such an order is to be granted only if the employer shows he is unable to comply with a standard for specific and limited reasons, the unavailability of professional or technical personnel, or of necessary materials or equipment, or because necessary construction or alteration of facilities cannot be completed in the time required. The economic implications of a standard for an employer are not to be considered in the determination as to whether a variance is to be allowed. The employees of such an employer are entitled to notice and hearing on such an order. Such an order may be issued in any given case for a maximum of 1 year and may not be renewed more than twice.

INSPECTION

The differences in the two versions of the bill with respect to inspection by the Secretary of Labor were not major, save in two respects. The Senate bill would have required an employer to make periodic self-inspections to be followed by a certification of the results to the Secretary of Labor. This would have faced an employer with the unfortunate choice of admitting a violation of a standard which would have subjected him to a citation under the act or subjecting himself to a charge of having made a false statement if he did not accurately report the condition or situation that was a violation of a standard under this act. The conferees adopted the principle of self-inspection. The Secretary may now provide for such self-inspection by regulation, but no certification of the results may be required.

Under the provisions of the Senate bill both a management and an employee representative had to be given an opportunity to accompany an inspector. The conferees adopted this principle rather than the provision of the House amendment under which an employee representative would have been given the opportunity to accompany an inspector only if the employer or his representative also accompanied the inspector.

CITATIONS FOR VIOLATIONS

The Senate bill provided that if, upon inspection or investigation, the Secretary or his authorized representative "determines" that an employer has violated mandatory requirements under the act, he shall "forthwith" issue a citation. The House amendment provided that if on the basis of any inspection or investigation the Secretary "believes" that an employer has violated such requirements, he shall issue a citation to the employer. The conference report provides that if the Secretary "believes" that an employer has violated such requirements he shall issue the citation with "reasonable promptness." In the absence of exceptional circumstances any delay is not expected to exceed 72 hours from the time the violation is detected by the inspector.

The Senate bill kept separate the proceedings for the issuance of the citation from those with respect to the imposition of penalties for violations. The House amendment combined proposed penalties with the issuance of the citation. The conference report follows the provisions of the Senate bill in this respect.

The House amendment prohibited issuance of a citation more than 3 months after the occurrence of any violation. The Senate bill had no such statute of limitations. The Senate receded with an amendment changing the 3 months to 6 months.

The Senate bill gave employees the right to appeal the time allowed for abatement of a violation and provided that the Commission should prescribe rules of procedure giving employees the opportunity to participate as parties. The House amendment restricted the right of appeal in such cases to the employer. The House receded with an amendment which provides that the employer shall have a right to reopen the proceedings for a rehearing in the event it is impossible to comply with the abatement requirements within the period provided for in the citation.

JUDICIAL PROCEEDINGS

Both the Senate bill and the House amendment provided for judicial review of Commission decisions. The Senate bill provided appeal rights to any person adversely affected or aggrieved by an order of the Commission. The House amendment limited appeal rights to the employer and the Secretary. The House amendment provided for judicial review in the court of appeals for the circuit where the violation occurred or where the employer had his principal office. The Senate bill also permitted review in the District of Columbia Court of Appeals. The House receded.

The Senate bill provided for administrative action to obtain relief for an employee discriminated against for asserting rights under this act, including reinstatement with back pay. The House bill contained no provision for obtaining such administrative relief; rather it provided civil and criminal penalties for employers who discriminate against employees in such cases. With respect to the first matter, the House receded with an amendment making specific the jurisdiction of the district courts for proceedings brought by the Secretary to restrain violations and other appropriate relief. With respect to the second matter dealing with civil and criminal penalties for employers, the House receded.

PENALTIES

The Senate bill provided that there shall be assessed a civil penalty of not more than $1,000 for each violation. The House amendment was similar unless the violation was determined not to be of a serious nature in which case a civil penalty of up to $1,000 was discretionary. The Senate bill provided for civil penalties of not more than $1,000 for each day in which an imminent danger order or final order of the Commission was violated. The House amendment also provided for a penalty of up to $1,000 for each day in which an order which has become final was violated. The Senate receded on each point.

The Senate bill provided criminal penalties for willful violations—not more than $10,000 and/or 6 months doubled after first conviction. The House amendment provided for a civil penalty of up to $10,000 for willful or repeated violations. The Senate receded on civil penalties and the House receded on criminal penalties with an amendment which requires that the willful violation of the standard or the rule, regulation or order result in death to an employee, for the employer to be subject to the criminal penalties provided in the subsection.

The House amendment provided no penalty for giving advance notice of any inspection to be conducted under the act. The Senate bill provided a fine not to exceed $1,000 and imprisonment for not more than 6 months or both for giving advanced notice. The House receded.

PROCEDURES TO COUNTERACT IMMINENT DANGERS

The Senate bill authorized the Secretary to seek a court order to remove or correct an imminent danger and require the withdrawal of endangered persons other than "those necessary to correct the danger, maintain the operating capacity of a continuous process operation or a permit a safe and orderly shutdown." The Senate bill contained no limitation on the duration of such a temporary restraining order, although the 10-day limit in the FRCP was applicable. The Senate bill permitted the Secretary to issue an administrative imminent danger shutdown order where there was insufficient time to obtain a court order. The House amendment authorized the Secretary to seek court orders to restrain conditions or practices which caused imminent dangers. A temporary restraining order under the House amendment was to remain in effect only 5 days. The House amendment contained no provision permitting the Secretary to issue an administrative imminent danger order. The Senate receded with an amendment adopting with minor changes the limitations on court authority mentioned in the quotation above.

EFFECT ON OTHER LAWS

There was a major difference in the two bills in the treatment of the proposed effect on other preexisting health and safety statutes. I think it appropriate to quote the conference report on this point.

The Senate bill said the act should not apply to working conditions with respect to which other Federal agencies exercise statutory authority affecting occupational safety and health, while the House amendment excluded employees whose working conditions were so regulated. The House language had an additional exclusion relating to employees whose safety and health were regulated by State agencies acting under section 274 of the Atomic Energy Act of 1954. The House receded on the first point; the Senate receded on the second.

The Senate bill provided that safety standards under any law administered by the Secretary of Labor—Walsh-Healy, Service Contract Act, Construction Safety Act, Arts and Humanities Act, and Longshore Safety—would be superseded when more effective standards are promulgated under this act, but until then they were deemed standards under the present act. The enforcement process of this act was thus added to the enforcement procedures of those other acts. The House amendment repealed and rescinded standards under the Walsh-Healy, the Service Contracts, and the Arts and Humanities Acts. All construction industry employers were exempted from this act and the entire industry brought under the Construction Safety Act.. That act was amended to make the enforcement provisions of this act applicable. Unlike the Senate bill which left the hearing of contract violation cases with the Secretary, the House amendment provided the hearing of such cases by the Safety and Health Commission. The House receded.

The conferees intend that the Secretary develop health and safety standards for construction workers covered by Public Law 91–54 pursuant to the provisions of that law and that he use the same mechanisms and resources for the development of health and safety standards for all the other construction workers newly covered by this act, including those engaged in alterations, repairs, painting and/or decorating.

It is understood by the conferees that in any enforcement proceedings brought under either this act or under such other acts, the principle of collateral estoppel will apply.

The Secretary was intended to have alternatives available to him. That is he may elect to pursue the procedure for enforcement laid out in either act and may seek to have imposed the penalty authorized by either act. He may not, however, pursue enforcement under one act and then—whether having failed or succeeded—attempt to pursue the procedure provided in the other act. The provisions for contract termination and blacklisting may be applied, of course, in appropriate cases and their imposition will not preclude the possibility of a civil penalty, in addition.

DUTIES OF EMPLOYERS AND EMPLOYEES

The Senate bill required workplaces to be free from "recognized hazards." The House amendment required such places to be free from "any hazards which are readily apparent and are causing or likely to cause death or serious bodily harm." The House provision was adopted with the Senate's "recognized hazard" term replacing the House's "readily apparent hazard."

The Senate bill required each employee to comply with occupational health and safety standards and the rules, regulations, and orders issued under this act. The House amendment had no comparable provision. The House receded.

The Senate bill made provision for the establishment of a National Institute for Occupational Safety and Health, and also established a National Commission on State Workmen's Compensation Laws, the latter to undertake a study and evaluation of the effectiveness of workmen's compensation statutes. Both the Institute and the Commission were accepted by the conference.

Steiger Explanation

House
12-17-70
pp. 11898-11900

Mr. STEIGER of Wisconsin. I thank the gentleman for his gracious comments.

Mr. Speaker, in this session of Congress the House and Senate have passed for the first time in our Nation's history comprehensive occupational safety and health legislation. The conference committee reported bill, which is now before the House, represents an unprecedented response by Congress to the need to help save the lives and protect the health of the working men and women throughout this great Nation.

One of the primary purposes of the bill is to set up a mechanism by which fair and effective occupational safety and health standards can be promulgated so that the many employers and employees throughout the Nation may be guided in their attempts to establish and maintain a safe and healthful work environment.

The conference reported bill is clearly based on the premise of this House that it is with the cooperation of both employers and employees that the act can most effectively meet the challenge of reducing and perhaps eliminating most of the occupational deaths, tragic injuries and diseases which take a large annual toll in terms of the human suffering and loss to the economy caused by these tragedies.

I feel that the conference reported bill is basically sound and provides fair and adequate procedures for the development of standards and their enforcement; I urge the House to vote favorably for the adoption of the conference reported bill.

APPLICABILITY

The coverage of this bill is as broad, generally speaking, as the authority vested in the Federal Government by the commerce clause of the Constitution. The terms of this bill will apply to all businesses having an effect on commerce except where another Federal agency other than the Department of Labor is exercising statutory authority to prescribe or enforce occupational safety and health standards or regulations. The bill also provides that occupational safety and health standards published under the various procurement laws and the Maritime Safety Act, which are administered by the Department of Labor, shall remain standards under those acts, at least for the time being. It is not the intent of the draftsmen of this legislation that double proceedings occur under one of those acts and under the omnibus Occupational Safety and Health Act which we are considering here today. For example, a proceeding could be pending before the Secretary of Labor for safety violations under the Construction Safety Act while at the same time a proceeding is pending before the Occupational Safety and Health Review Commission under the comprehensive Occupational Safety and Health Act.

Let me add a comment on what may appear to be an inconsistency between the last sentence of section 4(b)(2) and the expedited procedures set out in section 6 to adopt early interim standards.

The last sentence in section 4(b)(2) is included to insure that standards under existing laws will not be repealed by this enactment and will remain effective until superseded by the promulgation of standards under section 6a. At that time the newly promulgated standards will become standards under this Act and existing laws, thereby preserving remedies available under existing laws. To construe this provision otherwise would be to make the early standards-setting procedures in section 6(a) meaningless or a mere redundancy.

DUTIES

The conference bill takes the approach of this House to the general duty requirement that an employer maintain a safe and healthful working environment. The conference-reported bill recognizes the need for such a provision where there is no existing specific standard applicable to a given situation. However, this requirement is made realistic by its application only to situations where there are "recognized hazards" which are likely to cause or are causing serious injury or death. Such hazards are the type that can readily be detected on the basis of the basic human senses. Hazards which require technical or testing devices to detect them are not intended to be within the scope of the general duty requirement. It is also clear that the general duty requirement should not be used to set ad hoc standards. The bill already provides procedures for establishing temporary emergency standards. It is expected that the general duty requirement will be relied upon infrequently and that primary reliance will be placed on specific standards which will be promulgated under the act. After all, as I have already indicated, one of the primary purposes in enacting this legislation stems from the need to provide employers with health standards so that they might better protect the health and safety of the worker by providing the necessary machinery and protective devices in the workplace.

STANDARDS

The conference committee-reported bill provides for the promulgation of early standards by the Secretary of Labor without any hearing. However, these early standards would be limited to national consensus standards and established Federal standards. These early standards could only be adopted pursuant to the authority in section 6(a) within the first 2 years following the

day of enactment, and when adopted, would become effective immediately upon publication in the Federal Register.

The permanent standard-setting machinery is contained in the conference committee bill under section 6(b). The provisions require the Secretary to establish permanent standards by rule. It is contemplated by the draftsmen that the Secretary will base his decision upon a record which has been contributed to by public and private organizations as well as interested individuals. The permanent standard-setting machinery provides for a hearing upon request of an interested person following to judicial review, as are other standards promulgated under section 6, by an appropriate Federal court of appeals. The Secretary's standard will only be sustained by the court if it is supported by "substantial evidence on the record considered as a whole." Thus, the Secretary must have a record upon which to base his findings and to serve as the basis for judicial review. The act does not provide for an independent board for standard-setting as did the House bill. However, the court review based upon substantial evidence provides a sufficient element of fairness to satisfy me that conference report should be accepted.

As in the House-passed bill, the conference committee reported bill provides that upon publication of a permanent standard, the Secretary may provide for a delay in the effective date of that standard. Such a delay may not exceed 90 days. However, this is not intended to exclude the possibility that a particular standard may provide for graduated requirements to take effect progressively on specific dates even though the intervals between the effective dates of such graduated requirements may exceed 90 days. For example, a standard applicable to a particular industry could provide that, 90 days after issuance, the sound level in the workplace may not exceed X decibels; that 6 months after issuance, the sound level may not exceed X-5 decibels; and that, 1 year after issuance, the sound level may not exceed X-10 decibels.

TEMPORARY EMERGENCY STANDARDS

Section 6(c) provides for the expedited procedure for promulgating emergency standards in accordance with the desires of this House. It is intended that this procedure not be utilized to circumvent the regular standard-setting procedures. It should be used only for those limited situations where such emergency standards are necessary because employees are exposed to grave danger from substances or agents determined to be toxic or physically harmful agents, or new hazards. Section 6(c)(1)(B) makes it clear that it is also necessary that the Secretary determine that such a standard is necessary to protect employees from such danger. Thus, where the state of the act is incomplete or in some way lacking so that a determination cannot be made as to whether such a standard will protect employees, in such instances the Secretary would utilize the regular standard-setting procedures as provided in subsection 6(b) and not the emergency standard-setting authority.

INSPECTIONS AND INVESTIGATIONS

Under the bill the Secretary of Labor would be responsible for conducting inspections and investigations. There are two particular provisions regarding inspections on which I will comment. Subsection 8(e) requires the Secretary, in inspecting a facility, to make use of the knowledge of employees or their representatives by allowing them to accompany him and/or consult with him throughout the inspection. This provision, as well as a similar provision in the House bill, is intended as a specific aid to the Secretary and should be utilized by him for that purpose.

Section 8(f)(1) applies to situations where employees or their representative believe, in good faith and on a reasonable basis, that a violation of a standard exists which threatens significant physical harm, or that an imminent danger exists. It is expected that the Secretary will use his good judgment in determining whether there are reasonable grounds to believe that a violation exists and will not permit this procedure to be used as an harassment device.

Section 8(f)(1) also requires the Secretary to conduct such inspections as soon as practicable. This language requires the Secretary to act expeditiously. It also is intended to prevent serious disruptions in the systematic conduct of the Secretary's inspection program.

There may be other priorities which involve violations of a serious nature that are known and must be processed ahead of a given employee-requested inspection.

ENFORCEMENT

After an inspection or investigation, a citation may be issued for a violation of any safety or health requirement of the act. In the Senate bill, this citation

had to be issued "forthwith." The term, "forthwith," lent itself to an interpretation that would require the issuance of a citation on-the-spot before leaving the premises. The conference committee, however, changed this procedure to require the issuance of a citation with "reasonable promptness" after the completion of an investigation. The "reasonable promptness" standard will allow an investigator, before he issues a citation, to refer to regulations and guidelines issued by the Secretary, consider what is an appropriate abatement period in light of precedent, and consult with other officials about the facts of the case. The period, however, should be a brief interval between an inspection and the issuance of a citation, normally not exceeding 72 hours. The change brings the present language more in line with the citation provisions contained in the House bill.

Under the "penalties" provision, the distinction contained in the House bill between "serious" violations and "nonserious" violations is retained. Thus, there is no requirement that a penalty be assessed when the violation is not a serious one, but a penalty must be assessed where the violation is serious in nature.

ADVANCE NOTICE

The bill prohibits the giving of advance notice of an inspection "without authority from the Secretary or his designee," and violation of the provision carries a fine of not more than $1,000, or imprisonment of not more than 6 months, or both. It is clear from the language that giving advance notice of inspections is not prohibited where the Secretary believes such notice will further the interests of the act. However, there will be some cases where it will be important that no prior notice be given and therefore the penalty is provided for giving unauthorized notice.

PENALTY COLLECTION

It should also be made clear that the provision for judicial review and enforcement of the Commission's orders contained in section 11 are exclusive. Section 17(m) authorizing actions in the name of the United States for the collection of penalties should be construed narrowly and is intended to be limited to any collection process which may be necessary in order to actually collect the penalty.

RESEARCH AND TRAINING

As I mentioned at the outset, the need

for research in the area of occupational injuries and diseases is one of the primary objectives to be achieved by this legislation. In accord with this objective, the conference bill provides, as did the House-passed bill, for extensive research by the Secretary of Health, Education, and Welfare. This broad authority is contained in section 20 of the bill and section 22 specifically provides for the creation of a National Institute for Occupational Safety and Health Research in the Department of Health, Education, and Welfare. Among other specific directives to the Secretary of Health, Education, and Welfare, the bill requires the Secretary of Health, Education, and Welfare to publish current listings of workplace related toxic substances. Such a list should be of significant assistance in providing the information necessary for a broad based attack on the problem.

I am proud to have been able to play a part in the development of this historic legislation. As I have indicated, my colleagues and our staffs in the Congress who have labored to produce this legislation deserve the thanks of all working men and women throughout our land. And foremost in the list of those who deserve credit for this legislation is President Nixon, who not only presented to the Congress his own comprehensive occupational safety and health legislation, but also on numerous occasions reminded the Congress of the urgency and necessity for such legislation.

I believe that special credit should also be given to the long and tireless efforts of the men charged with the primary responsibility for administering the law, Secretary of Labor James Hodgson, and Under Secretary Larry S. Iberman who have given strong endorsement to the conference report.

EXPLANATION OF CHANGES MADE IN SENATE BILL

The Senate agreed to the conference agreement December 16. Senator Williams (D-NJ), floor manager of the bill, explained the major changes in the Senate bill and gave some indication of why various changes had been agreed to.

Senate
12-16-70
pp. 20279-20280

Mr. WILLIAMS. * * *

Mr. President, the Senate conferees on S. 2193, the Occupational Safety and Health Act of 1970, have met in five sessions with the conferees from the other body, and have reached agreement on a bill. This measure, which is long overdue, would for the first time provide for a comprehensive program to deal with the urgent problems of safety and health encountered in the workplace by our Nation's citizens.

When this bill was before the Senate 1 month ago, we clearly recognized that a strong Federal program was necessary to deal with the more than 14,000 industrial deaths and 2½ million job-related disabilities that occur each year, as well as the ever-increasing exposure of workers to substances whose toxic potential has never been adequately researched. As a consequence, the Senate passed this bill with only three dissenting votes.

In view of the 83 to 3 vote by which the Senate bill was approved, I am pleased to report that the bill agreed on in conference reflects, to a most unusual degree, the wishes of the Senate, as expressed during our action on this measure.

The conference agreement retains the basic features of the Senate bill, placing in the Secretary of Labor the clear responsibility for promulgating effective safety and health standards, applicable to specific hazards and industries. In exercising this responsibility, the Secretary would utilize and build upon the work already done by private industry and Government in the formulation of standards; and opportunity would be given, through advisory committees, and the hearing procedure, for affected employers and employees to have a voice in the standards-making process.

As in the Senate bill, inspections would

be made by the Labor Department, with authority to issue citations requiring the abatement of violations and to propose penalties, where appropriate. The conference agreement also contains the provision for an independent enforcement commission, which was adopted during Senate debate, on motion by Senator JAVITS. This provision was designed to separate the adjudication of violations from the other functions performed by the Secretary of Labor, in order to provide every assurance that fairness and due process would be fully served.

The conference agreement also contains the Senate bill's provisions which encourage State participation in the effort to bring safe and healthful conditions to the workplace, and which provide the workers and their representatives with an opportunity to participate in the standards-making and enforcement processes.

I might point out that the Senate bill contained a number of provisions that had no counterpart whatever in the House-passed bill. These include Senator JAVITS' proposals for a National Institute for Occupational Safety and Health to perform the all-important research functions which will be basic to this program's effectiveness, and a National Commission To Study the Problems of Workmen's Compensation, as well as Senator DOMINICK's proposal requiring the use of emergency locator beacons on certain small aircraft. All of these provisions remain in the bill agreed upon in conference.

Where the Senate conferees receded to the House, this was also done in accordance with views which had very substantial support in the Senate. I would cite in particular the bill's imminent danger provision. The Senate bill had provided that where an imminent danger was found to exist, the Secretary of Labor could not only go to court to obtain injunctive relief, but could, under certain circumstances, order the withdrawal of employees or closure of the plant for up to 72 hours. An amendment offered on the Senate floor by Senator SAXBE, which would permit all such imminent danger orders to be issued only by a court, failed by merely two votes. Under these circumstances, and in view of the insistence of the House Members on adhering to that portion of their bill which contained a provision similar to the Saxbe amendment, the Senate conferees felt warranted in receding to the House on this issue.

So I believe that in every respect we have been faithful to the wishes of the Senate, and in doing so, have brought back a bill which will be both strong and effective as well as fair and reasonable.

Mr. President, I am gratified that the administration announced its support yesterday of the bill agreed upon by the conference committee. I would also recall President Nixon's earlier remarks on this legislation in which he pointed out that "such a program ought to have been Federal law three generations ago. This was not done, and three generations of American workers have suffered because of this."

Mr. President, the legislation is now before us, and I urge immediate approval of the conference report.

APPENDIX I

SIGNIFICANT PARTS OF SENATE AND HOUSE DEBATE

The problem of interpreting a statute is primarily one of discovering the intention of the legislative body which enacted it. If the meaning of a provision is clear on its face, the courts go no further. Where, however, the language is ambiguous or conflicting, the courts will examine the legislative history of the measure in an effort to discover legislative intent.

The statements by Chairman Perkins (D-Ky) of the House Labor Committee and Congressman Steiger (R-Wis), sponsor of the Administration safety bill that originally passed the House, are reproduced in Appendix G. In addition, the editors have assembled the following statements made by members of Congress during debate on the Occupational Safety and Health Act.

Statements are grouped under the various provisions included in the Act. Citations are given in bold face type to the date of the Congressional Record (Vol. 116) and the page number at which they appear. Three asterisks (* * *) have been used to indicate the omission of text.

APPENDIX I-1

GENERAL DUTY

EDITORS' NOTE:—*The following comments were made by Congressman Steiger (R-Wis) in support of the general duty clause which was adopted in the final bill. The final version requires employers to keep workplaces free from "recognized hazards."*

**House
11-23-70
p. 10620**

Mr. STEIGER. * * *
The substitute recognizes that we are

not always going to have precise standards to cover all circumstances. Therefore a general requirement is included, but it is limited and made more specific by requiring employers to maintain working conditions which are free "from any hazards which are readily apparent and are causing or are likely to cause death or serious physical harm." It is patently unfair to require employers to supply every conceivable safety and health need for which no specific standards exist to guide them. By limiting this "general duty" requirement to apparent dangers, the substitute overcomes this element of unfairness and at the same time provides protection in serious situations which may not be covered by a precise standard.

297

APPENDIX I-2

EMPLOYEE RESPONSIBILITIES

EDITORS' NOTE:—*The following comments on employee responsibilities and the absence of a strike-pay provision were made by Senator Williams (D-NJ) during Senate debate.*

**Senate
11-16-70
p. 18250**

Mr. WILLIAMS * * *

I might point out, too, that in order to make clear that achieving the goals of a safe workplace is not a one-sided matter, we added in committee a provision placing upon employees, as well as employers, the obligation to comply with all applicable requirements under the act.

I should also add, despite some widespread contentions to the contrary, that the committee bill does not contain a so-called strike-pay provision. Rather than raising a possibility for endless disputes over whether employees were entitled to walk off the job with full pay, it was decided in committee to enhance the prospects of compliance by the employer through such means as giving the employees the right to request a special Labor Department investigation or inspection.

APPENDIX I-3

STANDARDS

EDITORS' NOTE:—*The following discussion concerns an amendment sponsored by Senator Dominick (R-Colo), which was adopted, to clarify the criteria to be used in setting standards.*

**Senate
11-17-70
p. 18355**

Mr. DOMINICK. Mr. President, I now send the amendment to the desk so that the clerk will have it in its modified form.

Mr. President, before we tried to get together on the exact language, we were discussing the problem that the language on page 39 and page 71, in setting standards and in setting criteria, tried to assure that, no matter what anybody was doing, the standard would protect him for the rest of his life against any foreseeable hazard.

What we were trying to do in the bill— unfortunately, we did not have the proper wording or the proper drafting—was to say that when we are dealing with toxic agents or physical agents, we ought to take such steps as are feasible and practical to provide an atmosphere within which a person's health or safety would not be affected. Unfortunately, we had language providing that anyone would be assured that no one would have a hazard, or at least, we would require the Secretary to set standards so stating, and that in the HEW standard there would be a requirement to proceed on that basis, so that no one would have any problem for the rest of his working life.

It was an unrealistic standard. As modified, we would be approaching the problem by looking at the problem and setting a standard or criterion which would not result in harm.

Mr. WILLIAMS of New Jersey. Mr. President, how much time do I have?

The PRESIDING OFFICER. The Chair is advised that the Senator from New Jersey has 2 minutes.

Mr. WILLIAMS of New Jersey. Two minutes.

As I understand this amendment, it will provide a continued direction to the Secretary that he shall be required to ·set the standard which most adequately and to the greatest extent feasible assures, on the basis of the best available evidence, that no employee will suffer any material impairment of health of functional capacity even if such employee has continual exposure to the hazard dealt with for the period of his working life.

Certainly that is the objective, and included within this concept of unimpaired health and functional capacity is pro-protection against diminished life expectancy.

Mr. DOMINICK. Mr. President, how much time do I have remaining?

The PRESIDING OFFICER. The Senator from Colorado has 7 minutes.

Mr. DOMINICK. Mr. President, I yield myself 3 minutes, for the purpose of having a colloquy with my colleague from New Jersey.

It is my understanding, if I may say so, that what we are doing now is to say that the Secretary has got to use his best efforts to promulgate the best available standards, and in so doing, that he should take into account that anyone working in toxic agents or physical agents which might be harmful may be subjected to such conditions for the rest of his working life, so that we can get at something which might not be toxic now, if he works in it a short time, but if he works in it the rest of his life it might be very dangerous; and we want to make sure that such things are taken into consideration in establishing standards; is that correct?

Mr. WILLIAMS of New Jersey. That is exactly correct.

Mr. DOMINICK. I appreciate the co-operation of my friend from New Jersey. I think we have worked it out to where it makes a lot of sense, at this point much more so than before.

Mr. WILLIAMS of New Jersey. I think it is clear, the objectives have been stated, and it strengthens the objectives of standards that will protect against physical impairment and loss of function.

The PRESIDING OFFICER. Do Senators yield back their remaining time?

Mr. DOMINICK. I yield back the remainder of my time.

Mr. WILLIAMS of New Jersey. I yield back the remainder of my time.

The PRESIDING OFFICER (Mr. CASE). All remaining time having been yielded back, the question is on agreeing, en bloc, to the amendments—No. 1054 and No. 1058—of the Senator from Colorado (Mr. DOMINICK), as modified.

The amendments were agreed to.

EDITORS' NOTE:—*Senator Javits (D-NY) introduced an amendment, which was adopted, to require the Secretary to explain a deviation from an existing national consensus standard.*

Senate
11-17-70
pp. 18355-18356

Mr. JAVITS. Mr. President, in proposing that amendment, I ask the Senator from New Jersey to state whether he agrees with me in the following: We have, under this amendment, the concept of a statement which will help us better to enforce the law where a deviation from an existing national consensus standard is promulgated by the Secretary.

A national consensus standard, under this act, is a standard which has been developed by one of two organizations at the present time: The American National Standards Institute or the Fire Underwriters Association.

In the first place, this amendment ought to be adopted so that the people will have an explanation of why the Secretary is doing what he is doing.

The other aspect of the matter is that the bill provides for a National Institute of Occupational Health and Safety, and it is important to assure these outside organizations, which are very important in this field, that the Institute is not designed in any way to preempt or limit the activity or importance of national consensus organizations such as the American National Standards Institute. These organizations have made valuable contributions in this field in the past, and I hope they will continue to do so in the future. This is so that they may be reassured that the Institute represents no threat to them.

The other point I should like to make with respect to reassuring these organizations is to confirm the fact that it is expected that the director of the new Institute will take full advantage of the extensive expertise represented by members of technical societies and private standards development organizations which serve an important purpose and which should continue to function in the private sector of occupational health and safety.

Mr. WILLIAMS of New Jersey. On the latter point, I would certainly agree that

that would be wise. Our hope is that that would come to pass.

The amendment reads:

Whenever a rule promulgated by the Secretary differs substantially from an existing national consensus standard, the Secretary shall include in the rule a statement.

Is that what he does—include it in the rule?

Mr. JAVITS. Mr. President, I modify my amendment to provide in the third line that "the Secretary shall publish in the Federal Reigster," instead of "include in the rule."

I agree with the Senator.

Mr. WILLIAMS of New Jersey. I certainly agree to the amendment offered by the Senator from New York.

The PRESIDING OFFICER. The question is on agreeing to the amendment, as modified.

The amendment, as modified, was agreed to, as follows:

"(7) Whenever a rule promulgated by the Secretary differs substantially from an existing national consensus standard, the Secretary shall publish in the Federal Register a statement of the reasons why the rule as adopted will better effectuate the purposes of this Act than the national consensus standard.

APPENDIX I-4

THE OCCUPATIONAL SAFETY AND HEALTH REVIEW COMMISSION

EDITORS' NOTE:—*The following comments were made on Senator Javits' (R-NY) amendment to create a review commission. Initially rejected by the Senate Labor Committee, the amendment was accepted by the Senate and retained in the final bill.*

Senate
11-17-70
pp. 18339-18340

Mr. JAVITS. * * *

Mr. President, if I may have the attention of Senators, I can explain what this is about very briefly.

The big issue on this bill—and certainly the Senate has made that clear by its votes—is the question of how it is to be enforced and how standards are to be promulgated. The amendment I have just called up deals with the matter of enforcement. The question of the promulgation of the standards remains in the Secretary, although there probably will be an amendment later to deal with that specific point, in a way different from that in which it was dealt in Senator DOMINICK'S substitute yesterday. But the key issue which has worried American business is, How is this very important piece of legislation to be enforced?

I am offering the administration's version of how it should be enforced. I introduced the administration's bill originally, and the provision I now offer as an amendment is consistent with the approval of that bill. It creates a review commission which will deal with all complaints referred to it by the Secretary and which will have the same type of authority that the Federal Trade Commission exercises: The power to issue a cease and desist order which, if challenged within a given period of time, can be reviewed by the Circuit Court of Appeals. Its operation is stayed if the Circuit Court of Appeals so orders. If the Secretary desires to enforce the order through the contempt power, similarly, he can go into court in order the get the Circuit Court of Appeals to enter an order for the specific purpose, and then that order can be enforced through the contempt powers of the Circuit Court of Appeals. It is the traditional Federal Trade Commission type of procedure.

Mr. HOLLAND. Mr. President, will the Senator yield for a question?

Mr. JAVITS. I yield.

Mr. HOLLAND. Would the commission which would be set up by the Senator's amendment be within the Labor Department and controlled by the Labor Department or would it be an independent commission?

Mr. JAVITS. Autonomous and independent. Perhaps it would be housed in the Labor Department, or administratively it might have employees who are common, but it is expressly set forth to be an independent commission, established for the purpose of dealing with these complaints and passing on them.

Mr. HOLLAND. I thank the Senator.

Mr. JAVITS. It would not be a Labor Department instrument. Indeed, I might say to my distinguished colleague that yesterday, when we were arguing the Dominick substitute, I made the point that a Secretary could set up, if he wished, a committee or commission—other Secretaries have—to exercise his power; but that commission would, as the Senator's question implies, be under his authority. That is not so under my amendment. This is an autonomous, independent commission which, without regard to the Secretary, can find for or against him on the basis of individual complaints.

Mr. HOLLAND. I thank the Senator. I shall support his amendment, because I believe that that kind of independent enforcement is required under the circumstances.

Mr. JAVITS. I thank my colleague very much.

Mr. President, one of the interesting things which comes out of this amendment, which interests me greatly, is the fact that I offered this amendment in committee as the "compromise." I had hoped that it would be accepted and supported. But it had the opposition, for reasons which absolutely escape me, of organized labor. One would think that organized labor wanted the certainty and the celerity which would come from this kind of enforcement, because there is speedier action here. It may be speedier action by as much as 18 months, in this way: The present scheme of enforcement requires the Secretary to go into court in order to enforce an order of enforcement which he makes. This order, which is made by the Commission, is self-enforcing unless stayed by the Court of Appeals. Immediately, there is a diminution of the time involved.

Second, this amendment provides that if the hearing examiner's report is not contested and the Commission does not order it reviewed, it becomes final, within the same procedures of the Commission—a very quick way of dealing with relatively minor situations.

It seems to me that this gives everything one would ask in the way of assurance, both to management and to labor. Yet, though management wanted it very much, organized labor apparently was opposed to it.

One final thing which is very interesting to me: The Administrative Procedure Act applies anyway, whether the Secretary is the enforcing agent or the Commission is the enforcing agent. So there is no diminution of the rights of anybody, nor denial of due process, and at the same time greater celerity is given and greater confidence that violations will be considered by a quasi-judicial authority expressly delegated for that purpose.

The importance of this particular measure is not so much in the absolutes which are involved. In an absolute sense, in view of the checks and balances which the judicial system imposes on the Secretary, one might think that enforcement by the Secretary would be more hedged in, more subject to judicial argument, and so forth, than even the determinations by this commission; but, as we all know, the climate in which things are done becomes critically important. We see that in many pieces of legislation. The business community feels deeply on this matter, which can be vexatious—there is no question about that and we must recognize it—as there can be all kinds of complaints and difficulties, and expensive difficulties, created for American business, so that apparently the business community feels an infinitely greater assurance with this kind of commission than with enforcement by the Secretary of Labor.

In my judgment, it would be better all around. I have been unable to understand up to now—perhaps those who oppose the amendment will enlighten me better than they did in committee—why it ran into an absolute, hard and unyielding opposition. As many Members have told me, if this particular amendment had been accepted in the Committee on Labor and Public Welfare, we would hardly be arguing about any part of this bill now as, generally speaking, we did balance out most of the bill pretty well, as the votes in the Senate have demonstrated.

Thus, again, quoting one of our Members, this is the nut in the coconut. This is what it is all about. It seems to me, in view of the fact that it will give a sense of greater assurance to the business community than enforcement by the Secretary of Labor, it certainly is not any tougher than his enforcement, in terms of the benefits which accrue from a piece of legislation like this to the worker, nor is it less advantageous to the worker because, if anything, it accelerates the time within which decisions can be made.

It seems to me this is the fair way to balance out the bill.

One other point which is critically important: What is the difference between a board to establish the standards and a commission to enforce them, and why, in my judgment, is it more important to have an autonomous and independent commission even than to have some form of board to promulgate certain standards?

The reason is this: The enforcement of orders is an adjudicatory act, whereas the establishment of standards is a deliberative act. There are serious penalties involved for the individual enterprise. It is a case by case proposition. It does not apply across the board to every member of industry. One particular rubber company, for example, can be materially disadvantaged by a finding against it in a given case, whereas established standards are an across-the-board proposition. It is entirely practical to be rather deliberate about that in hearings before the Secretary of Labor or officials of that Department. They can go into the thing deeply and if they want to contest it there is plenty of opportunity to go into court and contest the rule. But enforcement of an order or the making of an order is an adjudicatory action.

Therefore, I can understand that even people who would wish to go along with this bill in the main—and I am one of them—would draw back on the question of enforcement even if not on the question of promulgation of the standards.

My experience as a lawyer for many years tells me that I would feel entirely comfortable even if the Secretary promulgated the standards. I know that I would have plenty of time to contest them, but with respect to an order with regard to a violation, I would be worried if I were a lawyer for a particular concern. I would welcome the fact that we have more than one man and that we have an established practice of quasi-judicial character and a separation, a degree of autonomy in the commission which distinguishes it from the authorities who have done to investigating, the reporting, and so forth, in respect of the original complaint of the violation.

Mr. JAVITS. The panel would be three members appointed by the President for a specific term—2, 4, or 6 years. A term would normally be for 6 years. The analogies between the qualifications of members and the authority of the Commission, and so forth, would be with the Federal Trade Commission.

We used in the original text of the amendment the word "panel," but that seemed to water it down so that it did not represent it as it is. So we substituted the word "commission." That is the word used by the Senator from Colorado (Mr. DOMINICK) in his substitute, which we think is more accurately descriptive of an autonomous body which has tenure and quasi-judicial power.

Mr. WILLIAMS of New Jersey. From what areas would these members be selected?

Mr. JAVITS. That would depend on the President, but of course, the nominations would be subject to the advice and consent of the Senate so that the Senate could be a monitor, as it were, to see that they were people who had real qualifications to do the job.

Mr. WILLIAMS of New Jersey. In other words, there are no congressional guides for the selection of members of the Commission.

Mr. JAVITS. It will be done in accordance with the way it is done in other commissions of the same character. The protection there is confirmation by the Senate.

Mr. JAVITS. I might say to my colleague from New Jersey that we normally seek nominees with those qualifications for advisory committees but not for commissions. I believe, for example, that the authority of a commission should be the same authority as we would give to a judge. My view is that a broad range of business can be covered and the factors of judgment taken into consideration, as well as the weight of evidence, and so forth, which would be required; so that I believe we would be best advised to follow the traditional practice which we follow with many commissions, many of which deal with problems of considerable expertise. In the Interstate Commerce Commission and other agencies, the appointments are made by the President subject to the confirmation of the Senate, which gives us the safeguard we would require.

APPENDIX I-5

INSPECTIONS, INVESTIGATIONS, AND RECORD-KEEPING

EDITORS' NOTE:—*The following discussion by Congressman Waggonner (D-La) and Congressman Perkins, (D-Ky) which occurred during House debate on the bill, involves the Secretary's authorization to transfer inspection rights to his employees.*

House
11-24-70
pp. 10683-10684

Mr. WAGGONNER. * * *

All right, then going back to the inspection section, we have a definition of the word "Secretary." This language is rather tightly drawn. Is it possible that, when we talk about inspections, when we use only the word "Secretary," that employees of the Secretary could not conduct inspections?

Mr. PERKINS. Let me say to my distinguished friend that the word "Secretary" means his agents as well. We do not expect the Secretary himself to conduct inspections. His agents will conduct the investigations.

Mr. WAGGONNER. Does the gentleman feel we need an additional amendment to the definition of the word "Secretary"?

The CHAIRMAN. The time of the gentleman from Louisiana has expired.

(By unanimous consent, Mr. GROSS yielded his time to Mr. WAGGONNER.)

Mr. WAGGONNER. I refer the gentleman to the definition section, section 3 (1):

The term "Secretary" means the Secretary of Labor.

It does not say anything about his agents.

Mr. PERKINS. The legislation contemplates that the Secretary's agents will perform the inspections.

Mr. WAGGONNER. I beg to disagree.

Mr. PERKINS. That the Secretary may delegate his functions is clear.

Mr. WAGGONNER. I beg to disagree. When we talk about inspections we use only the word "Secretary."

Mr. PERKINS. It is provided in existing law that the Secretary may delegate functions.

Mr. WAGGONNER. Again I refer to the inspection section, page 57, section 9 (a):

In order to carry out the purposes of this Act, the Secretary, upon presenting appropriate credentials to the owner, operator, or agent in charge, is authorized—

To do certain things. It does not say anything about agents of the Secretary, and there is only one Secretary.

Mr. PERKINS. Mr. Chairman, will the gentleman yield further?

Mr. WAGGONNER. I am happy to yield further.

Mr. PERKINS. May I quote language from the Reorganization Plan No. 6:

The Secretary of Labor may from time to time make such provisions as he shall deem appropriate authorizing the performance by any other officer, or by any agency or employee, of the Department of Labor of any function of the Secretary, including any function transferred to the Secretary by the provisions of this reorganization plan.

Mr. WAGGONNER. None of the proposed amendments would affect that authority?

Mr. PERKINS. None of the amendments would affect that authority.

Mr. WAGGONNER. The proposed amendments.

Mr. PERKINS. That is correct.

Mr. WAGGONNER. I thank the gentleman for yielding.

EDITORS' NOTE:—*In the debate in the House that preceded the adoption of the Administration's bill, Congressman Galifianakis (D-NC) introduced questions he had asked Congressman Steiger (R-Wis) on the Secretary's right of entry. The questions and answers, which apply to the final version of the bill, follow, along with additional comments by Congressman Steiger.*

House
12-24-70
p. 10687

Mr. GALIFIANAKIS. * * *

Mr. Chairman, I asked the gentleman from Wisconsin (Mr. Steiger), who is the author of this bill, several pertinent questions and I included these questions and answers as a part of my remarks.

Following are the questions along with the answers:

Question. As I interpret Section 9(a) of H.R. 19200, until a Federal inspector has presented his credentials, he lacks the authority to enter and inspect a business or workplace. Is that correct?

Answer. It is. Section 9(a) provides in part that: "... the Secretary, upon presenting appropriate credentials to the owner, operator, or agent in charge, is authorized— (1) to enter without delay and at reasonable times ... and (2) to question ... and to inspect and investigate. ..."

So until the inspector has presented his credentials, he is not empowered to enter a business or workplace. I might add that this is a feature common to both H.R. 19200 and H.R. 16785.

Question. And the inspector not only must present those credentials, but he must present them to the owner, operator, or agent in charge, is that not correct?

Answer. It is.

Question. Then I would ask the gentleman this: is it legal, under the terms of H.R. 19200, for a low-ranking employee of a firm to leave a Federal inspector waiting at the entrance to a business simply by saying, "I am sorry, but I must locate the owner, operator, or agent in charge before you may present your credentials and enter." If that sort of evasion is legal under this bill, then we have lost the value of holding unannounced inspections.

Answer. My answer is, that such an evasion is not legal under H.R. 19200. Under my bill, it would constitute interference with a Federal inspector subject to the criminal penalties of Section 17(e). And I think the words "without delay," which appear in Section 9(a)(1) of H.R. 19200, make it a stronger bill in this regard than the committee version.

Question. This clarifies that important point. I have two other questions. First, I am bothered by the term, "agent in charge." Is it the gentleman's intent that whenever a business or workplace is inhabited, there is necessarily someone who is the "agent in charge?"

Answer. That is correct.

Question. And in the event that an "agent in charge" could not be located within a reasonable time, would the Federal inspector be able to gain entry by presenting his credentials to any other employee?

Answer. I would say so. In general, it is our intent in H.R. 19200 that the Federal inspector should gain entry to a business or workplace with an absolute minimum of delay.

Mr. Chairman, I appreciate the gentleman from Wisconsin's candor and his desire to meet every question that was asked. A I have studied H.R. 19200 in recent weeks, I have been impressed by the gentleman's work in shaping a straightforward piece of legislation which will do much to reduce the toll from on-the-job accidents.

Mr. STEIGER of Wisconsin. Mr. Chairman, section 9(a) of the bill provides that in carrying out the purposes of the act, the Secretary is authorized to enter and inspect a factory "upon presenting appropriate credentials to the owner, operator, or agent in charge." A question has been raised as to who exactly may be considered the agent in charge. For example, will the inspector have to wait outside the factory interminably while someone inside goes off to find "an agent in charge"? The way we envision this provision as operating is that the inspector will present himself at the factory entrance and he will ask to see the agent in charge. The inspector will present his credentials to any employee who presents himself as the agent in charge. Now, if no person shows up stating that he is the agent in charge, then we do not intend that, under those circumstances, the inspector is going to wait an inordinate amount of time for such an agent to show up; and we certainly do not expect the inspector to give up and go back to his office. If none of the employees, purporting to the agent in charge, shows up after a reasonable time, then we contemplate that the inspector, acting for the Secretary, could regard any employee as the agent in charge for the purpose of presenting credentials under the act.

I would add that in carrying out inspection duties under this act, the Secretary, of course, would have to act in accordance with applicable constitutional protections.

As to what is meant by a "reasonable time and manner" in connection with inspections, this I believe will have to be left to the interpretation of the Secretary and of the courts. This test of reasonableness will be applied on a case-by-case basis. But we could say that, in general, the term means during regular working hours and in a manner which does not unnecessarily disrupt normal business procedures.

APPENDIX I-6

IMMINENT DANGER

EDITORS' NOTE:—*The following comments concern an amendment, rejected by the Senate but included in the final bill, for plant closing for imminent danger.*

Senate
11-17-70
pp. 18334-18335

Mr. SCHWEIKER. * * *

The amendment which I am cosponsoring with the Senator from Ohio (Mr. SAXBE) would strike out this section, which is section 11(b). The effect of our amendment would be to require the Department of Labor to go to a Federal district judge and obtain a court order in all cases where it desires to order a plant closed down. Our amendment would not detract, in my opinion, from the safety features of this bill, but it would afford to employers—as well as employees who might be thrown out of work by some arbitrary shut-down—a greater right to be heard before the Federal Government took drastic action affecting them.

Mr. President, the closing down of an industrial plant is indeed a drastic remedy. If Congress is going to grant this power in this legislation,. then we must be sure that due process is observed through a judicial hearing. In the average case where the Department of Labor finds a real imminent danger in a plant, I would expect the employer to agree with the Department, and close the plant or the portion of the plant voluntarily himself. But if there is a difference of opinion between the Department and the employer, I feel the Department should have to sustain a burden of proof in persuading a Federal district judge that the closure of the plant is necessary. I believe that both the Department's side and the employer's side should be heard before such a drastic step is taken against the will of the employer and throwing employees out of work.

It must be remembered that we are speaking here of a situation of imminent danger. The bill defines "imminent danger" as "a condition or practice which could reasonably be expected to cause death or serious physical harm before such condition or practice can be abated."

Mr. President, I can hardly conceive of many instances when this whole provision—section 11—would actually come into play. Before this provision could apply, there would first have to be an imminent danger in the plant which was undetected by either the employer or the employees, or if it had been detected, received no corrective action or safety precautions. So we would have an imminent danger situation that was just sitting there awaiting the visit from a Federal inspector representing the Department of Labor.

Section 11 would not come into play until the Department of Labor representative advised the employer of the imminent danger and the employer refused to take any steps to safeguard his plant and his employees. This would be quite a rare occurrence, I believe. Employers do not want their plants to blow up any more than the employees do. But I am thinking that in some cases, the Department of Labor may not be infallible, and that the employer, if he has a real difference of opinion with the Department of Labor about the closing of his plant, should have a right to be heard by a judge. That is all our amendment would do.

Mr. SAXBE. * * *

What we are talking about is a danger that the management will not recognize because if it is recognized, management would immediately shut it down. I cannot fancy a situation where management would not close down a machine, an area, or a plant where an inspector, the Federal Government, or the Department of Labor comes in and says, "There is a situation that creates great danger to that man; danger to life and limb." I think in such a situation management would act immediately; so we are talking about the unique situation where there is serious disagreement as to whether there is imminent danger. I am referring to the situation where there is serious disagreement. Management says, "There is no danger here; I can explain it all; the inspector just does not understand what we are talking about. This pipe is not going to explode; this machine is safe."

In that instance there is a disagreement based perhaps on lack of knowledge or lack of understanding of the
situation. For years we have settled such
disputes in court and so on the very rare
occasions where management and an inspector disagree as to the extent of
danger I believe the court should have
the opportunity of making the decision
as to who is right, because if both man-

agement and the inspector agree there is
no problem, they are not going to court.
They both say, "Yes; there is danger.
Let us correct this situation." Then, it
never leaves the plant. So when the matter gets to court there is a disagreement.
We have traditionally settled disagree-
ments in court in this country, and I
suggest it is the way to settle disagree-
ments in this matter.

APPENDIX I-7

EFFECT ON OTHER LAWS

EDITORS' NOTE:—*The following
discussion concerns the effect of
the final bill on provisions of the
Construction Safety Act.*

House
12-17-70
pp. 11897-11898

Mr. KYL. Will the gentleman from
Wisconsin take just a moment to evaluate the provisions of this act as they relate to the construction industry?

Mr. STEIGER of Wisconsin. I shall be
happy to.

As the gentleman knows, in the House-
passed bill we had a provision which
would have had all construction handled
under Public Law 91-54, the Construction Safety Act. The conference committee recommendation is not as good, in
my judgment, as that passed by the
House. In fact, of all industries in this
Nation the construction industry is treated less well under the provisions of the
conference report.

I would refer the gentleman from Iowa
to page H11811, in which there is a discussion of the construction safety concept.

What we have now under this conference report is, first, the continuation
of the Construction Safety Act; Public
Law 91-54, to cover contractors who have
Government contracts. Then we have
this omnibus safety and health bill to
cover all non-Government contracts.

There is a danger of there being dual
standards and a duplicating enforcement
procedure. But I believe the conference
report, may I say to the gentleman from
Iowa, has a protection, particularly in
the language I will read now:

The conferees intend that the Secretary
develop health and safety standards for construction workers covered by Public Law 91-
54 pursuant to the provisions of that law
and that he use the same mechanisms and
resources for the development of health and
safety standards for all the other construction workers newly covered by this Act, including those engaged in alterations, repairs,
painting and/or decorating.

The report goes on to say:

It is understood by the Conferees that in
any enforcement proceedings brought under
either this Act or under such other Acts, the
principle of collateral estoppel will apply.

So one cannot go one route and then
change his mind and decide he wants to
go another.

Mr. KYL. Mr. Speaker, will the gentleman yield further?

Mr. STEIGER of Wisconsin. I am
happy to yield further.

Mr. KYL. Would the gentleman in the
well and the chairman of the committee go so far at this point as to say in
the RECORD that it is the purpose, the
intent of the committee of conference to
indicate to the administrative branch
that there should be no duplication and
that the dual law now on the books so
far as construction is concerned must
be treated administratively so there is
no undue burden placed upon this one
industry.

Mr. STEIGER of Wisconsin. I would
answer the gentleman from Iowa by saying yes. It would be my best judgment
that it is the intent of the conferees—
and the distinguished gentleman from
Kentucky can correct me if he disagrees—first, there should be no duplication; second, there should be as little
burden on that industry in terms of how
it is operated as there is on any other
industry; and third, I think we should

all agree that the Secretary of Labor in working with the advisory committee created under Public Law 91–54 can work toward an effective coordination between the two acts.

Mr. PERKINS. Mr. Speaker, will the gentleman yield to me?

Mr. STEIGER of Wisconsin. I yield to the chairman.

Mr. PERKINS. I think the gentleman from Wisconsin has correctly stated the intent of the conferees. We did not take the House provision on construction safety but took the Senate provision. At the same time we used language in the statement of the managers to make clear that with respect to the imposition of penalties for the violation of a standard promulgated, pursuant to Public Law 91–54 by an employer covered by that act where the Secretary proceeded under one act and failed—or succeeded—he then could not resort to the penalty proceedings in the other act with respect to a construction contractor covered by Public Law 91–54.

Mr. SCHERLE. Will my distinguished colleague yield?

Mr. STEIGER of Wisconsin. I yield to the gentleman from Iowa.

Mr. SCHERLE. Is my understanding correct that if the Secretary of Labor assesses a civil penalty or if under the jurisdiction of the court there is a criminal penalty for a violation of a Government construction contract, the provisions of the occupational health and safety bill 2193 will apply?

Mr. STEIGER of Wisconsin. If I understood the gentleman's question correctly, you are asking me if there is a civil penalty. Is that correct?

Mr. SCHERLE. In one case and, of course, a criminal penalty if it is so adjudicated by a court.

Mr. STEIGER of Wisconsin. I am not sure I can correctly answer you. Let us back up for a minute. As we have drafted the conference report, the Secretary makes a choice. He can decide in the case of a Government contract to rely exclusively on Public Law 91–54, in which case he goes into court for an adjudication of the penalty. Non-Government contracts are covered under the omnibus act.

The gentleman from New Jersey was seeking recognition in order to clarify that further.

Mr. SCHERLE. If my colleague from Wisconsin will yield, I would like to continue this colloquy with the gentleman from New Jersey for the primary reason of establishing legislative history. Would the gentleman from New Jersey care to reply?

Mr. DANIELS of New Jersey. I would like to point out that the Senate version in the Senate bill contains civil as well as criminal penalties for violation of standards. The House bill merely provided for civil penalties and only a criminal penalty for willful violation. As a result of a compromise, the conferees agreed on civil penalties only and a criminal penalty of $10,000 and/or 6 months in prison on the first conviction and $20,000 and 1 year on a conviction after that but only if the violation results in the death of an employee.

Mr. STEIGER of Wisconsin. May I say that that does not answer the distinguished gentleman from Iowa's question. What he is interested in is the question as to whether or not if there is a civil penalty applied for a Government construction contract firm, then where does he go?

Mr. SCHERLE. Will this be under the Construction Safety Act or will it be adjudicated under the occupational health and safety bill, which is compromise legislation?

Mr. DANIELS of New Jersey. If the Secretary proceeds under the Government Construction Health and Safety Act, then it is confined to that act.

I think the gentleman from Wisconsin answered that question earlier that if the Secretary——

The SPEAKER pro tempore. The time of the gentleman from Wisconsin has expired.

Mr. PERKINS. Mr. Speaker, I yield the distinguished gentleman 5 additional minutes.

Mr. DANIELS of New Jersey. If the Secretary elects to proceed under the construction public safety provision and a decision is made thereunder, it becomes more or less res adjudicata so far as proceeding under this particular bill that we are considering today.

Mr. SCHERLE. Mr. Speaker, if the gentleman from Wisconsin will yield further, and in order to simplify my question, I am trying to find out if the Secretary of Labor assesses a civil penalty for a violation under a Government construction contract, does adjudication apply to this compromise legislation?

Mr. STEIGER of Wisconsin. My answer to the gentleman is that the Secretary does not apply penalties. He decides either to use Public Law 91–54, which is the courts, or he decides to go the route of this bill which is the Commission. He cannot go both ways. The construction industry in my judgment would be treated in a manner that ensures that he makes a decision whichever way he wants to go. The Secretary does the inspection, but the Commission would have to enforce it and assess a civil penalty for a violation of the standards.

Mr. SCHERLE. And, would that be covered under this compromise legislation?

Mr. STEIGER of Wisconsin. He can proceed under this act; that is correct.

Mr. SCHERLE. And the construction industry would be entirely removed from the legislation which is now law with refernce to construction safety?

Mr. STEIGER of Wisconsin. No; they would not be removed, but the Secretary has the choice as to which route he wants to take. That is why I do not think the construction industry was treated equitably under the conference report.

Mr. SCHERLE. Let me say in conclusion that I feel sorry for the construction industry, particularly the way they were treated in this conference committee. I would hope that some decisive legislation will be implemented shortly after the next Congress convenes to establish uniform standards so at least these unfortunate people will know exactly where they stand and what they can expect insofar as rules, regulations and guidelines are concerned.

Mr. STEIGER of Wisconsin. I think it is the express intent of the conference that the Secretary of Labor will proceed initially under this act; and the Commission's findings of fact will be binding upon the Secretary as well as upon the employer in determining whether an additional remedy should be imposed pursuant to other statutory authority.

Appendix I-8

STATE JURISDICTION AND STATE PLANS

EDITORS' NOTE:—*The following comments by Congressman Steiger (R-Wis) relate to provisions retained in the final bill for state plans and grants. Section 21 in the House bill became Section 23 in the final measure.*

House
11-23-70
pp. 10621-10622

Mr. STEIGER. * * *

Section 21(g) of the substitute authorizes the Secretary to make grants to States having plans which he has approved in order to assist these States in administering and enforcing their programs. The Federal grant authorized here may be up to 50 percent of a State's total costs. The section provides that any variation in the percentage of costs granted to different States shall be determined on the basis of objective criteria. One positive consideration in determining the amount of a grant should be the effort expended by a particular State in the field of employee safety and health prior to its application for a grant. It is intended that States which take the lead in this area and develop effective programs should receive special consideration in the making of Federal grants.

The substitute would not require a State to adopt any particular standard setting and enforcement procedures in order for its plan to be approved by the Secretary. It is only necessary that the State comply with the criteria set forth in section 18(c) of the substitute. Central to these requirements is the provision of section 18(c)(2) which requires that a plan provide for the development and enforcement of standards which are at least as effective as the Federal standards to be promulgated under the act. A State plan must also designate an agency or agencies which will administer the plan, and assure the legal authority, personnel, and funds necessary for it to carry out its administrative and enforcement activities.

EFFECT ON BUILDING CODES

The substitute will not supplant local building codes. It is conceivable that there will be some overlap between certain standards developed under the bill and local regulations which cover the same substantive areas. For example, a standard might be promulgated by the Federal Occupational Safety and Health Board dealing with the necessity for, or placement of, fire exits in a plant. A local building code might also have regulations in this area. Whether the Federal standard would apply would depend upon the existence and operation of an applicable State plan. In addition, in the promulgation of such a Federal standard, it would be appropriate to consult local building codes and building safety officials in an effort to accommodate those codes as far a possible.

As far as requiring major remodeling of buildings, the setting of standards contemplates taking into account "feasibility." Further, the substitute provides for the granting of variances from standards.

EDITORS' NOTE:—*States would be required to show compelling local conditions to justify a deviation from a national standard for products nationally distributed, under an amendment agreed to by both Houses. The following comments were made by the sponsors— Senator Saxbe (R-Ohio) and Congressman Railsback (R-Ill).*

Senate
11-17-70
p. 18354

Mr. SAXBE. Mr. President, this is an amendment which applies to those who manufacture machinery products that go into interstate commerce, specifically applying to those who manufacture movable equipment such as dirt movers, tractors, and other heavy equipment. If, after the expiration of the initial stage of this bill, each of the States were permitted to set differing safety standards for dirt movers, it would place a tremendous burden on interstate commerce. This amendment provides that they may do so because there may be circumstances that would so require, but the words are put in, "compelling local conditions," and, second, that they "do not unduly burden interstate commerce."

This amendment is offered so that we do not have differing safety regulations on equipment moving from State to State in interstate commerce and to try

to prevent States from making unreasonable limitations on certain type of equipment.

I have discussed the amendment with the manager of the bill, and I believe it is acceptable to him.

House
11-23-70
p. 10638

Mr. RAILSBACK. Mr. Chairman, at the appropriate time I intend to offer an amendment which I believe will strengthen the legislation that we now have under consideration.

Mr. Chairman, a main purpose of this legislation is to strengthen State programs concerning industrial or in-plant safety. Traditionally, industrial safety programs have been aimed at the design and arrangement of the plant itself and the establishment of safety rules and practices to be followed by the employees. The bills before us today, however, are even more inclusive. They cover all types of products which might be used on worksites and would permit each State to issue design standards for the safety of these products.

The difficulty with product design standards is that products are frequently mass produced on a national market basis and without any particular plant or worksite in mind. Contrasted with a plant, which is nearly always custom designed and laid out, some products which might be used in that plant are often not custom designed by instead are of a uniform design and are nationally distributed and sold. Thus a forklift or tractor, or even a lawn mower, are all often used in or around a plant or worksite and yet are seldom designed or manufactured for any particular customer. These products are designed for a national market. The problem which I hope to avoid would arise when under this legislation the States promulgate standards which deal with the design of such products. It would be possible to have each of the 50 States enact a varying standard and thus require the product manufacturer to custom build an unnecessarily expensive and slightly different model of his product for each of the 50 States. Even if the manufacturer did this it would not solve the problem a user of the product would have where he brought the product into several States with varying standards and might have to customize it for use in each of those States.

My amendment would specify that with respect to the standards which a State may promulgate, the standards should not present an undue burden on interstate commerce and should only be applied to the area of product safety when a compelling local condition can be shown, unless there is no national or Federal standard applicable. In other words, where a product is built to a Federal standard, it should not have to be custom-built to varying State standards, either by the manufacturer or the user, unless required by compelling local conditions.

It should be noted that may amendment does not deny the States the right to issue product design standards, it only requires that there be a sufficient showing of compelling local conditions which would justify the deviation from a national standard. In this regard, I note the recommendation of the National Commission on Product Safety, created by Public Law 90–146 in 1967:

That a mandatory Federal safety standard for a consumer product preempt any State or local standard, with appropriate provision for exemption where clear and compelling conditions in the State make it necessary.

The Product Safety Commission, in explaining its recommendation stated:

States seldom impose safety standards for consumer products. Where requirements apply to product safety, these vary considerably. For this reason, many manufacturers cannot produce for a national market except by designing different models for individual States. Ultimately, consumers pay the wasteful cost of several models being produced where one would do.

I think that we could all agree with such reasoning.

The Commission concluded that:

With a provision for exemption of State regulations that do not unduly burden interstate commerce, national safety standards for unreasonably hazardous consumer products can be expected to enhance protection for the public and conserve time, money, effort, and resources. At the same time, the possibility of exemptions will leave States free to develop innovative safety methods and to satisfy unusual local needs.

This is exactly the approach which my amendment is intended to take.

EDITORS' NOTE:—*The following comments concern an amendment by Senator Cook (R-Ky), which was adopted, to provide for court*

consideration of the Secretary's rejection of a state plan on the basis of substantial evidence, rather than a finding that the disapproval of the plan was arbitrary and capricious.

Senate
11-17-70
p. 18354

Mr. COOK. Mr. President, on page 69 of the act as presently drafted appears the sentence:

Unless the court finds that the Secretary's decision in rejecting a proposed State plan or withdrawing his approval of such a plan to be arbitrary and capricious, the court shall affirm the Secretary's decision.

I have proposed a change in my amendment, so that the language would read:

Unless the court finds that the Secretary's decision in rejecting a proposed State plan or withdrawing his approval of such a plan is not supported by substantial evidence the court shall affirm the Secretary's decision.

The amendment merely states that an action will lie in regard to a State plan based on substantial evidence, and not based on the negative plea of arbitrary and capricious.

I think all Members of the Senate who have had an opportunity to practice law will state that they know of very few cases which anyone has won based on arbitrary and capricious action. In the first place, if the regulations provide that the Secretary can do it, and if he does it within the regulations, then obviously it is not arbitrary and capricious.

I have talked with the manager of the bill in this regard. This is the same language that was adopted by the Senate in the Coal Mine Safety Act. I believe the manager of the bill is perfectly willing to accept the amendment.

Mr. WILLIAMS of New Jersey. Mr. President, that is correct. We accept the amendment.

The PRESIDING OFFICER. If there be no further discussion, the question is on agreeing to the amendment.

The amendment was agreed to.

EDITORS' NOTE:—*During Senate debate, Senator Javits (R-NY) sought to clarify the right of states to grant variances from standards with the approval of the Secretary.*

Senate
11-17-70
p. 18356

Mr. JAVITS. Mr. President, in the same connection, with regard to State plans, a number of States apparently want to have this question answered, and that is that State plans—this is for the purpose of legislative history—may contain appropriate provisions for granting variances as is provided by this bill for the Secretary under section 6(d). In other words, it is to make clear that whatever State plan the Secretary approves may have the same opportunity for the State to make variances as he retains under this legislation.

Perhaps I have not made myself clear. Under this measure, the Secretary may authorize variances by section 6(d) in the Federal standards for particular firms. The State can submit a total plan under certain restrictions and criteria, and so forth. It is not clear from the bill that a State plan may also contain a similar variance provision.

Mr. WILLIAMS of New Jersey. Certainly, that should follow. Where there is a State plan, there should be an opportunity for a variance as under the Federal program.

Mr. JAVITS. That is correct.

Mr. WILLIAMS of New Jersey. I find nothing unacceptable about it. In other words, there should be a similarity of opportunity for a variance under a State plan.

Mr. JAVITS. That is correct. In other words, it is not mandatory. A Secretary might not agree in a given case at the State level. But a State plan may include a similar provision with respect to section 6(d), with respect to variances.

EDITORS' NOTE:—*Both the Senate and the House adopted amendments relating to state enforcement of occupational health and safety laws before the effective date of federal standards. The following comments relate to the House amendment, which was accepted by the conferees.*

House
11-24-70
p. 10684

Mr. HATHAWAY. Mr. Chairman, this amendment, which would be put in the section of the substitute pertaining to the States making application to enforce their own occupational health and safety laws. In view of the fact that there may be an hiatus between the effective date of the Federal standard and the time when the Secretary will actually be geared up to enforce that standard, I believe it would be advisable in that interim period, which from past experience may take up to 2 years, to allow the States to continue to enforce their own standards with respect to the area covered by the Federal standards.

That is the only purpose of this amendment. This amendment was offered in another form and accepted in the other body. I believe it is a worthwhile amendment.

Mr. STEIGER of Wisconsin. Mr. Chairman, will the gentleman yield?

Mr. HATHAWAY. I yield to the gentleman from Wisconsin.

Mr. STEIGER of Wisconsin. I appreciate the gentleman from Maine yielding.

This amendment, may I ask the gentleman, is not identical to that offered in the other body to the Senate passed bill?

Mr. HATHAWAY. That is correct; it is not identical.

Mr. STEIGER of Wisconsin. Would the gentleman be willing to briefly say what are the differences between the two?

Mr. HATHAWAY. The amendment which was offered in the other body was restricted to standards that are not in conflict with the Federal standard, and it said that a State standard which was stronger than the Federal standard would not be in conflict. But this restricts the field of application beyond that which I believe the Secretary would like to have and would need to have.

If, for example, you had a Federal standard that said workbenches should be 3 feet apart and if there were a State standard that said they should be 2½ feet apart, then under the Senate amendment that was approved and agreed to, the State standard could not be effective, because it would be in conflict. The Secretary may say "We had better have a 2½-foot standard at least until the 3-foot standard is ready to be enforced." That is why I deleted that language from the Senate amendment.

Mr. STEIGER of Wisconsin. I appreciate that explanation. I discussed this with the gentleman from Florida, and we both concur that the amendment does make sense, and we would accept it.

Mr. HATHAWAY. I thank the gentleman.

The CHAIRMAN. The question is on the amendment offered by the gentleman from Maine to the amendment in the nature of a substitute offered by the gentleman from Wisconsin.

The amendment to the amendment in the nature of a substitute was agreed to.

SAFETY AND HEALTH STANDARDS

Text of regulations prescribing safety-health standards on Walsh-Healey (federal-supply) contracts. Issued by Labor Secretary, effective May 20, 1969; revised Secs. 50-204.7 and 50-204.10 (c)-(d) effective February 23, 1970.

PART 50–204—SAFETY AND HEALTH STANDARDS FOR FEDERAL SUPPLY CONTRACTS

Safety and Health Standards

Following notice and opportunity for public participation, on January 17, 1969, a revision of Part 50–204 of Title 41, Code of Federal Regulations, and an amendment of § 50–201.502 of the same title were published in the FEDERAL REGISTER at 34 F.R. 788–796. On February 14, 1969, a document was published in the FEDERAL REGISTER at 34 F.R. 2207 postponing the effective date of the rules until May 17, 1969. The purpose of the postponement was to permit a careful review of the rules by the present Secretary of Labor. Further notice and general public participation were found unnecessary in view of the previous opportunities afforded, although an advisory committee with a broad representation of labor, management, and public groups interested in occupational safety and health was appointed to assist in the review and to make recommendations concerning the rules.

Subpart A—Scope and Application
Sec.
50–204.1 Scope and application.
50.204.1a Variations.

Subpart B—General Safety and Health Standards
50–204.2 General safety and health standards; incorporation by reference.
50–204.3 Material handling and storage.
50–204.4 Tools and equipment.
50–204.5 Machine guarding.
50–204.6 Medical services and first aid.
50–204.7 Personal protective equipment.
50–204.8 Use of compressed air.
50–204.10 Occupational noise exposure.

Subpart C—Radiation Standards
50–204.20 Radiation—Definitions.
50–204.21 Exposure of individuals to radiation in restricted areas.
50–204.22 Exposure to airborne radioactive material.
50–204.23 Precautionary procedures and personnel monitoring.
50–204.24 Caution signs, labels and signals.
50–204.25 Exceptions from posting requirements.
50–204.26 Exemptions for radioactive materials packaged for shipment.
50–204.27 Instruction of personnel posting.
50–204.28 Storage of radioactive materials.
50–204.29 Waste disposal.
50–204.30 Notification of incidents.
50–204.31 Reports of overexposure and excessive levels and concentrations.
50–204.32 Records.
50–204.33 Disclosure to former employee of individual employee's record.
50–204.34 AEC licensees—AEC contractors operating AEC plants and facilities—AEC-agreement State licensees or registrants.
50–204.35 Application for variation from radiation levels.
50–204.36 Radiation standards for mining.

Subpart D—Gases, Vapors, Fumes, Dusts, and Mists
Sec.
50–204.50 Gases, vapors, fumes, dusts, and mists.
50–204.65 Inspection of compressed gas cylinders.
50–204.66 Acetylene.
50–204.67 Oxygen.
50–204.68 Hydrogen.
50–204.69 Nitrous oxide.
50–204.70 Compressed gases.
50–204.71 Safety relief devices for compressed gas containers.
50–204.72 Safe practices for welding and cutting on containers which have held combustibles.

Subpart E—Transportation Safety
50–204.75 Transportation safety.

AUTHORITY: The provisions of this Part 50–204 issued under secs. 1, 4, 49 Stat. 2036, 2038, as amended; 41 U.S.C. 35, 38; 5 U.S.C. 556.

Subpart A—Scope and Application

§ 50–204.1 Scope and Application.

(a) The Walsh-Healey Public Contracts Act requires that contracts entered into by any agency of the United States for the manufacture or furnishing of materials, supplies, articles, and equipment in any amount exceeding $10,000 must contain, among other provisions, a stipulation that "no part of such contract will be performed nor will any of the materials, supplies, articles, or equipment to be manufactured or furnished under said contract be manufactured or fabricated in any plants, factories, buildings, or surroundings or under working conditions which are unsanitary or hazardous or dangerous to the health and safety of employees engaged in the performance of said contract. Compliance with the safety, sanitary, and factory inspection laws of the State in which the work or part thereof is to be performed shall be prima-facie evidence of compliance with this subsection." (sec. 1(e), 49 Stat. 2036, 41 U.S.C. 35(e)). This Part 50–204 expresses the Secretary of Labor's interpretation and application of this provision with regard to certain particular working conditions. In addition, §§ 50–204.27, 50–204.30, 50–204.31, 50–204.32, 50–204.33, and 50–204.36 contain requirements concerning the instruction of personnel, notification of incidents, reports of exposures, and maintenance and disclosure of records.

(b) Except in the conduct of formal enforcement proceedings provided for in Part 50–203 of this chapter and as otherwise provided in this part, every investigator conducting investigations and every officer of the Department of Labor determining whether there are or have been violations of the safety and health requirements of the Walsh-Healey Public Contracts Act and of any contract subject thereto, and whether a settlement of the resulting issues should be made without resort to administrative or court litigation, shall treat a failure to comply with, or violation of, any of the safety and health measures contained in this Part 50–204 as resulting in working conditions which are "unsanitary or hazardous or dangerous to the health and safety of employees" within the meaning of section 1(e) of the Act and the contract stipulation it requires. Every such investigator or every such officer shall have technical competence in safety, industrial hygiene, or both as may be appropriate, in the matters under investigation or consideration.

(c) Whenever any applicable standard in this Part 50–204 is relied upon by the Department of Labor in a formal enforcement proceeding under section 5 of the Walsh-Healey Public Contracts Act to support a finding of violation of the safety and health provisions of the Act and of a contract subject thereto, any respondent in the proceeding shall have the right and shall be afforded the opportunity to challenge the legality, fairness or propriety of any such reliance.

(d) The standards expressed in this Part 50–204 are for application to ordinary employment situations; compliance with them shall not relieve anyone from the obligation to provide protection for the health and safety of his employees in unusual employment situations. Neither do such standards purport to describe all of the working conditions which are unsanitary or hazardous or dangerous to the health and safety of employees. Where such other working conditions may be found to be unsanitary or hazardous or dangerous to the health and safety of employees, professionally accepted safety and health practices will be used.

(e) Compliance with the standards expressed in this Part 50–204 is not intended, and shall not be deemed, to relieve anyone from any other obligation he may have to protect the health and safety of his employees, arising from sources other than the Walsh-Healey Public Contracts Act, such as State, local law or collective bargaining agreement.

(f) Whenever this part adopts by reference standards, specifications and codes published and available elsewhere, it only serves to adopt the substantive, technical portions of such standards, specifications and codes.

§ 50–204.1a Variations.

(a) The safety and health standards expressed in this part are intended for the application of section 1(e) of the Walsh-Healey Public Contracts Act to ordinary employment situations. The Director of the Bureau of Labor Standards may apply variations from the provisions of this part in enforcing the Act whenever he finds that, under the particular facts and circumstances involved, the plants, factories, buildings, surroundings, or working conditions are not unsanitary or hazardous or dangerous to the health and safety of the employees involved. Interested persons may request such a variation by making application therefor to the Director, Bureau of Labor Standards, U.S. Department of Labor, Washington, D.C. 20210.

(b) The provisions of paragraph (a) of this section shall not apply to §§ 50–204.35 and 204.36 which contain separate and specific variations procedures.

(c) Requests for exceptions or exemptions from the safety and health standards required by the Walsh-Healey Public Contracts Act, as permitted under section 6 of the Act, are processed under § 50–201.601 of this chapter.

Subpart B—General Safety and Health Standards

§ 50–204.2 General safety and health standards; incorporation by reference.

(a) Every contractor shall protect the safety and health of his employees by complying with the applicable standards, specifications, and codes developed and published by the following organizations:

American National Standards Institute Incorporated.

National Fire Protection Association.

American Society of Mechanical Engineers.

American Society for Testing and Material.

United States Governmental Agencies, including by way of illustration the following publications of the indicated agencies;

(1) U.S. Department of Labor

Title 29 (CFR):

Part 1501—Safety and Health Regulations for Ship Repairing.

Part 1502—Safety and Health Regulations for Shipbuilding.

Part 1503—Safety and Health Regulations for Shipbreaking.

Part 1504—Safety and Health Regulations for Longshoring.

(2) **U.S. Department of Interior, Bureau of Mines**

(i) Safety Code for Bituminous Coal and Lignite Mines of the United States, Part I—Underground Mines, and Part II—Strip Mines.

(ii) Safety Code for Anthracite Mines of the United States, Part I—Underground Mines, and Part II—Strip Mines.

(iii) Safety Standards for Surface Auger Mining.

(iv) Respiratory Protective Devices Approved by the Bureau of Mines, Information Circular 8281.

(3) **U.S. Department of Transportation.**

49 CFR 171-179 and 14 CFR 103 Hazardous materials regulation—Transportation cf compressed gases.

(4) **U.S. Department of Health, Education, and Welfare, Public Health Service.**

(i) Publication No. 24—Manual of Individual Water Supply Systems.

(ii) Publication No. 526—Manual of Septic-Tank Practices.

(iii) Publication No. 546—The Vending of Food and Beverages.

(iv) Publication No. 934—Food Service Sanitation Manual.

(v) Publication No. 956—Drinking Water Standards.

(vi) Publication No. 1183—A Sanitary Standard for Manufactured Ice.

(vii) Publication No. 1518—Working with Silver Solder.

(5) **U.S. Department of Defense.**

(i) AFM 127-100—Air Force—Explosives Safety Manual.

(ii) AMCR 385-224—Army Material Command—AMC Safety Manual.

(iii) NAVORD OP5—Navy—Ammunition Ashore, Handling, Stowing, and Shipping.

(6) **U.S. Department of Agriculture.**

Respiratory Devices for Protection against Certain Pesticides—ARS 33-76-2.

(b) Information as to the standards, specifications, and codes applicable to a particular contract or invitation for bids and as to the places where such documents and those incorporated by reference in other sections of this part may be obtained and is available at the Office of the Director of the Bureau of Labor Standards, U.S. Department of Labor, Railway Labor Building, Washington, D.C. 20210, and at any of the following regional offices of the Bureau:

1. North Atlantic Region, 341 Ninth Avenue, Room 920, New York, N.Y. 10001 (Connecticut, Maine, Massachusetts, New Hampshire, New York, Rhode Island, Vermont, New Jersey and Puerto Rico).

2. Middle Atlantic Region, Room 410, Penn Square Building, Juniper and Filbert Streets, Philadelphia, Pa. 19107 (Delaware, District of Columbia, Maryland, North Carolina, Pennsylvania, Virginia, and West Virginia).

3. South Atlantic Region, 1371 Peachtree Street NE., Suite 723, Atlanta, Ga. 30309 (Alabama, Florida, Georgia, Mississippi, South Carolina and Tennessee).

4. Great Lakes Region, 848 Federal Office Building, 219 South Dearborn Street, Chicago, Ill. 60604 (Illinois, Indiana, Kentucky, Michigan, Minnesota, Ohio and Wisconsin).

5. Mid-Western Region, 1906 Federal Office Building, 911 Walnut Street, Kansas City, Mo. 64106 (Colorado, Iowa, Kansas, Missouri, Montana, Nebraska, North Dakota, South Dakota, Utah, and Wyoming).

6. West Gulf Region, Room 601, Mayflower Building, 411 North Akard Street, Dallas, Tex. 75201 (Arkansas, Louisiana, New Mexico, Oklahoma, and Texas).

7. Pacific Region, 10353 Federal Building, 450 Golden Gate Avenue, Box 36017, San Francisco, Calif. 94102 (Alaska, Arizona, California, Hawaii, Idaho, Nevada, Oregon, Washington and Guam).

(c) In applying the safety and health standards referred to in paragraph (a) of this section the Secretary may add to, strengthen or otherwise modify any standards whenever he considers that the standards do not adequately protect the safety and health of employees as required by the Walsh-Healey Public Contracts Act.

§ 50-204.3 Material handling and storage.

(a) Where mechanical handling equipment is used, sufficient safe clearances shall be allowed for aisles, at loading docks, through doorways and wherever turns or passage must be made. Aisles and passageways shall be kept clear and in good repair, with no obstruction across or in aisles that could create a hazard. Permanent aisles and passageways shall be appropriately marked.

(b) Storage of material shall not create a hazard. Bags, containers, bundles, etc. stored in tiers shall be stacked, blocked, interlocked and limited in height so that they are stable and secure against sliding or collapse.

(c) Storage areas shall be kept free from accumulation of materials that constitute hazards from tripping, fire, explosion, or pest harborage. Vegetation control will be exercised when necessary.

(d) Proper drainage shall be provided.

(e) Clearance signs to warn of clearance limits shall be provided.

(f) Derail and/or bumper blocks shall be provided on spur railroad tracks where a rolling car could contact other cars being worked, enter a building, work or traffic area.

(g) Covers and/or guard rails shall be provided to protect personnel from the hazards of open pits, tanks, vats, ditches, etc.

§ 50–204.4   Tools and equipment.

Each employer shall be responsible for the safe condition of tools and equipment used by employees, including tools and equipment which may be furnished by employees.

§ 50–204.5   Machine guarding.

(a) One or more methods of machine guarding shall be provided to protect the operator and other employees in the machine area from hazards such as those created by point of operation, in going nip points, rotating parts, flying chips and sparks. Examples of guarding methods are—Barrier guards, two hand tripping devices, electronic safety devices, etc.

(b) General requirements for machine guards. Guards shall be affixed to the machine where possible and secured elsewhere if for any reason attachment to the machine is not possible. The guard shall be such that it does not offer an accident hazard in itself.

(c) Point of Operation Guarding.

(1) Point of operation is the area on a machine where work is actually performed upon the material being processed.

(2) Where existing standards prepared by organizations listed in § 50–204.2 provide for point of operation guarding such standards shall prevail. Other types of machines for which there are no specific standards, and the operation exposes an employee to injury, the point of operation shall be guarded. The guarding device shall be so designed and constructed so as to prevent the operator from having any part of his body in the danger zone during the operating cycle.

(3) Special hand tools for placing and removing material shall be such as to permit easy handling of material without the operator placing a hand in the danger zone. Such tools shall not be in lieu of other guarding required by this section, but can only be used to supplement protection provided.

(4) The following are some of the machines which usually require point of operation guarding:

Guillotine cutters.
Shears.
Alligator shears.
Power presses.
Milling machines.
Power saws.
Jointers.
Portable power tools.
Forming rolls and calenders.

(d) Revolving drums, barrels and containers shall be guarded by an enclosure which is interlocked· with the drive mechanism, so that the barrel, drum or container cannot revolve unless the guard enclosure is in place.

(e) When the periphery of the blades of a fan is less than seven (7) feet above the floor or working level, the blades shall be guarded. The guard shall have openings no larger than one half ($\frac{1}{2}$) inch.

(f) Machines designed for a fixed location shall be securely anchored to prevent walking or moving.

§ 50–204.6   Medical services and first aid.

(a) The employer shall ensure the ready availability of medical personnel for advice and consultation on matters of plant health.

(b) In the absence of an infirmary, clinic or hospital in near proximity to the work place which is used for the treatment of all injured employees, a person or persons shall be adequately trained to render first aid. First aid supplies approved by the consulting physician shall be readily available.

(c) Where the eyes or body of any person may be exposed to injurious corrosive materials, suitable facilities for quick drenching or flushing of the eyes and body shall be provided within the work area for immediate emergency use.

§ 50–204.7   Personal protective equipment.

Protective equipment, including personal protective equipment for eyes, face, head, and extremities, protective clothing, respiratory devices, and protective shields and barriers, shall be provided, used, and maintained in a sanitary and reliable condition wherever it is necessary by reason of hazards of processes or environment, chemical hazards, radiological hazards, or mechanical irritants encountered in a manner capable of causing injury or impairment in function of any part of the body through absorption, inhalation or physical contact. Where employees provide their own protective equipment, the employer shall be responsible to assure its adequacy, including proper maintenance and sanitation of such equipment. All personal protective equipment shall be of safe design and construction for the work to be performed.

§ 50–204.8 Use of compressed air.

Compressed air shall not be used for cleaning purposes except where reduced to less than 30 p.s.i. and then only with effective chip guarding and personal protective equipment.

§ 50–204.10 Occupational noise exposure.

(a) Protection against the effects of noise exposure shall be provided when the sound levels exceed those shown in Table I of this section when measured on the A scale of a standard sound level meter at slow response. When noise levels are determined by octave band analysis, the equivalent A-weighted sound level may be determined as follows:

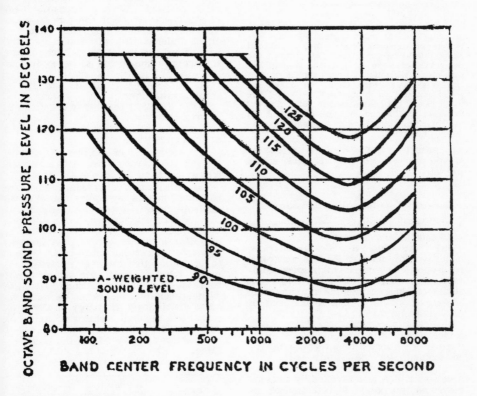

Equivalent sound level contours. Octave band sound pressure levels may be converted to the equivalent A-weighted sound level by plotting them on this graph and noting the A-weighted sound level corresponding to the point of highest penetration into the sound level contours. This equivalent A-weighted sound level, which may differ from the actual A-weighted sound level of the noise, is used to determine exposure limits from Table I.

(b) When employees are subjected to sound exceeding those listed in Table I of this section, feasible administrative or engineering controls shall be utilized. If such controls fail to reduce sound levels within the levels of the table, personal protective equipment shall be provided and used to reduce sound levels within the levels of the table.

(c) If the variations in noise level involve maxima at intervals of 1 second or less, it is to be considered continuous.

(d) In all cases where the sound levels exceed the values shown herein, a continuing, effective hearing conservation program shall be administered.

TABLE I

PERMISSIBLE NOISE EXPOSURES [1]

Duration per day, hours	Sound level dBA slow response
8	90
6	92
4	95
3	97
2	100
1½	102
1	105
½	110
¼ or less	115

[1] When the daily noise exposure is composed of two or more periods of noise exposure of different levels, their combined effect should be considered, rather than the individual effect of each. If the sum of the following fractions: $C1/T1 + C2/T2 * * * Cn/Tn$ exceeds unity, then, the mixed exposure should be considered to exceed the limit value. Cn indicates the total time of exposure at a specified noise level, and Tn indicates the total time of exposure permitted at that level.

Exposure to impulsive or impact noise should not exceed 140 dB peak sound pressure level.

Subpart C—Radiation Standards

§ 50–204.20   Radiation—definitions.

As used in this subpart:

(a) "Radiation" includes alpha rays, beta rays, gamma rays, neutrons, high-speed electrons, high-speed protons, and other atomic particles; but such term does not include sound or radio waves, or visible light, or infrared or ultraviolet light.

(b) "Radioactive material" means any material which emits, by spontaneous nuclear disintegration, corpuscular or electromagnetic emanations.

(c) "Restricted area" means any area access to which is controlled by the employer for purposes of protection of individuals from exposure to radiation or radioactive materials.

(d) "Unrestricted area" means any area access to which is not controlled by the employer for purposes of protection of individuals from exposure to radiation or radioactive materials.

(e) "Dose" means the quantity of ionizing radiation absorbed, per unit of mass, by the body or by any portion of the body. When the provisions in this subpart specify a dose during a period of time, the dose is the total quantity of radiation absorbed, per unit of mass, by the body or by any portion of the body during such period of time. Several different units of dose are in current use. Definitions of units used in this subpart are set forth in paragraphs (f) and (g) of this section.

(f) "Rad" means a measure of the dose of any ionizing radiation to body tissues in terms of the energy absorbed per unit of mass of the tissue. One rad is the dose corresponding to the absorption of 100 ergs per gram of tissue (1 millirad (mrad) = 0.001 rad).

(g) "Rem" means a measure of the dose of any ionizing radiation to body tissue in terms of its estimated biological effect relative to a dose of 1 roentgen (r) of X-rays (1 millirem (mrem) = 0.001 rem). The relation of the rem to other dose units depends upon the biological effect under consideration and upon the conditions for irradiation. Each of the following is considered to be equivalent to a dose of 1 rem:

(1) A dose of 1 rad due to X- or gamma radiation;

(2) A dose of 1 rad due to X-, gamma, or beta radiation;

(3) A dose of 0.1 rad due to neutrons or high energy protons;

(4) A dose of 0.05 rad due to particles heavier than protons and with sufficient energy to reach the lens of the eye;

(5) If it is more convenient to measure the neutron flux, or equivalent, than to determine the neutron dose in rads, as provided in subparagraph (3) of this paragraph, 1 rem of neutron radiation may, for purposes of the provisions in this subpart be assumed to be equivalent to 14 million neutrons per square centimeter incident upon the body; or, if there is sufficient information to estimate with reasonable accuracy the approximate distribution in energy of the neutrons, the incident number of neutrons per square centimeter equivalent to 1 rem may be estimated from the following table:

NEUTRON FLUX DOSE EQUIVALENTS

Neutron energy (million electron volts [Mev])	Number of neutrons per square centimeter equivalent to a dose of 1 rem (neutrons/cm²)	Average flux to deliver 100 millirem in 40 hours (neutrons/cm² per sec.)
Thermal	970×10⁶	670
0.0001	720×10⁶	500
0.005	820×10⁶	570
0.02	400×10⁶	280
0.1	120×10⁶	80
0.5	43×10⁶	30
1.0	26×10⁶	18
2.5	29×10⁶	20
5.0	26×10⁶	18
7.5	24×10⁶	17
10	24×10⁶	17
10 to 30	14×10⁶	10

(h) For determining exposures to X- or gamma rays up to 3 Mev., the dose limits specified in this part may be assumed to be equivalent to the "air dose". For the purpose of this subpart "air dose" means that the dose is measured by a properly calibrated appropriate instrument in air at or near the body surface in the region of the highest dosage rate.

§ 50–204.21 Exposure of individuals to radiation in restricted areas.

(a) Except as provided in paragraph (b) of this section, no employer shall possess, use, or transfer sources of ionizing radiation in such a manner as to cause any individual in a restricted area to receive in any period of one calendar quarter from sources in the employer's possession or control a dose in excess of the limits specified in the following table:

	Rems per calendar quarter
1. Whole body: Head and trunk; active blood-forming organs; lens of eyes; or gonads	1¼
2. Hands and forearms; feet and ankles	18¾
3. Skin of whole body	7½

(b) An employer may permit an individual in a restricted area to receive doses to the whole body greater than those permitted under paragraph (a) of this section, so long as:

(1) During any calendar quarter the dose to the whole body shall not exceed 3 rems; and

(2) The dose to the whole body, when added to the accumulated occupational dose to the whole body, shall not exceed 5 (N–18) rems, where "N" equals the individual's age in years at his last birthday; and

(3) The employer maintains adequate past and current exposure records which show that the addition of such a dose will not cause the individual to exceed the amount authorized in this paragraph. As used in this paragraph "Dose to the whole body" shall be deemed to include any dose to the whole body, gonad, active bloodforming organs, head and trunk, or lens of the eye.

(c) No employer shall permit any employee who is under 18 years of age to receive in any period of one calendar quarter a dose in excess of 10 percent of the limits specified in the table in paragraph (a) of this section.

(d) "Calendar quarter" means any 3-month period determined as follows:

(1) The first period of any year may begin on any date in January: Provided, That the second, third, and fourth periods accordingly begin on the same date in April, July, and October, respectively, and that the fourth period extends into January of the succeeding year, if necessary to complete a 3-month quarter. During the first year of use of this method of determination, the first period for that year shall also include any additional days in January preceding the starting date for the first period; or

(2) The first period in a calendar year of 13 complete, consecutive calendar weeks; the second period in a calendar year of 13 complete, consecutive calendar weeks; the third period in a calendar year of 13 complete, consecutive calendar weeks; the fourth period in a calendar year of 13 complete, consecutive calendar weeks. If at the end of a calendar year there are any days not falling within a complete calendar week of that year, such days shall be included within the last complete calendar week of that year. If at the beginning of any calendar year there are days not falling within a complete calendar week of that year, such days shall be included within the last complete calendar week of the previous year; or

(3) The four periods in a calendar year may consist of the first 14 complete, consecutive calendar weeks; the next 12 complete, consecutive calendar weeks, the next 14 complete, consecutive calendar weeks, and the last 12 complete, consecutive calendar weeks. If at the end of a calendar year there are any days not falling within a complete calendar week of that year, such days shall be included (for purposes of this part) within the last complete calendar week of the year. If at the beginning of any calendar year there are days not falling within a complete calendar week of that year, such days shall be included (for purposes of this part) within the last complete week of the previous year.

(e) No employer shall change the method used by him to determine calendar quarters except at the beginning of a calendar year.

§ 50–204.22 Exposure to airborne radioactive material.

(a) No employer shall possess, use or transport radioactive material in such a manner as to cause any employee, within a restricted area, to be exposed to airborne radioactive material in an average concentration in excess of the limits specified in Table I of Appendix B to 10 CFR Part 20. The limits given in Table I are for exposure to the concentrations specified for 40 hours in any workweek of 7 consecutive days. In any such period where the number of hours of exposure is less than 40, the limits specified in the table may be increased proportionately. In any such period where the number of hours of exposure is greater than 40, the limits specified in the table shall be decreased proportionately.

(b) No employer shall possess, use, or transfer radioactive material in such a manner as to cause any individual within a restricted area, who is under 18 years of age to be exposed to airborne radioactive material in an average concentration in excess of the limits specified in Table II of Appendix B to 10 CFR Part 20. For purposes of this paragraph, concentrations may be averaged over periods not greater than 1 week.

(c) "Exposed" as used in this section means that the individual is present in an airborne concentration. No allowance shall be made for the use of protective clothing or equipment, or particle size, except as authorized by the Director, Bureau of Labor Standards.

§ 50–204.23 Precautionary procedures and personnel monitoring.

(a) Every employer shall make such surveys as may be necessary for him to comply with the provisions in this subpart. "Survey" means an evaluation of the radiation hazards incident to the production, use, release, disposal, or presence of radioactive materials or other sources of radiation under a specific set of conditions. When appropriate, such evaluation includes a physical survey of the location of materials and equipment, and measurements of levels of radiation or concentrations of radioactive material present.

(b) Every employer shall supply appropriate personnel monitoring equipment, such as film badges, pocket chambers, pocket dosimeters, or film rings, to, and shall require the use of such equipment by:

(1) Each employee who enters a restricted area under such circumstances that he receives, or is likely to receive, a dose in any calendar quarter in excess of 25 percent of the applicable value specified in paragraph (a) of § 50–204.21; and

(2) Each employee under 18 years of age who enters a restricted area under such circumstances that he receives, or is likely to receive, a dose in any calendar quarter in excess of 5 percent of the applicable value specified in paragraph (a) of § 50–204.21; and

(3) Each employee who enters a high radiation area.

(c) As used in this subpart:

(1) "Personnel monitoring equipment" means devices designed to be worn or carried by an individual for the purpose of measuring the dose received (e.g., film badges, pocket chambers, pocket dosimeters, film rings, etc.);

(2) "Radiation area" means any area, accessible to personnel, in which there exists radiation at such levels that a major portion of the body could receive in any one hour a dose in excess of 5 millirem, or in any 5 consecutive days a dose in excess of 100 millirem; and

(3) "High radiation area" means any area, accessible to personnel, in which there exists radiation at such levels that a major portion of the body could receive in any one hour a dose in excess of 100 millirem.

§ 50–204.24 Caution signs, labels, and signals.

(a) *General.* (1) Symbols prescribed by this section shall use the conventional radiation caution colors (magenta or purple on yellow background). The symbol prescribed by this section is the conventional three-bladed design:

RADIATION SYMBOL

1. Cross-hatched area is to be magenta or purple.

2. Background is to be yellow.

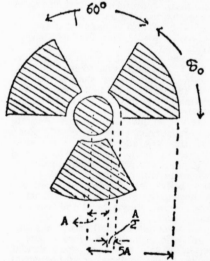

(2) In addition to the contents of signs and labels prescribed in this section, employers may provide on or near such signs and labels any additional information which may be appropriate in aiding individuals to minimize exposure to radiation or to radioactive material.

(b) *Radiation areas.* Each radiation area shall be conspicuously posted with a sign or signs bearing the radiation caution symbol and the words:

CAUTION [2]
RADIATION AREA

(c) *High radiation area.* (1) Each high radiation area shall be conspicuously posted with a sign or signs bearing the radiation caution symbol and the words:

CAUTION [2]
HIGH RADIATION AREA

(2) Each high radiation area shall be equipped with a control device which shall either cause the level of radiation to be reduced below that at which an individual might receive a dose of 100 millirems in 1 hour upon entry into the area or shall energize a conspicuous visible or audible alarm signal in such a manner that the individual entering and the employer or a supervisor of the activity are made aware of the entry. In the case of a high radiation area established for a period of 30 days or less, such control device is not required.

(d) *Airborne radioactivity area.* (1) As used in the provisions of this subpart, "airborne radioactivity area" means (i) any room, enclosure, or operating area in which airborne radioactive materials, composed wholly or partly of radioactive material, exist in concentrations in excess of the amounts specified in column 1 of Table 1 of Appendix B to 10 CFR Part 20 or (ii) any room, enclosure, or operating area in which airborne radioactive materials exist in concentrations which, averaged over the number of hours in any week during which individuals are in the area, exceed 25 percent of the amounts specified in column 1 of the described Table 1.

(2) Each airborne radioactivity area shall be conspicuously posted with a sign or signs bearing the radiation caution symbol and the words:

CAUTION [2]
AIRBORNE RADIOACTIVITY AREA

(e) *Additional requirements.* (1) Each area or room in which radioactive material is used or stored and which contains any radioactive material (other than natural uranium or thorium) in any amount exceeding 10 times the quantity of such material specified in Appendix C to 10 CFR Part 20 shall be conspiciously posted with a sign or signs bearing the radiation caution symbol and the words:

CAUTION [2]
RADIOACTIVE MATERIALS

(2) Each area or room in which natural uranium or thorium is used or

stored in an amount exceeding 100 times the quantity specified in Appendix C to 10 CFR Part 20 shall be conspicuously posted with a sign or signs bearing the radiation caution symbol and the words:

CAUTION [2]
RADIOACTIVE MATERIALS

(f) *Containers.* (1) Each container in which is transported, stored, or used a quantity of any radioactive material (other than natural uranium or thorium) greater than the quantity of such material specified in Appendix C to 10 CFR Part 20 shall bear a durable, clearly visible label bearing the radiation caution symbol and the words:

CAUTION [2]
RADIOACTIVE MATERIALS

(2) Each container in which natural uranium or thorium is transported, stored, or used in a quantity greater than 10 times the quantity specified in Appendix C to 10 CFR Part 20 shall bear a durable, clearly visible label bearing the radiation caution symbol and the words:

CAUTION [2]
RADIOACTIVE MATERIALS

(3) Notwithstanding the provisions of subparagraphs (1) and (2) of this paragraph a label shall not be required:

(i) If the concentration of the material in the container does not exceed that specified in column 2 of the described Table 1, or

(ii) For laboratory containers, such as beakers, flasks, and tests tubes, used transiently in laboratory procedures, when the user is present.

(4) Where containers are used for storage, the labels required in this paragraph shall state also the quantities and kinds of radioactive materials in the containers and the date of measurement of the quantities.

§ 50–204.25 Exceptions from posting requirements.

Notwithstanding the provisions of § 50–204.24:

(a) A room or area is not required to be posted with a caution sign because of the presence of a sealed source, provided the radiation level 12 inches from the surface of the source container or housing does not exceed 5 millirem per hour.

(b) Rooms or other areas in on-site medical facilities are not required to be posted with caution signs because of the presence of patients containing radioactive material, provided that there are personnel in attendance who shall take the precautions necessary to prevent the exposure of any individual to radiation

----

[2] Or "Danger".

or radioactive material in excess of the limits established in the provisions of this subpart.

(c) Caution signs are not required to be posted at areas or rooms containing radioactive materials for periods of less than 8 hours: *Provided,* That (1) the materials are constantly attended during such periods by an individual who shall take the precautions necessary to prevent the exposure of any individual to radiation or radioactive materials in excess of the limits established in the provisions of this subpart; and (2) such area or room is subject to the employer's control.

§ 50–204.26　Exemptions for radioactive materials packaged for shipment.

Radioactive materials packaged and labeled in accordance with regulations of the Department of Transportation shall be exempt from the labeling and posting requirements during shipment, provided that the inside containers are labeled in accordance with the provisions of § 50–204.24.

§ 50–204.27　Instruction of personnel posting.

Employers regulated by the AEC shall be governed by "§ 20.206" (10 CFR Part 20) standards. Employers in a State named in § 50–204.34(c) shall be governed by the requirements of the laws and regulations of that State. All other employers shall be regulated by the following:

(a) All individuals working in or frequenting any portion of a radiation area shall be informed of the occurrence of radioactive materials or of radiation in such portions of the radiation area; shall be instructed in the safety problems associated with exposure to such materials or radiation and in precautions or devices to minimize exposure; shall be instructed in the applicable provisions of this subpart for the protection of employees from exposure to radiation or radioactive materials; and shall be advised of reports of radiation exposure which employees may request pursuant to the regulations in this part.

(d) Each employer to whom this subpart applies shall post a current copy of its provisions and a copy of the operating procedures applicable to the work under contract conspicuously in such locations as to ensure that employees working in or frequenting radiation areas will observe these documents on the way to and from their place of employment, or shall keep such documents available for examination of employees upon request.

§ 50–204.28　Storage of radioactive materials.

Radioactive materials stored in a non-radiation area shall be secured against unauthorized removal from the place of storage.

§ 50–204.29　Waste disposal.

No employer shall dispose of radioactive material except by transfer to an authorized recipient, or in a manner approved by the Atomic Energy Commission or a State named in § 50–204.34(c).

§ 50–204.30　Notification of incidents.

(a) *Immediate notification.* Each employer shall immediately notify the Regional Director of the appropriate Wage and Labor Standards Administration, Office of Occupational Safety of the Bureau of Labor Standards of the U.S. Department of Labor, for employees not protected by AEC by means of 10 CFR Part 20, § 50–204.34(b) of this part, or the requirements of the laws and regulations of States named in § 50–204.34 (c), by telephone or telegraph of any incident involving radiation which may have caused or threatens to cause:

(1) Exposure of the whole body of any individual to 25 rems or more of radiation; exposure of the skin of the whole body of any individual to 150 rems or more of radiation; or exposure of the feet, ankles, hands, or forearms of any individual to 375 rems or more of radiation; or

(2) The release of radioactive material in concentrations which, if averaged over a period of 24 hours, would exceed 5,000 times the limit specified for such materials in Table II of Appendix B to 10 CFR Part 20.

(3) A loss of 1 working week or more of the operation of any facilities affected; or

(4) Damage to property in excess of $100,000.

(b) *Twenty-four hour notification.* Each employer shall within 24 hours following its occurrence notify the Regional Director of the appropriate Wage and Labor Standards Administration, Office of Occupational Safety of the Bureau of Labor Standards of the U.S. Department of Labor, for employees not protected by AEC by means of 10 CFR Part 20, § 50–204.34(b) of this part, or the requirements of the laws and applicable regulations of States named in § 50–204.34(c), by telephone or telegraph of any incident involving radiation which may have caused or threatens to cause:

(1) Exposure of the whole body of any individual to 5 rems or more of radiation; exposure of the skin of the whole

body of any individual to 30 rems or more of radiation; or exposure of the feet, ankles, hands, or forearms to 75 rems or more of radiation; or

(2) A loss of 1 day or more of the operation of any facilities; or

(3) Damage to property in excess of $10,000.

§ 50–204.31 Reports of overexposure and excessive levels and concentrations.

(a) In addition to any notification required by § 50–204.30 each employer shall make a report in writing within 30 days to the Regional Director of the appropriate Wage and Labor Standards Administration, Office of Occupational Safety of the Bureau of Labor Standards of the U.S. Department of Labor, for employees not protected by AEC by means of 10 CFR Part 20, or under section 50–204.34(b) of this part, or the requirements of the laws and regulations of States named in § 50–204.34(c), of each exposure of an individual to radiation or concentrations of radioactive material in excess of any applicable limit in this subpart. Each report required under this paragraph shall describe the extent of exposure of persons to radiation or to radioactive material; levels of radiation and concentrations of radioactive material involved, the cause of the exposure, levels of concentrations; and corrective steps taken or planned to assure against a recurrence.

(b) In any case where an employer is required pursuant to the provisions of this section to report to the U.S. Department of Labor any exposure of an individual to radiation or to concentrations of radioactive material, the employer shall also notify such individual of the nature and extent of exposure. Such notice shall be in writing and shall contain the following statement: "You should preserve this report for future reference."

§ 50–204.32 Records.

(a) Every employer shall maintain records of the radiation exposure of all employees for whom personnel monitoring is required under § 50–204.23 and advise each of his employees of his individual exposure on at least an annual basis.

(b) Every employer shall maintain records in the same units used in tables in § 50–204.21 and Appendix B to 10 CFR Part 20.

§ 50–204.33 Disclosure to former employee of individual employee's record.

(a) At the request of a former employee an employer shall furnish to the employee a report of the employee's exposure to radiation as shown in records maintained by the employer pursuant to § 50–204.32(a). Such report shall be furnished within 30 days from the time the request is made, and shall cover each calendar quarter of the individual's employment involving exposure to radiation or such lesser period as may be requested by the employee. The report shall also include the results of any calculations and analysis of radioactive material deposited in the body of the employee. The report shall be in writing and contain the following statement: "You should preserve this report for future reference."

(b) The former employee's request should include appropriate identifying data, such as social security number and dates and locations of employment.

§ 50–204.34 AEC licensees—AEC contractors operating AEC plants and facilities—AEC agreement State licensees or registrants.

(a) Any employer who possesses or uses source material, byproduct material, or special nuclear material, as defined in the Atomic Energy Act of 1954, as amended, under a license issued by the Atomic Energy Commission and in accordance with the requirements of 10 CFR Part 20 shall be deemed to be in compliance with the requirements of this subpart with respect to such possession and use.

(b) AEC contractors operating AEC plants and facilities: Any employer who possesses or uses source material, byproduct material, special nuclear material, or other radiation sources under a contract with the Atomic Energy Commission for the operation of AEC plants and facilities and in accordance with the standards, procedures, and other requirements for radiation protection established by the Commission for such contract pursuant to the Atomic Energy Act of 1954 as amended (42 U.S.C. 2011 et seq.), shall be deemed to be in compliance with the requirements of this subpart with respect to such possession and use.

(c) AEC-agreement State licensees or registrants:

(1) *Atomic Energy Act Sources.* Any employer who possesses or uses source material, byproduct material, or special nuclear material, as defined in the Atomic Energy Act of 1954, as amended (42 U.S.C. 2011 et seq.), and has either registered such sources with, or is operating under a license issued by, a State which has an agreement in effect with the Atomic Energy Commission pursuant to section 274(b) (42 U.S.C. 2021(b)) of the Atomic Energy Act of 1954, as amended, and in accordance with the requirements

of that State's laws and regulations shall be deemed to be in compliance with the radiation requirements of this part, insofar as his possession and use of such material is concerned, unless the Secretary of Labor, after conference with the Atomic Energy Commission, shall determine that the State's program for control of these radiation sources is incompatible with the requirements of this part. Such agreements currently are in effect only in the States of Alabama, Arkansas, California, Kansas, Kentucky, Florida, Mississippi, New Hampshire, New York, North Carolina, Texas, Tennessee, Oregon, Idaho, Arizona, Colorado, Louisiana, Nebraska, and Washington.

(2) *Other sources.* Any employer who possesses or uses radiation sources other than source material, byproduct material, or special nuclear material, as defined in the Atomic Energy Act of 1954, as amended (42 U.S.C. 2011 et seq.), and has either registered such sources with, or is operating under a license issued by a State which has an agreement in effect with the Atomic Energy Commission pursuant to section 274(b) (42 U.S.C. 2021(b)) of the Atomic Energy Act of 1954, as amended, and in accordance with the requirements of that State's laws and regulations shall be deemed to be in compliance with the radiation requirements of this part, insofar as his possession and use of such material is concerned, provided the State's program for control of these radiation sources is the subject of a currently effective determination by the Secretary of Labor that such program is compatible with the requirements of this part. Such determinations currently are in effect only in the States of Alabama, Arkansas, California, Kansas, Kentucky, Florida, Mississippi, New Hampshire, New York, North Carolina, Texas, Tennessee, Oregon, Idaho, Arizona, Colorado, Louisiana, Nebraska, and Washington.

§ 50–204.35   Application for variations from radiation levels.

(a) In accordance with policy expressed in the Federal Radiation Council's memorandum concerning radiation protection guidance for Federal agencies (25 F.R. 4402), the Director, Bureau of Labor Standards may from time to time grant permission to employers to vary from the limitations contained in §§ 50–204.21 and 50–204.22 when the extent of variation is clearly specified and it is demonstrated to his satisfaction that (1) such variation is necessary to obtain a beneficial use of radiation or atomic energy, (2) such benefit is of sufficient value to warrant the variation, (3) employees will not be exposed to an undue hazard, and (4) appropriate actions will be taken to protect the health and safety of such employees.

(b) Applications for such variations should be filed with the Director, Bureau of Labor Standards, U.S. Department of Labor, Washington, D.C. 20210.

§ 50–204.36   Radiation standards for mining.

(a) For the purpose of this section, a "working level" is defined as any combination of radon daughters in 1 liter of air which will result in the ultimate emission of 1.3×10^5 million electron volts of potential alpha energy. The numerical value of the "working level" is derived from the alpha energy released by the total decay of short-lived radon daughter products in equilibrium with 100 pico-curies of radon 222 per liter of air. A working level month is defined as the exposure received by a worker breathing air at one working level concentration for $4\frac{1}{3}$ weeks of 40 hours each.

(b) (1) Occupational exposure to radon daughters in mines shall be controlled so that no individual will receive an exposure of more than 2 working level months in any calendar quarter and no more than 4 working level months in any calendar year. Actual exposures shall be kept as far below these values as practicable.

(2) In enforcing this section, the Director of the Bureau of Labor Standards may at any stage approve variations in individual cases from the limitation set forth in subparagraph (1) of this paragraph to comply with the requirements of the Act upon a showing to the satisfaction of the Director by an employer having a mine with conditions resulting in an exposure of more than 4 working level months but not more than 12 working level months in any 12 consecutive months that (i) under the particular facts and circumstances involved the working conditions of the employees so exposed are such that their health and safety are protected, and (ii) the employer has a bona fide plan to reduce the levels of exposure to those specified in subparagraph (1) of this paragraph as soon as practicable, but in no event later than January 1, 1971.

(3) Whenever a variation under subparagraph (2) of this paragraph is sought, a request therefor should be submitted in writing to the Director of the Bureau of Labor Standards, U.S. Department of Labor, Washington, D.C. 20210, within 90 days following the end of the calendar quarter or year, as the case may be.

(c) (1) For uranium mines, records of environmental concentrations in the occupied parts of the mine, and of the time spent in each area by each person involved in underground work shall be established and maintained. These records shall be in sufficient detail to permit calculations of the exposures, in units of working level months, of the individuals and shall be available for inspection by the Secretary of Labor or his authorized agents.

(2) For other than uranium mines and for surface workers in all mines, subparagraph (1) of this paragraph will be applicable: *Provided, however,* That if no environmental sample shows a concentration greater than 0.33 working level in any occupied part of the mine, the maintenance of individual occupancy records and the calculation of individual exposures will not be required.

(d) (1) At the request of an employee (or former employee) a report of the employee's exposure to radiation as shown in records maintained by the employer pursuant to paragraph (c) of this section, shall be furnished to him. The report shall be in writing and contain the following statement:

This report is furnished to you under the provisions of the U.S. Department of Labor, Radiation Safety and Health Standards (41 CFR 50–204.36). You should preserve this report for future reference.

(2) The former employee's request should include appropriate identifying data, such as social security number and dates and locations of employment.

Subpart D—Gases, Vapors, Fumes, Dusts, and Mists

§ 50–204.50 Gases, vapors, fumes, dusts, and mists.

(a) Exposures by inhalation, ingestion, skin absorption, or contact to any material or substance (1) at a concentration above those specified in the "Threshold Limit Values of Airborne Contaminants for 1968" of the American Conference of Governmental Industrial Hygienists, except for the USASI Standards listed in Table I of this section and except for the values of mineral dusts listed in Table II of this section, and (2) concentrations above those specified in Table I and II of this section, shall be avoided, or protective equipment shall be provided and used.

(b) To achieve compliance with paragraph (a), feasible administrative or engineering controls must first be determined and implemented in all cases. In cases where protective equipment, or protective equipment in addition to other measures is used as the method of protecting the employee, such protection must be approved for each specific application by a competent industrial hygienist or other technically qualified source.

TABLE I

	8-hour time weighted average
Toluene (Z37.12–1967)	200 p.p.m.
Formaldehyde (Z37.16–1967)	3 p.p.m.
Carbon tetrachloride (Z37.17–1967).	10 p.p.m.
Trichloroethylene (Z37.19–1967)	100 p.p.m.
Tetrachloroethylene (Z37.22–1967).	100 p.p.m.
Hydrogen fluoride (Z37.28–1966)	3 p.p.m.
Fluoride dust as F (Z37.28–1966)	2.5 mg/M^3
Carbon disulfide (Z37.3–1968)	20 p.p.m.

	Acceptable ceiling concentration
Hydrogen sulfide (Z37.2–1966)	20 p.p.m.

TABLE II
MINERAL DUSTS

Substance	Mppcf [*]	Mg/M^3
Silica:		
Crystalline—		
Quartz (Respirable)	250 [f]	10mg/M^{3m}
	$\frac{\%SiO_2+5}$	$\frac{\%SiO_2+2}$
Quartz (Total Dust)		30mg/M^3
		$\frac{\%SiO_2+2}$
Cristobalite: Use ½ the value calculated from the count or mass formulae for quartz.		
Tridymite: Use ½ the value calculated from the formulae for quartz.		
Amorphous, including natural diatomaceous earth	20	80mg/M^3
		$\frac{\%SiO_2}$
Tremolite	5	20mg/M^3
		$\frac{\%SiO_2}$
Silicates (less than 1% crystalline silica):		
Asbestos—12 fibers per milliliter greater than 5 microns in length [j] or	2	
Mica	20	
Soapstone	20	
Talc	20	
Portland Cement	50	
Graphite (natural)	15	
Coal Dust (Respirable fraction less than 5% SiO_2)		2.4mg/M^3
		or
For more than 5% SiO_2		10mg/M^3
		$\frac{\%SiO_2+2}$
Inert or Nuisance Dust:		
Respirable Fraction	15	5mg/M^3
Total Dust	50	15mg/M^3

NOTE: Conversion factors

mppcf$\times$35.3 = million particles per cubic meter
= particles per c.c.

[*] Millions of particles per cubic foot of air, based on impinger samples counted by light-field technics.

[f] The percentage of crystalline silica in the formula is the amount determined from air-borne samples, except in those instances in which other methods have been shown to be applicable.

[j] As determined by the membrane filter method at 430 X phase contrast magnification.

[m] Both concentration and percent quartz for the application of this limit are to be determined from the fraction passing a size-selector with the following characteristics:

Aerodynamic diameter (unit density sphere)	% passing selector
2	90
2.5	75
3.5	50
5.0	25
10	0
	0

The measurements under this note refer to the use of an AEC instrument. If the respirable fraction of coal dust is determined with a MRE the figure corresponding to that of 2.4 Mg/M³ in the table for coal dust is 4.5 Mg/M³.

§ 50–204.65 Inspection of compressed gas cylinders.

Each contractor shall determine that compressed gas cylinders under his control are in a safe condition to the extent that this can be determined by visual inspection. Visual and other inspections shall be conducted as prescribed in the Hazardous Materials Regulations of the Department of Transportation (49 CFR Parts 171–179 and 14 CFR Part 103). Where those regulations are not applicable, visual and other inspections shall be conducted in accordance with Compressed Gas Association Pamphlets C–6–198 and C–8–1962.

§ 50–204.66 Acetylene.

(a) The in-plant transfer, handling, storage, and utilization of acetylene in cylinders shall be in accordance with Compressed Gas Association Pamphlet G–1–1966.

(b) The piped systems for the in-plant transfer and distribution of acetylene shall be designed, installed, maintained, and operated in accordance with Compressed Gas Association Pamphlet G–1.3–1959.

(c) Plants for the generation of acetylene and the charging (filling) of acetylene cylinders shall be designed, constructed, and tested in accordance with the standards prescribed in Compressed Gas Association Pamphlet G–1.4–1966.

§ 50–204.67 Oxygen.

The in-plant transfer, handling, storage, and utilization of oxygen as a liquid or a compressed gas shall be in accordance with Compressed Gas Association Pamphlet G–4–1962.

§ 50–204.68 Hydrogen.

The in-plant transfer, handling, storage, and utilization of hydrogen shall be in accordance with Compressed Gas Association Pamphlets G–5.1–1961 and G–5.2–1966.

§ 50–204.69 Nitrous oxide.

The piped systems for the in-plant transfer and distribution of nitrous oxide shall be designed, installed, maintained, and operated in accordance with Compressed Gas Association Pamphlet G–8.1–1964.

§ 50–204.70 Compressed gases.

The in-plant handling, storage, and utilization of all compressed gases in cylinders, portable tanks, rail tankcars, or motor vehicle cargo tanks shall be in accordance with Compressed Gas Association Pamphlet P–1–1965.

§ 50–204.71 Safety relief devices for compressed gas containers.

Compressed gas cylinders, portable tanks, and cargo tanks shall have pressure relief devices installed and maintained in accordance with Compressed Gas Association Pamphlets S–1.1–1963 and 1965 addenda and S–1.2–1963.

§ 50–204.72 Safe practices for welding and cutting on containers which have held combustibles.

Welding or cutting, or both, on containers which have held flammable or combustible solids, liquids, or gases, or have contained substances which may produce flammable vapors or gases will not be attempted until the containers have been thoroughly cleaned, purged, or inerted in strict accordance with the rules and procedures embodied in American Welding Society Pamphlet A–6.0–65, edition of 1965.

Subpart E—Transportation Safety

§ 50–204.75 Transportation safety.

Any requirements of the U.S. Department of Transportation under 49 CFR Parts 171–179 and Parts 390–397 and 14 CFR Part 103 shall be applied to transportation under contracts which are subject to the Walsh-Healey Public Contracts Act. See also § 204.2(a)(3) of this part. When such requirements are not otherwise applicable, Chapters 10, 11, 12, and 14 of the Uniform Vehicle Code of the National Committee on Uniform Traffic Laws and Ordnances, 1962 edition, shall be applied whenever pertinent.

(Secs. 1, 4, 49 Stat. 2036, 2038, as amended; 41 U.S.C. 35, 38)

The following is a listing of addresses where the Standards, Specifications, and Codes referred to in Part 50-204.2 of the Safety and Health Standards for Federal Supply Contracts may be obtained.

(1) AMERICAN NATIONAL STANDARDS INSTITUTE, INC.
1430 Broadway
New York, N.Y. 10018

Individual standards on safety and related subjects available at the above address.

(2) NATIONAL FIRE PROTECTION ASSOCIATION
60 Batterymarch Street
Boston, Mass. 02110

National Fire Codes are available in 10 volumes with individual codes, standards, and practices also available in pamphlet form.

VOLUME I	Flammable Liquids
VOLUME II	Gases
VOLUME III	Combustible Solids, Dusts, and Explosives
VOLUME IV	Building Construction and Facilities
VOLUME V	Electrical
VOLUME VI	Sprinklers, Fire Pumps and Water Tanks
VOLUME VII	Alarm and Special Extinguishing System
VOLUME VIII	Portable and Manual Fire Control Equipment
VOLUME IX	Occupancy Standards and Process Hazards
VOLUME X	Transportation

(3) AMERICAN SOCIETY OF MECHANICAL ENGINEERS
United Engineering Center
345 East 47th Street
New York, N.Y. 10017

Boiler and Pressure Vessel Code
Section VII — Recommended Rules for Care of Power Boilers

Section VIII — Unfired Pressure Vessels

(4) AMERICAN SOCIETY FOR TESTING AND MATERIALS
1916 Race Street
Philadelphia, Pa. 19103

Various material testing codes, standards, and procedures to be used with reference to the mechanics of testing.

(5) U.S. DEPARTMENT OF LABOR
Bureau of Labor Standards
Washington, D. C. 20210

Title 29(CFR):

Part 1501 — Safety and Health Regulations for Ship Repairing
Part 1502 — Safety and Health Regulations for Shipbuilding
Part 1503 — Safety and Health Regulations for Shipbreaking
Part 1504 — Safety and Health Regulations for Longshoring

Single copies available free from the above address or at Regional Offices, listed in 50-204.

(6) U.S. DEPARTMENT OF THE INTERIOR
Bureau of Mines
Washington, D. C. 20240

Safety Code for Bituminous Coal and Lignite Mines of the United States.
Part I — Underground Mines
Part II — Strip Mines

Safety Code for Anthracite Mines of the United States.
Part I — Underground Mines
Part II — Strip Mines

Single copies available free from:
U.S. DEPARTMENT OF THE INTERIOR
Bureau of Mines
223 Federal Building
Wilkes Barre, Pa. 18700

Recommended — Safety Standards for Surface Auger Mining
Information Circular 7845
Available from:
U.S. DEPARTMENT OF THE INTERIOR
Bureau of Mines
Washington, D. C. 20240

Respiratory Protective Devices Approved by the BUREAU OF MINES, Information Circular 8281.

(7) U.S. DEPARTMENT OF TRANSPORTATION
800 Independence Avenue SW.
Washington, D. C. 20590
49 CFR 171-179 and 14 CFR 103
Hazardous Materials Regulation — Transportation of Compressed Gases.

49 CFR 171-179

14 CFR is available in single copies from:

> FEDERAL AVIATION
> ADMINISTRATION
> 800 Independence Avenue SW.
> Washington, D. C. 20590

(8) U.S. DEPARTMENT OF HEALTH,
EDUCATION, AND WELFARE
Public Health Service
Washington, D. C. 20203

Publication No.   24 — Manual of
Individual Water Supply System
Publication No.   526 — Manual of
Septic-Tank Practices
Publication No.   546 — The Vending
of Food and Beverages
Publication No. 934 — Food Service
Sanitation Manual
Publication No.   956 — Drinking Water
Standards
Publication No. 1183 — A Sanitary
Standard for Manufactured Ice
Publication No. 1518 — Working with
Silver Solder

(9) U.S. DEPARTMENT OF DEFENSE
Department of the Air Force
AFDASBA
Washington, D. C. 20330

AFM-127-100 Air Force — Explosives
Safety Manual
U.S. Department of the Army
Headquarters, U.S. Army Materiel
Command
Washington, D. C. 20315
AMCR 385-224 — AMC Safety Manual
U.S. Department of the Navy
Washington, D. C. 20350
NAVORD OP5 — Navy — Ammunition
Ashore, Handling, Stowing, and
Shipping

Available from:

> Commanding Officer
> Naval Publications and Forms Center
> 5801 Tabor Avenue
> Philadelphia, Pa. 19120

(10) U.S. DEPARTMENT OF AGRICULTURE
Entomology Research Division
Pesticide Research Branch
Agriculture Research Center
Beltsville, Md. 20705
Respiratory devices for protection against

certain pesticides — ARS 33 -76-2 available at above address.

(11) U.S. ATOMIC ENERGY COMMISSION
Washington, D. C. 20545

10CFR20 — Standards for Protection
Against Radiation

(12) COMPRESSED GAS ASSOCIATION
500 Fifth Avenue
New York, N.Y. 10036

Available at above address:
C-6   Standards for Visual Inspection
of Compressed Gas Cylinders
C-8   Standards for Requalification of
ICC-3HT Cylinders
G-1   Acetylene
G-1.3 Acetylene Transmission for
Chemical Synthesis
G-1.4 Standard for Acetylene Cylinder
Charging Plants
G-4   Oxygen
G-5.1 Standard for Gaseous Hydrogen
at Consumer Sites
G-5.2 Tentative Standard for Liquefied
Hydrogen Systems at
Consumer Sites
G-8.1 Standard for the Installation of
Nitrous Oxide Systems at
Consumer Sites
P-1   Safe Handling of Compressed
Gases
S-1.1 Safety Relief Device Standards
For Compressed Gas
Cylinders
S-1.2 Safety Relief Device Standards
For Cargo and Portable Tanks.

(13) AMERICAN CONFERENCE OF
GOVERNMENTAL INDUSTRIAL
HYGIENISTS
1014 Broadway
Cincinnati, Ohio 45202
Threshold Limit Values of Airborne
Contaminants for 1968

(14) NATIONAL COMMITTEE ON
UNIFORM TRAFFIC LAWS AND
ORDINANCES
525 School Street SW.
Washington, D. C. 20024

Uniform Vehicle Code

(15) AMERICAN WELDING SOCIETY
345 East 47th Street
New York, N.Y.

INDEX

A

Abatement orders, affirmance or modification by Review Commission 55
Acetylene
—Walsh-Healey Act, safety standards 326
Accident prevention, training and education programs under Act 82
Addresses, articles, statements
—see also Legislative history of Act
—Abel, I. W. 43
—Dent, John P. 84
—Dominick, Peter H. 35, 90
—Egeberg, Roger 77
—Gidel, Robert D. 28
—Gordon, Jerome B. 13, 63
—Green, Edith 84
—Hathaway, William D. 67
—Hodgson, James D. 43
—Javits, Jacob K. 13, 56, 82, 87
—Johnson, Lyndon B. 16
—Meany, George 43
—Perkins, Carl D. 25, 27, 39
—Pyle, Howard 41
—Saxbe, William B. 45, 61
—Schweiker, Richard 60
—Schultz, George P. 13, 73
—Steiger, William A. 25, 28, 46, 55
—Williams, Harrison A., Jr. 35, 43, 61
Administrative review, see Occupational Safety and Health Review Commission
Advance notice of inspections
—ban on under Act 45
—state safety plans, condition to approval 69
Agriculture Department, directory 328
Alarm and special extinguishing systems, NFPA National Fire Codes 30
American Conference of Govermental Industrial Hygienists
—directory 328
—National Institute for Occupational Safety and Health, relation to 81
—proprietary safety standards 31
—role in standards-setting 25
American National Standards Institute, Inc.
—advisory boards 30
—"American National Standards," method of adoption 30
—Board of Standards Review 30
—Consumer Council 29
—directory 327

—injuries and illness, proposed reporting system 66
—injury and death statistics 63
—Member Body Council 29
—National Institute for Occupational Safety and Health, relation to 81
—revised procedures for standards-setting 31
—role in standards-setting 25, 29
—standards committees 30
—structure 29
American Society for Testing and Materials
—directory 327
—role in standards-setting 25
American Society of Mechanical Engineers
—directory 327
—role in standards-setting 25
American Welding Society
—directory 328
—role in standards-setting 25
Apparatus and equipment
—"Inspection Survey Guide," Bureau of Labor Standards handbook 28
Arts and Humanities Act
—safety standards under, continuing application pending new standards under OSHA 16, 26, 91
Asbestosis, employee exposure to 14
Associated General Contractors, proprietary safety standards 32
Atomic energy
—federal safety programs preceding OSHA 14
—radiation, employee exposure to 14
—Walsh-Healey Act, radiation standards 318 et seq.
Atomic Energy Commission, directory 328

B

Boilers, heaters and cooling equipment, pressure vessels and piping
—"Inspection Survey Guide," Bureau of Labor Standards handbook 28
Building and construction
—Construction Safety Act, see Construction Safety Act
—Davis-Bacon Act, safety provisions 15
—federal safety programs preceding OSHA 14

329